D1387999

DIOCESE OF
THOROLD &
LYTTELTON
LIBRARY
WINCHESTER

Three Centuries
of Mission

'...to impart the full benefits of her apostolical government'. Bishops Azariah and Motoda, first Indian and Japanese Anglican bishops, commemorated in stained-glass windows commissioned to mark the Society's 250th anniversary

Three Centuries of Mission

The United Society for the Propagation of the Gospel 1701–2000

Daniel O'Connor and others

CONTINUUM
London and New York

Continuum
The Tower Building, 11 York Road, London SE1 7NX
370 Lexington Avenue, New York, NY 10017-6503, USA

ISBN 0 8264 4989 1 (Hb)
ISBN 0 8264 4988 3 (Pb)

British Library Cataloguing-in-Publication Data
A catalogue record for this book is available from the British Library.

Printed and bound in Great Britain by the Bath Press.

Contents

CONTENTS

CONTENTS

4. (a, b, c) KING'S COLLEGE, NEW YORK; BISHOP'S COLLEGE, CALCUTTA; KAFIR INSTITUTION, GRAHAMSTOWN
Engraved illustrations in Pascoe, pp. 775, 789 and 785.

5. (a) GEORGE UGLOW POPE
The statue stands on the Marina, Chennai (Madras), South India. Photograph (1999) by Wide-Angle, Chennai.

5. (b) TIRUNELVELI CONGREGATION
Engraved illustrations in the 1866 SPG Report.

6. EMIGRANTS AT LIVERPOOL
Engraved illustration in the 1869 SPG Report.

7. AUSTRALIAN 'PIONEER MISSIONARY'
Engraved illustration in the 1872 SPG Report.

8. (a) SLAVE, CONVOY, CENTRAL AFRICA
Drawing in the Society's Archive (UMCA A1 (I)A) at Rhodes House Library, Oxford.

8. (b) CECIL AND LUCY MAJALIWA AND FAMILY
Photograph (1886?) in the Society's Archive (UMCA Album 22, page 4, no. 44) at Rhodes House Library, Oxford.

9. (a) ZENANA AND MEDICAL WORKERS, DELHI
Photograph (1877) of Dr Bose (male), Mrs Davies and Misses Engelmann, Floyd, Straig, Beacon, Bland, Tonnochy, Pousaz, Boyd, Orr, Brown, M. King, Hannay, L. King, in the Society's Archive at Rhodes House Library, Oxford.

9. (b) PURDAH WOMEN AT DISPENSARY
Photograph (n.d.) of Delhi or Rewari hospital, in the Society's Archive (Photograph 684) at Rhodes House Library, Oxford.

10. (a) ROLAND ALLEN AND THEOLOGICAL STUDENTS, PEKING
Photograph taken before the Boxer Rebellion of 1900. Reproduced courtesy of Hubert Allen.

10. (b) CODRINGTON THEOLOGICAL STUDENTS
Photograph (1961) in the Society's Archive (Photograph 1707) at Rhodes House Library, Oxford.

11. ASHRAM ART
The Visit of the Magi, by Alfred Thomas, from the SPG publication *The Life of Christ by an Indian Artist*, London, 1948, facing p. 10.

12. MEMBERS OF THE COLLEGE OF THE ASCENSION
Photograph (1988) taken for USPG publicity, in the Society's Archive at Partnership House, London.

13. (a) C. F. ANDREWS WITH GANDHI AND TAGORE
Watercolour by Abanindranath Tagore, at Santiniketan, West Bengal, reproduced with permission.

13. (b) ARTHUR SHEARLY CRIPPS
The photograph appears as the frontispiece to D. V. Steere's *God's Irregular: Arthur Shearly Cripps*, published by SPCK, London 1973, earlier provenance not recorded. Reproduced by courtesy of SPCK.

14. (a) ST PETER AND ST PAUL'S CHURCH, KANGHWA, KOREA
Local Cultural Property No. 111. Photograph made available by the Revd Dr Jeong-ku
Lee, and by permission of Bishop Matthew Chong, Diocese of Seoul.

14. (b) MEHRAULI CHURCH, NORTH INDIA
Drawing by the architect, A. Coore, printed as frontispiece in *Delhi*, July 1927.

15. (a) UMCA DISPENSARY, LIKOMA ISLAND
Photograph (*c.* 1900) in the Society's Archive (UMCA Album 10, p. 43) at Rhodes
House Library, Oxford.

15. (b) CHINESE MEDICAL STUDENTS, SHANTUNG
Photographic illustration in the 1920 SPG Report.

16. (a) ST NICHOLAS SCHOOL FOR THE BLIND, PENANG
Photograph (1970) in the Society's Archive (1999.068, MAL/WMA/ED/76) at
Partnership House, London.

16. (b) LEPROSY CENTRE, SEOUL
Photograph (1970) of Mother Phoebe SHC, Bishop Paul Lee and leprosy patient; also
Lawrence Park and Sr Catherine SHC. In the Society's Archive (1999.068, KOR/SEO/
ME/6a) at Partnership House, London.

17. MISSIONARIES ON TOUR
(a) North China. Photographic illustration in 1924 SPG Report.

(b) South Africa, Archdeacon Leary. Lantern slide in the Society's Archive (Box 12,
no. 3) at Rhodes House Library, Oxford.

(c) Zambia, hospital orderly, Chipili photograph (1920s) in the Society's Archive
(Photograph 167) at Rhodes House Library, Oxford.

(d) Kuching, Jemal Sananda, Vicar of Simanggang. Photograph by John Crowe (1978) in
the Society's Archive (1999.068 Kuching JC/5/3) at Partnership House, London.

18. MISSIONARY FAMILIES
(a) Photograph of Wendy and Frances Copland at Mandla, Central India (Christmas Day
1950). Reproduced courtesy of Wendy and Charles Copland, Kirriemuir, Scotland.

(b) William Sweetnam and family at their 'Summer Vicarage', Diocese of Caledonia,
Canada. Photographic illustration in 1925 SPG Report.

19. MISSION FUNDRAISING
(a) 'Sunday collection for the SPG', *Punch* cartoon (22 February 1896), drawing by du
Maurier. Reproduced with permission of *Punch* Ltd.

(b) UMCA supporters' meeting, Leigh-on-Sea, England (1950). Photograph courtesy of
Stella Hale.

(c) 1998 London Marathon sponsored runners (the Revds Peter and Mary Vickers and
Ben Humphreys).

20. CHURCH OF THE FUTURE
Bishop Dinis Sengulane and Niassa children. Photograph (1979) by W. T. W. Whiffen
in the Society's Archive (1999.215, Sengulane, D/155b) at Partnership House, London.

Foreword by the Archbishop of Canterbury

As President of the United Society for the Propagation of the Gospel, I warmly welcome this new history. A worthy successor to earlier official histories, it updates the story and makes a valuable contribution to our celebration of the Society's three hundred years in mission.

Daniel O'Connor and his essayists have left us indebted to them in several ways. Much of this part of the story of the modern missionary movement has never been told before. It is fascinating, and deserves a wide readership. It also makes a significant contribution to contemporary historical studies. The earlier official histories, of 1901 and 1951, were written when British imperialism was still largely intact, and they shared the generally unquestioning attitude of people in the British Isles to USPG's inevitable association with it. This book is different. Many of the essays are by scholars, women and men, from Africa, Asia, North America and the Pacific, and reveal a range of points of view, contributing significantly to what is a serious attempt at a re-reading of the Society's history.

I am sure that many people, students of mission and members of the Churches of our Communion, will welcome this book, and I hope that the Society and its supporters in these islands will, in rediscovering their missionary roots, find inspiration to share in God's mission in the new century.

✠ George Cantuar

Preface

This account of the history of the United Society for the Propagation of the Gospel was written to mark the tercentenary in 2001. Several accounts have preceded it, including a series of more concise offerings, the first as early as 1730, most recently Margaret Dewey's spirited *The Messengers* of 1975, and also two monumental accounts, C. F. Pascoe's *Two Hundred Years of the SPG*, of 1901, some 1800 densely-printed pages, and H. P. Thompson's *Into All Lands*, bringing the story to 1950. A committee chaired by the Revd David Tuck and with a mercifully light touch gave me helpful advice and few instructions beyond that there should be a disproportionate emphasis on the last 50 years. The committee agreed that it would be good to devote half the book to a series of contributions by other writers who could offer a range of perspectives and interpretations and, with only a couple of years for the entire project, it has been a relief as well as a pleasure to have had fourteen such co-workers.

There was a considerable constraint upon length, when compared with Pascoe and Thompson, so that the immensely detailed record that they produced was impossible on this occasion. Pascoe referred to every clerical missionary of the Society (though few non-clerical!) between 1701 and 1900, and Thompson appears to have tried to add all who served to 1950. I have had to be content with making a selection of exemplary individuals and interesting events, inevitably a more arbitrary procedure. Perhaps, however, by including a Prologue about a little-known individual, whose missionary career was cut cruelly short, tribute is paid to the many unnamed here.

There have been other developments since Thompson's volume besides another 50 years of the Society's history to record. One of these has been a great deal of new research and writing of which account needs to be taken where possible. This includes an increasing amount by scholars in the countries and Churches with which the Society has been associated, not all of it easy of access because often published locally and written in other than English – in Malagasy, for example, or Tamil. Added to this, the Society's archives are now explored more extensively by secular scholars, so that interesting and often illuminating work is appearing well beyond the circle of faith. I have often over the past two years, nevertheless, dreamed of having the assistance of a large research team to open up many as yet unexplored aspects of the history.

A related development has been in shifting perspectives, so that, for example, disentangling mission from imperial and colonial history is now as essential as it is impossible! That, of course, goes for every other branch of European mission history as much as it does for Anglican, although of course each strand provides its own interesting modulations. While anxious to avoid the absurd jargon and the superficiality of much current 'post-colonial' study, we do now need to include a reading of the Society's texts for their gaps, absences and ellipses, silences and closures, for we will only discern the grand narrative of the propagation of the Gospel, if at all, beyond such a reading. A relevant remark of Desmond Tutu's, nevertheless, including a glorious metaphor, was quoted to the Society's Overseas Committee on 21 September 1980, 'I cannot understand you Europeans, always leaning over backwards to beat your breasts. You did a good job, don't run it down!' A remark like that comes best from the sort of person who might be chosen to chair a Truth and Reconciliation Commission in somewhere like 1990s' South Africa.

A somewhat more domestic missiographical corrective has been attempted here. Recent work on the history of the Church of England shows how the Oxford Movement was written up by a writing down of the preceding High Church tradition. So in mission history the advent of William Carey and the 'Missionary Awakening' that Eugene Stock, in his history of the CMS, located in 1786, have in volume after recent volume consigned the first century of the Society's history to a prehistoric darkness. The eighteenth-century Society was much more interesting than this would imply, in a distinctive first of three centuries of mission, hence our title.

For generous assistance with the costs of this project, I thank the Carnegie Trust for the Universities of Scotland, the University of Edinburgh (for a Research Travel Grant) and the St Luke's College Foundation. I am also most grateful for the hospitality of the Cowley Fathers in Westminster and of Bob Jeffery in Oxford on numerous expeditions to consult the Society's archives.

I place on record here also my gratitude for the willing co-operation of the fourteen essayists whose work so richly enhances this volume.

With regard to my own part in it, I record my thanks for much assistance to John Pinfold and his colleagues at the Rhodes House Library, Oxford, and Colin Rowe and Elizabeth Williams at the Mission Studies Library at Partnership House, London. Many members of the staff of the Society have been generous with their help and guidance, including the Secretary and Deputy Secretary, Munawar Rumalshah and Michael Hart, but in a category quite unique has been the Society's Archivist, Catherine Wakeling, without whose expertise and unwearying help this task could not have been completed, and I am extremely grateful.

I thank the Venerable Society for entrusting me with this assignment, and my wife, Juliet, for her loving support.

Daniel O'Connor
Elie, Epiphany 2000

Abbreviations

ACC	Anglican Consultative Council
AMEC	American Methodist Episcopal Church
AMPLA	Anglican–Methodist Project in Latin America
BCC	British Council of Churches
BCMS	Bible Churchmen's Missionary Society
CBMS	Conference of British Missionary Societies
CHSKH	Chung Hua Sheng Kung Huei (Holy Catholic Church of China)
CI(P)BC	Church of India (Pakistan), Burma and Ceylon
CMD	Cambridge Mission to Delhi
CMS	Church Mission(ary) Society
CNI	Church of North India
CPCA	Church of the Province of Central Africa
CPEA	Church of the Province of East Africa
CPSA	Church of the Province of South(ern) Africa
CPSS	Christa Prema Seva Sangha (Society of the Love and Service of Christ)
CR	Community of the Resurrection
CSI	Church of South India
CSS	Christa Seva Sangha (Society of the Service of Christ)
CWM	Council for World Mission
CWME	(WCC's) Commission for World Mission and Evangelism
CWW	Committee for Women's Work
DFMM	Delhi Female Medical Mission
ECUSA	Episcopal Church of the USA
I-CA	Inter-Church Aid (later Christian Aid)
IMC	International Missionary Council

JCMA	Junior Clergy Missionary Association
LMS	London Missionary Society
MMS	Methodist Missionary Society
NSKK	Nippon Sei Ko Kai (Holy Catholic Church in Japan)
OMC	Oxford Mission to Calcutta
PWM	Partnership for World Mission
SAMS	South American Missionary Society
SPCK	Society for Promoting Christian Knowledge
SSJE	Society of St John the Evangelist
SSM	Society of the Sacred Mission
SVMU	Student Volunteer Missionary Union
UMCA	Universities' Mission to Central Africa
URC	United Reformed Church
WCC	World Council of Churches
WMA	Women's Mission Association

PART 1

The Society in changing times

SECTION 1

The eighteenth century

Prologue: a global perspective

We begin with a missionary. Patrick Gordon was the Society's first, together with George Keith. He sailed with Keith on the *Centurion* on 24 April 1702, the latter having been appointed to investigate the missionary needs of North America. Gordon was a young, educated Scot, a son of the Episcopalian rector of Banchory Devenick, an MA, like Keith, of Aberdeen and a Fellow of the Royal Society. He had been a naval chaplain for some six years, and was appointed by the Society to the parish of Jamaica, Long Island.[1]

His Fellowship had probably been a reward for his *Geography Anatomiz'd*, originally published in 1693, a bold attempt to give an overview of the entire 'terraquaeous globe'. Gordon adds some interesting missiological considerations which make him in some respects a herald of the Society. The 'sad Truth' is, he explains, that only five-thirtieths of humanity belong to the Greek, Roman and Protestant churches, while six-thirtieths are 'Jews, Turks and Saracens', and nineteen 'Blind and gross Idolaters'.[2] Prospects for a propagation of the gospel are, however, good, for England has 'a footing' through 'a Trade or Factories' all over the world, not only in North America and the Caribbean, but in many other regions, on the Coast of Coromandel, in the Gulf of Bengal, in Arabia Felix, in the Kingdom of Siam and in China, on the Gold Coast and the Coast of Barbary. In an Appendix, Gordon adds 'Some proposals for the Propagation of the blessed Gospel in all *Pagan* countries'.[3] These proposals, for both a broad programme of missionary language-study, and fund-raising in the entire householding population of England, found their way on to the agenda of an early meeting of the Society, but appear to have got no further.[4] Initially written for schools and young gentlemen with time on their hands, Gordon's book had an enormous vogue, twenty editions appearing by 1754, others later, also French and Italian editions. It is supported by a series of maps, and tables of both physical and human features, mountains and seas, native peoples and bishoprics across 'the Surface of the Earthly Ball'.

In a third edition, in 1702, Gordon's survey has gained new significance, for in a new Epistle Dedicatory he rejoices that, like the Roman Catholic Church with its Sacred Congregation for the Propagation of the Faith, established in 1622, the Church of England 'may now boast of a settled Society *de propaganda Fide* as well as *they*', so that 'our implacable Adversaries can no longer upbraid us with a supine Neglect of our Heathen American Neighbours'. This new Society is as near official as may be, the Archbishop of Canterbury being 'the *main Spring* that animates that *truly Christian* body'.

Patrick Gordon's own part in the realization of his missionary vision was tragically cut short. After a voyage of 43 days, during which he and Keith were guests 'at free cost' at the table of a fellow-passenger, the Governor of New England, and he avoided seasickness like a 'thorough . . . Seaman', which of course he was, he made for his new parish, where he gained the immediate good opinion both of the Church and among the Dissenters for his 'Abilities, Sobriety & Prudence', but then contracted a fever, and, a few days later, died.[5] His ideas were by then, however, published abroad, a global vision for the propagation of the Gospel.

I

⊷⇒◎⇐⊷

The mission of an Ancient Regime Church

The Society for the Propagation of the Gospel in Foreign Parts came into being with a Charter granted by William III on 16 June 1701. It followed English charters to 'conquer, occupy and possess' lands occupied by 'heathens and infidels, in whatsoever part of the world', which went back to 1482.[1] The Bishop of St Asaph thought the new Charter was timely, for the European 'Discoveries' of the previous two centuries were a door opened by God, while the Society's seal, bearing the text from Acts, 'Come over and help us', suggested an invitation, which was indeed sometimes the case.[2]

By 1701, British expansion and success in wars with its colonizing Roman Catholic rivals, France and Spain, saw the thirteen colonies in the eastern woodlands of North America under British control if not entirely wrested from their original inhabitants, while, further north, much of Acadia was occupied and Newfoundland about to be. Several Caribbean islands were also British possessions, with Britain soon to be a net exporter of slaves and the islands on the threshold of great economic significance. There were also, as Gordon had indicated, British 'factories', trading stations, in Africa and Asia by this time. With people from Britain thus widely spread and neighbour to native peoples and slaves, the Church of England saw itself as having new pastoral and missionary responsibilities. The Charter refers to the lack of provision at that time for the propagation of the Gospel and for the Church's ministry in the 'Plantations, Colonies and Factories beyond the Seas'. Hence, the new organization, 'one Body Politic and Corporate', such a society being the only means a Church of the Ancient Regime had to respond to new needs. The Charter gave authority 'for ever' thereafter to collect and administer funds for 'the better Support and Maintenance of an Orthodox Clergy in Foreign Parts'.

The reference here to 'an Orthodox clergy' is a helpful clue to the Society's character. The term 'orthodox' referred to the High Church tradition articulated in the sixteenth century by Richard Hooker and reinforced by the Caroline Divines of the earlier seventeenth. The Society and SPCK were to become an important *locus* of this tradition throughout the eighteenth century and onwards.[3] It included a high view of the Church, of church order and apostolic succession, liturgy and sacraments, exemplified in an early decision that 'no Bibles be sent by the Society into the Plantations without Common Prayer Books bound up with them.'[4] An important consequence, though not fully realized until the nineteenth century, was the understanding that a missionary was answerable to the Church and the bishop to which he or she was sent, only secondarily to the Society. Accompanying this high ecclesiology was a political theology which saw Church and state intimately associated, theologically and practically two aspects of a single national community. It was in this tradition that the Charter was framed and the Society emerged. It led to the assumption that where British sovereignty prevailed, SPG had a responsibility. It also gave the Society a very powerful start, with much of the weight of both Church and state behind it. The Archbishop of Canterbury reported to the March 1702 meeting that Queen Anne had told him that she would be 'always ready to do . . . [her] part in Promoting and Encouraging so Good a Work', and she was indeed a strong supporter. In 1711 she authorized a first Royal Letter requiring every parish in England to raise 'a liberal contribution' for the Society's work, these Letters being issued at intervals thereafter until 1853.[5] With such a theological basis, and such prestigious support, it is easy to see why the Society became 'the Venerable Society' within a year or two of its inception. It was set up, however, on assumptions that advancing secularization was to render less and less sustainable over the next two hundred years, creating endless puzzles for its leadership, while the location of its mission principally in British colonial and imperial domains was to bring many problems and uncomfortable contradictions to its operations.

There had of course been Church of England missionary initiatives from the beginning of English transatlantic adventures. The first permanent settlement of colonists in America was in 1606, and the first celebration of Holy Communion in 1607, but early initiatives were relatively limited both geographically and in their resources. It was a decision of 1634 extending the responsibilities of the Bishop of London to 'our British Foreign Plantations' that began to establish the context of the Society. On Henry Compton's becoming Bishop of London in 1675 and finding there were 'scarce four ministers of the Church of England in all the vast tract of America', these responsibilities began to be seriously addressed. The year following, thanks to Compton's influence at Court and membership of the Lords of Trade and Plantations, instructions were issued to colonial governors which set in place an extraordinarily strong structure to sustain the Church's mission. These were to apply to colonial governors well into the nineteenth century, and required each to ensure that throughout his colony public worship was offered and sacraments administered according to the Book of Common Prayer. To this end, an adequate number of parishes was to be established, with churches and houses for the clergy built and maintained 'at the Common Charge'. In addition, the governor must see that 'a competent proportion of lands be assign'd to . . . [each clergyman] for a glebe and exercise of his industry'. Initially it was usual for 200 acres to be assigned, with 100 for a parish schoolmaster. We find the Society within its first year of operation calling upon governors to implement these instructions.[6] Although they were sometimes ignored, they gave the essential economic base to the Society's work for much of the first two centuries, in North America and the Caribbean, and later also in New Zealand, Australia and South Africa.[7] This support was supplemented from 1774 by parliamentary grants of land for the Church in Canada, the Clergy Reserves, these eventually tailing off in the 1840s. The Society's need of additional funds was in consequence modest, and these were often provided from Queen Anne's Bounty, to pay for passages, the box of books that every missionary was given, with further batches often sent later, a basic missionary stipend until the local church was able to provide it and support for missionary widows and orphans.

A further element in Compton's very effective assumption of his responsibilities was the appointment from 1689 of Commissaries, his clerical representatives in the various colonies. Crucial for the creation of SPG was his appointment of Thomas Bray in 1696 as Commissary for Maryland. Bray, with his vision and extraordinary organizational talent, and with Maryland as something of a laboratory, began to see the wider needs of the Church in foreign parts, and how they might be met. His first step was, with four friends, to establish on 8 March 1699 a Society for Promoting Christian Knowledge (SPCK). This voluntary and essentially private society would, in addition to the tasks it set itself in England, raise funds to provide books, libraries and schools to strengthen and enrich the mission of the Church in its colonial parishes. The more substantial task of personnel for the mission required a more substantial organization and this Bray secured by means of the Royal Charter, devised in consultation with his SPCK friends, the Archbishop of Canterbury, Thomas Tenison, and Bishop Compton, and with leverage from Convocation. Like SPCK, the SPG was voluntary, but the Charter gave it authority, with accountability to the Lord Chancellor, to receive, manage and disburse public as well as private funds in order to maintain an orthodox clergy. It also provided a constitution which had the Archbishop of Canterbury appointed annually as President and chairing the monthly meeting, and nine senior English and Welsh bishops, the four principal theological professors at Oxford and Cambridge and some 86 others, including many eminent and influential laity, colonial governors among them, to direct its work. Others were soon added, including, by 1705, clergy and laity representing every diocese in England and Wales and several of the larger cities, while a branch of SPG was established in Dublin in 1714, including as members the two archbishops of the Church of Ireland, all the bishops and three laity. Over 40 leading members of the reformed Churches on the European continent were also made members, the link being provided by H. W. Ludolf and A. W. Bohme, secretary and chaplain respectively at the English court to Prince George, Danish husband of Queen Anne.[8]

The Archbishop of Canterbury and his colleagues in the Society appear to have taken up their new responsibilities with energy and with 'meticulous and superior planning', as the detailed accounts of their business in the *Journal*, reporting the monthly – sometimes fortnightly – meetings, indicate.[9] The growing number of members soon necessitated a Standing Committee, and this usually met, about twenty attending, at the Archbishop's Library at St Martin-in-the-Fields, London. They also needed a Secretary. The first, from 1701 to 1716, was a layman, John Chamberlayne, a graduate of Oxford and Leiden, a renowned linguist and a lawyer. He received his mail at 'St Paul's Coffee House in St Paul's Churchyard'. He was also Secretary to Queen Anne's Bounty Commission, Secretary of the SPCK, an active member of the Society for the Reformation of Manners and a Fellow of the Royal Society, for which he wrote learned papers; he was also gentleman waiter to Prince George of Denmark and gentleman of the Privy Chamber, first to Queen Anne and then to George I. Two Treasurers were appointed and, hardly surprisingly, within a year, the Society agreed to provide Chamberlayne with the assistance of a Messenger, William Carter, at £20 per year, the staff staying at this level more or less throughout the eighteenth century. An early task was to gather information; maps were acquired and interviews with colonial governors currently in London were supplemented by George Keith's mission of inquiry to America. Keith had previously lived as a Quaker in Pennsylvania, subsequently conforming in England, where he wrote *A Pilgrim's Progress from Quakerism to Christianity*, so he was well qualified for the tour of over a year that he undertook. His expenses were paid by 'eminent merchants' who were approached for contributions by members of the Society and the Dean of Lincoln applied to the Lord High Admiral for a berth for him on one of 'Her Majesty's ships to Virginia'. This was the *Centurion*, to which Bishop Compton appointed him chaplain for the voyage. It was soon necessary, of course, for SPG to formalize its procedures with missionaries, but it continued throughout the century to function with this close personal involvement of members of the Society in London and their contacts.

Keith's return prompted the first Report, in 1704, the Report being an annual feature thereafter to the present day. This first one covered all aspects of SPG's emerging concerns but emphasized the priority of work among Native Americans, to whom the first missionary had by now been sent. To the report of work done were added appeals for subscriptions and for missionaries.

A feature from 1702 was the Anniversary Sermon preached in a London church every February by a nominee of the Archbishop, invariably through the eighteenth century an English, Irish or Welsh bishop or senior clergyman, the printed version being widely distributed in Britain, Ireland and the colonies. The sermons were often significant statements, and provide some indication of the mind of the Society. The very first, in 1702, refers to the mission to Native Americans, as many do subsequently into the 1770s, advocating education and a civilizing mission, and identifying the rapacity of the settlers as the chief obstacle to the conversion of the indigenous people. George Berkeley's sermon in 1732 was perhaps the most fierce on this, suggesting that the settlers from the beginning had 'imigrate[d] Jews rather than Christians', imagining, as indeed they quite literally did, that they had a right to treat the Native Americans as 'Canaanites or Amalekites'.[10] Slavery was the other major theme of the sermons during the century, with regular references to the slaves' grievous and pitiable state. William Beveridge in 1707 was convinced that God would never have allowed 'such multitudes . . . [to be] brought out of Africa every Year, and made Slaves to Christians in America, but that he designed they should be there all taught the Principles of the Christian Religion', and some sent back as missionaries to Africa. The greed, wickedness and folly of the slave owners is regularly castigated, as is their refusal to acknowledge the slaves' 'immortal souls' and their 'right to be admitted to the Sacraments'. As early as the 1766 sermon, William Warburton denounced the slave trade as contrary to 'both divine and human Law', though the hints of Bielby Porteus in the 1783 sermon at the possibility of emancipation were firmly rejected by the Society. The terrible treatment of both Native Americans and slaves regularly led to the suggestion in the sermons that SPG should begin by trying to convert the English planters.[11] The other regularly recurring theme, referred to below, is the British government's denial of a bishop for America to renew the 'perpetual succession from the Apostles', the denial being 'a manifest injustice and oppression'.[12] These calls for a bishop evoked angry resentment among the Society's dissenting detractors in America from the early 1750s, best answered, Bishop Drummond suggested in 1754, by the comportment of 'a peacable, pure clergy'. The sermons themselves show surprisingly little animus towards the opponents of British rule throughout the most turbulent period, the 1770s, though the annual Reports were very bitter at what was happening to the missionaries.

An extraordinary diplomatic mission to London took place in 1710 of four Native Americans, known as 'The Indian Kings', three of them Mohawk. This episode, their reception by the Queen with all 'the symbolic theatre of state', and the 'unique . . . cultural impact' of the event has been described as a transformative moment in the 'dawning awareness of Britain's imperial destiny'.[13] SPG's involvement was notable. The four kings asked Queen Anne for more missionaries, and she referred them to the Archbishop and the Society. Also notable was the perception of SPG's significance in one of the more striking productions in the nascent literature of empire which accompanied the episode, Elkanah Settle's *Pindaric Poem, on the Propagation of the Gospel in Foreign Parts*.[14] For Settle, the Society's Charter signalled a revival of 'Apostolic Fervour' and marked 'An Epoch worthy of the British State',

> Since English Zeal o'er swelling Oceans bore
> The Saviour, & his Cross to th' Indian Shore.

This was something of an outsider's view – Settle was simply an onlooker upon the Society, a popular London poet. An insider's view some twenty years later, that of the Secretary, David Humphreys, in his *Historical Account*, confirms that the Society's role is to ensure that the 'mighty English Empire' emerging in America 'should be Christian'. Humphrey's vision is couched in the idiom of the Augustan Age. SPG's missionaries are guiding the colonial settlers from their 'former Rudeness . . . [to] become a religious, sober and polite People . . . [with] a manifest Change in . . . [their] Manners . . . [amounting to a] Reformation'. It is a serious vision, finding a place for the slaves as, quoting the Bishop of London, 'truly a Part of our own Nation', while the Society is represented as King William III's 'most valuable Legacy and greatest Blessing . . . to his American Subjects'.[15]

Settle's vision of 'the English Mitre . . . in Foreign Temples worn', indicates SPG's great problem in colonial America, the refusal of the British government to accede to its constantly repeated requests for a bishop or bishops. Only an act of the English Parliament could secure this, and this was denied throughout the Society's 70 years in America, leading to the absurd necessity of sending Americans to England for ordination, and to a weakened and incomplete Church until after Independence. The Society first called for a bishop in 1703, and constantly thereafter, with an American Colonial Bishops Fund established in 1717. One of the most energetic advocates was Archbishop Secker during the 1760s, urged on by a group of largely ex-Dissenter American clergy, in particular Thomas Chandler, Samuel Johnson and Henry Caner. The British government, pursuing its own domestic political interests, remained unmoved. Only with Independence did the American Church get its first bishop, and then not from the Church of England but from the small, persecuted Episcopal Church in Scotland, where a 'free, valid and purely ecclesiastical' episcopacy was made available in 1784, along with ideas for a constitutional and synodical Church. Throughout SPG's 70 years in America, the High Church polity which in some respects gave such great advantages to the Society's mission, in this regard betrayed it.

The year of the 'Indian Kings'' visit to London witnessed also the initiation of one of the most difficult challenges that SPG had to face. In April 1710, General Christopher Codrington, one of the wealthiest planters in the Caribbean, died, bequeathing a large plantation on Barbados and 300 slaves to the Society. His will, though unclear and a playground for lawyers for years to come, indicated that he wanted SPG to maintain the plantation, the profits going towards the Christianizing of the slaves, their education and health care, as an example for other planters to follow, and towards establishing a college, the purpose of which was regularly disputed from its inception in 1745. How well or badly SPG handled this unenviable responsibility is discussed in Titus's essay in this volume. Through most of the eighteenth century, it was regarded as eccentrically humanitarian.[16] By the 1790s, this was changing, the Society being pre-eminently in the sights of the abolitionists by this time.[17]

Elsewhere in the Caribbean, in the Bahamas from 1733, and on the Mosquito Shore in what is now Nicaragua from 1748, the Society had a handful of missionaries building up a Church of settlers, slaves and free blacks in the former, and of indigenous people in the latter.

The Society undertook a number of other, small ventures in the eighteenth century. In Europe, trading posts in Amsterdam and Moscow were supported with personnel or books from 1702, while warm relations with some of the reformed Churches led to support at various times for Protestant galley slaves in France and persecuted Palatines, for the Protestants of the Vaudois Churches and the University of Debritzen in Hungary. In India, SPCK took up the support of Lutheran missionary work, in a small way from 1706, more substantially from 1728. SPG contributed some small assistance, and was acknowledged as the inspiration of 'Christian Princes' on the European continent, amongst whom it was assumed was the King of Denmark, patron of this first German pietist mission work, that of Ziegenbalg and Plutschau.[18] The Society's only work in Africa in the eighteenth century was at a trading station at Cape Coast, referred to later, and a brief disastrous attempt to resettle a party of ex-slaves in Sierra Leone in the 1780s. In 1790, SPG started to supply schoolteachers, men and women, to work among the children of convicts transported from England to Australia.

It is with the Society's work in North America, however, in what became the United States, and in Canada, that most of the following account is concerned.

2

⊹⇒◎⇐⊹

Thomas Bray's Apostolic Charity

Thomas Bray's role in the formation of the Society was remarkable. 'I am called a *Projector* . . . on . . . account of these Designs I am continually forming', he remarked in 1699, at a time when several were in process of formation.[1] Within three years several very substantial projects had been implemented, a properly functioning Church in Maryland, the SPCK, the SPG and, at least in essentials, the charity for slave education known as Dr Bray's Associates. This brief but extraordinary phase of organizational creativity is best seen and understood, however, in the longer sweep of Bray's life.

From humble origins on a small farm in the parish of Chirbury in Shropshire in 1658, by way of the village school and the grammar school at the nearby town of Oswestry, Bray went up to Oxford in 1675 as a 'poor student' of All Souls College. His education there opened the way to ordination in 1681, and to the parish of Sheldon in the diocese of Coventry and Lichfield in 1690. It was here that he began to develop a lifelong missionary concern, that of catechesis. In 1696 he published *Catechetical Lectures on the Preliminary Questions and Answers of the Church Catechism, in four volumes*, dedicated to his diocesan, William Lloyd, who in a visitation had emphasized to his clergy the importance of catechizing. Bray's concern here, of course, was with Christian formation in an English country parish such as his own at that time. Among other features of his *Lectures*, three are important here. First, the identification of children and young people as more open to teaching than older people, and thus potentially 'a choice *Society* of . . . young Disciples . . . [a] *little Leaven* . . . [that] would soon season the *whole Lump*'. Catechesis had always been, of course, an element in mission, a part of the way into the life of faith, but here Bray clearly saw its additional significance in

15

revitalizing or re-evangelizing the existing Church. Second, there was a stress on the family as a place where faith was transmitted, learned and practised. Third, Bray emphasized the worshipping and eucharistic community as an essential end of mission. In this he again emphasized the leading role that his 'young Disciples' should take as the nucleus of a body of communicants and leaders in a revitalized worship, offering them the very latest aid by including in the first volume 'Psalms . . . out of the New Version of Mr. *Brady* and Mr. *Tate*', which had just been published that year. All these three elements in his *Catechetical Lectures* we will see Bray applying to the Church's missionary task in America. In an injunction of 1695, the Archbishop of Canterbury had called for regular catechizing throughout the Church of England. Bray's special interest clearly answered to a wide need, and the first volume sold 3000 copies, with large orders for the second.

Meanwhile, a wider field was opening for him. In autumn 1695, Bishop Compton agreed with the Governor of Maryland to appoint a Commissary, and he immediately approached Bray, who also immediately hired a curate to look after his parish so that he could, at least initially, base himself in London. With a population in Maryland at the time of some 25,000 settlers in some 30 parishes, but with these not as yet endowed and only eight of them supplied with missionaries, Bray's immediate task was to recruit clergy as missionaries, provide books and libraries for them and their parishes, and secure adequate financing for 'a Legal and Established Maintenance'.[2]

With the first of these, Bray was remarkably successful. Within three years, 21 clergy had been recruited for Maryland. During the next few years he was instrumental in over a hundred others leaving for various parts of America and the Caribbean.

An illuminating disclosure of Bray's mind and heart accompanied this new responsibility. This was the sermon he preached at the Advent Ordination in 1697, when Bishop Compton ordained six of these missionaries at the newly reopened St Paul's Cathedral in London. Bray's sermon, prefaced with a 'General View of the English Colonies . . . with respect to Religion', was published subsequently with the title *Apostolic Charity, its Nature and Excellence Considered in a Discourse upon Daniel 12.3*. The preface itself is interesting, and, like Gordon's book of 1700, though more narrowly conceived, not entirely dissimilar from William Carey's *Enquiry* of a century later. There are tables of information on some seventeen colonies, on the inadequate provision of churches, ministers and schoolmasters, libraries and free schools, including schools for 'Indian Youth', and an outburst of indignation that England, 'so much enrich'd' with profits from these colonies, and in sorry contrast with 'Mahometans

... Papists', and the Dutch, has so far done so little in mission, 'a melancholy consideration to such as have any true Love of God, or the Souls of Men'.

The sermon itself continually alludes to the text from Daniel, on the honour of those who 'lead many to righteousness', Bray defining 'righteousness' as 'Justice and Equity between Man and Man', and as 'the whole Christian Religion'. He also twice refers to the Great Commission in St Matthew's Gospel as the authority for the apostolic task of 'Evangelizing Mankind . . . [that is] incumbent upon every Christian Church and Nation'. Bray shares the European view that had prevailed from pre-Christian times, of 'the other' as 'Barbarous & Savage'.[3] Humankind is in a state of 'wicked Apostacy', of 'Inhumanity, Savageness and Brutality; whereby they are Beasts of Prey to each other'. In the computation of 'skilful Geographers', and using the data Gordon also used, nineteen thirtieths of the earth are inhabited by 'Idolaters . . . ignorant of the true God', not to mention the 'Idolatrous and other destructive Heresies . . . brought into Christendom itself'. The work of Christ is as 'an Ambassador Extraordinary', who proposes 'Terms of Reconciliation, and . . . [invites] Mankind home to God . . . and their Happiness'. The task of the missionary is 'the Conversion of Mankind . . . to enlighten them with a full and bright Knowledge of their Creator, Redeemer and Sanctifier . . . to stamp upon their Souls . . . [the] lovely Image of God', and the effect, echoing one of Bray's favourite writers, Erasmus, in his *Ecclesiastes*, 'the most Wild and Savage of Men . . . [will] become Innocent, Mild and Sociable'. There is a further task, among the settlers, of re-evangelization, 'to carry on to Perfection the . . . [instruction] and Conversion of Christians'. In this mission, the Church of England has a particular responsibility, being 'a Church so pure in its Doctrine, & so Heavenly in its Worship', making it 'the fittest in the World to be the Model to the New Acquisitions'. The nation owes this both as 'a grateful Return for that Blessed Light of the Gospel that has shone' among the English, and also for being 'so enriched by the Commerce and Commodities of so many Barbarous and Pagan Countries'. It is also timely, following the Glorious Revolution of 1688 and 'the little less than Miraculous Deliverances . . . received in the Preservation of our Religion and Liberties'. Mission is the special responsibility of the clergy, who are 'not only ordained and separated for this Work, but the Instructing, Inlightening and Informing of the World . . . is peculiarly the Pastor's Province'. They must have a thorough understanding of 'the Nature, Terms and Conditions of the Covenant of Grace, and the Nature of Christ's Mediation, through which it was obtained'. At the same time, they 'cannot now work Miracles . . . [and]

are left to the Ordinary means of Converting the World, *namely*, the Common Measures of God's Holy Spirit accompanying our own hard Study'. Bray takes the opportunity to attack the writings of 'Atheists, Deists, Socinians and Antinomians', which will spread 'Destruction and Ruin amongst the Souls of Men to the World's End', and to promote his concern for Christian schools, colleges and libraries, 'directly tending to the Everlasting Happiness of the Souls of Men'. All who engage in any aspect of this work, either directly or through their 'Wealth and Substance' are 'a sort of Apostles'. Seven hundred and fifty copies of *Apostolic Charity* were published and distributed.

With regard to books and libraries, the needs of Maryland led Bray into a project which was to be a major passion and achievement. He put the idea of the provision of books and libraries for Maryland first to Bishop Compton, and it was then endorsed by the two Archbishops and four senior bishops, who saw it as a means both to 'propagate Christian Knowledge' and also to encourage 'some of the more studious and virtuous persons out of the Universities to undertake the ministry in those parts, and . . . be a means of rendering them useful when they are there'. A pamphlet by Bray publicized the idea in December 1695, *Proposals for encouraging Learning and Religion in the Foreign Plantations*, many thousands of copies being printed over the next few years. The scheme gained widespread support, including that of Princess Anne, whose donation enabled Bray to plan a library for the new capital of Maryland, to be named Annapolis in her honour. He further elaborated his ideas in his *Bibliotheca Parochialis* of 1697, suggesting that the libraries needed to include secular titles to equip the missionaries for 'a very inquisitive age'. Later that year, his scheme was expanded to cover 'both . . . home and abroad', with 'Lending Libraries', a new idea of Bray's, to support the poorer clergy, some 400 of them, he estimates, 'in all the Deaneries of *England*'. Two years on, Bray was able to report £2500 spent on libraries and books in America and the Caribbean, 30 libraries functioning and another 70 begun.

It was in order to get this aspect of his activity and concern into a permanently organized form that Bray with his four friends, laymen of influence in business and the law, formed themselves into the SPCK. In this way, many of Bray's schemes for libraries in Britain and abroad, the publishing of books, the provision of schools and a great deal more, were given a means of continuity and permanence, in what was to be a sister organization to SPG.

By the autumn of 1699, the Maryland Church Act, to provide a settlement of the Church there, was sufficiently advanced by the Lords of the Council of Trade to allow and indeed require Bray to visit

Maryland, which he did, though only for two months, in early 1700. Here, he had to guide the Act through the Maryland Assembly, where he was strongly though ineffectually opposed by 'the Quakers openly and the Papists Covertly', before returning to see it through its final stages in London.[4] Bray had no quarrel or intention to 'intermeddle' with the 'Independency . . . [that seemed] to be the Religion of the Country', but only with the obstructive Quakers and Roman Catholics. His involvement saw Maryland's parishes securely endowed with a tithe on the tobacco crop, in addition to glebe land. Before leaving, he carried out a formal Visitation of the clergy, in which he laid down guidelines for the mission and ministry of the Church, full of echoes of his *Catechetical Lectures*. He clearly intended his visit as a first step towards permanent residence as Commissary. Over the next three or four years, however, problems in funding the post of Commissary proved insurmountable, and Bray's hopes of returning gradually faded, underlined by his return to his country parish of Sheldon in 1704.

Bray's visit to Maryland had shown him that the relative constitutional informality of the SPCK was inadequate to some of the chief needs of the Church in America and the Caribbean, especially with regard to maintaining missionaries. These required a chartered body. Although the proposal for this was backed by a resolution of the Lower House of Convocation, and initiated at a meeting of SPCK, and with 'the best persons in the Kingdom' secured as 'friends to . . . [the] design', the achievement of bringing the chartered Society into being belonged entirely to Bray. At the beginning of April 1701, he wrote and signed the petition to King William for a charter, citing his own recent observations in America in support of the project. He then prepared the first draft of the Charter itself and laid it before SPCK on 5 May for revision before submission to the King. Receiving it back from the Crown Offices duly signed and sealed on 16 June, he was right to call it 'my' SPG Charter. The first meeting of the Society was then summoned by the Archbishop, and Bray's energetic and creative role was complete.

His further involvement in the business of the Society, now with a permanent chairman in the person of the Archbishop and a formally appointed Secretary, was relatively slight. For the first year or two, he attended many of the monthly meetings, and until his return to Sheldon in 1704 was clearly very active on the Committee for Receiving Proposals, established in 1702 as the Standing Committee to prepare the business of the monthly meeting, while the Secretary wrote to him from time to time over the next few years for his opinion or advice. When the third Secretary of the Society, Humphreys, published his *Historical Account* in 1730, the year of Bray's death, the only reference was to his work as Commissary. Bray's vital part in things was only reaffirmed by the Society in a 'Historical Summary' published in the 1851 Report. The reasons for his earlier dropping out of SPG's memory are not clear.

What is clear is that Bray's gifts as a 'Projector' were far from exhausted by 1701. Despite much sorrow in his home life back at Sheldon with the death of two of his children, he returned, on his appointment to St Botolph's, Aldgate, in London in 1706, to a life bubbling with 'pious, useful and charitable' projects, many of them effectively fulfilled, though none of as great and enduring significance as those launched around 1700. The scheme for the amelioration of black slavery by evangelization and education that he had formed and discussed with the King's Secretary, Abel Tassin, in 1699, remained in abeyance until a gift from the latter enabled the establishment of Dr Bray's Associates in 1717. In addition to the Associates' chief work with slaves in America, which continued until 1777, they used the organization to secure grants for the foundation of the new colony of Georgia in 1733, three years after Bray's death, to fulfil a concern of his to establish a settlement for 'honest poor Distressed' English debtors and their families.

Though Bray's association with the Society dwindled, his concern for the mission of the Church in America in particular was lifelong, through his 'singular Affection for the whole Province' of Maryland.[5] The fullest and most interesting expression of this arose in response to the philosopher Dean of Derry, George Berkeley's *Proposal for . . . Converting the Savage Americans to Christianity* of 1724. His proposal was to establish a college in Bermuda to train young Native Americans as missionaries to their own people, a plan which, though eventually abandoned, attracted large promises of government funding. Bray was stung by Berkeley's 'Libel' that 'none but Illiterate Creatures' had gone as missionaries hitherto, which seemed to disparage all that he and the Society had been doing both in selecting missionaries and providing libraries for them. Perhaps this called out Berkeley's subsequent observation in his Anniversary Sermon of 1732 on the missionaries' 'Sobriety of Manners, discreet Behaviour, and . . . competent Degree of Useful Knowledge'. Bray was also upset at his 'Aspersions . . . for Neglecting the Conversion of the Heathen'. As for his 'incongruous' plan for 'this Utopian Seminary' in Bermuda, Bray indicated that a similar experiment, the Brafferton at William and Mary College in Virginia, had failed. He devoted ten pages to numbered criticisms of Berkeley's proposal, based on queries he put to his friends in Maryland, the chief one being that the Native Americans selected as missionaries would be alienated culturally in Bermuda and, returning to their own people, who were 'infinitely Tenacious of their own Customs', would be resented and rejected. 'Good God!' Bray exploded, 'What a Fatal Blow will this Man have given to the Propagation of the Gospel in Foreign Parts'. To 'prevent so fatal a Mischief', Bray presented his own proposals, addressed to his Maryland friends, stressing the importance of understanding 'the Nature and Situation of Mind, and Condition of Life, of the People to be Converted', supporting his arguments by the example of the Jesuits, and of the Presbyterian John Eliot among the Pequot people in New England in the previous century, quoting from the 'Royal Commentaries of Peru', and, at great length, from the 'excellent' writings of the Carmelite Thomas à Jesu. Bray's chief counter proposal was that to convert the Native Americans and rescue them 'from a Savage to a Civil and Human Life . . . Artificers in the Quality of Catechists' should be settled in their vicinity. Their life would draw the Native Americans from 'Roam[ing] about in the Woods, Hunting after Prey as the Wild Beasts do', into a settled, pastoral life, the men cultivating orchards, vineyards and gardens, the women making bread, butter and cheese, brewing, spinning and weaving, this life providing natural opportunities for catechizing them. He seems not to have been aware that some Native Americans in fact were horticulturalists. There is no record of the response of Bray's Maryland correspondents to his proposals, though, significantly they were echoed in Native American requests a few years later 'for missionaries to help in Husbandry', which suggests that he was on to something.[6]

Bray clearly had little patience with the view, whatever its motivation, that had designated Native American tribes as 'Nations'. Their itinerating, he believed, was uncivilized, and as such militated against their reception of the Gospel. In his critique of Berkeley's proposal, he picks on the term 'Nation', commenting, 'as some call them, and as they love to be so esteemed, though, God knows, some of them are like Gangs of Strolling Gypsies'. That view, attaching the Gospel to Western notions of civilization, and intent on 'reducing' the Native Americans to 'civility', had been the established procedure of Eliot and others for the best part of a century.[7] In it is delineated much of the theory of the missionary movement of the next two centuries, an interesting exception being described in Sohmer's chapter in this volume. His explosion against Berkeley, nevertheless, suggests some awareness, exceedingly rare at the time, of the need for discernment when cultural issues were concerned.

In this intervention just three years before his death on 15 February 1730, Bray took the opportunity to suggest an application of the funds of Dr Bray's Associates to the needs of 'the Negroes in our Plantations'. These were 'as much a part of the Pastoral Charge as the Planters themselves', but it was to the latter that Bray addressed his suggestions, and in particular to such 'Heads of Families among the Planters' as were 'tinctur'd with some Sense of Religion'. The Associates could provide them with such necessary books as *A Short, Plain and Delightful Method of Family Religion*. Could not these heads of families, 'being Priests, as it were, in their own Families . . . set up a Course of Family Religion and Worship in their Houses', and include in it all their slaves, both domestic and field, 'these poor Heathen having Souls Immortal and Precious as their own?'. Bray recommended once again, as in his Sheldon days, 'the Collection of Psalms . . . adapted to the Catechumens' as likely to be attractive to 'the Youth . . . both White and Black'. His further recommendations were already known in Maryland, to instruct and admit the slaves to the Sacrament, adding 'It may rejoyce our very hearts to behold minds so enlightened in bodies so dark.'

Bray's most creative and significant years, from the Society's point of view, came when he was in his early forties. His apostolic charity seems never thereafter to have deserted him.

3

⊱⋯⊰⊚⊱⋯⊰

Orthodox clergy, schoolmasters, two creditable white women and a surgeon

SPG's missionary appointments in the eighteenth century fell into a number of categories. There were the clergy, who were to work among the settlers, indigenous people and slaves in the emerging parish system, occasionally with an itinerating role. These were usually known as missionaries, sometimes ministers, while a number appointed to work among the slaves were called catechists. Laity were appointed to the position of schoolmaster, reader and catechist, within a parish and in association with a missionary. Women were also recruited in America by Dr Bray's Associates as teachers of the children of slaves, in Philadelphia, for example, working with the Society's catechist in the 1740s and in Williamsburg in 1760 on Benjamin Franklin's advice, while the Society in 1797 directed Codrington to employ Mary Howard and Mrs Reid, 'two Creditable white Women . . . for the sole purpose of teaching the young Negroes to Read & instructing them in principles of Religion'. The one medical post for this period, also at Codrington, was not always held by a Society missionary, though the first to hold it was, a clergyman with 'due testimonials of his skill in *Physic* and *Surgery*', but a disaster in other respects.[1]

With regard to recruitment, Bray had already shown what was possible as Commissary for Maryland. In the course of seven years from his appointment in 1695, he found and sent a total of 129 missionaries to America and the Caribbean. Much the same rate of recruitment followed in the Society's early years, though it was no longer Bray's responsibility. With close episcopal involvement in the Society, not only English but also Irish and Welsh, it was possible to broadcast the need for missionaries widely. By 1706, the Report was being used to encourage 'such Clergymen as have a mind to be employed in this Apostolical Work' to 'give in their names to their respective Bishops'.

23

Selection was thorough. Testimonials were required, covering a candidate's 'temper . . . prudence . . . learning . . . sober and pious conversation . . . zeal for the Christian religion and diligence in his holy calling'. SPG also sought confirmation of the candidate's orthodoxy, meaning doctrinal and canonical conformity, and also 'affection to the present government'. The attestor was asked to avoid recommendation 'out of favour or affection, or any other worldly consideration', but only with 'a sincere Regard to the Honour of Almighty God and our Blessed Saviour'. Testimonials were to be endorsed by the diocesan bishop or three communicants. A candidate was required to 'read Prayers and preach before some of the Members of the Society'.[2] Thus, William Cordiner read prayers at St Alphege Church in London on the Friday, All Saints Day, 1707, and preached at St Austin's the following Sunday on a text provided by the Committee.

This thorough process may help to explain the low failure rate among SPG's missionaries. There were, of course, exceptions, like the excessively materialistic William Dunn, who in 1707 asked the Society to send his salary to him in goods that he could sell at great profit, six dozen pairs of women's lambskin gloves, 'Roles & weirs for head Dresses Fashionable . . . [and] 12 pair of leather clogs for Women', a sidelight on the aspirations and needs of a colonial society. More common exceptions were those like John Winteley, accused of being 'a Whoremonger and a drunkard'. These examples from America are from the south, where Church of England clergy had a reputation for worldliness, but a very careful examination of all the clergy in South Carolina during the period concludes that, while about 10 per cent, amongst whom SPG had its share, made themselves liable to dismissal, a number, including more than its share from the Society, served with distinction, and 'the average minister was capable and well behaved'.[3] Very few in Canada or in the West Indies were ever dismissed. With regard to the Society's concern for the doctrinal and canonical correctness of its missionaries, no secessions from the ranks of the clergy took place during the period, while 'affection to the present government', underwritten by the ordination oath of loyalty, proved a very costly orthodoxy to many of those in America in the 1770s.

Initially, mission preparation was the responsibility of the individual concerned, supported by a set of 'Instructions', first published in 1706. These required that 'from the Time of their Admission, they lodge not in any Public House; but at some Bookseller's, or in other private and reputable Families', and employ their time until sailing 'usefully, in Reading Prayers, and Preaching . . . in hearing others Read and Preach; or in such Studies as may tend to fit them for their Employment'. There was a proposal in 1707 for a college for mission preparation on the Isle of Man but this was not taken up. Bray himself when Rector of St Botolph's took a number of younger men for preparation. His idea was that they should spend at least a year at this. They would study 'the whole System of Theology, Positive, Practical & Pastoral', giving 'a Proof of their Fitness for the Mission by the Experience had of their Industry, prudent Behaviour, and good Conduct'. He also 'put them upon a catechetical exercise on Sunday evenings' in the parish church, and arranged 'Preaching to our poor Prisoners in Two of the most forlorn Prisons in the Outparts' of London, this 'the better to inure them to the most distasteful part of their Office, and to bring them to a Temper of Mind, and facility of Expression to the level and low Capacities of the most Ignorant'. He hoped that the missionaries, in thus preaching the Gospel to the poor, would 'derive a Blessing from above upon their Ministry, as well as render them rationally ever after more useful in the same'.[4] Later in the century, mission preparation was seen as one of the roles of Codrington College, while King's College, New York, later Columbia University, was established in 1758 to train, among others, 'good and able Missionaries'.

A missionary and family might wait six months in London for a ship. During this time he was required to 'constantly attend the Standing Committee'. Before leaving, he was to visit his new Metropolitan and Diocesan, the Archbishop of Canterbury and the Bishop of London, 'to receive their Paternal Benediction and Instructions'.

There is no formal record of outfitting these early missionaries, though Bray was concerned to supply one of them with 'Gown, Cassock and Hat', and they could be granted something like £20 to cover 'equipping'.[5] Much more important from his distinctive point of view was to provide every missionary with a generous box of books. The 1702 *Journal* includes a list of 52 volumes, headed 'Bibliotheca Missionarum', a very solid body of divinity, including biblical commentaries, the Fathers, Aquinas, Herbert's *A Priest to the Temple* and, of course, for an Orthodox clergy, Hooker's *Ecclesiastical Polity*. A revised list was included in the 1705 *Journal*. Individual missionaries were also provided with books and tracts for distribution, for example, 50 copies of a tract against the Quakers, one hundred copies of a sermon on the Book of Common Prayer.

Stipend and expenses were also agreed in advance, and provision agreed for a missionary's wife and children 'in case he Dies'. Stipends amounted to £50 sterling, better than an English curate's average £35, but much less than a pluralist English incumbent's £300, though glebe guaranteed a good subsistence. Stipends were reduced as local provision increased. Missionaries to the Native Americans were paid £100, sometimes £150. Schoolmasters were very poorly paid, between £10 and £30, and were compelled to find other work as well, as town clerks and the like; William Forster at Westchester also practised 'Surgery and other Employments', while Daniel Denton at Oyster Bay, with responsibility for seven small children and a 'weakly woman . . . not brought up to hard usage', ran a tavern and brewhouse; others managed to secure school fees from the wealthier parents in their parish.[6]

Instructions relating to the voyage out perhaps reflect Bray's unhappy experience on his own earlier voyage to Maryland in the company of a parson who drank late in the Round House and Steerage and was suspected of consorting with lewd women on the ship. The instructions required the missionaries to demean themselves 'so as to become remarkable Examples of Piety and Virtue to the Ship's Company', prevailing if possible with the Captain to have Morning and Evening Prayer said daily, 'Preaching and Catechizing every Lord's Day', and throughout the voyage instructing, exhorting, admonishing and reproving with 'Seriousness and Prudence'. With such instructions observed, no ship can have been unaware that it had an SPG missionary aboard, one such being John Wesley who, on a long and stormy voyage to America in 1736, spent many hours in prayer and other godly exercises with a party of 26 Moravians on board.

Instructions for the missionaries in their country of work included twelve that refer to their personal ascesis in 'Propagating the Gospel of our Lord and Saviour'. These included a recommendation of periodic meetings for mutual advice and assistance, taken up strongly in regional conventions in America. The twelfth advised 'avoiding all Names of Distinction', that is, identification with political or church parties, preserving unity 'as a Body of Brethren . . . united under the Superior Episcopal Order, and all engaged in the same great Design of Propagating the Gospel', advice much reiterated in the nineteenth century and into the twentieth, as Evangelicals and Tractarians created just such 'Distinctions'.[7] A further fourteen related to missionary duties, liturgical, sacramental, catechetical, homiletic and pastoral. There are specific notes on convincing and reclaiming 'with a Spirit of Meekness and Gentleness . . . those that oppose us, or dissent from us', supplemented in 1735 by an instruction relating specifically to America, 'to promote loyalty'. Another, on 'instructing the Heathens and Infidels', required that they proceed, in a contemporary variant on a classic Catholic missiology, from 'the Principles of Natural Religion' to 'the Certainty of . . . Revelation . . . contained in the Holy Scriptures'. There are instructions on distributing tracts and books. The widows of missionaries are encouraged to set up schools, as Mrs Tizard did on Eleuthera in the Bahamas in 1770, and succeeded in reforming many of the children who had learned to curse their parents as soon as they could speak. A final group of instructions requires 'a constant and regular Correspondence with the Society', and the return every six months of *Notitia Parochialis*, specified statistics of their mission and its results.

Schoolmasters were also selected after careful enquiry. An early intention was that they should be in deacon's orders, but the growth of local recruitment soon rendered this impracticable. Catechists were appointed to work among Native Americans and slaves from 1704, and were usually appointed locally, and often, as it became possible, from within these communities. A set of fourteen instructions was published in 1706 for schoolmasters employed by SPG, the end being 'the instructing and disposing Children to believe and live as Christians'. Rote learning of the catechism was not enough, 'Sense and Meaning' needed to be understood, and 'kind and gentle Methods' were encouraged. The children's intelligent and reverent participation in liturgy, always a strong concern of Bray's, was emphasized. Regular consultation with the missionary was required and, again, a six-monthly return, *Notitia Scholastica*, to be sent to the Society.

Just over 410 ordained missionaries appeared on SPG's lists in the eighteenth century, mostly working in America and the Caribbean. In addition to the 309 in the (now) United States, fifteen worked in Newfoundland, 38 in Nova Scotia, eleven in New Brunswick, six in Lower Canada and three in Upper Canada, while in the Caribbean there were nineteen at Codrington and twenty in the Bahamas and Jamaica; there were also four in Central America, now Nicaragua, and three in West Africa. Some fifteen refugee-missionaries from the (now) United States around 1776 went on to work further north or in the Caribbean. Though many of the lay agents – schoolmasters, readers and catechists – contributed significantly to SPG's work, their number is more difficult to compute, with perhaps a quarter or third as many of these as there were clergy. At mid-century there were seventeen Society schoolmasters and 58 clergy in America. Some lay appointees of course went on to ordination.

Who, then, were these ordained SPG missionaries? Unique was the West African, Philip Quaque, at the British trading station at Cape Coast from 1765 and on the Society's list for 50 years, the first African in Anglican orders, deeply devoted to his task but, for much of the time, unimaginatively supported by the Society, indeed, scandalously ignored, his letters unanswered for years on end, though plainly cheered by kindly letters from Samuel Johnson in Connecticut.[8] Quaque had been identified for this work, and sent to England for training and ordination by the Society's first Cape Coast chaplain, Thomas Thompson. The largest single group of missionaries, perhaps a third of the total, was from England, their birthplace sometimes given, more often their ordination or the fact that they were 'ex-curate' of a particular parish, Ashington, Epworth, Horsham, Kendal, Petersfield or Pickering. There were significant minorities from elsewhere. SPG appointed 'numerous' Scots clergy in the century, including its first two missionaries, Gordon and Keith, and the first colonial bishop, Charles Inglis, born in Ireland but of a long line of Scottish Episcopalians. Keith was joined by John Talbot, a Cambridge Fellow who had had a parish in England but hailed from Montgomeryshire in Wales, and there must have been about 50 Welsh on the Society's list by 1750. About twenty on the list during the century are specified as Irish, but the total must have been considerably greater. There were also over 50 largely from a Dissenting background in America who successfully made the crossing to and from England for ordination, while there was also a handful born of missionary parents, while a few born of settler parents in the Caribbean and Canada were appearing on the list before the end of the century. There were also those who had been originally continental European Protestants from France, Germany, Sweden and Switzerland, like the intelligent and dedicated missionary, Francis le Jau, a Huguenot, born in France, a graduate of Trinity College, Dublin, and a Canon of St Paul's Cathedral, London, who worked for a year in St Kitts in the Leeward Islands and fifteen years in South Carolina. There was also a handful of former Roman Catholic priests, like Robert Norris, from Bath in England, Charles Boschi, described as 'formerly a Franciscan Fryer', and Michael Houdin, who acted as one of the chaplains to Wolfe's army in the capture of Quebec.

Among the lay agents recruitment was soon largely but never exclusively local, and also from a variety of backgrounds, the founding schoolmaster of the slaves' school in New York among the more exotic, appearing first in the Society's records in 'Orders made on board the Gallies of France' (1699) as 'the illustrious Mr Elias Neau who has since been delivered from his Bonds'.[9] Most of the schoolmasters at this time were recruited in Britain or from among the settler communities, but a number of Mohawk were trained by the missionaries as teachers and readers, and employed at SPG's expense. This was still seen as 'important to the rising generation' when a grant was made for this work at Kingston, Ontario, in 1792.

The majority of missionaries from Britain were from among the excessive numbers of poorer clergy with little or no expectation of ever escaping the poverty at the bottom of the Church's essentially class-determined structure. The books and libraries that Bray was so effective in supplying were in part intended as 'a necessary Encouragement . . . [to] induce a Learned and Sober Minister to go into the Service of the Church in . . . [the] Plantations . . . considering that few men of Fortunes . . . will go into such Remote Parts'.[10] Probably all had attended a university or college, most being graduates of, in the British Isles, Oxford or Cambridge, Trinity College, Dublin, or Aberdeen, Edinburgh, Glasgow or St Andrews.[11] Bray was concerned that these 'young Divines or Candidates for Orders in our Universities' should know about the libraries he was setting up in America and elsewhere, to encourage them to offer for missionary work. Most of the Society's missionaries originating in America were graduates of Yale or Harvard, some from William and Mary College and the College in Philadelphia, a few of the later ones from King's College, New York. Some of the missionaries clearly kept abreast of the thought of their times, Samuel Johnson in his conversations with George Berkeley at Newport, Rhode Island, being a distinguished case in point, and in fact several of the New England ex-Dissenting clergy were respected intellectuals. William Gordon, the missionary at Exhuma in the Bahamas in the 1790s, found that the refugee gentry were in their leisure hours reading the works of Mandeville, Gibbon, Voltaire, Rousseau and Hume, and had 'acquired a great tincture of infidelity', and he wondered if the Society might find 'a conversible Clergyman' able to take them on, and also supply some 'modern books of divinity in a good style', adding that 'ancient books would not be relished'.[12]

Finally, some reference should be made to the conditions under which the missionaries and their families lived and worked. The Atlantic crossing to America and the Caribbean, of course, made a hazardous beginning. That one-fifth of those who attempted the double crossing from America for ordination during the eighteenth century were lost at sea says almost all that needs to be said, though things were made worse by hostilities with the French which carried away a number of missionaries and their families as prisoners, some never to see America. On a voyage at its best, as Keith and Gordon experienced at the beginning, 'the great cabin' could be 'like a college for good discourse, both in matters theological and philosophical', but other missionaries, a group from Wales, for example, used to second-class citizenship, complained that they were 'in no respect better accommodated than the most common ordinary sailors'.[13] In the earlier years in particular, in America, the well-being of the missionaries and their families, often with seven or eight children, might well be in the hands of a poor congregation unable to provide much support, though SPG's own provision and the pressure it was able to exert on governors in many cases compensated. A much greater source of difficulty were the periodic uprisings of Native Americans, when houses and possessions would be destroyed and missionaries and their families forced to evacuate to safer areas. Disruption came likewise with the upheaval of the 1770s, when, for example, John Stuart had his house 'frequently broken open by Mobs', saw his church 'plundered by the Rebels . . . [and] afterwards employed as a Tavern', and, after release from imprisonment, had to make his way with his wife and three small children to Canada on foot.[14] It is not surprising that some missionaries only stayed for two or three years, but impressive how many persevered for their entire lives. Those settlers who became missionaries, of course, often worked for SPG for 40 or 50 years, like Henry Caner, 'Father of the American Clergy', who worked for the Society for 50 years in New England before seeking refuge in Nova Scotia in 1776, or Samuel Andrews who, after working in Connecticut for 24 years, went north to New Brunswick for a further 32. Others, too, originally from the British Isles, often stayed for the rest of their lives, like Edward Vaughan of Llandaff who worked in New Jersey for 30 years, dying there and bequeathing his property to the Society, James Honyman, born in Scotland, who worked in New England for 50 years, and James Balfour in the much less hospitable climate of Newfoundland for 37 years. Most who worked at Codrington, in the much more artificial society of a plantation, only stayed for an average of five years, as was also the case in the unhealthy climate of the Bahamas, where a number of missionaries died after working there only a year or so. On the Mosquito Shore of Nicaragua, also, none of SPG's missionaries managed more than about a year, except the remarkable ex-Moravian, Christian Frederick Post who, with his wife, after working for 30 years among Native Americans in Pennsylvania, served for twenty years as the Society's effective catechist among the indigenous people of the Shore, leaving, when he died, as his wife had predicted, 'nothing . . . but a beggar's staff', and a firmly rooted community of local Christians. The community was still flourishing, with 'a wonderful degree of enthusiasm and love for Mother Church', in the 1940s, when it passed from Society support to that of the ECUSA Diocese of Panama.[15]

4

⟡⟶○⟵⟡

Red, black and white – the Society in mission

In 1660, the Council for Foreign Plantations had been instructed by Charles II that Native Americans and African slaves 'be invited to the Christian Faith' and 'taught the knowledge of God and . . . the mysteries of Salvation'.[1] It is hardly suprising, then, that there were from the Society's inception these elements in its mission, mission to the indigenous inhabitants of North America, to the enslaved Africans there and in the Caribbean, and to the European settlers in both regions.

Bray had always had the first of these in mind, 'to civilize and convert' Native Americans 'in every Province', and the Charter required that provision be made for this. The first practical move came in response to a request from the Governor of New York considered at the third monthly meeting of the Society, in September 1701, to send two missionaries to work among the 'Five Nations' of the Iroquois, including the Mohawk. These being strategically located between the British colonies on the coast and the French in Canada, the mission would from the official point of view be 'for Improving the Interest of England' as well as 'for the Propagation of the Reformed Religion'.[2] From the Native American perspective, the issue was one of survival by accommodation to a stronger power. It entailed the surrender of land by a 'Deed, from the Five Nations to the King, of their Beaver Hunting Grounds', but with retention of hunting rights. There is no indication that they quoted the text, 'Come over and help us', though there are several references to the Mohawk leaders asking for missionaries and schoolteachers, most strikingly in the case of the 'Four Kings' during their London visit in 1710. The outcome of this particular mission, described in Anderson's essay in this volume, included the baptism of the majority of the Mohawk over the next half century, and a continuation of Society support well into the nineteenth, as they were progressively cheated of land they had been granted after their migration to Upper Canada.

The 1706 Report makes a distinction between Spanish evangelizing tactics in southern North America and what was going on in the British-occupied areas. In the former, 'the poor Natives' were brought to baptism by 'such violent Measures as could not possibly persuade or convince any Rational Creature. For, contrary to the Gospel Spirit of Meekness and Charity, they used all the Engines of Terror, Force and Cruelty in such a barbarous Manner, that their own Authors have made grievous Complaints of them'. The 'Spirit of the Reformed Protestant Religion', was quite another matter in the view of SPG, with 'not one Instance . . . of hunting poor Souls into a forced Conversion', these 'softer, milder ways' leaving 'those barbarous People more free and unprejudiced, and fitter to receive the Impressions of Christian Faith and Knowledge when by Degrees they should be made upon them'. The underlying issue of land, though, was crucial, and no doubt affected and in many cases negated the Society's efforts. The missionaries seem to have only dimly appreciated the courage and determination with which the Native Americans resisted the theft of their lands. Almost invariably it was assumed to be 'the fierce and cruel tempers of these poor Barbarians' that roused them to 'Vengeance, to Murder and Massacre'.[3]

SPG's records indicate the outstanding commitment and contribution of such converts as Thayendanegea and a series of Mohawk schoolmasters and readers. They also indicate the Society's substantial translation programme, several of its more able missionaries, Andrews, Barclay, Ogilvie, Inglis, Doty, Stuart and Addison, being engaged in this, and the strong support of laity such as Sir William Johnson, 'Colonel of the Six Nations', and Colonel Daniel Claus, both made members of the Society.

The Society's missionaries were involved with some 46 Native American tribes in all. Some endeavours were less successful than that with the Mohawk, for example that in South Carolina among the Yamasee prior to the Yamasee War of 1715.[4] The first missionary there, Samuel Thomas, arrived specifically to work with Native Americans in 1702. Some of his early successors, Le Jau and his schoolmaster, Benjamin Dennis, Robert Maule, Francis Varnod and Gideon Johnson, the Commissary, took a serious interest in the character and culture of the Yamasee, in the perspective of current 'Age of Reason' theories. Though they thought the indigenous population were 'much Inclined to Idleness', they saw much to admire, evidences perhaps of the 'noble savage'. Le Jau found them 'very quiet, sweet humour'd and patient, content with little which are great Dispositions to be true Christians'.[5] At the same time, 'They make us ashamed by their life, Conversation and Sense of Religion quite different from ours'. Maule noted a distinctive tribal virtue, describing them as 'Lovers of Justice and Equity'. Several of these missionaries were plainly looking for and found those evidences of natural religion to which SPG's *Instructions for Missionaries* had drawn attention, both in Yamasee ideas of 'the being of God and Immortality of the Soul', and in echoes they claimed to find of the Creation and Flood in local belief and ritual. Such discoveries reported to the Society in 1710 and 1711 took the missionaries nowhere, however, for they were already being overtaken by the growing estrangement of the Yamasee, chiefly because of what Le Jau called the 'many Enormities & Injustices' of the Indian trade, and the traders' enslavement of Indian women and children, the men taken prisoner being 'burnt most barbarously', all of which provoked the Yamasee War of 1715 and brought this early missionary endeavour to a close.[6] Expanding European occupation was accompanied by growing violence against Native Americans and the seizure of their land in what was to be over the next two centuries 'America's holocaust', and this of course frustrated many subsequent missionary endeavours amongst them.[7]

SPG established schools for Native American children, in Virginia, New England, Pennsylvania, New Jersey and New York and also further north, in Nova Scotia in the 1760s and New Brunswick in the 1790s. Remarkably, in spite of the colonizing process, and presumably as a strategy of survival, Native Americans did accept baptism in most areas, though never in large numbers, the Naragansetts in Rhode Island, in a striking reversal, expressing their gratitude by a gift of land to the Society in 1746.

Despite attempts to understand indigenous religion in the case of South Carolina, the attempts made to understand local languages were largely in order to advance Christian education and to incorporate new Christians into the liturgical life of the Church. This was done most extensively in the case of the Mohawk, with translations of a hornbook, a Primer, selected chapters of the Old and New Testaments, Thayenda-negea's St Mark, a *Compendious History of the Bible* prepared by John Stuart in 1774, the Book of Common Prayer and an exposition of the Catechism. Enabling the Mohawk Christians to keep to their own language, Andrews observed in a letter to the Society in 1713, was also some preservative against their learning the vices of the settlers.

There are a striking number of missionary accounts of Native Americans taking part in public worship according to the Book of Common Prayer, as well as engaging in private and family prayer. 'Many of the Indians . . . seem to have a serious & habitual sense of Religion;

they regularly attend Divine Worship, and participate frequently of the Lord's Supper, and tho' at this season they are all out upon the hunt several of the principals come near 60 miles to communicate at Christmas', while the 40 children in school in that case were making 'a considerable Progress in Psalmody'.[8]

In 1767, the missionary Thomas Wood, having compiled a Micmac grammar and translated portions of the Book of Common Prayer, conducted the first service in St Paul's, Halifax, for a Micmac congregation in the presence of the governor and many officers. Accounts of such events and treasured gifts of eucharistic vessels underline, no doubt, colonial co-option but also the full incorporation of converts into the liturgical life of the Church. In worship, at least, the Society thus brought into close Christian community peoples that were generally deeply and increasingly alienated.

⋅⟶⟨⟨⟨⟩⟩⟩⟵⋅

Regarding the African slave population, European planters in the Caribbean began to establish a purely racial slavery by the mid-seventeenth century, and on the American mainland it was seen as an economic necessity by the end of the century. The English Restoration had marked a turning point, with Parliament's legitimation of the slave as chattel, property and merchandise, to be controlled 'with strict severity'. While this seemed to be contradicted by the royal instruction that slaves be 'invited to the Christian faith', care was taken to specify in the Virginian Assembly in 1667, and in the other colonial legislatures subsequently, that 'the conferring of baptism . . . [did] not alter the condition of the person as to his bondage or freedom'.[9] Only the Quakers questioned slavery at this time, SPG and other Christian bodies finding scriptural warrant for accepting it in their interpretation of St Paul.[10] While there are frequent references in missionary reports to 'these poor people . . . poor negroes . . . poor creatures', the Society regularly recommended the purchase of slaves to farm a missionary's glebe or as domestics, the latter like the slave Toby, sent to London in mid-century by a missionary as a gift for the wife of the Secretary, Philip Bearcroft.[11]

SPG's mission was the first to the African slave population in English colonial America, to be followed by a Moravian mission. It was, of course, an almost impossible assignment, as Bishop Secker acknowledged in the sermon of 1741, because of 'the strong Prejudice . . . [the slaves] must have against Teachers from among those whom they serve so unwillingly', so that 'it . . . [could] not be wondered, if the Progress made in their Conversion prove but slow'. A second obstacle was the opposition of most of the slaveholders, on the grounds that either it took up valuable time or it gave the slaves wrong ideas about themselves. Regularly the missionaries had to remind them that slaves were equal to them in the sight of God. 'Many Masters can't be persuaded that Negroes and Indians are otherwise than Beasts, and use them like such,' Le Jau complained to the Secretary in a letter of 22 March 1709, but, he added, 'I endeavour to let them know better things'. At the same time, he was among those missionaries who suggested to the owners that Christian faith made slaves better workers.

This aspect of SPG's mission also began with its first missionary in South Carolina, Samuel Thomas, and a number of baptisms followed. Thomas was encouraged by his estimate that 80 per cent of the African slaves (presumably largely those born in America) could speak English, and that 'many of them . . . [were] desirous of Christian knowledge'.[12] In 1702 he reported that he had taught twenty of them to read while catechizing them. Catechizing by Society missionaries was often very thorough, a two-year preparation for baptism, and this combined with teaching literacy in a process of careful nurture and slow growth were marks of SPG's approach at its best. There was also much less effective work among slaves, as an inquiry by the Bishop of London in Virginia and Maryland in 1724 elicited, but few of the clergy involved were Society missionaries. This inquiry may nevertheless have inspired the Secretary's circular of the following year encouraging the missionaries in 'so good a work'. By then, one of the most sustained and effective applications of SPG's approach was well advanced, the work of the schoolmaster Elias Neau, who had opened a 'Catechizing School' in New York in 1704. By July 1707, he reported over a hundred slaves attending, the next year more than two hundred. Neau went from house to house, persuading the owners to send their slaves every Monday, Wednesday and Friday at 4 p.m. to his house where he taught them the Lord's Prayer, followed by the Creed, recited facing eastward, and Catechism. They were subsequently examined in Trinity Church. Some could not read, but 'could yet by Memory repeat the History of the Creation of the World, the Flood, the giving of the Law, the Birth, Miracles and Crucifixion of our Lord, and the chief Articles and Doctrines of Christianity'. In all, several hundreds under Neau's instruction became communicants. After his death in 1722, the school was carried on by other Society missionaries, frequently with 40 to 60 candidates for baptism annually, and continued to the War of Independence. SPG attached much hope to Neau's school as exemplary, and also provided the bulk of the funding for a further advance in slave education, the establishment of a school at Charlestown in South Carolina in 1743, in defiance of a state law of 1740 against teaching slaves to write. An aim was the training of black missionaries, though this was not very successful. The teaching in this case was 'by *Negro* Schoolmasters, Home-born & equally Property as other Slaves, but educated for this Service, & employed in it during their Lives'. Two black teenagers were purchased by the Society for this work. One of them, Harry, 'an Excellent Genius', proved very effective, teaching children through the day and adults in the evening, and the School for Negroes flourished in his care for over twenty years.[13]

Most of SPG's missionaries had responsibilites towards the settler communities as well as the slaves, and the balance of this varied. An early glimpse is of Francis Varnod finding seventeen slaves among the 50 communicants at his first Christmas in South Carolina in 1723. Clement Hall at Edenton, North Carolina, baptized some 5840 white and 355 black parishioners over some seven years from 1744, while Samuel Frink's church in Savannah, Georgia, had 680 settler and 520 slave members in 1767. Further north, in Philadelphia, George Ross baptized on one occasion twelve adult slaves 'who were publicly examined before the congregation and answered to the admiration of all that heard them'. The 1742 Report continues, 'the like sight had never before been seen in the Church', though it soon became a common one, the 1747 Report recording in consequence the appointment of William Sturgeon as 'Catechist to the Negroes'. Providing a somewhat different perspective, Samuel Johnson commented in Stratford, Connecticut in 1751 that 'as far as . . . [he could] find, where the Dissenters have baptized one we have baptized two, if not three or four negroes or Indians, and I have four or five communicants'.[14]

A number of Society missionaries in Nova Scotia and New Brunswick from the 1780s, several themselves refugees, ministered to the often quite large groups of ex-slaves who were also refugees there. The 1784 Report refers to 'many hundreds' of Christians among them, some of them 'constant communicants', others being baptized in their new settlements. SPG opened schools for them at Tracadie and Birchtown. Strikingly, the community at the former was led by a black Reader, Demsy Jordan, trained at the Catechizing School in New York, and he and his work recur in Society reports for many years, for example that of 1822, when a special grant was made for his work, until his death, recorded in the 1859 Report.

In the British Caribbean, 1.6 million slaves were imported in the course of the eighteenth century, where the system was run 'at a new pitch of intensive organization and commercialization', the slave population rising from just over 100,000 to nearly 600,000 in the period. In the small island of Barbados, just 144 square miles, the slave population in the same period almost doubled to about 80,000. The white minority, 15,000 in 1700, maintained its position by a climate of racial fear and a punishment regime 'severe and humiliating'.[15] What one Anniversary Sermon called 'this outrage on humanity' was continuously problematic for the Society because of its Codrington responsibilities, bringing what another called 'a load of guilt'.[16] On top of the fundamental problem of the outrageousness of the system, the Society had to contend with a dominant view in England through much of the eighteenth century that it was not outrageous. It was also frustrated by the contradiction between its own better aspirations and the consistently hard-nosed commercial calculations of its managers on the spot. Archbishop Secker confessed that he was out of his depth with the practicalities of SPG's responsibilities, with 'the technical Terms & Form of Merchants Accounts, which I understand not', and indeed the entire enterprise, 'We do not understand the affair'.[17] The most thorough study of this, the most fully documented of Caribbean sugar plantations, concludes that it was a case of 'perplexed Anglican prelates . . . doing their ignorant best', although another non-Caribbean assessment calls it 'an experiment in Anglican altruism . . . a missionary ideal attempting to penetrate a regime of slavery'.[18]

In 1727, the Bishop of London delivered an 'Address to Serious Christians' in England in support of the Society's work among slaves, in particular to secure funds to appoint more specialist Catechists for this work. He made the point that the slaves 'contribute much by their Labour to the Support of our Government', while, speaking of 'the inestimable Value of a Soul', he claimed, 'The Souls for which I am now pleading . . . are truly a Part of our own Nation'. Much of the ambiguity of an Ancient Regime Church in mission is exemplified there.

⊷══◐═⊶

The Society had from the beginning regarded its work among the white, settler communities in America as very important. At its meeting on 28 April 1710, when the four Iroquois 'kings' visiting London were formally welcomed by SPG, it was agreed that the missionary task did 'chiefly and principally relate to the conversion of heathen and infidels'. The decision at that time, however, to 'stop . . . the sending of any more Missionaries among Christians' except in special circumstances, was not implemented, and the Society continued as long as it was deemed necessary or proved possible to direct a large part of its attention to the colonists. There were a number of compelling reasons for this.

One was to improve the witness borne by the English settlers to Native Americans and slaves. The missionaries to the Mohawk often commented on the destructive effect of settler behaviour as being 'very

37

unchristian, particularly in taking away their Land from them without a Purchase', while the Secretary, Humphreys, noted more generally that,

> It would be ineffectual to begin with an Attempt to convert the Indians and Negroes, and to let our own People continue in their gross Ignorance, or Supine Negligence of all the Duties of Christianity: For both the former Sorts of Men, would necessarily take their first Impressions concerning Christianity from the English; and when they found them pay so little Obedience to the Laws of the Gospel, must either neglect it as an unprofitable Labour, or hate it as a heavy Imposition.[19]

The missionary theory was impeccable, the implications of the 'Laws of the Gospel' hardly imagined among slave owners and inside a violent, land-hungry colonialism.

There were however, other compelling reasons for work among the settlers. The Charter had noted that provision of clergy and schoolmasters for the embryonic parish system was 'very mean', with many settlers 'abandoned to Atheism and Infidelity'. As Humphreys put it in 1730,

> The first Planters, those of the British Nation especially, as coming from a Country blessed with the purest Religion, and truest Liberty, retained some remembrance of both, and lives through the force of that, in those wild Parts, among the Savages and Woods, in human Civility and Decency, tho' I cannot say, in Christian Order.

These, having been 'once Christians, at least their Parents', SPG's task in this aspect was to re-evangelize the Church. A mission of this sort was, Samuel Johnson suggested to the Secretary in 1755, 'perhaps as great a charity as even *in partibus infidelium*'.[20]

News of the formation of the Society soon spread among the settlers, and 'very earnest Letters', memorials and petitions were often received in London. A Philadelphia vestry solicited help in the 'propagation of the sacred Gospel' among its own colonialist parishioners 'in these remote and dark Corners of the Earth', while requests from both Monmouth County and Salem, New Jersey, quoted Acts 16.9, 'Come over and help us', as on the Society's seal.

The missionary's first step, often, was to secure the support of local worthies, as George Ross seems to have done somewhat sycophantically, preaching whenever he could create the opportunity before the 'Governor and Justices' and in the County Courthouse. Otherwise, it was a matter of visiting settlers in their homes, these often widely scattered even in what was known as a town, perhaps only a handful of houses scattered over several miles.

In Long Island in 1704, John Thomas discovered the people 'wholly unacquainted with the Blessed Sacrament for five and fifty years together', while the same year Thomas Crawford in Pennsylvania found the people 'very ignorant', not one man in the county understanding 'how the Common Prayer Book was to be read', so that he was 'forced to instruct them privately at home, in the Method of reading the Liturgy'. Sometimes the missionaries' reception was very good. James Honyman's original house meetings in Providence in 1704, for example, grew so fast that they had to move out into 'the open fields' for worship. Elsewhere in New England, under Dissenter influence, the missionaries were initially resisted, with fines, imprisonment and boycotts. Evan Evans was able to bring a special contribution, the liturgy in Welsh, to a community of Welsh speakers in Pennsylvania in 1716 who had been 'bred up Members of the Church of England', but had 'unhappily fallen into Quakerism for Want of a Minister'. The libraries provided by the Society, with books and tracts like 'Dr Beveridge's Sermon of the Excellency and Usefulness of the Common Prayer', were an important resource. Robert Maule noted that they made 'the whole People in general more inquisitive about their Spiritual Concernment'. Schools were another aspect of the re-evangelization, because, as one applicant to the Society put it, if children continued 'to be deprived of Opportunities of being instructed, Christianity . . . [would] decay insensibly . . . [leaving] a Generation . . . as ignorant as the Native Indians'. Many churches were built, occasionally timber-framed and clapboarded, but often of stone or brick and with a steeple, a wooden altar inside, with a railed chancel, a 'decent Pulpit and Reading Desk' and a royal coat of arms. John Lyon in Pennsylvania in 1774 was ministering 'in an old ruinous church in the forest to a considerable number of poor people', but by this time there were many large and handsome churches, evidence of the close identification with educated and prosperous groups in the towns, like the church in New York for which Sir William Johnson provided in 1773 'a neat organ which cost him £100'.

As early as 1730, Humphrey had concluded that SPG's efforts were producing 'a religious, sober and polite People'.[21] This re-evangelization, in other words, was broadly conceived.

> The genius of Thomas Bray and his successors lies in their complete understanding of the frontier problem of intellectual poverty in all its ramifications. With superb intelligence, they took steps to remedy this colonial poverty of the mind and soul . . . Their major objective

was the equalization of Christian culture on both sides of the Atlantic.[22]

Some of this endeavour found expression in the specificities of 'the Moderate Enlightenment', in which the Society's William Smith, first Provost of the College of Philadelphia, was a major figure, aiming through education 'to make better Men and better Citizens', but SPG aimed at this much more widely through the influence of the entire body of educated missionaries, and the schools and libraries that the Society and SPCK brought to eighteenth-century America.[23] The Society's gifts of books to colleges over which it had no control and almost no influence, Yale and Harvard, for example, and the 1500 books for King's College, New York, in 1749, are suggestive of the scope of the re-evangelization attempted.

In this mission in eighteenth-century America, the strong political component, the intention to replicate the Church's political hegemony in England, found expression in the Secretary's reference in 1730 'to . . . [settling] an Establishment'. The political culture of America was developing, however, in a very different direction, as Calam's essay in this volume indicates. This was only too evident in the very plural religious situation with which SPG missionaries were confronted in some colonies, vigorous in its diversity and with a rising political content. It was represented in a spectrum from relatively respectable 'Dissent', Presbyterians and Independents, through to every sort of 'impudent . . . Enthusiastick . . . Sectarist'. Humphreys said New England 'swarmed' with them, as did Pennsylvania, and missionaries' reports refer to Anabaptists, Antinomians, Antipaedobaptists, Arrians, Bowlists, Brownists, Conformitants or Formalists, Davisonians, Dunkers or Dippers, Eutychians, Familists, Gortonists, Levellers, Mountain Men, Muggletonians, New Born, New Lights, Old Lights, Quakers, including Foxonians, Rogereens, Sabbatarians, Sandemanians and Sandemanians Bastard, among others. The official *Instructions for the Missionaries* called for the reclamation of these groups with 'a Spirit of Meekness and Gentleness', though this did not always obtain, George Keith, for example, in the earliest period, incessantly attacked the Quakers in speeches and pamphlets. Much, indeed, of the literature produced by the missionaries in America was polemical, as, for example, their part in a 'decade of torrid controversy' in the *Boston Gazette* in the 1760s.[24] Many of the missionaries, however, and some of the Dissenters, seem to have approached things more irenically. Dissenters in New Jersey, for example, contributed to the cost of building a Church of England church at Amwell in 1753 and later of repairing it, and others at

Maidenhead loaned their Meeting House to the Church of England congregation in 1763.

There are frequent reports of Dissenters worshipping in the missionaries' churches, and of many, even from 'rigid dissenting families', transferring their allegiance, while Evan Evans'evening lectures in Philadelphia attracted many young people, chiefly Quakers 'who dared not appear in the Day time, at the publick Service of the Church, for fear of disobliging their Parents or Masters . . . [but] would stand under the Church Windows at Night and hearken', many subsequently being baptized. One-fifth of all SPG's ordained missionaries were American-born and had been brought up Dissenters, among them Samuel Seabury, father of the first American bishop. The most spectacular case was the group of gifted Congregationalists, led by the President of Yale, Timothy Cutler, with Samuel Johnson and others, who travelled to London for ordination in 1724 and returned with their honorary Oxford DDs, Johnson later becoming the first President of the Society-supported King's College, New York. Not all ex-Dissenters had such effective later ministries, a group of parishioners in South Carolina complaining that their ex-Presbyterian rector, Ebenezer Taylor, tended in the liturgy to lapse 'into a long and unmannerly Expostulation with God Almighty after the Method of the meanest and most ignorant of the Presbyterians'. Undoubtedly, though, large numbers were, in Humphrey's phrase, 'engaged . . . to a Conformity'.[25] The Church's 'formal and mannerly' liturgy, and its image as a 'dependable, rational representative of Christianity', were attractive and, to many, a welcome alternative to the 'Awakenings'.[26] Certainly, the Church grew impressively among the settlers, not least between 1760 and 1775, the number of licensed clergy nearly doubling over that of the previous fifteen years. An increasing number of the clergy during this period were American-born, especially in New England. Similarly, while in the 1750s, only 21 churches were built, a further 90 were added in the 1760s, with congregations growing to fill them. The Church's involvement in education, with institutions like King's College, New York, opened in 1754, and the College of Philadelphia in 1755, aided the perception of the Church as a local institution. As such, it is not surprising that it survived the upheaval of American Independence remarkably strongly.

While the issue of Dissent was very central to the concerns of SPG missionaries, a much less difficult phenomenon was the growing number of continental European settlers, both in America and later in the century further north, amongst them Calvinists, Lutherans and Moravians. The Church of England viewed these Churches positively – they were, after all, represented in the membership of the Society in London. The chief concern seems to have been to assist in their institutional survival, with little attempt to force them into Church of England ways.[27] John Wesley's journal for Sunday 30 October 1737, during his brief time as an SPG missionary at Savannah, himself a thorough High Churchman, provides a glimpse,

> The first English prayers lasted from five to half-past six. The Italian, which I read to a few Vaudois, began at nine. The second service for the English (including the Sermon and the Holy Communion) continued from half an hour past ten to half an hour past twelve. The French service began at one . . . About three I began the English service . . . about six the service of the Moravians, so-called.

There were clearly, nevertheless, in some cases, efforts to bring individuals and groups into 'a uniform and public Worship'.[28] To this end, the Society provided several versions of the Book of Common Prayer, for example, in 'Low Dutch' for the Dutch in New York, in French, with Bibles also, for French settlers in New York, South Carolina and Halifax, and in German, called 'High Dutch', for the Palatines in New York and Germans in Virginia, Nova Scotia and Montreal. This was not always successful. In South Carolina, a group of former Huguenots encouraged their clergy to revert, the Commissary complaining that the heart of one of them was 'not with us, but at Geneva or Elsewhere'.[29] Many, however, like some of the Dutch of New York, became deeply committed to their new Church. Likewise, a number of ministers of Lutheran and other congregations sought Anglican orders, something like a dozen travelling to England for ordination and becoming Society missionaries during this period.

In 1776, when America declared itself independent, about a third of the clergy, some 73, were on SPG's list. Of these, over 40, mindful of the oath of allegiance to the English sovereign taken at the time of their ordination, fled with their families, either to England or further north. Many of these, in the process, suffered grievously at the hands of the Patriots, and a number died. One was locked in a room to contemplate a picture of Oliver Cromwell before becoming a refugee. Some, however, stayed, and were among the hundred or so clergy who, with large numbers of the laity, supported the Patriot cause. Two-thirds of the 55 signatories to the Declaration of Independence were what were by then beginning to be called Protestant Episcopalians, members of an emerging sister Church to the Church of England, busily reforming itself on republican lines and proving its resilience and vitality.

Further north, in Newfoundland, Nova Scotia and New Brunswick, where the first missionaries had arrived in 1703, they had found things much less advanced, the communities newer and less developed, conditions very harsh, with only a handful of missionaries in place at any given time. By the mid-century, small and often very poor settlements of fishing families and businesses were supplemented by larger schemes of settlement launched by the Board of Trade and Plantations, Halifax becoming the main centre. Waves of French, German and Swiss Protestant immigrants were followed later by thousands of usually destitute refugees from America, who created an almost overwhelming situation for the few missionaries, but loyalist clergy among the refugees were an added resource. The consecration of Charles Inglis as Bishop of Nova Scotia at Lambeth in 1787, himself a refugee from New York, where he had sparred in pamphlets with Tom Paine, consolidated the mission of the Church in that vast region, and an SPG missionary thus became the first bishop of an English colony. Inglis's diocese included Upper and Lower Canada at first. Here, the pioneer missionaries were some of the chaplains with Wolfe's army, including Michael Houdin, who appears to have had a key role as an intelligence officer at Quebec, and those who were missionaries to the British army's Mohawk allies, John Doty, John Ogilvie and John Stuart, the last known as the 'Father of the Church in Canada', along with a small number of new missionaries sent by the Society.

⌖

Thus did the High Church Society propagate the Gospel in the eighteenth century. There was a highly significant but not easily computable 'transit of culture' involved in the case of America, but there were also, thanks to the systematic information embodied in the *Notitia Parochialis*, plain numerical facts to be noted, making clear that the Society's missionaries baptized more non-Christians (and the *Notitia* were most fully completed in regard to Native American and black parishioners) than were baptized in the first 40 or 50 years of the evangelical revival of the nineteenth century.[30] In relation to indigenous North Americans, that propagation had to contend increasingly with the barbarities of white settlement in the continent, so that its limited successes were remarkable enough. That is perhaps even more true of the slave population both there and in the Caribbean. When account has been taken not only of the appalling context of that propagation but also of the evident later attraction of other forms of 'slave religion', SPG's endeavours nevertheless laid the foundations of that 'dedication and unfeigned loyalty that blacks . . . [subsequently showed] to the Episcopal Church for 200 years', and without doubt to Caribbean Anglicanism also, because it was and is 'a catholic institution . . . divine and in place before racial inequality'.[31] This also, of course, may help to explain how that High Church propagation, encumbered as it was with the political theology of England's Ancient Regime, yet carried through a re-evangelization that made the Society, by its 'nursing care and protection', as the Preface to their Prayer Book put it, 'the first builder of . . . [the] ecclesiastical foundations' of the Protestant Episcopal Church in the United States.[32]

SECTION 2

The nineteenth century

5

⚬⟹⟸⚬

Greater Britain

There was a moment in the world's history when Britain can be described as its only workshop, its only massive importer and exporter, its only carrier, its only imperialist . . . An entire world economy was . . . built . . . around Britain, and this country therefore temporarily rose to a position of global influence and power unparalleled by any state of its relative size before or since, and unlikely to be paralleled by any state in the foreseeable future.[1]

It is the earlier nineteenth century that is alluded to chiefly here, although Britain's political reach outlived its economic considerably, with the colonial empire at its widest in the 1920s. While the Bishop of Ripon, in his Anniversary Sermon of 1841, was able to rejoice that 'the sun now never sets upon the Kingdom of the Saviour', the empire as the context for SPG's work, as indeed for that of the numerous additional British mission agencies which came into being from the 1790s, was problematic – exemplified in the fact that the posts of Secretary of State for War and the Colonies were combined between 1794 and 1854.

Part of the situation which faced the Society and other British mission agencies was the vast number of the colonized, something like a quarter of all humanity as the century advanced. Some of these peoples fared particularly badly under colonization. An illustration from the 1820s in the first issue of SPG's monthly, *The Mission Field*, was an engraved portrait of a woman called Shanawdith. She was the last survivor of the aboriginal Boeothic people of Newfoundland, who were driven away by the settlers from their familiar shores and rivers, where they had sources of food, into extinction. Shanawdith herself died in 1825.[2] Gradually supplanted from their homes and land as the occupation advanced

47

westwards, and increasingly confined to reserves, the only significant remnants of the 'First Nation' Canadians in the later decades of the century were in British Columbia. As a writer in the January 1899 *Mission Field* put it, 'the Indians move their wigwams further west, but civilization is on their track'. Similar experiences of displacement, dispossession and destruction accompanied colonization elsewhere. SPG's first missionary in Western Australia, George King, commented in the 1844 Report,

> We have usurped their well-stocked hunting grounds, taken possession of their fisheries, and ploughed up the very staff of life, which the rich valleys naturally yielded, in the bulbs and roots so genial to native life.[3]

With none of this sensitivity, the Bishop of Grahamstown gave his view of the South African situation in the 1860 Report:

> The change that has taken place in British Kaffraria during the last 12 months is indeed surprising, the country, which before was filled with savages being (with the exception of the Mission Stations and Crown Reserves) subdivided into farms occupied chiefly by English. In all directions, farmhouses are seen instead of Kafir kraals, and the country is being filled with life.

In many places, it was being filled with death, in what plainly amounted to genocide.[4] In Australia in 1869, a Society missionary, J. K. Black, referred to the 'wholesale massacres' of native Australians by the colonists, and in fact only 3 per cent of the aboriginal inhabitants of Australia survived the era of colonization, 13 per cent in New Zealand and none in Tasmania. Further into the Pacific, the September 1858 *Mission Field* carried a report of the 'slaughter' of islanders by English and French intruders, while the 1871 Report identifies a growing 'slave trade', accompanied by 'contempt and injury', inflicted on the people of Melanesia.

SPG and other mission agencies were confronted with vastly larger native populations in India and China, where British imperial dominance and influence presented a different sort of context for mission. In India, and in a variant form in China, it was not so much colonial settlement as economic exploitation, often of a very ruthless and destructive type, bringing about for example the industrial devastation of Bengal in the first half of the nineteenth century, accompanied by immense suffering, and the swamping of China with narcotics, which was liable to blight the relationship of missionary to local population.

With the abolition of slavery, its replacement, indenture, was another aspect of the colonial scene in the nineteenth century. Some three million people from India and large numbers from China and elsewhere were shipped about the colonies – to Fiji, Guyana, the West Indies, East Africa, Natal, Malaya, Mauritius, etc. – to work for colonial agricultural interests, only a minority ever returning to their native countries. Some of these, particularly from South India, were Christians. Known as 'coolies', these uprooted peoples in what was nothing less than a new system of slavery provided another field of missionary encounter and service.

The diversity of the peoples encountered is suggested in an account of Guyana in the February 1870 *Mission Field*. Described as 'an epitome of the Church's work', something of the globalizing character and effect of 'Greater Britain' is evident here. In addition to the various 'tribes of aboriginal Indians', amongst whom SPG missionaries had worked continuously and with some success since 1835, there were,

> Englishmen, natives of the North American Union, French, Dutch, Portuguese, Creoles, emancipated Negroes, and Negroes imported since emancipation from the West Indies and from Africa, Mohammedan and Hindu Coolies from Calcutta, Madras and Bombay, with immigrants from China, Madeira, Malta, the Azores and the Cape de Verde Islands.

Emigration from Britain, which had accompanied the 'First British Empire' in eighteenth-century America and the Caribbean, accompanied the second on a much greater scale, and much more widely, some fifteen million people leaving Britain and Ireland in the nineteenth century for, in particular, Canada and the United States, Australia, New Zealand and South Africa. The Charter made emigrants as much a concern of the Society as the colonized.

Most of the earlier emigration was involuntary, an aspect of 'confinement, that massive phenomenon . . . across eighteenth-century Europe', which from the previous century in England had entailed the poor being 'banished and conveyed to the New-found Land, the East and West Indies'.[5] Thus, SPG's earliest involvements in Australia were to provide a book grant for the first Government chaplain to convicts at Botany Bay in 1787 and, from 1794, schoolteachers, men and women, to work among the convicts' children on Norfolk Island. A slightly later glimpse of this particular emigrant people occurs in the 1839 Report, quoting a

House of Commons Report on Transportation. With recurring reference to 'the depravity of the lower orders', and pointing out that the proportion of convict men to convict women was seventeen to one, they are described as constituting

> a peasantry unlike any other in the world, a peasantry without domestic feelings or affections, without parents or relations, without wives, children or homes; one more strange and less attached to the soil they till, than the negro slaves of a planter.

Very often, it was a peasantry in leg-irons or chains. SPG pressure in Parliament contributed to the abolition of this brutal institution, transportation to Australia, in 1852.

Other cases and types of involuntary emigration show up from time to time in the Society's records. Thus, in 1827, the Bishop of Nova Scotia, on his first visit to Bermuda, part of his diocese, reported finding 'many hundreds of convicts' there, at the dockyard; he requests SPG to provide a chaplain. Somewhat different was the practice of sending pupils from the St John's Wood Clergy Orphans School to train as 'clerical students' at Bishop's College, Calcutta, from the 1820s, though they went with the consent of their guardians – orphans generally were sent in large numbers to the colonies after 1830. In 1858 the Society's files contain a proposal from Sir Thomas Phillips to transport to India 'able-bodied men and women from workhouses' to staff 'a vast number of . . . settlements and fortresses in India as a defence against Russia and a potent method of evangelism', a proposal that SPG appears to have ignored.

The Society provides a very interesting picture of the later, voluntary waves of emigration from Britain, these acquiring the features of a mass movement from the time of the Irish famine in the late 1840s, including many Protestants from there. The 1848 Report refers to 'scarcity . . . great straitness and distress' in Ireland, the highlands of Scotland and parts of England, leading to emigration 'beyond all former precedent', with 116,000 sailing to the British colonies that year in addition to 142,000 to the United States. The following year, SPG set up with SPCK an Emigrants' Spiritual Aid Fund. This entailed appointing a Chaplain to Emigrants at Liverpool, with further appointments to the port of London and ports across the Atlantic, endowment for an immigrants' hospital in New York, appointment of missionaries in transit as chaplain to the ship in which they sailed, provision for shipboard libraries and a system of commendation to the colonial Church. In the cadences of the missionary

St Paul, the Chaplain at Liverpool, J. W. Welsh, in 1862, gave thanks for God's watchful care over his work on the River Mersey,

> in perils of sickness, and perils of waters. Twice have I been seized with ship cholera, and twice have I been immersed in the river, and obliged to swim for my life. I have been exposed to every kind of accident, every form of danger, every change of weather, in open boats, in a treacherous river.

He would often accompany a ship as far as the open sea, assembling the people on deck for prayers, 'the whole 400 voices joining heartily . . . [in] the 100th Psalm', perhaps baptizing infants born since the emigrants had left home, ministering communion to upwards of a hundred, and parting from his temporary congregation after raising three cheers, 'for the Queen, the Church, and Old England'. In the June 1857 *Mission Field*, he noted large numbers of 'infidels, downright avowed infidels' emigrating to Australia, 'mechanics . . . chiefly from Manchester, Rochdale and London', about 400 leaving weekly, while 'the character of those who proceed to Canada . . . [was] exceedingly promising . . . small farmers, farm labourers . . . almost exclusively members of our Church, and therefore most enthusiastically loyal to our gracious Queen'. In the 1863 Report, he noted that recent emigrants had been 'first-class people, not as formerly the refuse of the country', and referred to how 'Thousands of the suffering mill-hands in Lancashire are hoping to be enabled to emigrate during the present year.' In great tides – 'in numbers without parallel' into Canada according to the 1882 Report – this process continued well into the twentieth century.

⋅⊷═◉═⊶⋅

In early Society responses to this second empire, expressed in the Anniversary Sermons, attention was largely on the mercantile aspect of British expansion, suggesting to the preachers simply widening horizons for mission. Already, however, in 1798, the Bishop of Carlisle had seen the negative side of this:

> God knows, that the rapaciousness of commerce, the thirst for wealth, or the desire of conquest, are not well calculated to prejudice . . . [the colonized] in favour of a Religion which they may suppose to authorize such excesses – or at least not to condemn them – and he whom we term savage and unenlightened, hath yet sufficient both of reason and acuteness to urge the objection in its strongest form. –

51

'What, he will ask, is this better religion, which does not make better men?'

The Bishop hoped that the presence of SPG's missionaries might modify the question. The Bishop of Norwich, in his 1810 sermon, was more positive. Citing a work of Richard Raikes, *Considerations on the Alliance between 'Christianity and Commerce'*, he suggested that British merchants, being 'the Honourable of the earth', were 'peculiarly qualified to "prepare the way of the Lord".' A slightly later Bishop of Carlisle in the 1812 Sermon contrasted the 'mastery and dominion' exercised by the merchant and colonizer with the 'different arts' of the 'blameless' missionary.

The contrast was exemplified in practice in one of the Society's first missionaries in Bengal, Thomas Christian, who, going on a 'laborious journey' among the hill tribes, 'might have performed the journey with greater ease and security by accompanying the Collector of the district', but, Bishop Heber explained to the Society, 'declined the offer, apprehending that the bustle and parade attending an official progress would interfere with his means of obtaining access to the people, and with the discharge of those lowly duties to which he . . . [had] devoted himself'. Perhaps that is why the local people saw him, according to another SPG missionary, 'in the light of a superior being'.[6]

Such distinctions between missionary and imperialist continued to be implied and expressed in the Anniversary Sermons, the Bishop of Gloucester, for example, in 1825, urging the avoidance of 'everything which may appear to connect the cause of religion with the power of the sword'. Bishop Samuel Wilberforce, one of SPG's most energetic supporters, spoke in mid-century of 'an ungodly colonization', but one which the Society had acted to redeem, like an 'Angel of Mercy'.

> It is no light blessing to have been permitted to accompany everywhere throughout the world England's too irreligious colonization with the blessed seed of the Church's life.[7]

Britain's widening dominion was often regarded in the Society as providential. To Bishop Blomfield, in the 1827 sermon, it was 'a great door' of missionary opportunity, opening on to

> An empire so vast, so interspersed amidst the different nations of the world, so unaccountable in its growth, so singular in its structure, as fully to justify a belief that Providence has ordained it for some

purpose of vast importance to mankind; and . . . a commerce so wonderfully extended and extending that we may seem to discern the finger of the Most High.[8]

The Bishop of Carlisle's gloomy evaluation of 1798 was as negative as the Anniversary Sermons got. They were much more likely to tend the other way, as in the Bishop of Gloucester and Bristol's suggestion in 1836 that 'the arm of the Lord' was discernible in the 'wonderful success of our countrymen in military and naval warfare', because it 'enable[d] this country to propagate among the inhabitants of . . . [our] vast colonial dependencies the pure religion of Christ's Gospel'. To the Bishop of Chichester in 1848, Britain's 'vast . . . colonial dependencies' meant that 'the parting command of the Saviour' seemed to be addressed 'with awful emphasis' to the Church of England.

While the Anniversary Sermons ceased to be published regularly after the mid-century, and we lose this source for the Society's mind, it is clear that as the century advanced into the high imperial period of the later decades, missionary opinion in all denominations took the empire for granted as a providential opportunity, with 'England's Duty' a new main theme, as in a sermon printed with the 1877 Report. In the 1886 Ramsden Sermon, G. U. Pope, a former missionary, expressed the liberal imperial position in classic form,

This Empire cannot in these days hold together, unless there is in us wisdom and disinterestedness, and a love of justice and moderation.

There were, as Bishop Westcott put it in a pamphlet slightly later, 'Obligations of Empire', and in someone like Westcott this shaded into a sort of liberal internationalism. Others associated with the Society seem to have been comfortable with something much more chauvinistic, and there was a certain amount of shuffling between the two positions, represented during the 1880s in contributions to the *Mission Field* with titles like 'The Spiritual Counterpart to Imperial Destiny', and Bishop Lightfoot's 'The Imperial Destiny of Great Britain', while the Secretary at the turn of the century, H. W. Tucker, gathered up these ambiguities in the Society's position in a pamphlet entitled 'The Spiritual Expansion of the Empire'.

A very different note, however, was also being struck by this time. Archbishop Benson, in his sermon at the 1890 anniversary, spoke of his 'great aspiration and desire . . . that there should be peoples . . . whom we can go to in another form than that of masters'.

We want to deal with them in such ways as shall make them, as far as possible, true, independent, active Christian nations, having their own constitutions, their own Churches, built up according to those methods which most suit their national characters . . . It is clear that as there were Oriental and Occidental and Northern European and Southern European Churches, all following on old apostolic lines, so there will be Indian, Japanese and other churches.

A preliminary step was suggested by John Stephenson the year following, in an address to the Liverpool Clerical Society, quoted in the Report, where he suggested that 'reparation' for slavery, for the opium trade, for the scramble for and partition of Africa, ought to be the leading motive in mission to 'the heathen'. This was an early expression of what became a significant motive for mission in the next century.

Considering the extent of the Society's commitment to the re-evangelization of settlers, surprisingly little attention is paid to this topic in the sermons. The Bishop of Rochester had observed in 1795 how the lot of the poor settlers in Nova Scotia was gradually improving, while the Bishop of Ripon in 1841 drew attention to 'the rapid tide of emigration', but these are rare references. Perhaps the most significant observation was that of Bishop Selwyn, who suggested in a Society pamphlet on the Melanesian Mission that 'the surest way to spread the Gospel . . . [was] by building up the colonial churches as missionary centres'. A dichotomizing approach, however, was more common. One of the Organizing Secretaries observed in the 1870 Report that it was easier to raise funds for what he called 'direct mission', while Archbishop Maclagan of York provided a similar explanation in preaching to the Society prior to the 1898 Lambeth Conference. 'Missions of Recovery' were not as 'interesting' as 'Missions of Discovery'. The latter had 'an element of heroism, of Christian romance'.

Among the 'Missions of Discovery', those in India got quite the most attention, especially in the earlier sermons. The 'duty of attempting the propagation of the gospel among our Mahometan and Gentoo subjects in India' had been proposed by Joseph White in a sermon at Oxford in July 1784, and this was referred to by Bishop Thurlow in his Anniversary Sermon of 1786, a year in which a range of other missionary stirrings also occurred in Britain.[9] Acknowledging the long-standing work of the 'worthy' SPCK in India, Thurlow suggested there was room for SPG there also. With large tracts of India now added to the British Empire, the inhabitants, 'so many millions of rational beings, unhappily deluded by error', were justly entitled 'to all the privileges of fellow-subjects'. It was necessary, though, to start with a fully constituted Church.

When the gospel of Christ Jesus shall become the established religion of Britons throughout Indostan, we may then hope assuredly to see the purity of evangelical truth . . . in the hearts of the unenlightened natives.

The Society's part in the ensuing long campaign to overturn the East India Company's opposition to missions, in which William Wilberforce took a well-known later part, is reflected in nine further Anniversary Sermons, which dealt substantially with the issue prior to the eventual creation of the Diocese of Calcutta in 1814. Most of these sermons reflect the very negative attitudes to Indian religious tradition character-istic of contemporary evangelicalism, and see India sunk in idolatry. Few follow William Cleaver of Chester in suggesting in the 1794 sermon ways in which Hinduism and Islam 'connect with the theology of the Gospel', although Henry Ryder of Gloucester, in 1819, in a sermon littered with wide-ranging and relevant footnotes, sees already great significance in the work of the Hindu reformer, Ram Mohun Roy, whom by this time Bishop Middleton of Calcutta had befriended.[10]

The note struck in Benson's sermon of 1890 sounds in a number of other places. One such had been Bishop R. S. Copleston of Colombo's pre-Lambeth sermon for SPG, attached to the 1878 Report, on 'The Obligations of Christianity and Civilization to the Heathen'. Acknowl-edging his debt to the missionary ideas of B. F. Westcott, Copleston looked beyond a colonial or imperial Christianity.

Our Anglican Church is . . . entering on a new phase of existence, as she passes from being the Church of the Anglo-Saxon race to being the Church of many races, and peoples and tongues . . . [with] many native Churches, free and living their own life, yet bound to us in close communion.

Turning to the particular case of his own Church in Ceylon, the Bishop acknowledged that all four of the main groups, Singhalese, Tamil, Burgher and English, were all 'striving to assume English civilization', though he recognized that the poor, to whom characteristically the Gospel was preached, had no part in this. While contact with the Church of England was important as his Church's means of access to Christian tradition, Copleston suggested that the rich cultural hybridity of the early Church suggested a better way forward.

If it is God's will that in their turn, those which we now call native races, should bring to light, in the course of their own divinely guided life, aspects of the Christ-life which the old peoples have missed, then we must be careful how we insist on uniformity, lest in any way we crush . . . this divine originality of the Churches. We owe them nurture, but we also owe them freedom.

The Indian Bishops in their conference of January 1883, quoted in that year's Report, had a similar vision, of an Indian Church working out 'her own spiritual life . . . [bearing] spiritual fruit of her own . . . [contributing] her own spiritual gifts to the wealth of the Universal Church'. Archbishop Benson, at the Society's Annual Meeting the following year, citing Las Casas and the contemporary Bishop of Lahore, T. V. French, affirmed 'the real spirit of Missions', in which 'the whole history of the world is looked upon as the ancient Christians looked upon it − as a preparation for the Gospel, not a thing to be despised or thrown away'.

If the Society continued to honour very fully its chartered obligation to British settlers throughout the colonies, another, and, at least in these last examples, far-sighted commitment attached to its mission to the colonized.

6

⋄⇥═◗ ◖═⇤⋄

The nineteenth-century Society

Just as SPG originated with a remarkably creative individual, Thomas Bray, so its revival after the withdrawal from America owed a great deal to one man, Joshua Watson, 'one of the Society's most stedfast friends', as the Report put it at the time of his death in 1855. A wealthy layman, Watson gave up his business interests in 1814 in order to devote himself wholly to the service of the Church. Living in the then village of Hackney on the edge of London, he and his group of High Church friends became known as the Hackney Phalanx.[1] Watson was involved in a range of new initiatives, King's College, London, which educated some of SPG's missionaries, especially for India, the National Society, the Church Building Society and Additional Curates Society, among others. It was, however, by his membership of the two older societies, SPG and SPCK, being elected Treasurer of the latter in 1814, that Watson was able to move the Society to greater effectiveness, while his conviction, shared with the Phalanx, of the place of the bishop in the propagation of the Gospel, gave a distinctive focus to this.

Improved effectiveness was doubtless overdue. Although the work of the Society had grown somewhat in Canada and the Caribbean after American Independence, and there had been a fresh though abortive initiative in West Africa and small beginnings in Australia, there was little sense of urgency. For example, the Secretary, William Morice objected to the appointment of the first bishops in Canada because 'the whole system of the Society's quiet proceedings was changed and much unreasonable trouble thrown upon the Secretary.'[2] A younger Secretary, Anthony Hamilton, took over soon after Watson began to get involved, and SPG started to respond more energetically to the perceived requirements of the emerging 'Greater Britain'.

One of the first steps was to get the Society to support Watson's Hackney friend, the new, first Bishop of Calcutta, Thomas Middleton. He needed help especially to establish Bishop's College, Calcutta, as a key instrument of the Church in India. Middleton regarded preaching as inadequate as a means of mission and, well before Alexander Duff, saw the need for educational institutions to prepare 'the Native Mind to comprehend the importance and the truth of the doctrines proposed to them'.[3] Bishop's College would play a central part, train Indian converts for ordination and produce Christian literature in the learned and vernacular languages of India. Initial offers of funds, including SPG's £5000 in early 1818, encouraged Middleton to begin to implement his scheme. For its fuller financing, Watson worked through another close friend, the Archbishop of Canterbury, to put through the Society's application for a Royal Letter in 1819, which raised nearly £50,000, quite the largest sum since the inception of the letters in 1711. SPG then sent another of the Hackney circle, the exceptionally gifted W. H. Mill, to be the College's first principal.

Others shared with Watson in efforts at making the Society more effective. Together with SPG and SPCK, the Church Missionary Society (CMS) had made a grant towards Bishop's College. Founded in 1799, CMS was at this time viewed disapprovingly in Hackney circles as politically dangerous, being 'a popular organization, independent of the laws of the country'.[4] This did not prevent its Secretary, Josiah Pratt, who was also a member of SPG, from publishing anonymously in 1820 his *Propaganda*, best interpreted as an attempt by a well-wisher to coax an overcautious SPG into new missionary endeavour.

Watson himself made numerous other contributions to the Society's development. An important and characteristic one relating to India was to effect the transfer between 1817 and 1825 of the mission in South India from SPCK to SPG, thus ensuring that the work which SPCK had begun in 1728 using Lutheran missionaries would be taken forward by missionaries in Anglican orders. The foundation was thus laid for SPG's most admired nineteenth-century venture in India, the mission in Tirunelveli.

The secularizing process in Britain reflected in the Test and Corporation Acts of 1828 was further signalled by the government's withdrawal of its support for the Church in Canada through the Clergy Reserves during the 1830s. This led the Society, no doubt correctly, to suggest parallels with the government's suspension of the Irish bishoprics which occasioned John Keble's sermon of 1833 on 'National Apostasy'. A number of Anniversary Sermons reflect similar indignation over the withdrawal of the Reserves, while the 1837 and 1838 Reports speak of this as 'an act of national sin and folly' and 'a heinous national sin'. SPG's response, however, was practical as well as rhetorical. The hard-working new Secretary, A. M. Campbell, supported by energetic preaching and speaking tours by Bishop John Inglis of Nova Scotia and Samuel Wilberforce, helped the Society to accept the need to cultivate popular lay support to compensate for waning state support. This was not familiar territory, and not all approved. To promote the new approach, but also to claim the continuing support of government wherever possible, a large public meeting was held in London in June 1838. The Archbishop of Canterbury saw this as 'the beginning of a great effort that will be made in this country in support of . . . [the] Society'. The London meeting was followed by some 144 local ones which led to the widespread formation of parochial associations and district committees, with over 7000 parishes recruited. This ensured a large increase in SPG's income, which then rose steadily for the next 35 years. It was accompanied by the huge proliferation of missionary literature and general consciousness-raising which marked the Society's work thereafter. Though all this had its roots in SPG's endeavours in the very different circumstances of the eighteenth century, in, for example, its widely distributed Anniversary Sermons and Reports, it was a time of unprecedented expansion in the British missionary movement, with the Society, now competing with several other mission agencies, including CMS, all of them together beginning to make that quite exceptional impact on the popular consciousness of Victorian Britain which characterized the rest of the century.

In this new situation, SPG sought to define itself more clearly as the Church of England in mission. One way it did so was by the creation of an Archbishops' Board of Examiners in 1846, whereby the missionaries supported by the Society were recognized as missionaries of the Church. Even so, Bishop Selwyn of New Zealand, preaching at Cambridge in 1854, suggested that England had 'enlarged her empire, but . . . had not extended her church', and this was 'evil', and he paid a particularly overheated tribute to the Society for remedying the Church's failure.[5] Reinforcement of the Church of England's ownership of the Society was further emphasized by a Supplementary Charter in 1882. While the Monthly Meeting had had a continuous life from 1701, and continued into the second half of the twentieth century, its shrinking importance was underlined by this Supplementary Charter's provision for every diocese to be represented on the Standing Committee, now also given executive power.

The 1840 Report, referring to the changed circumstances of the Society over the previous two years, suggested that it was now practicable to consider a 'measure for the endowment of Bishoprics for the Colonies'. At this time, only ten such bishoprics had been created, among them Sydney, covering the whole of Australia, and which Bishop Broughton wished to divide, his cause being pressed in London by his friend, Watson. Shaw's chapter in this volume describes the Society's support for Broughton. The need for many more bishoprics was expressed by the Bishop of London, C. J. Blomfield, in a letter of April 1840 to the Archbishop of Canterbury. The time had come for the Church of England

> to impart the full benefits of her apostolical government . . . to those distant parts of the British Empire where, if the Christian religion is professed at all, it is left to depend . . . upon the energies of individual piety and zeal, without being enshrined in the sanctuary of a rightly-constituted Church, the only sure and trust-worthy instrument of its perpetuation and efficiency.

Blomfield also pointed out that the state was an increasingly uncertain support to the Church in this as in other regards. To meet this situation and need, the Colonial Bishoprics Fund was established the following year. This was the responsibility of the entire body of English and Irish bishops, but 'under the immediate auspices of this Society', as W. E. Gladstone, the Fund's Treasurer for the next 50 years, later put it.[6] The Fund established and endowed 33 bishoprics over the next twenty years, the number of missionaries doubling or trebling in all dioceses to which bishops were sent, with a further 54 before the end of the century. The earlier dioceses created were chiefly in areas of large-scale colonial settlement, the later largely in those of imperial control and beyond. SPG, with SPCK, contributed something like a quarter of the Fund's income for the rest of the century, with many additional grants and special appeals for particular emerging dioceses, and with SPG's Secretary, initially the capable Ernest Hawkins, acting as secretary. The Fund in fact became quite soon 'practically an appendage of SPG', for its purpose accorded fully with the High Church missiology of the Society.[7]

The consecration of the early colonial bishops had been a semi-private affair in the Lambeth Palace Chapel. Middleton's had been, like his subsequent entry into Calcutta, a covert operation, out of wildly exaggerated fears of enraging Bengal's Hindu population. It was a concession a few years later for Mrs Heber to be allowed to take two friends to her husband's consecration. After the launching of the Fund, however, they became major public events in Westminster Abbey or St Paul's Cathedral or at Canterbury, that of Bishop Gray for Cape Town and three new Australian diocesans at the Abbey in 1847 being the first in the new style. The colonial bishops remained, however, something of a breed apart in the public mind, especially those seen as real missionary bishops, presented as heroes in the Society's burgeoning publications. Though they were usually closely identified with the colonial authorities and sailed about the empire as guests of the Royal Navy, and came from the same élite sector as the English bishops, the Bishop of Labuan 'and a few others' were reported in *The Times* in 1867 as arriving for the first Lambeth Conference, not like the English diocesans in their coaches, but on foot, 'as became the more primitive habits of missionary life'.[8]

By then, nevertheless, and despite the oddity of colonial bishops, the notion of a worldwide Anglican Communion had been fermenting for some years, not least thanks to Joshua Watson's hospitality in England to bishops from America and Canada and his friendship with others scattered about the world. SPG's anniversary celebrations of 1851–2 advanced the process, with a number of bishops present from Scotland, the colonies and the USA. Bishop McCoskry of Michigan noted, preaching on the text 'And all ye are brethren', that there had never been 'such a union of the different parts and members of Christ's family since the Reformation as we have here this day'. The term 'Anglican Communion' appears to have been used for the first time at this anniversary, and a proposal for an 'Anglican Council of Bishops' was made at the time by Bishop de Lancey of New York. Looking back in 1888, Bishop Lightfoot commented that 'if there had been no SPG there would, humanly speaking, have been no Lambeth Conference.'[9]

The entry of the Society into the market for lay support probably only served to widen the gulf between itself and CMS. The latter, from its founding in 1799 under the cold disapproval of those in authority in the Church, had expanded in its first two decades with remarkable success in both funding and missionary recruiting, a clear response to the Evangelical Revival and ably guided by its Secretary, Josiah Pratt. Its 'repeated conflicts with the colonial bishops during the period 1820–50', and Venn's views on the separation between Church and mission, undoubtedly served to accentuate the difference between the two societies.[10] The formation of the Archbishop's Board of Examiners must have done the same. While established to conform to 'the wise and comprehensive spirit of the Church of England, and most emphatically repudiating all party bias', it was bound to differentiate it further from the committed voluntarism of the CMS.

The Oxford Movement and its controversies complicated the Society's role during these years, forcing it to steer 'a wavering course between the sensitive consciences of two opposing sets of supporters', while its many identifications with the movement, specifically with Keble, Manning, Newman, Pusey and Liddon, for example, only served to deepen the divide with CMS.[11] The first attempt to unite them had been made by Bishop Heber, and his proposals were taken up by Bishop Blomfield in mid-century. There were occasional instances of mutual recognition and co-operation in the mission field, for example in Tirunelveli, and even in England, as when Venn persuaded reluctant colleagues in CMS to take up a suggestion of SPG's Secretary, W. T. Bullock, to promote jointly a Day of Intercession in 1872. Only the previous year, at the Anniversary Meeting, the Bishop of Ely had extolled the Society, 'thoroughly true to the Church in . . . its co-extensiveness, a truly comprehensive and a truly Anglican body', but the religious competition which characterized Victorian England was becoming particularly acute during the 1870s, and this, and the many eruptions over ritualism, no doubt helped to reinforce their continuing separation. When Archbishop Benson addressed the Missionary Conference of the Anglican Communion on 29 May 1894, he acknowledged that the unification of the two societies was a Utopian project achievable only in an unspecified future.[12]

The missionary endeavours of the Church of England were further fragmented with the founding of the Universities' Mission to Central Africa (UMCA) in 1857. SPG was concerned that its own recruiting would be damaged if UMCA became a separate project. 'Month after month, the Society renews its appeal to our two Universities . . . whence its need of well-trained Missionaries might be supplied', said the 1857 Report, as the new mission was in process of formation, implying a prior claim and perhaps anxiety and irritation. Certainly that was not the whole of SPG's response. Some of its chief supporters, among them Gladstone and Wilberforce, were enthusiastic about the new mission, while the 1861 Report, referring to the consecration of Bishop Mackenzie, alluded to 'this great Christian enterprise', which would be watched 'with hopeful attention and deep sympathy'. The hope in these earlier years, though, was that UMCA would soon merge with SPG, and so the Society took on both the financial support of a UMCA priest and its first native deacon, John Swedi, and some of its administrative support in London. The merger, though, had to wait more than a hundred years. While Livingstone's overriding intention had been to undermine the East African slave trade with Christianity and commerce, the plan that actually evolved seemed as much intended to fulfil the Tractarian dream for a missionary bishop beyond the 'blighting influence' of the Establishment, and this had the effect of consolidating UMCA's particular, societal character over against SPG's self-understanding as ecclesial, and reinforced their separate existences.[13]

A similar issue arose when the rather unsubtle later Secretary, H. W. Tucker, complained in 1880 that the Oxford Mission to Calcutta, finding university support poor, as UMCA had done, was 'appealing outside the University' and becoming 'another Missionary claimant on the alms of the whole Church'. Other missionary diversification was much more acceptable. The Scottish Episcopal Church assumed responsibility for the new diocese of St John's, Kaffraria, in South Africa in 1873 in an amicable partnership with SPG; the promoters of the Cambridge Mission to Delhi in 1877, in Tucker's view, 'showed practical wisdom in allying themselves with the SPG, and strengthening . . . the old Mission of the Society at Delhi', though this proved a rather uncomfortable alliance initially; while the Dublin University Mission to Chota Nagpur in 1891 was established, to Tucker's satisfaction, as 'in no sense a distinct organisation'.[14] The case of the missions to Melanesia, New Guinea and Borneo were different again. While SPG helped fund the first two in their early years, they were acknowledged as the responsibility of the Australian Board of Mission from its inception in 1850. The Borneo venture started as a more or less private initiative, which the Society had to take over in 1853.

The Cambridge Mission to Delhi (CMD), founded in 1877, had a special, and indeed unique character, and though small it added a strong new strand to mission associated with SPG. Conceived largely in correspondence between B. F. Westcott at Cambridge and T. V. French in the Diocese of Lahore, but with other distinguished Cambridge theologians, J. B. Lightfoot and F. J. A. Hort also on the founding body, the Mission was envisaged as a means to a serious engagement with the Indian religious tradition, which would create 'a new Alexandria' in Delhi.[15] Out of the work of CMD's Cambridge Brotherhood, and not least through its college, St Stephen's, it was hoped that an Indian Christianity would emerge 'as thoroughly Hindu as Christian'. The vision, unique for the nineteenth-century missionary movement, had, despite its 'orientalist' tendencies, a series of striking realizations in the twentieth century.

Further diversification followed from the Oxford Movement and the revival of the religious life in the Church of England. Some of the new religious orders established overseas branches quite independently of the Society, most, though, with various degrees of collaboration, like the Society of St John the Evangelist, the Society of the Sacred Mission, the Community of the Resurrection, the Order of the Holy Paraclete and the Community of St Mary the Virgin. Others were set up by bishops and SPG missionaries as indigenous communities or missionary sisterhoods and brotherhoods, others continuing to be inaugurated through the twentieth century.

An independent development in Britain particularly important for SPG was the creation of St Augustine's College, Canterbury, in 1848. Sometimes called a missionary college, sometimes a colonial church college, St Augustine's was designed to pay 'the debt . . . [owed] to the heathen world', and to meet the rapidly growing need for ordained missionaries created by the pace of emigration.[16] Students were prepared at Canterbury and ordained overseas. The College soon came to include also a number of students recruited overseas. This and a cluster of smaller institutions about the country, at Warminster, Burgh and St Bees, for example, enabled large numbers of those unable to afford university and ordination in England to respond to the missionary enthusiasm that marked the period. Typical in this regard, early in the present century, was George Appleton, son of a cook and a gardener, subsequently a colonial archbishop. The Colonial Clergy Act of 1819 had ensured that this would be a disadvantaged class in relation to the Church of England and its clergy. Nevertheless, St Augustine's and the smaller colleges sent over 1000 to missionary work during the approximately 100 years of their existence, the largest number going to Canada, then South Africa, India, Australia and the West Indies.[17] Figures in SPG's 1899 Report exemplify the College's importance to the Society, with fifteen clergy sent overseas, twelve of them graduates of Cambridge, Dublin, Durham and Oxford, and sixteen laity, fourteen of them from St Augustine's. The College had its own constitution but the Society provided continuous funding and special grants such as one in 1853 to pay a lecturer in oriental studies, also staff from among its former missionaries, while the majority of students were assisted by and many became missionaries of SPG.

St Augustine's broadened the class composition of the ordained missionary community, while a 'Ladies Association for the Promotion of Female Education among the Heathen', later known as the Women's Mission Association (WMA), added a further dimension to the Society's work. The first meeting was in London on 11 May 1866. From its inception 'in connexion with the Mission of the SPG', the Association grew rapidly, with over 200 branches in England, Ireland, Scotland and Wales within the first ten years, and with its own monthly publication, *The Grain of Mustard Seed*, five years later.

The Association began by improving support for existing work, for SPG had sent women teachers to Australia and Canada from the end of the eighteenth century, and other girls' and women's education had been initiated by 'the quiet work of missionary wives', and sisters and daughters, in, for example India and Ceylon, South Africa, Borneo, Sarawak and Melanesia. Such were the schools run by Bishop Caldwell's daughters and T. Brotherton's sister in Tirunelveli, and by Harriette McDougall, the Bishop's wife, in Sarawak.[18] Kirkwood's chapter in this volume describes these and many other instances. Within the first two years, additional women were recruited for some of these countries and also for Burma, Madagascar and Mauritius, with, in some cases, initial training at St Denys' Home, Warminster. At the 1888 Lambeth Conference, Bishop Webb of Grahamstown, a former Society missionary, claimed that it was 'now . . . everywhere recognized that a Mission cannot be fully organized . . . without women on its staff of workers'. By the end of the century the Association supported approximately 100 missionaries and a similar number of native teachers.

In addition to the recruitment of teachers and, later, medical workers, and their financial support, other elements in the Association's work included the raising of funds for scholarships and bursaries in their schools, and the collection and despatch of parcels of 'Native Clothing', though these latter were not restricted to those being educated, but might go to an entire congregation.[19] It was an intensely serious, prayerful project, with book lists provided for reading aloud at working parties.

This new development was of great significance in its impact on indigenous societies, bringing large numbers of women and girls to Christian faith and into the transformations that their societies were undergoing. At its worst, it was part of 'the politics of exploitation', as in South Africa, but more generally in Africa it was recognized as 'empowering', while at its best it made a contribution to national renaissance, as in Japan and India, and, in Victorian Britain opened up new career and vocational opportunities to women.[20]

Looking back at the 1890 anniversary, Archbishop Benson, as we have seen, saw the need for new, post-imperial attitudes. He nevertheless saw that already much had been and was being achieved.

> Through the work of this Society there are taking place some of the most marvellous changes that have ever taken place since the world began.

It was a considerable claim, but a fair reflection of the mood and judgement of the Society and its supporters at this time.

7

⋯⊶⊙⊶⋯

Mission in Greater Britain and beyond

Some of the most significant missionary developments of the nineteenth century were entirely indigenous, and not easily discerned in missionary reports, for, as Henry Callaway noted in South Africa, 'Those who receive the Word from the missionary do not lock it up in their bosoms, but repeat it to their friends.' Thus, also, Africans baptized and confirmed while working in the Rand mines, returned home to the east coast and, long before the establishment of a Diocese of Lebombo in 1893, 'began a work of preaching and conversion'.[1] In addition to this sort of development, SPG's own work extended throughout the entire 'Greater Britain', and beyond, often stretching its resources alarmingly. It began with a series of continuities.

In British North America, unlike the United States with its 'purely spiritual episcopacy', it was inescapably a continuation, for the Bishop of Nova Scotia from 1787 until 1816, the Loyalist refugee from colonial New York, Charles Inglis, was committed to Pitt's objective of an Anglican establishment capable of withstanding 'the blasts of French catholicism on the one hand, and American radical dissent on the other'.[2] The Society in 1800 noted the dangerous politics of the Dissenters and of the books they circulated, *The Rights of Man*, *The Age of Reason*, *Volney on the Ruin of Empires* and *A False Representation of the French Revolution*, 'with scandalous invectives against all the Crowned Heads in Europe, and against the British Administration in particular'. Government support for a Church that was a bulwark against all this was generous, including the Clergy Reserves, one-seventh of the land in each township set aside as an endowment. Much of the government funding of the Church was administered – and supplemented – by the Society, which also helped to ease the progressive alienation of the

66

Reserves from the 1830s through to 1858.[3] The novelty of dealing with a colonial bishop did not come easily to the Society, and, despite flattering accounts of Inglis in the Reports, William Morice, the Secretary, tended to act as though he did not exist, for example appointing missionaries without consultation.[4] By the beginning of the nineteenth century, there were two dioceses in Canada, and Society involvement and support began to grow. Of the over four thousand ordained missionaries recruited by SPG during the nineteenth century, more than a third, some 1600, went to work in Canada, with perhaps two-thirds as many lay missionaries, chiefly teachers, especially in the earlier decades, including 32 schoolmistresses by 1830. SPG's ordained missionaries dominate standard histories of the the Anglican Church in Canada.[5] Their work was predominantly with the colonial settlers and took a variety of forms. These included ministering to immigrants at the plague-infested Quarantine Station at Grosse Ile, where a series of Society missionaries worked and died of cholera, much pioneering in very difficult conditions for both missionaries and their wives, navigating the rugged Labrador coast, travelling with dog teams or on snowshoes or in canoes and pressing ever westwards as the Hudson's Bay Company extended its interests, as new waves of immigrants arrived, including the thousands of prospectors joining in the Cariboo Gold Rush of 1858 and others later at Kootenay and Klondike. The Canadian-Pacific Railway, completed in 1885, transformed the development of the west, and this was marked with the appointment in 1892 of a Society missionary to work among Chinese arriving in Vancouver from across the Pacific, later also among the Japanese there. The Bishop of Nova Scotia, speaking at the London meeting of the Society in June 1831, had no doubt that SPG's work with immigrants was 'of a Missionary character', for they endured 'all the toils and privations to which primitive professors were subject'. As in eighteenth-century America, the task was re-evangelization, the immigrants being 'often as much without God in the world, as the remote tribes who have never heard the sounds of salvation'.

Support of these missionaries often lasted only two or three years, until local churches assumed the responsibility. Very substantial, often crucial funding went into the endowment of a series of institutions across the country, beginning with King's College, Windsor, Nova Scotia, Canada's first university of British origin, which educated some 250 ordinands in the course of the century, 'in the western limit of the Empire', as the 1822 Report noted, answering to Bishop's College, Calcutta, in the eastern. The Church's self-support took a significant step when Hawkins, on the first overseas tour of a Secretary, arrived in 1848 to negotiate with the then four bishops the gradual reduction of Society funding. By mid-century, the 'Church of England in Canada' consisted of eight dioceses. The 1851 Quebec Conference of Bishops suggested that 'the Church in these colonies . . . [owed] under God, its existence and means of usefulness' to SPG. At the end of the century, the Society was still making itself useful. There were then 24 dioceses, with a General Synod formed in 1893, and although the Church was by then supporting its own first missionaries in other parts of the world, ever-increasing migration induced the Society to continue some funding and to send its largest number of ordained missionaries ever to Canada, some 240, in the final decade of the century.

Similar accounts could be given of SPG support for the colonial Church in Australia, New Zealand and South Africa and numerous smaller areas of settlement like Tristan da Cunha and among the descendants of the *Bounty* mutineers on Pitcairn Island. The majority of the Society's 560 ordained-missionary appointments in nineteenth-century South Africa, 460 in Australia and Tasmania, and 110 in New Zealand, worked among the settlers, with, again, particularly large numbers appointed in the 1890s. Missionary reports are full of graphic accounts, of encounters with often impoverished settlers, some of these devout Christians, others, as was reported in 1844, for example in the Australian outback, 'in a state of perfect ungodliness'. These often proved very responsive to the missionaries and their efforts to help them, like one poor woman discovered by the missionary F. P. Strickland: 'See, children,' she said to her family, 'this is one of the Clergymen I have told you about that live in dear old England – who could have thought that one of them would have sought us out in this wilderness?'[6] Beyond helping establish the expanding number of dioceses, SPG's main funding was to enable the bishops to initiate work in these new areas of settlement, the Society being, in the words of Bishop Barker of New South Wales, 'for many years . . . the great sole channel for diffusing the bounty of England through this dry and thirsty land'.[7] By 1882, funding support to Australia was phased out, except for work with the indigenous population and among Melanesian and Chinese migrant workers, and the endowment of bishoprics.

New Zealand saw SPG first extending the medical element in its work beyond what was done at Codrington. From 1842, it funded two doctors who taught medicine and surgery at St John's College, Auckland. Other early support included that from 1848 of F. T. McDougall in Borneo, later first Bishop of Labuan, who was a qualified doctor and exercised his medical skills there for twenty years. John Strachan's medical skills in Tirunelveli from 1861 were such that he was sent to

Madras and Edinburgh for advanced study, returning to describe his work in his report of 1872:

> Every day in the week, except Sundays, about 150 patients assemble at the Dispensary. It is a picturesque and interesting group. Mahom-medans, Christians, Brahmins . . . Chanars . . . Pariahs . . . are all sitting together, suffering from disease common to all, and thus bearing witness (notwithstanding caste distinctions) to a common humanity. Tickets are given as they arrive, and in that order they are seen. The day's work commences with two short religious services, one for the men and one for the women . . . I usually begin to prescribe about 6.30, and keep it up continuously until 11 o'clock . . . Some of the ignorant natives in these parts think that a God has descended amongst them. May God give me grace to show, the loving, gentle, sympathizing character of our blessed Lord and Saviour Jesus Christ!

Students of St Augustine's College were given some medical training at a Canterbury hospital, as perhaps D. J. H. Ibbetson had been, who set off on horseback in Australia to conduct services in the wool-sheds in the outback, taking with him 'a few drugs, and . . . Cox's *Companion to the Medicine Chest*', and who later reported administering rhubarb powder and brandy to a sick station carpenter before preaching to him.[8]

In the background to the encounter with indigenous medical practice must have been the standard castigation fixed by Macaulay's 1835 Minute on Education of 'medical doctrines which would disgrace an English farrier', but a missionary doctor like Henry Callaway at Springvale in South Africa seems to have preferred persuasion to condemnation. When a 'native doctor . . . came to express his great grief' at the death of one of Callaway's congregation whom he had been treating, Callaway 'had a long conversation with him on medicines and diseases, and pointed out to him how rash and uncertain their mode of practice' was.[9]

Women missionaries increasingly found areas of opportunity in medical work as the century advanced, as in Fitzgerald's essay in this volume. Local people were also trained, either in the lay agent category, as 'medical evangelists', or as doctors, and by the end of the century SPG was supporting medical missions in most areas where it worked among indigenous people.

In 1860, Hawkins told Bishop Selwyn in New Zealand that the Society would rather 'contribute towards the maintenance of Missionaries for the native people than for British Colonists'.[10] Mission among the indigenous populations in areas of colonial settlement was far from easy, for these were the marginalized victims of the process, often resisting and fighting bravely against their dispossessors, in periodic local 'Black Wars' in Australia and in land wars also in Canada, southern Africa and New Zealand. Some missionaries did stand up for the local people. Selwyn was abused in the *Taranaki Herald* in 1855 for defending Maoris accused of murder, who 'appeal[ed] to his sympathies through the medium of a dark skin'. Meanwhile, Hawkins gave what help he could from London, objecting to the government land dealings in Waitara which precipitated the First Taranaki War.[11] In Australia, also in the 1860s, a Society missionary, J. K. Black, in the *Port Denison Times*, denounced 'the abominable atrocities', and 'indiscriminate slaughter' of the indigenous people of North Queensland. In Canada, Church leaders held the government responsible for provoking the North-West Rebellion of 1885, though they seem to have been more concerned at the disruption of settler communities than justice for the First Nation people. One Society missionary, George McKay, was rewarded with an archdeaconry for his role as chaplain to the 'Canadian loyal forces'. These situations must have been very difficult for indigenous Christians, for example for the very small group of Maoris in New Zealand who were by this time ordained, George Mutu, Riwai te Ahu and Pirimona Te Karari, the last of these being falsely attacked in the settler press as an 'ordained rebel'.[12] Similarly in South Africa, where resistance was widespread and general, an agonizing conflict of loyalties faced, for example, the young Christian converts, the chiefs' sons and daughters educated at Zonnebloem College at the Cape, at the time of the Ninth Frontier War of 1877–78, 'torn . . . between the expectations of their new colonial masters and the call of their kinsfolk to fight to recover their land and their freedom'. Nathaniel Mahale did not join the 'rebels' but was accused nevertheless by the settler press of being a traitor and was forced into hiding, while Edmund Sandile did join them, was captured and exiled from his people for ten years. Others, like those the Church of the Province of Southern Africa (CPSA) Calendar calls the 'Martyrs of Mbokothwana', died, it has been suggested, because they were perceived to be 'the lackeys of a colonial government' and as such 'martyrs of imperialism'. An unambiguous case was that of Bernard Mizeki, catechist and martyr in Mashonaland, dying in the violence of a resistance movement in 1895.[13]

In spite of Hawkins' aspirations, the Society's work among these indigenous peoples in the areas of major British colonial settlement was a relatively small part of what was done. Not all the bishops showed an interest in or gave much encouragement to it, and in some cases, as in Canada, when missionaries left, they failed to follow up this ministry and mission.[14]

The continuation of the Mohawk story is one aspect of this work. A series of devoted missionaries continued to minister to what one of them, John Strachan, in 1829, called 'the feeble remains of the five nations'. Theirs was still, after a century, a missionary-led Church, though with plenty of devout communicants and a group of Society-paid local catechists and readers. A programme of Gospel translation by two Mohawk catechists, Aaron Hill and Joseph Brant, and the missionary Robert Addison, who worked among them for 37 years, was overtaken in the 1820s by requests for Bibles in English, which many now spoke. In all of these colonial contexts, missionaries reported requests for schools and education in English. Through these requests, they gained the impression that the indigenous people were saying 'Come over and help us.'[15] While the missionary John Good in British Columbia in the 1860s and 1870s wrote of his friendship with native people, easiest when they were not yet 'contaminated by intercourse with white men . . . [by whom they were] so fearfully brutalized and betrayed', and of his appreciation of their culture and language, even he saw the only feasible good outcome as 'civilization and Christianity'. The Society's chief instrument for this process was what was called the 'industrial school'. With little attention or respect given to indigenous culture, these were intended to assist the integration of indigenous Christians into the emerging hegemonic culture. Among them was the Poonindie Institution established by Matthew Hale in South Australia in 1850, though his successor, Octavius Hammond, was despondent in 1857 at the rate at which the community were dying off. There were numerous industrial schools in South Africa, including the first in the Zulu community, started by J. W. Colenso at Ekukanyeni in 1857, from which several detailed reports appeared in *The Mission Field*. From the later 1860s they often provided a means of fulfilling the missionary vocation of members of the Ladies' Association, for example in enabling 'native women . . . [to change] that heathen kraal into a Christian home'.[16] Some of these schools provided more academic teaching, like St Matthew's School, Keiskama Hoek, leading to the ministry, teaching, nursing or government service.

In these regions of colonial settlement, the Church was only rooted effectively enough among local people to produce its own priests in New Zealand and South Africa. The first in South Africa was Paulus Masiza in 1870, with 42 by 1899, 8 per cent of the Society's South African list. By contrast, when James Noble died in North-West Australia in 1941, he was the only Australian aboriginal ever to have been ordained in the Anglican Church. Greater evidence of success, as measured by the proportion of indigenous priests ordained and supported by the Society, occurs in some other areas, a majority, 57 per cent in Madagascar, and only a slightly smaller proportion in Mauritius, Japan, West Africa and South Asia. In Ceylon, the Bishop of Colombo was claiming in the 1865 Report pastors 'furnished by the races of this island . . . as faithful and true as England itself could furnish'. Perhaps the most instructive case is that of Madagascar. Not being anyone's colony until the French seized control from the Malagasy ruler in 1895, the Society, from 1864, was clearly operating in 'regions beyond' the British Empire. Perhaps it was this freedom from imperial association that, both before and after 1895, attracted such an unusually high proportion of local men to ordination.

In India, by 1816, Bishop Middleton had not only established a mutually respectful relationship with Ram Mohun Roy, the most eminent Indian of the period, so different from the self-defeating rancour of the Serampore Baptists in their approach to Roy, but, as we have seen, had begun to develop a missionary strategy resting on his hopes for Bishop's College, which opened in 1820.[17] In all, the Society supported over 600 ordained missionaries in India, Burma and Ceylon during the nineteenth century. Nearly a third of these were Indian, only a minority educated at Bishop's College, but some fulfilment of Middleton's hopes nevertheless. By mid-century, one-third of all the Society's funding was going to India, by the end, one-half, in particular and increasingly into education and medical work. In the immensity and diversity of Indian society and religion, many of the Society's endeavours were infinitesimal and in some cases short-lived. Bishop's College itself, in its chief purpose, to train Indians for ordination, only came into its own long after its foundation, though its impact and that of some of its staff on the intellectual ferment of nineteenth-century Bengal was not insignificant.

Much of SPG's work, as that of most missions, was directed to people and groups at or near the bottom of the caste system, India's own 'colonialism within colonialism', and this helps to explain the successes it achieved.[18] The Society's missionaries were close to the imperial rulers, most of their bishops being senior officials in the Indian Ecclesiastical Establishment, paid out of Indian taxation, but this gave them a borrowed authority to act as the protectors of the outcaste and tribal peoples against their older colonial masters, the higher castes. To Indian eyes, of course, denominational distinctions cannot have been at all obvious, and this identification with imperial power probably served the interest of other missionaries also. Certainly, American Presbyterians in the Punjab were under instruction from their Board of Foreign Missions to work in close harmony with British officials.[19] If shunned by the higher castes, the missionaries seem often to have appeared as liberators to non-Brahmins, outcastes and tribals. The missions in Nandyal and Tirunelveli, the latter described in Kumaradoss's essay in this volume, were cases in point, and proved enduringly significant in this regard, the latter constantly reported in the Society's literature, with large new accessions as the century advanced, like the 30,000 reported in 1878.[20] Half of SPG's ordained missionaries here were Tamils. Elsewhere in the British Indian Empire, in Ceylon especially, the proportion was almost as high.

A striking aspect of the Society's work in this region was educational. J. E. Marks in Burma saw some 9000 boys through St John's College, Rangoon, from its foundation in 1864, his work modelled on that of Arnold of Rugby. The June 1889 *Mission Field* listed another seven schools founded by him in Burma.

The impact of the Society's work upon women, especially through education, and upon their place in and impact on their own rapidly changing societies, was marked in India, with schools from an early stage in Delhi, others in Calcutta, Chota Nagpur and Cawnpore within twenty years of the launch of the Ladies Association, new schools in Tirunelveli and teacher training in Bombay. Throughout all Asia also, this work was significant, through institutions like St Mary's SPG School, Rangoon, begun in 1865, and, very soon, four other girls' schools in Burma, along with St Faith's School, Peking, begun in 1890, one former pupil being the first woman to be employed in the Chinese Embassy in London, others going on to the staff of the Union Medical College and the National University. Alice Hoar reported in 1875 'a Japanese gentleman' in Tokyo providing rent-free accommodation in his house for her first school; work advanced through Ladies' Association missionaries and soon expanded into a training school for women evangelists, a high school, industrial school, orphanage and, by 1888, a twenty-bed hospital.

In the West Indies, the Society continued active beyond emancipation, with one strikingly moving innovation. Earlier in the century, however, while there is no doubt that the Society in the eighteenth century had led the Caribbean in ameliorating the conditions of the slaves, it approached emancipation only falteringly and hesitantly, continuing to affirm a role at Codrington 'in every way coincident with the colonial interest', under the hostile gaze of the abolitionists and the most publicized plantation in the empire. Even after the British government committed itself in 1823 to eventual emancipation, managers on the spot continued to ignore SPG in London so that the whip was still used in the field, women could still be flogged, no record of punishments was kept and manumissions were extremely rare. By the time the Emancipation Act became effective, however, on 1 August 1834, the Society estates had developed a workable pattern for freedom, and could now be hailed, even by the abolitionists, as 'pioneers in the great work of emancipation'.[21]

It was the appointment in 1824 of another member of the Hackney Phalanx as the first Bishop of Barbados, William Hart Coleridge, and his judicious and strong leadership which moved the Society along and carried the emancipation and apprenticeship process through, most successfully at Codrington, less so elsewhere in his diocese, and created this workable pattern for freedom. It was for this, indeed, that the British government had appointed him, and his achievement was remarkable. The resultant highly paternalistic, 'almost feudal' system that emerged, in close conformity with the subsequent Masters and Servants Act of 1840, had a range of decent welfare provisions for the ex-slaves in the highly stratified and repressive but somewhat less grotesque colonial society that then began to develop. The outcome at Codrington was an 'obviously happy . . . Negro tenantry'.[22]

SPG marked emancipation by launching a major appeal for a Negro Instruction Fund. Aided by a Royal Letter, grants from Parliament, SPCK and others, the Society was able to raise over £170,000 to provide churches, clergy and catechists, schools and teachers in the region between 1835 and 1850. It was all very necessary throughout the Carribbean, with its poverty and hunger and its enduringly despotic plantocracy.

Society literature through most of the remainder of the century describes lowly and devout congregations of communicants across the growing number of dioceses in the Caribbean, the 'disendowed Church in most of the West Indian islands . . . [resting] on the pence of the negro peasantry'.[23] From the 1830s to 1900, SPG had some 300 ordained missionaries in the West Indies, with a further 113 in the contiguous area of Guyana, a handful of them black, and another handful brought from India, including Tirunelveli, to work among the Indian indentured labourers. In the Bahamas, Anglo-Catholic bishops and SPG missionaries helped a distinctively Bahamian cultural identity to develop, with similar hybridities emerging elsewhere in the region. Thus, Walter Page's plans in 1874 for his congregation to sing 'Onward, Christian soldiers' in a festal procession were overtaken by a brisk rendition of 'Heigh, ho! Heigh ho! Johnny come blow the organ', after the first few yards, 'a song by the black sailors at heaving anchor'. Bishop Venables had perhaps been bowing to the inevitable then, when, in 1868, he told the Secretary that he was establishing

a more elastic system with the uneducated poor of our Out Islands . . . [recognizing] all as members of the Church who will accept the Sacraments at the hands of the clergyman whenever he may visit them, but . . . [leaving] them at other times to carry on their worship in their own way . . . not fettering them with the Prayer Book.

Meanwhile, some missionaries such as William Harte and Richard Rawle, later first Bishop of Trinidad, made brave efforts against the prevailing plantocratic culture within the life of the Church, but were only marginally effective against its deep racist structures which tended on the whole to serve the consolidation of colonial power in the Caribbean at large.[24]

To mark the third jubilee of SPG, Rawle, then Principal of Codrington, persuaded the Church in the West Indies to initiate a mission to West Africa, as Bishop Beveridge's Anniversary Sermon of 1707 had proposed. The first missionaries, H. J. Leacock, an English priest, who died within a few months of his arrival, and J. H. A. Duport, a black West Indian layman, both trained at Codrington, arrived to work in the Rio Pongas, now part of Gambia, in 1856. SPG funding supported the venture, the white missionary being paid six times as much as the black initially, though this was largely corrected later. They were helped on arrival by Lt Buck RN, commanding HMS *Myrmidon*, and Captain Fletcher of the 1st West India Regiment, who took them to meet the local chief, 'the renowned Kennybeck Ali'. Leacock reported, 'The Captain told him of my profession . . . and stated that Her Britannic Majesty's Government highly approved of my mission . . . the mention of our beloved Victoria acted like a charm.'[25]

As Leacock lay dying, Duport read Lancelot Andrewes's 'Litany for the Dying' for him. His English successor died on arrival after four days' journey in an open boat, and a third English missionary superintendent after a short time. Duport was put in charge in 1863 and did distinguished evangelistic, educational and translation work until his death in 1873. Society funding for this venture increased over the years as the poverty of the Church in the West Indies gradually deepened. Strikingly, eight black missionary priests served here during the rest of the century, as compared with only seven on SPG's list for the whole of the West Indies.[26] Though it proved as much the Black Man's as the White Man's Grave, several of the former, Duport, and also S. Cole, J. B. McEwen and J. W. T. Turpin, gave many years of able and effective service, Canon McEwen 30 years. They represented an impressive turnaround, for if these missionaries' forbears had appeared at all in SPG's records, it would have been as Christian names only on the baptism lists in the slave plantations.

8

⋄⇒◎⇐⋄

'Our own hard study'

Thomas Bray had recognized that 'Converting the World' would entail 'the Common Measure of God's Holy Spirit accompanying our own hard Study'. Hard study had not been lacking in the eighteenth century, for example among SPG missionaries and their local co-workers who translated the Bible and Prayer Book into several Native American languages, and others engaged in apologetics among the settlers in North America. The nineteenth century, however, witnessed a great extension, not least of translation work, many hundreds of texts being prepared in over 60 languages, and numerous other literary contributions to the propagation of the Gospel.[1]

Much effective propagation was, of course, carried on by intelligent, educated and thoughtful missionaries working in a non-literary mode, like Walter Chalmers, who reported on the first fruits of the Dayak mission in Borneo,

> I spoke to Nyanda of our mutual descent from Adam and Eve. He was much struck, and told many of his friends that I was 'one flesh with them'. He has been assured in a dream that what I said was true.[2]

Hard study nevertheless was a significant aspect of the Society's work, none more impressive than that of W. H. Mill (1792–1853), first Principal of Bishop's College, Calcutta, from 1820 until crippling illness finally forced his withdrawal in 1838.[3] A Scot, though born in Hackney, Mill devoted much of his eleven years at Cambridge before going to India to oriental studies. Study also filled his time in Calcutta, along with anxious care for his students. 'My own attention,' as he explained in an early letter to the Secretary, on 29 July 1822, 'has been from the beginning chiefly devoted to the Sanskrit, the ancient brahminical language, in which all the terms of Hindu religion and philosophy are contained, and by which alone we can hope to understand that singular system of opinions, to which the whole of this vast population is enslaved.'

At the request of Bishop Heber, Mill's first task was to prepare Sanskrit versions of the Decalogue and the Apostles', Nicene and Athanasian Creeds. The problems he encountered in this led to collaboration with the Sanskrit scholar, H. H. Wilson, in publishing a *Proposed Version of Theological Terms* in 1828. This stimulated a varied response, including a little-known letter from Ram Mohun Roy, whose principal suggestion they accepted. At this point, however, Mill's work took off in a completely new direction. Though what followed only hinted at a more harmonious relation to India's religious and cultural heritage, it disclosed a profound grasp and appreciation of it. In 1828, Mill's Hindu pandit, Ramachandra, presented him with some Sanskrit verses in praise of Jesus Christ, which he regarded as only a preliminary fragment. The pandit's creativity failing, however, Mill took over the project, recalling the Apostle Paul at Athens as the model for his new hermeneutics. Incorporating Ramachandra's introductory stanzas, he published over the next nine years in four cantos the 5028 stanzas of his *Christa-Sangita, or the sacred history of our Lord Jesus Christ in Sanscrit verse*. In this, abandoning his earlier, painstaking exposition of Christianity as simply one more theological–philosophical system, and mining with inspired boldness many rich Sanskrit seams, he presented through this great poem his proclamation of Christ as the 'great saviour' and life in the Church as a way of salvation.

Mill was not the first missionary to work in Sanskrit. A number of Roman Catholics, including de Nobili and Jean Calmette in the seventeenth and eighteenth centuries, essentially sympathetic towards the system, had preceded him with great skill. William Carey also, aggressively unsympathetic to it, seeing brahminical power as 'a masterpiece of policy unequalled in the annals of ecclesiastical domination', had completed his translation of the Bible into Sanskrit in 1816.[4] The received view of Christian Sanskritists nearly two centuries later, nevertheless, was that Mill's work was unsurpassed in its poetic and interpretative power. At the time of its publication, almost all of the devotees at the Kalighat temple in Calcutta to whom Mill offered a copy, against all normal expectation, accepted one, and he was hailed in a 'Tribute of the Pandits' shortly before his departure from India as 'a new Kalidasa', after the greatest of India's poets. The Society welcomed his work as 'the most valuable boon that has ever proceeded from a European pen'.[5]

In the flood of occidentalism which characterized Calcutta for many years from the 1830s, reinforced by views such as those of the Church of Scotland missionary, Alexander Duff, who saw Sanskrit itself as evil, 'a stupendous system of error', Mill's work remained known and admired only in limited circles, while Bishop's College only partially fulfilled Middleton's dream of a 'University of the East'. Part of the unfulfilment included diversion into wholly irrelevant Oxford Movement polarization. The austere next principal caricatured the evangelical Bishop Wilson as carrying out his visitations in 'feather bed palanquins', while the bishop described himself as 'worn out . . . [by] nine years of miserable thwarting'.[6] In the life and work of two immensely learned Indian members of staff later in the century, however, both missionaries of SPG, the Gospel was again propagated through hard study. Here we can only deal with one of these, though the other, Nilakantha Nehemiah Goreh (1825–95), who had found Mill's *Christa-Sangita* indispensable for his own spiritual life after he became a Christian in the mid-1840s, brought formidable intellectual powers to his life as a 'scholar-saint and ascetic'.[7]

Krishna Mohan Banerjea (1813–85), a student of Mill's during the missionary's last two years at Bishop's College, was an SPG missionary for 34 years from the time he joined the staff of the College in 1851. Already, by the time of his baptism by Duff in 1832, he was an outstanding figure, a former student of both Hare and Derozio and a leader of the reforming intellectual movement, Young Bengal. His ordination in 1839 as the first Bengali to take Anglican orders only served to broaden and deepen the vast range of his interests and concerns so that 'hard study' is a somewhat restrictive expression in his case and he remained and developed as a characteristic renaissance figure, involved, as the nationalist newspaper, the *Bengalee*, said at the time of his death, 'in every phase of the Bengal Renaissance'.

He was, presumably, one of the 1837 Report's 'five promising youths . . . rescued from the gulf of infidel metaphysical pantheism', whom Bishop Wilson visited at the College. Wilson was struck by their 'heartfelt . . . love to the divine Saviour', and also by their oral translation of Homer, Xenophon, Cicero and Ovid, and their expositions of Paley and others.[8] Duff suggested that with Krishna Mohan's ordination 'the process of indigenous self-propagation may be said to have begun'.[9] Ordained, Krishna Mohan's preaching and ministry to young people attracted the title 'Kristobando's Girija' to his charge, Christ Church, Cornwallis Street. The 1870 Report provides a later glimpse of him as a missionary, preaching to 'the heathen Pundits . . . [and] the poor people at Bathietollah' by a form of musical recitation known as *obhinoy*.

Krishna Mohan was no pliant servant of the imperial Church. He resigned the first of the canonries at St Paul's Cathedral on learning that a higher stipend was to be attached to the second which was to go to an English priest. Bishop Wilson attributed this to 'conceit and unthankfulness'.[10] He continued to be concerned at the racism in the Church, whereby, as he put it, the native Christians were treated like 'spiritual ryots or villeins', the foreign missionaries acting like 'barons and zemindars'. In consequence, he became involved in one of the earliest indigenous movements in Indian Christianity following the uprising of 1857, being elected in 1868 first President of the Bengal Christian Association for 'the Protection of the Rights of Indian Christians', later known as the Calcutta Christo Somaj.[11]

Krishna Mohan was, however, far from confined to church circles after his ordination. He was much concerned with social reform, particularly regarding female education and caste, working through such organizations as the Society for the Acquisition of General Knowledge, the Bengal Social Service Association, Calcutta University, where he was President of the Faculty of Arts, and Calcutta Corporation. He also shared in the growing political movement. Some of the earliest meetings leading up to the formation of the Bengal British India Society in 1843 took place in his house, and he was later President in turn of the Indian League and the Indian Association, precursors of the Indian National Congress. His presence as a Christian gave 'a non-sectarian . . . character', as the nationalist Surendranath Banerjea put it, to 'what was the first great political demonstration of the middle class community in Bengal'.

Despite his many-sided activity, Krishna Mohan remained a respected scholar. Much of his earlier work, to about 1865, was apologetic, most importantly in his *Dialogues on Hindu Philosophy*. SPG welcomed the English version in the 1861 Report, and paid for the publication of the Bengali version. Presented as a dialogue between a group of Brahmins and one of their number converted to Christianity, it is a sensitive disclosure of the terms and implications of conversion in contemporary Bengal. That he kept in touch with his roots is evident in the series of Sanskrit texts that he published over some 30 years, although he was wary of the imperialist uses to which oriental studies could be put. The theological work of his later years was undoubtedly the most important, published as *The Arian Witness* in 1875, followed by two supplementary essays in 1880 and *The Relation Between Christianity and Hinduism* in 1881. Unusually conciliatory and proposing a Vedic preparation for Christ, his thinking suggested a freshly constructive propagation of the Gospel such as the founders of the Cambridge Mission to Delhi, Westcott, Lightfoot and Hort, were at this time hoping to see, and which achieved wider acceptance only in the later twentieth century.

For two Society missionaries in South India, Robert Caldwell and George Uglow Pope, hard study was a central aspect of their influential work. Again, we can only deal with one of these, though the other, Pope, was highly effective in an evangelization that brought harmony between castes, and is still honoured in Tamil Nadu for his editions of three Tamil classics, *Tirukural*, *Naladiyar* and *Tiruvasagam*, still in print 160 years later and still considered authoritative.[12] Caldwell, after developing an interest in comparative philology while a student at Glasgow University, arrived in Madras as a London Missionary Society (LMS) missionary in 1837. English education was being established, not least by his friend John Anderson, founder of Madras Christian College, but Caldwell was convinced that 'the masses . . . [could] only be reached through the vernacular', and so devoted his early years in Madras to studying Tamil language and literature.[13] Attracted to the High Church tradition of Hooker and Waterland, he was ordained by Bishop Spencer of Madras in 1841, and became his missionary chaplain. Following the example of the earlier, German, missionaries in their village missions, of living 'nearly on a level with the natives and among the natives', Caldwell settled at Idaiyangudi in Tirunelveli, where he was to work for over 50 years, initially as an SPG missionary and from 1877 as Bishop.

To understand the context of his missionary task, Caldwell did pioneering work in two fields, which issued in numerous publications but especially in *A Comparative Grammar of the Dravidian or South-Indian Family of Languages* (1856), a painstaking and brilliant work, filling a great lacuna in the state of knowledge about India at that time, and *A Political and General History of the District of Tinnevelly . . . from the Earliest Period to . . . 1801* (1881). All was put at the service of the missionary task, and he played a leading part in the revision of the Tamil Book of Common Prayer and the Tamil Bible, and wrote on mission issues in, for example, *Lectures on Tinnevelly Mission* (1857), 'The Languages of India in Relation to Missionary Work' (1875) and *Evangelistic Work among the Higher Classes and Castes in Tinnevelly* (1876).

Caldwell's missionary task was chiefly with a caste community, the Shanars. He saw this in broad terms. 'The old East is at last waking up,' he wrote in 1857, and he clearly envisaged the Christian Church and community graduating from their traditional Shanar occupation as palmyra-climbers and toddy-tappers to become a new élite in this awakening society. Towards the end of his long working life in Tirunelveli, he concluded that this was happening, and that the Shanars now occupied 'a very high place amongst the most progressive tribes and castes in Southern India'.

There were, however, additional, unforeseen consequences. For

Caldwell, the greatest obstacle to Christian conversion in India was Brahminism and its 'fossilising caste rules', so his establishing a 'South-Indian Family of Languages' under the name he devised, 'Dravidian', was a way of affirming an identity among non-Brahmins in the south in opposition to the traditional Brahmin colonists with their social dominance and its sustaining ideologies. While he offended the Tamils with his disparagement of ancient Dravidian religion, his establishment of their separate and independent linguistic and cultural identity nevertheless served not only to consolidate the 'Tinnevelly' Church but also to launch a Dravidian movement broader than he can have envisaged, some revivalist aspects of which were far from his intentions, but within a cultural renewal, the Tamil Renaissance, in which he, and his Society colleague, G. U. Pope, are still honoured.

Alice Hoar's work among young Japanese women in the 1870s, referred to above, was another extremely interesting case of the significance and influence of educated missionaries, for the 'Japanese gentleman' who offered her hospitality and encouragement in her work was Fukuzawa Yukichi, the most influential figure in the modernization movement in the Meiji Era. Though he never became a Christian, he was very close to three Society missionaries in particular, admiring much of what they stood for as representatives of the Western civilization he so much admired, but also in carrying out their evangelism with 'a positive attitude to Japanese culture, tradition and even religion'.[14] In addition to Alice Hoar, these were Arthur Lloyd, former Dean of Peterhouse, Cambridge, who ran the English Department of Fukuzawa's Keio School, with the right to teach Christianity, and above all A. C. Shaw, who, with W. B. Wright, was SPG's first missionary to Japan, arriving in 1873, a Canadian and a graduate of Trinity College, Toronto. Fukuzawa asked Shaw to tutor his children, and built him a house next to his own, and they remained close friends for 27 years. Fukuzawa's relationship with all three, Hoar, Lloyd and Shaw, was, in fact, 'a family relationship'. He saw the Society missionaries' 'learning' as crucially significant for his contribution to Japan's modernization, and they were, as he put it in an editorial in his influential newspaper, *Jijishimpo*, in October 1890, 'torches that lead along the path of right'.[15] From the missionaries' perspective, the friendship of this great Japanese gave them encouragement and insights about a fast-changing Japanese society that advanced the equally speedy emergence of a Japanese Church, the Nippon Sei Ko Kwai (NSKK), with its first priest, a student of Shaw, John Toshimichi Imai, in 1889.

Most hard study by missionaries in Africa in the nineteenth century was devoted to the understanding of languages. Edward Steere's work on 'the language of Zanzibar', Swahili, and his biblical translations in the 1860s and 1870s, with frequent consultation on Arabic questions with William Kay, retired Principal of Bishop's College, Calcutta, were among the most significant. These endeavours were fundamental for the development of Swahili as a trans-tribal language in Church and society in East Africa.

In one exceptional case, biblical interpretation in the missionary context of Africa proved of great significance. This was in the work of John William Colenso (1814–83).[16] Even before going to South Africa, though, chiefly under the influence of F. D. Maurice, to whom his future wife had introduced him, Colenso's missionary approach was evident in his *Village Sermons*,

> By . . . meeting the heathen half way . . . upon the grounds of our common humanity, and with the recollection that that humanity is now blessed and redeemed in Christ . . . we may look for far greater success in missionary labours, and far more stability in the converts that may be made, than by seeking to make all things new to them – to uproot altogether their old religion, scoffing at the things which they hold most sacred.

His consecration as first Bishop of Natal in 1853 provided the opportunity to put this missionary approach to the test. His earliest years were largely devoted to learning the Zulu language, compiling dictionaries and grammars and translating the Bible and Prayer Book. He became increasingly convinced of the error of the prevailing missionary approach with its dismissal of the religious inheritance of African people and its emphasis on the wrath of God, and a substitutionary doctrine of the atonement, which he called 'a corruption of Christianity'. His considered response was *St Paul's Epistle to the Romans, newly translated and explained from a missionary point of view* (1861) where he suggested that teaching 'the truths of our holy religion to intelligent adult natives' was 'a sifting process for the opinions of any teacher'.

> The state of everlasting torment after death of . . . the whole heathen world, as many teach, is naturally so amazing and overwhelming . . . that it quite shuts out the cardinal doctrines of the Gospel, the Fatherly relation to us of the Faithful Creator. The conscience . . . does not answer to such denunciations of indiscriminate wrath, and cannot, therefore, appreciate what is represented as Redeeming Love, offering a way of escape.

By the time Colenso's *Romans* was published, he was already occupied with further challenging work, examining the Pentateuch in the light of contemporary scholarship and geological discoveries, but also in the light of the questioning of a Zulu convert, who had asked of the story of the Flood and Noah's Ark, 'Is all this true?' Elaborating on the question, asking for example how the animals got from Mount Ararat to their subsequent habitats – especially in the case of flightless birds such as the dodo of Mauritius and the apteryx of New Zealand – Colenso said that he 'dared not, as a servant of the God of Truth, urge my brother man to believe that which . . . I knew to be untrue as a matter-of-fact historical narrative'. This missionary context of his studies in the Pentateuch and Joshua, published in five volumes between 1862 and 1865, gave a distinctive character to his handling of a burning issue of the age.

Colenso's fundamental assumption here of the essential intelligence, humanity and dignity of the Zulu, whose queries were to be answered with integrity, flew in the face of prevailing views on the inferiority of 'heathen' and 'primitive' peoples. It also enabled him, a few years later, to transcend the prevailing paternalistic politics, which he had originally supported, and to take a stand against the current deceitful and violent British seizures of land in Natal, his sermon of protest in 1879 being described as 'one of the great sermons of the world', an example of 'the true rhetoric of integrity'.[17]

The tragedy was that, in the reaction which Colenso's hard study brought upon his head, his insights and arguments about mission were entirely overlooked. With few reasons given, but with a great deal of abuse, he was denounced as a heretic in 1856 and excommunicated by Bishop Gray of Cape Town in January 1866. Thanks to the still inchoate legal status of the Anglican Church in South Africa, he was able to continue as Bishop of Natal, alongside a bishopric of Maritzburg that Gray then created, but his isolation meant that his missionary vision was never taken seriously. Fortunately, a handful of other missionaries, including SPG's Henry Callaway, shared something of Colenso's view of the culture and capacity of the local people, and Callaway's labours brought the first two Zulus, William Negwensa and Umpengula Mbanda, to ordination in 1871, Callaway referring to the latter as 'a very superior mind'.[18] One good that might be said to have derived from Colenso's story was that Robert Gray was able to bring this problem of inchoateness to the first Lambeth Conference in 1867, and the structural coherence of the Anglican Communion was advanced.[19]

Throughout the Colenso controversy, the Society attempted to follow a principle of expressing no judgement and deferring to the judgement of the Church. Organizing Secretaries in both Chester and

Durham dioceses reported in 1870 that SPG had 'given offence on both sides', which suggests that this virtuous fence-sitting was working. Fence-sitting, though, cannot have been easy initially, for Colenso had been very active in the Society in England before going to South Africa, as editor of two of the new journals created in the 1840s, and clearly the Society was enthusiastic about his early work in South Africa, the *Mission Field* in the 1850s carrying long accounts of his work at Ekukanyeni, while his proposal to develop a more missionary style of episcopate in 1860 brought offers of generous Society grants. Advised, however, by the English bishops in February 1863 to withdraw its confidence and withhold its grants, SPG was bound to comply. At least thereafter the Society was silent on the matter, though it could prevent neither Prime Minister Gladstone at the 1867 Anniversary Meeting going on about 'colonial churches . . . [running] off in all directions into the wild fields of space . . . [in a] spirit of division and egotism', nor Dean Stanley, at a meeting just before Colenso died, criticizing the Society's lack of sympathy and praising both Colenso's scholarship and his identification with African interests, and suggesting that,

> posterity will say that, among the propagators of the Gospel in the nineteenth century, the Bishop of Natal was not the least efficient.

Posterity took exactly a century to reach this conclusion.[20] Colenso's hard study brought much trouble upon him, but it made him one of the 'intellectual princes of the nineteenth-century missionary movement' in Africa, indicating the terms on which an African Church could be expected to emerge.[21]

SECTION 3

1900-47

9

The Society 1900–47

Two interesting events occurred in South Africa in 1900. The long-serving missionary at St Augustine's, Rorke's Drift, Charles Johnson, was visited in the thick of the Boer War by General Bethune and his assistant, Captain Lord de la Warr, and with his wife, Margaret, accompanied them to Ngudu, 'taking with them a Union Jack of their own making, which they hoisted on the fort'. This footnote in Pascoe provides a glimpse of the way the Church functioned within colonialism. The same year, there was an introduction to the way colonialism functioned within the Church. On Sunday 26 August 1900, James Mata Dwane, of the royal Xhosa house of the Amantinde, led his followers into Grahamstown Cathedral and the *Umzi wase Tiyopia*, more widely known as the Order of Ethiopia, was welcomed into the fellowship of the CPSA. Goedhals' account of the Order occurs later in this volume. The Society provided initial funding and missionary personnel to advance this 'creative synthesis' of African and Anglican traditions.[1] The aspiration for an African Christianity represented in the Order was long in the fulfilling, with the Order finally granted its first bishop, Sigqibo Dwane, grandson of the founder, in 1982. Other African aspirations within the CPSA in the first half of the century, such as James Calata and Hazel Maimane's African Catholic Church movement, were invariably firmly suppressed by the white episcopate.[2]

Certainly, at the bicentennial celebrations in London, the Society was encouraged by one of its most consistent supporters, Randall Davidson, soon to be Archbishop of Canterbury, to look 'fearlessly and hopefully out upon the . . . wide varieties of form and development in liturgy and life which . . . based firmly upon the ordered system which has come down to us from primitive days . . . before the coming century has run its course, are bound to show themselves in new-born churches the world through'.[3] There was a long way to go, though, and the imperialist enthusiasms that had taken off in the 1880s continued strongly in SPG as in other British mission agencies. J. A. Hobson referred in his *Imperialism* in 1902 to 'religious and philanthropic agencies' which, for all their real achievements and good faith, were having the effect of 'mystification', allowing imperialism to escape general recognition for the 'narrow, sordid' thing that it was. He cited only one agency, the Society, quoting Lord Hugh Cecil's 'naive' call to 'sanctify the spirit of Imperialism' at the Annual Meeting in May 1900. Hobson's views were corroborated in India at the time in an observation on 'modern missionaries', that 'to non-Christians their mission appears to be much less religious than commercial or political'.[4] The scope for this was in an ever-wider British Empire, at its widest in the 1920s, with parts of both east and south-west Africa added at the conclusion of the 1914–18 war, the former adding to UMCA's work, the latter, following a genocidal German colonialism among the Herero, to SPG's.

The Society's Secretaries in this period were a series of ex-colonial bishops and an ex-colonial archdeacon, starting with H. H. Montgomery (1902–18), his distinctive vision and objectives described in this volume in Maughan's essay. His seemingly easy accommodation to the imperialistic mood of the times was perhaps somewhat modified by his promotion of the place of women in SPG's work. He also promoted the use of typewriters and telephones, in the Society's first purpose-built office in Tufton Street. This must have been a shock to such an older member of staff as E. Davies, who had copied all important letters by hand for 42 years. Montgomery was also vigorous in extending SPG organizationally, and in strengthening the base of support in England, especially through increasing the number of area secretaries from 50 to over 100. Montgomery's successor, G. L. King (1918–24), oversaw a Second Supplementary Charter in 1921. This authorized retrospectively work in such regions beyond British imperial control as China, Japan, Korea, Madagascar and Mozambique, and eventually, as resources and capacity permitted, and as the missionary imperative was reinterpreted, in Britain itself. King also oversaw the founding in 1923 of the College of the Ascension at Selly Oak for the preparation of women missionaries. The Society had hesitated to be associated with the Nonconformist agencies at Selly Oak, but was persuaded of the significance of Selly Oak as a mission-training centre by Charles Gore, former Bishop of Birmingham. The next Secretary, S. Waddy (1924–37), was notable for his energetic leadership, which no doubt helped contribute to what he called 'in a true sense *annus mirabilis* of our Society', 1926, with a highest ever list of 1516 missionaries, including 432 indigenous clergy and 403 women, and to a high point in funds received. Waddy's later years and those of his successors, N. B. Hudson (1938–40) and J. Dauglish (1941–4), were preoccupied with managing the retrenchments that the economic situation in the 1930s entailed in both Britain and many other countries where SPG was engaged, and the much reduced operation during the Second World War, responsibility taken up and developed by B. C. Roberts (1944–57) with great gifts of judgement and far-sightedness.

The overall policy for this period was to reduce support for work among colonial settlers, and to increase it for indigenous communities. Emigration from Britain, moderated only by the two World Wars and the economic depression of the 1930s, continued in millions well into the second half of the century, to Australia, Canada, New Zealand and southern Africa, especially Rhodesia, but the Society decreased its involvement. This is very clear in regard to missionary numbers, with the largest number of missionaries by 1926, some 700, in south and east Asia, about half this number in southern Africa, some increase in the West Indies and only 150 in Canada and Australia together. There was one innovation in work among settlers, that taken up by women missionaries in Canada among settler but also First Nation children. This shift is equally clear in funding, with grants to Australian dioceses, largely to complete episcopal endowments, tapering off during the period, and an end to grants to Canada finally in 1940. Such state support of the Church that still obtained largely ended during this period, in India partially in 1927, finally in 1947, in British Guiana in 1944, with only the clergy of Barbados still paid out of island revenues in 1950. Various arrangements with the colonial authorities, however, increased the Church's widespread involvement in education for indigenous communities, while annually from 1896 the Society itself had had substantial additional resources for school buildings, as well as for churches and hospitals, from the Marriott Bequest.

Education was given a high priority at the Edinburgh 1910 World Missionary Conference, and was very significant for SPG during this period, developed on a very large scale. Many of the schools and colleges concerned were of course founded in the nineteenth century, but considerable expansion of this side of SPG's work came in this period. Thus, a retrospect in 1950 of the Society's work in the Gold Coast, begun in 1904, describes both the 'SPG Grammar School' at Cape Coast, now known as Adisadel College, and 'hundreds of village schools . . . at the other end of the scale'.[5] The UMCA's St Andrew's College, originally, from 1871, at Kiungani, Zanzibar, later at Minaki, likewise sat on the shoulders of a vast number of village schools. St Andrew's was, as Bishop Tozer had intended a 'School of the Prophets', producing almost the entire indigenous clergy and later leadership of the Church in much of East Africa. It was an educating clergy. The 'Apostle', Kolumba Msigala, for example, himself went on from a theological course there at the beginning of this period to a ministry of evangelism accompanied by the opening of numerous schools as an instrument of his vision of 'Christianity and Christian "modernisation"' for his country.[6] He gives us a glimpse of this in telling the story of Chief Undi who begged for a school,

> I asked him, 'Very well, but why do you want a school so much and yet you refuse our religion?' And he replied, 'Ah! do not say that. Your religion profits us in two ways. (1) Your religion builds up a town. (2) Your religion brings civilisation. For this reason we want it, that we also may become people of importance'.[7]

Kiungani itself had this wider function, creating a new élite in the early decades of the century who were, among other things, the founders of the first modern political organizations of Africans in the region.

> The quality of Kiungani's education was unequalled in East Africa at this time. Boys entered after four year's education elsewhere. They were taught in Swahili, but expected to read in English. The curriculum emphasised religion and was not unlike that of an English school.

A modern Tanzanian assessment suggests that 'this "English" quality was Kiungani's virtue, for it meant that the school tried to give its pupils the best education its teachers knew, not a specially restricted education "for Africans only". It produced, and was meant to produce, young men who often thought like Europeans, but at least it produced young men who had the knowledge and confidence to criticise Europeans.'[8]

The story could be repeated for many areas where the Society worked, though we should note also such variants as the respected educational work of the blind missionary, W. H. Jackson, among the blind in Burma, and the Blind School at Ranchi in North India and similar educational endeavours among the most disadvantaged in many other places. A system, though, based on vast numbers of village-level schools – missions provided 85 per cent of schools in Africa – building up to impressive and prestigious tertiary institutions was almost universal in the Society's work. No pinnacle was more impressive and prestigious than CMD's St Stephen's College, Delhi, established in 1881. It was recognized by 1900 that such institutions did not generally produce converts, but that in the context of the country's rising national movement they bore a valuable witness to Christianity. St Stephen's itself, under the brilliant Indian leadership of S. K. Rudra, which began unusually early, in 1907, bore additional witness to the notion of a learning community transcending India's religious divisions, and also to the possibility of a missionary institution supporting nationalism. Gandhi planned the Non-Cooperation Movement in the Principal's house with the assistance of Rudra and a Society missionary, C. F. Andrews. That this small college produced during this period future Presidents of both India and Pakistan, as well as a future Vice-President of Tanzania, is some indication of the role such institutions performed.[9]

Rudra's leadership at this level was virtually unique for this period, but at the 'other end of the scale', at the level of village evangelism and village schools, the work of indigenous Christians was very significant. This had become a well-established system in, for example, Tirunelveli, in the second half of the nineteenth century, taking over the practice from the Roman Catholics, and even using the eighteenth-century Jesuit Beschi's catechists' manual, the *Vediar-olukkam*, only slightly modified. The missionary list for South Asia in 1900 records, alongside some 700 ordained missionaries (290 of them native clergy) and 100 women missionaries from Britain, approximately 2500 'lay agents', catechists, teachers, Bible women or female catechists and readers. Clearly there were many more, in Africa for example, but they are only vaguely if at all accounted for in SPG's lists, since the Society's responsibility was generally only indirect, through diocesan block grants. While lay agency was sometimes criticized in India for creating dependency among the agents, it more commonly awoke possibilities in the individuals concerned and so 'introduced a new culture into . . . outcaste communities'. The testimony here from Ghana, in Pobee's essay in this volume, with reports from South Africa and UMCA areas carrying many similar testimonies, indicates that organized indigenous teaching and catechizing of this sort, as earlier in India, contributed substantially to the propagation of the Gospel and its outworking in society in the first half of the twentieth century.[10]

Despite this, and despite the vision of distinctive provincial and national Churches voiced at the turn of the century by Benson, Copleston, Davidson and Westcott, leadership by indigenous clergy was advanced only slowly in the first half of the twentieth century, and SPG's practice did not always match its rhetoric. Just as the 'high imperial' mood had gradually undermined and compromised the ideal of the self-governing Church in the work of CMS and UMCA by the early twentieth century, so in SPG progress also seems to have slowed.[11] This is the more surprising when one notes, for example, that as early as 1865 local congregational leaders in Tirunelveli had been calling for a 'Native Bishop . . . [and] a chance to attain independent existence'.[12] Nothing had come of this, but Tirunelveli was nevertheless still relatively one of the Society's more progressive areas, the bishop writing to the Secretary in 1910,

> Since the beginning of this year, I have thrown more responsibility upon the *Indian* clergy and placed them in charge of Districts, increasing their powers of administration and authority.[13]

Raising local clergy in new areas of work often went ahead quite quickly. The first ordinations took place within ten years of work restarting in the Gold Coast in 1904 and in south-west Africa in 1924, while by 1925 the dioceses that the Society was supporting in south and south-east Asia had a majority of local clergy, a third in southern Africa. Encouraging self-support and self-propagation among the Karens of Burma was another success, enabling the Church there to grow and to endure under impressive local leadership during the Second World War.

Entrusting non-white clergy with much responsibility and leadership was, however, another matter, and still very rare. The SPG missionary, L. Fuller CR, in Johannesburg in 1907, expressed an attitude that was common early in the century,

> You cannot leave the Natives to work by themselves; it is not fair – they want a backbone and the white to help them, and then they do wonderfully well.

The language is not unlike that of Bishop Lefroy of Lahore in arguing unsuccessfully in the same year against S. K. Rudra's appointment as Principal of St Stephen's College, Delhi, on the basis of a belief in 'Western effectiveness and energy and grit and grip', though Lefroy later unreservedly supported Rudra.[14] Even more destructive, perhaps, was the mistrust that pervaded relationships within colonialism, as in the case of the UMCA missionary H. A. M. Cox, who, around 1909, mistrusted the saintly Leonard Kamungu in money matters, and the case also of V. S. Azariah, the first Indian bishop in the Anglican Church in India, who, though in an 'overall . . . harmonious' relationship with the Society, was caused 'much injury' by mistrust. Montgomery encouraged such attitudes with his declaration that 'the Hindu is inherently untruthful'.[15]

Other factors also occasionally militated against indigenous advancement. Not least among these was the opposition of local people against one of their own being placed over them. This occurred particularly vociferously in the case of Azariah, though this was not the whole of that story. Two years before being consecrated, he had told the Edinburgh 1910 conference, 'We shall learn to walk only by walking – perchance only by falling and learning from our mistakes, but never by being kept in leading strings until we arrive at maturity', yet Azariah seems not to have wanted other Indian clergy walking alongside himself.[16]

That, of course, does not account for the twenty-year wait for the next Indian bishop, S. K. Tarafdar, as assistant in Calcutta diocese in 1935. What does, perhaps, was the general climate of the period indicated above, and which a Bengali missionary of the Society, S. A. C. Ghose, had described as 'a vast heritage of accumulated prejudice against the Indian as such'.[17] This was reflected in the efforts of SPG's India subcommittee to block Azariah's appointment, a 'recently ordained priest of no marked distinction'. The rejection in this case of the views of the bishops on the spot, Whitehead and Copleston, is a measure of the 'accumulated prejudice' active in the Society at the time, though the subcommittee was overruled by Montgomery and Archbishop Davidson.[18] Similarly, the French colonial spirit seemed to have rubbed off on the Church in Madagascar, where, with 60 Malagasies among the 65 clergy by 1939, the greatest responsibility conferred, on Paul Tsimilanja, was that of rural dean. Japan, beyond the corrosions of colonialism, had taken the first step towards a Japanese episcopate in 1908, but war and an earthquake created unavoidable delays until, with Society grants towards their stipends, Bishops Motoda and Naide were consecrated in 1923. China, however, in an area of relatively early CMS work, Chekiang, had acquired its first Anglican bishop, Shen Tsai-sen, in 1918. North China, where SPG worked, had to wait until the eve of the Communist revolution before its two English bishops handed over to Chinese leadership.

There were, of course, many missionaries trying to transcend colonial attitudes, as was the case with R. Freeman in Central India, who tried to do so through identification with the poor of his parish, though he was humiliated at his failure to be able to live on less than Rs.15 per month, something like twice the income of most of them. On his death in 1937, a friend and former colleague wrote,

Ronald was a brilliant Cambridge scholar, a man of exceptional courage, enterprise and devotion. He married a former Matron of

the Purulia Leper Home, and went with her to the . . . little town of
Malegaru to start work for lepers . . . They were building up a centre
of Christian love and justice . . . when Ronald contracted dysentery
and after a month of intense suffering, died . . . at the age of 34 . . . I
remember when Ronald first went to his leper-work, how struck I
was that no one thought anything of it. I think that is a great tribute
to Christianity. It is taken for granted, as a normal and accepted
thing, that a first-class scholar and thinker should devote himself to
the . . . most degraded section of the population.[19]

The context of Freeman's work was the Diocese of Nasik, in which a
group of women missionaries, Latham, Kenyon, Young and Broomfield,
and their Indian colleagues, were similarly working among leprosy
patients. There also Bishop Loyd, a former Society missionary, was at
this same time launching, with the Society, the 'Nasik Scheme' to build
up a staff of Indian clergy independent of funding from England. They
were a good way behind Tirunelveli, 'the classical example of Indian
self-government within the Anglican Church', where, by this time,

Not even the Bishop can dominate proceedings, and the control of
administration and policy is very largely Indian.[20]

Nasik, though, was more typical at this time, with the missionary still
dominant, at best doing things sacrificially for others.

Loyd had contributed an essay to *Essays Catholic and Missionary*, edited
by the Warden of the College of the Ascension, E. R. Morgan, in 1928,
in which he identified much work in his diocese in which 'the Indian
must of necessity be to a large extent in a position of pupillage and
subordination'. The *Essays* had an encouraging Preface proposing that
'the theory of Catholic Order . . . [in] Anglican Catholicism . . . ensures
unity without endangering initiative', and concluded with a piece by the
Secretary, Waddy, suggesting that Churches overseas were at a turning
point in their development. Only one of the essays suggests that
indigenous leadership had any part to play in this. Typical is W. J.
Clissold, a missionary at Molepolele in Bechuanaland, full of admiration
for the local catechists, for their 'spiritual influence' and the 'mystical
element' in their work, but sure that 'intellectual and administrative'
tasks were beyond them. Only G. Callaway SSJE, a Society missionary
in South Africa, thought that for 'English Catholics' to serve under an
African bishop would be a great opportunity to bear witness to the
reality of their faith. It was an opportunity that no Anglican in South
Africa would enjoy for many years to come.

The Second World War brought calamity for many SPG-related Christians particularly in south-east and east Asia. The outcome for the NSKK, noted below, can stand for the many other Anglican dioceses and provinces which were victims of Japan's vision of a 'Greater East Asia', for there was much suffering, martyrdom and heroic ministry under often oppressive conditions. While the Society's missionaries faced considerable trials, with internment in some cases and death in others, the majority withdrew from the war regions, and it was the indigenous Christians who bore the brunt, but who also, as in the case of Japan, threw up a leadership which, in the longer run, strengthened the Churches for their growing independence in the second half of the century.

A very major preoccupation of SPG throughout the period was with ecumenical issues, chiefly regarding the search for unity in South India, where a relatively successful accommodation of missionary expertise to indigenous aspiration was achieved, leading up to the inauguration of the Church of South India (CSI) in 1947. Throughout the process in India, a series of SPG missionaries and bishops closely associated with the Society played a leading role in support of reunion, a much lesser number in opposing it. First among the former was H. A. Whitehead, who after fifteen years on the Society's list as Principal of Bishop's College, Calcutta, was Bishop of Madras from 1899 to 1922 and, as such, 'the outstanding Anglican reunion leader in South India'. A 'determined Tractarian' when he arrived in Madras, a decision of the Episcopal Synod in 1900 encouraging co-operation with other denominations launched Whitehead into a rapidly deepening commitment to organic union, by a road which lay 'in a general recognition of all that is good and true in other churches'.[21] Two concerns proved to be a constant theme of others also as the movement developed. One was the missionary significance of reunion, reflected in the 1908 Lambeth belief in the 'waste of force' inherent in disunity. The other was the special case for unity in India, where, for example, the organic unity guaranteed by the historic episcopate could reduce the danger of caste Churches. Indian Christians added their own Indian perspectives. For example, one of the leading negotiators, Meshach Peter, whose father was a pastor in the Reformed Church, an uncle an Anglican, his grandfather and mother Lutherans and his wife from a Congregationalist family, said, 'I love them all. Why should we not get together.' These issues were highlighted at the landmark conference of Indian Christians at Tranquebar in 1919, a conference led and inspired by Samuel Azariah. Increasingly a 'convinced Anglican', Azariah played a crucial role in the process until his death in 1945. The other key Anglican was E. J. Palmer, who as a committed

Tractarian had taken a leading part in SPG's Junior Clergy Missionary Association (JCMA) in England prior to his appointment as Bishop of Bombay in 1909. Described as 'the greatest theological mind applied to the South Indian union problem', Palmer's constitutional work to transform the established Church of England in India into a disestablished, synodical Church of India, completed in 1927, was a step essential to Anglican participation in the ecumenical process. Palmer made a continuous contribution to the union negotiations even after his retirement in 1929, so that 'during the 1930s his influence . . . was felt almost as strongly as before'. Other SPG missionaries, most of whom became bishops, made their contribution in the negotiating committee, among them R. A. Manuel, a Tamil, H. Pakenham-Walsh, F. J. Western, G. N. L. Hall, P. Loyd and A. M. Hollis. They were consistently strongly supported by the Metropolitan, Foss Westcott. They were all from the 'Catholic' end of the Anglican spectrum, some decidedly, but all would have endorsed Palmer's observation, in his *Challenge of an Indian Experience* of 1933, on how the Indian context had strengthened and shaped his own commitment to reunion, and all would have heard, as he had, Indian Christians saying, 'Your learned advice may help us much, but nothing that you can do can stop us.'

For the Society in England, other voices were more likely to predominate. The first clear indication was in connection with the Edinburgh 1910 conference. A Remonstrance signed by 900 Incorporated Members sought to prevent SPG's participation in this exercise in 'undenominationalism'. Montgomery and 34 others did in fact attend, but the warning sign was there, that many of the Society's supporters were opposed to this sort of ecumenism. This was further underlined in what was known as the 'Kikuyu Crisis' of 1913, in which protest erupted at news of a service of Holy Communion in which Anglican missionaries of the CMS had shared with Baptists, Methodists and Presbyterians at a conference in Kenya, with rumours of the formation of some sort of missionary federation. The eruption was made more explosive by an ill-informed Bishop of Zanzibar, F. Weston, writing of heresy and schism. Over a hundred letters to *The Times*, about 50 pamphlets and a report from the Consultative Committee of the Lambeth Conference, requested by Archbishop Randall Davidson, ensued, along with a limerick on Weston,

> There once was a Zanzibarbarian
> Who thought the whole world had turned Arian
> So he called upon Randall
> For Bell, Book & Candle,
> But Randall lay low like a wary 'un.[22]

An ancient-regime church in mission. It is a 'tantalizing conjecture' that the military chaplain praying on the right of Benjamin West's *Death of Wolfe* was the Society missionary, Michael Houdin

Above: The altarpiece in the Chapel at Cyrene, Zimbabwe, including an African Christ the High Priest, Simon of Cyrene, and the martyrs Bernard Mizeki and Manche Masemola

Below: '...building, carpentering, tinkering, writing, teaching and preaching... It is as well to be busy, as otherwise one might have time to think of fever.' Memorial window in an English parish church (St Aidan's, West Hartlepool) to a former curate, Arthur Fraser Sim, who died after eighteen months in Central Africa.

'...to rescue them from a savage to a civil and human life'. Mohawk children and their schoolmaster

..indubitably the best-known Indian in the annals of the Society'. *Thayendanegea*, also known as Captain Joseph Brant, translator of St Mark's Gospel into the Mohawk language

'...to make better men and better citizens'.
King's College (later Columbia University), New York;
Bishop's College, Calcutta; Kafir Institution, Grahamstown

Statue of George Pope, editor of Tamil Saiva classics, erected by the Tamilnadu State Government, Madras, 1968

'The strength of the Christian cause in India is in these missions.' A Tirunelveli congregation in the 1860s

'...scarcity – great straitness and distress'. Emigrants at Liverpool in the 1860s

'...waiting till his billie boiled'. A 'pioneer missionary' in Australia, as depicted in the 1872 Report

'... this atrocious traffic'. Arab and Swahili slave-raiding. Drawing by one of the survivors of Mackenzie's mission party

'...making Cecil a Bishop ... he would be admirable'. Cecil Majaliwa and his family, Zanzibar

'...the benefit of minds and bodies as well as souls'. UMCA dispensary, Likoma Island,
c.1900; Chinese medical students at Shantung Christian University, 1920

'...*the diversification of care*'. School for the blind, Penang, 1970; leprosy centre, Seoul, 1970

This particular excitement evaporated with the onset of the First World War, but had served as both a further rallying point for Anglo-Catholics in England, and a further indication of the great gap between many in England and missionaries overseas in pursuit of reunion with non-episcopal Churches. This gap was underlined two years later when Whitehead had to respond to Montgomery's anxious letters, with threats of grants being withheld, over plans for co-operation in the Women's Christian College, Madras. Whitehead told Montgomery not to be 'frightened by a shadow'. Anglican encouragement outside India for the ecumenical endeavours in South India was probably at its strongest at Lambeth 1920, at which Azariah, Palmer and Western took a leading part, Palmer being largely responsible for the Encyclical 'Appeal to all Christian People'. Lambeth 1930's recognition that the proposed Church of South India would be autonomous and not a part of the Anglican Communion, though with limited intercommunion, evolving over time into a fuller version, did little to calm Anglo-Catholic anxieties. Thereafter, news of occasional intercommunion among the negotiators further roused the opponents of the process, including some in the Province, Bishop Carpenter-Garnier of Colombo and members of the Oxford Mission to Calcutta (OMC) in particular. It also roused Palmer in a letter to *The Times* of 5 January 1933 to claim that 'the acid test of a church's life is whether it does convert pagans', and he was sure that the non-episcopal Churches in India passed the test as well as the episcopal. SPG at this stage took legal advice, and was told the Charter would only allow support for the proposed Church out of its General Fund if it met Anglican criteria laid down in the Lambeth Conference. As the plan reached its final stages in the 1940s, the controversy reached its peak in the Church of England, and it was clear that only limited recognition would be available from the Anglican Communion. Archbishop Temple ruled that the 'going out' of the four Anglican dioceses concerned, Dornakal, Madras, Tinnevelly and Travancore and Cochin, from the Anglican Communion into the CSI would not be an act of schism, despite T. S. Eliot seeing it as 'the greatest crisis in the Church of England since the Reformation'. Meanwhile, the Church of India, Burma and Ceylon (CIBC) voted in support of the final scheme. Determined Anglo-Catholic pressure within and towards SPG suggests that the limited support offered by the Society at the time of the union in 1947 was all that was possible. This took the form of a Special Fund, to protect the consciences of those opposed to the union, agreed by 58 votes to 19 in the Standing Committee. This was proposed by Archbishop Fisher, who added that 'the withdrawal of the Anglican element' from the Church would be an 'act of treachery'.[23] His strong leadership at this point, but much more the patient dedication of the Society's missionaries and bishops in India who had espoused this cause in the face of growing opposition, helped to secure a respected place for the Church of South India among the Churches, in accordance with what Azariah at Tranquebar had called 'the rule in practice for nineteen centuries', something, as Manuel had promised, 'Indian and Catholic'.

10

'Atheists of empire'

Contesting the widespread enthusiasm for 'imperial Christianity' at the beginning of the century was a small number of Society missionaries who have been called 'atheists of empire'.[1] The first notable one appeared in China. American Episcopalian and then CMS missionaries had entered China in the aftermath of the First Opium War and the Treaty of Nanking of 1842, SPG missionaries in 1863 after the Second Opium War. Continuous Society work began with the arrival of C. P. Scott and M. Greenwood in Shantung in 1874. They spent their earlier years learning the language, enjoying the hospitality initially of John Nevius, an American Presbyterian missionary with radical ideas about the creation of an indigenous Church. Following Scott's consecration as Missionary Bishop of North China in 1880, SPG's missionary numbers grew, some 30 men and women added in the 1880s and 1890s, including Chang Ching Lan, the first ordained Chinese on the Society's list. These were only a tiny element in the 'rapid increase in the number of missionaries' that Bishop Scott referred to in a letter to the Secretary in December 1892. To Scott, this accounted 'in the most natural and straightforward way for the multiplication of the instances of friction between the Chinese and the foreigners', instances which issued finally in the Boxer Rising of 1900, in which over 200 missionaries and some 35,000 Chinese Christians, 'secondary foreign devils' in Boxer terminology, were killed. A later Chinese commentator described this as 'the most important religious uprising in the world as a whole to take place this century'.[2]

Among the missionaries of the Society's North China Mission was Roland Allen, appointed in 1895 to the charge of the embryonic Theological School in Peking to prepare young men for work as catechists with a view to later ordination.[3] He was also Chaplain to the

British Legation in the city. By the time the Boxer Rising reached Peking in April 1900, three SPG missionaries had been killed, Sydney Brooks at Ping Yin, Harry Norman and Charles Robinson at Yung Ch'ing. Allen provided a graphic account of the rising in three articles for the *Cornhill Magazine* and a book published the following year, *The Siege of the Peking Legations*, this last including a description of his final days with his students in early June before encouraging them to leave the city under cover of night and make their way home to their families,

> Parting from them was terrible. I prayed with them, commended them to God, and sent them away, and fairly broke down . . . Whilst the Church has amongst her members such Christians as these she cannot fail to make progress – she must win the world.

Allen then withdrew from the school, soon to be in ruins like the rest of the Mission property, and took refuge in the British Legation. Here he acted as chaplain and assisted in look-out duties during the several weeks of the siege, until the arrival of the massive military relief column put together by the Europeans, Russians, Americans and Japanese, the British providing a number of Indian regiments. In his articles and book, Allen devotes much attention to the causes of the uprising. The Chinese had 'plenty of justification . . . [in the] territorial aggressions of the Powers . . . [which had made them] the slaves of a foreign despotism'. They saw the missionary as 'a political agent, sent out to buy the hearts of the people, and so to prepare the way for a foreign dominion', and the converts as 'willing dupes and allies of the foreign invasion'. He argues that the 4000 Chinese Christians admitted into the Legations saved the situation by the work they did in building the defences, despite very inferior rations. There are bits of bravado, as when waiting in suspense for a Boxer attack 'reminded one of the Eights at Oxford', but plainly the whole experience was setting Allen thinking, particularly about missionary methods. It was essential to disengage the missionary project from the imperial, and also to stop 'trying to force upon the Chinese . . . the arbitrary dictates of autocratic church government'. Above all, a new method was required whereby a small Anglican mission might hope to 'provide such a vast area with a properly ordered Church life', in a Church 'openly and undeniably Chinese', in which 'the fundamental principles of the Christian religion' would be grafted 'upon the sound stock of Confucian morality'.[4]

Perhaps Allen had heard from Bishop Scott something of the missionary methods advocated by Scott's old friend Nevius, who had died two years before Allen's arrival in China. Certainly Allen wrote about the

'Nevius Method' later. He also discussed and criticized the ideas of Henry Venn later, but makes no reference to them at this time, although some of his colleagues in North China were aware of them. His own explanation of the origin of his new ideas indicates that they sprang essentially out of his reflection on the Boxer Rising itself.[5]

After a recuperative leave in Britain, Allen returned to North China in 1902 where he began to implement some of his new ideas, working at Yung Ch'ing with the local congregation and with one of the catechists whom he had taught earlier in Peking, Wang Shu Tien, 'a very excellent and able man'.[6] Essentially, the missionary must avoid the impression of being 'a ruler set over the converts by a foreign power', must be 'always retiring from the people in order to prepare the way for final retirement', pressing full responsibility on the local Christians under a 'new code . . . [which] should embody as much as possible of the ancient customary law', treating them as a Church and refusing to do anything that other, local members could do.[7]

After only two months in his new work, Allen wrote that he could see 'no reason why it should be necessary to keep a foreigner here more than a year or two longer, and even now I think the continual presence of a foreigner rather a disadvantage than otherwise'.[8] The matter was taken out of his hands, however, for a few months later Allen was invalided home, never to return to China, but convinced that he had discovered 'a compelling truth'.[9] To this he was to devote his entire energies until his death in 1947, first in his 1912 classic *Missionary Methods: St Paul's or Ours?*. This was essentially a critique of the culture of imperialism as it pervaded and undermined the Church's mission, expressed in a missionary dominance which he contrasted with what he saw in St Paul. He elaborated this Pauline alternative over against the imperialism he had seen in the Church, 'the most deep-rooted of all imperialism'.[10] Further insights came in the light of the serious clergy shortages throughout the Anglican Communion in the 1920s, which led to fierce criticism of the system of a paid clergy which had the Church bound to 'the chariot wheels of Mammon', so that in too many places it was dependent on outside help. This led in turn to his advocacy of what he called 'voluntary clergy', and, beyond this, to a call for deeper trust in the work of the Holy Spirit. In books, articles and addresses as he travelled about the Anglican Communion during the rest of his life, he pressed and developed his ideas, while in correspondence he harangued and hounded church leaders, though often with a vehemence that was self-defeating.[11]

Allen terminated his formal connection with SPG on leaving China. There was clearly uneasiness in the Society with so comprehensive a dismissal of standard missionary practice, and such a fierce denunciation of the imperial mentality in missionary work. The review of his *Missionary Methods* in the July 1912 *East and West* was a sweeping dismissal, missing his vision of Churches rooted in their own culture and context, while the Society's Editorial Secretary, C. H. Robinson, in the opening section of his *History of Christian Missions* of 1915, entitled 'St Paul's Missionary Methods', without referring to Allen by name, is at pains to reject his arguments. His ideas did nevertheless make some headway. Bishop Whitehead of Madras had written the Preface, and his assistant bishop, Azariah, wrote to Mrs Whitehead that Allen's 'fearless conclusions' suited his own 'militant spirit'. Also in India, P. N. F. Young of the Delhi Mission was soon 'bombarding our Missions in India . . . [on] a non-professional ministry'.[12] One of the most serious appropriations of his ideas was, as we shall see, in the new context of China after the Communist revolution. Other significant responses came through a post-colonial rereading of his work after its republication in the 1960s, for example in regard to work in Nicaragua, the work of Bishop Harris in Alaska, of Bishop Cáceres-Villavicencio in Ecuador and of a Roman Catholic, Vincent Donovan, among the Masai in Tanzania, while his 'teaching' was commended as a basis for indigenization and shared ministry at the 1984 Anglican Consultative Council (ACC) meeting in Nigeria.

One missionary who admired and commended Allen's ideas, a near contemporary, was himself another of the Society's 'atheists of empire'.[13] This was Arthur Shearly Cripps, in Rhodesia, or Mashonaland as he invariably called it, on the missionary list from 1900 to 1926. He was, among other things, a prophetic poet. The poetry takes us wonderfully close to this missionary's heart, while the more prosaic files of the Aborigines Protection Society and the Fabian Colonial Bureau, and many others, bear witness to other aspects of his lifelong opposition to colonialism, presented here in M. Steele's essay in this volume.

Among Cripps's poems is one of 1934 to honour another SPG missionary, beginning,

> Behold a Lazarus of Bethany,
> Who breathes (in this world), that world's air,
> And moves as one almost too glad to be –
> Of the Immortals' blessedness aware.[14]

This was Charles Freer Andrews. Cripps had met Andrews for the first time that year. Andrews had by then been active as the most remarkable of the Society's 'atheists of empire' for some 30 years, indeed virtually from the day of his first arrival in India in 1904. On the morning after his arrival in Delhi, he later recalled, the first doubts were sown,

> I sat in church before the service began, and opened the Urdu Prayer Book. These were the words I saw – 'Edward VI. Ke dusre sal men Parliament ke hukm se' (in the second year of King Edward VI by order of Parliament).

Andrews says that his heart sank within him. Was that 'fateful order of Parliament . . . [of 1549] to go on finding fresh fields and pastures new of spiritual usurpation *ad infinitum?*' There were also instructive first impressions outside the church – 'the policemen saluting, the people salaaming . . . everyone making way'.

> I thought at first it was all directed towards my companion, who was well known in Delhi. But no! all was exactly the same when I was alone. It was due to the simple fact that I was a Sahib.[15]

Andrews arrived in India at the 'high noon of empire', during the viceroyalty of Lord Curzon. Of the 36 years that he spent there, he was an SPG missionary for the first ten, as a member of the Cambridge Brotherhood in Delhi and a teacher at St Stephen's College.[16] In the course of that ten years, he moved from a rather bewildered admiration for British rule to a total commitment to the cause of Indian independence. Nothing did more to bring about this change than his friendship with a colleague at the College, the Bengali Christian, S. K. Rudra. Andrews' capacity for deep and unreserved friendships across the normally unbridgeable racial divide, starting with this friendship with Rudra, was crucial in helping him to appreciate the feelings of a subject people and the facts of subjugation.

For Andrews, as a missionary in the more formal sense, his chief concern was to promote the development of an Indian Church, and he did this on a number of fronts, introducing new ideas through articles in mission and Christian journals and in books. His first book, *North India* of 1906, in the series of Handbooks of English Church Expansion, was constructed round this theme of interracial friendship in the life of the missionary; his second, *The Renaissance in India* of 1912, for a mission-study series in Britain, was a sympathetic survey of contemporary Hindu and Muslim reform movements, too sympathetic for the editor of the series, who edited out some of the sympathy, to Andrews' annoyance. The generally hostile reaction in the mission community and amongst many North Indian Christians to much that he wrote is a measure of the rarity then of a missionary questioning the colonial mind-set. The former group was up in arms at SPG's Summer School in England in 1912 at his advocacy of interracial marriage among Christians, proposed in a series of articles in *The East and the West*. Among Indian Christians, he found strong support among the educated and independently minded, while a number of younger missionaries were encouraged by his fresh ideas, and with Rudra's help he ran a series of 'Indian Schools of Study' for them. Among his other church involvements was the part he took in the vigorous debate in the Mission leading up to Rudra's appointment as Principal of the College in 1907. Legend long said that Andrews fought alone for Rudra, but in fact most of the Delhi missionaries and the entire Cambridge Committee were in favour of his appointment. It was nevertheless a revolutionary move among missionary institutions. Also far in advance of its time were Andrews' pleas for the theology taught to Indian ordinands to be contextualized, something that only came about long after Indian independence. Associated with this were his attempts to present his friend, Sadhu Sundar Singh, as a model for Christian ministry in India, and to encourage an authentic Indian theology, in particular by publishing extracts from the then little-known writings of Brahmabandhav Upadhyaya. In a debate initiated by Bishop Whitehead about the missionary significance of colleges like St Stephen's, he argued, and convinced Montgomery during a visit to India in 1907, that, though they produced few conversions, they provided opportunities to influence the 'educated classes' in the shaping of the emerging nation. A 'Church of the poor' would be, in his view, a vital but later priority.

Andrews' role as an activist in the Indian national movement began remarkably soon after his arrival as a missionary. He started with a letter in the *Civil and Military Gazette* in 1906, a newspaper of which the Kipling family were proprietors. Andrews criticized a correspondence that was being conducted in highly racist terms. This caught the attention of the nationalists, and led to invitations to write in their newspapers and journals. Andrews never looked back, writing hundred of articles throughout the rest of his life, on every conceivable aspect of the national movement, establishing a unique role as a Christian voice within Indian nationalism. Encouraged by the nationalists, he attended the December 1906 meeting of the Indian National Congress, and began to make the sort of personal contacts that were also important for his role, and indeed led directly to his first meeting with Gandhi in South Africa in 1914.

Attending the 1906 Congress meetings also led to the first strains in his relationship with his Delhi Mission colleagues. Though he always affirmed their liberal support of his new-found commitment, it is clear that his increasing preoccupation with it and the much travelling about

India that followed, and his absence from the work for which he had been appointed, created irritation, envy and disapproval. So, too, did his increasingly deep association with Hindus and Muslims in the movement. Though post-colonial Christianity saw his friendships with people of other faiths as exemplary, most missionaries and North Indian Christians at the time found them incomprehensible. With widespread criticism of his friendships and involvements, and his own increasing discomfort at the Churches' close identification with imperial power, Andrews decided to resign from his missionary appointment and throw in his lot with the nationalists, seeing this as an opportunity to bear a Christian witness within the 'political nation'. He was confirmed in this decision by encounters with SPG's India subcommittee on a visit to London in 1912. This was the committee that a few months earlier had objected to Azariah's consecration. Andrews accompanied Rudra to the subcommittee to seek support for changes to the constitution of the College. In the negotiation over this, Rudra was subjected to a series of highly offensive snubs by members of the committee, whom even Montgomery described as 'old fogies'. Rudra was also bypassed at one point by Montgomery himself, who preferred to consult an English missionary, and Andrews demanded an apology. He was furious at his friend's treatment, and, though the constitution was revised as Rudra and he had wished, this certainly strengthened his decision in 1914 to resign from SPG.

So, too, did his visit to South Africa to meet Gandhi in early 1914. He had gone with a warning from the nationalist leader, Gokhale, that what he saw there would be a great shock to his Christianity, and so it was. His long-held views about the contradiction between 'European racial arrogance' and 'the vision of Christ, the meek and lowly Son of Man' were confirmed decisively. He concluded that 'the West' was in a state of virtual apostasy, worshipping only 'Money and Race', while 'the meek and lowly Christ' was to be discerned 'more outside the Church than in it', among, for example, 'the little group of Indian passive resisters fresh from prison – Hindus almost all of them'. In a sermon in Lahore Cathedral in May 1914, on his return to India, he summarized both his own sense of a calling to disengage from the Church with its imperial associations and a vision of a coming Church of the poor. Turning first in an original way to the much used analogy between contemporary Western hegemony and the Roman Empire, he depicts Jesus as rejecting the rich and cultured world of Chorazin, Bethsaida and Capernaum, 'the direct social outgrowth of the great Roman system of government', for 'the simple, child-like peasant poor . . . the poor, tired labourers . . . half-famished'. He says that his visit to South Africa, and subsequently to England on the verge of the First World War, raised the question, whether the modern, aggressive, wealthy nations of the world, armed to the teeth against each other, trafficking in the souls of men for gain, can be for long the dwelling place of the meek and lowly Christ; whether the hour may not be near when He will say unto them . . . 'Woe unto you', and will turn instead to the poor and down-trodden peoples of the earth and say unto them, 'Come unto me.'

The ensuing 26 years of Andrews' life in India are well known, not least his close association throughout that period with the two greatest leaders of the national movement, Gandhi and Tagore, and his many contributions to it. Perhaps his greatest was the campaign he waged for the abolition of indenture, the system which took poor Indians as 'coolies' to work throughout the British Empire. By his campaign, 'virtually on his own', he brought about its abolition, 'a reform almost equal to the abolition of slavery', and earned the title *Deenabandhu*, 'friend of the poor'.[17] His associations with SPG after 1914 were slight. Montgomery dreaded his calling if he visited London, for the uncomfortable questions he raised. At the same time, his continuing confession of Christ, strengthening with the years, and marked by a return to his priestly ministry shortly before his death, was an influential witness within the emerging nation. Gandhi called him, long after he had left the Society, 'the pattern of the ideal missionary' and 'love incarnate', while Tagore said that nowhere had he seen 'such a triumph of Christianity'. In independent India, schools and other institutions were named after him, a postage stamp was issued in his honour and a National Seminar held in New Delhi at the centenary of his birth.

There were few other Society missionaries in this class of 'atheists of empire'. The report on 'Missions and Governments' at the Edinburgh 1910 conference noted that missionaries willing to give time or thought to the question were 'very few indeed'. Though a number, like P. N. F. Young in Delhi and G. A. West in Burma later, sought to take up some of Allen's ideas on ministry, his underlying critique of the culture of imperialism seems to have been almost entirely ignored, except by David Paton, whose *Christian Missions and the Judgement of God* of 1953, with due acknowledgement to Allen, saw the bigger picture to which the Siege of Peking had alerted Allen at the beginning of the century.[18] Andrews had many admirers and supporters for what he was doing, though few in the missionary community who were willing to make a stand on the issues that concerned him. One who did, in a cautious way, calling Andrews his guru, was SPG's J. C. Winslow, who worked with Gandhi on a number of occasions, and whose young Oxbridge companions at his *Christa Seva*

Sangha ashram in Pune got somewhat out of hand while he was on furlough in 1930, with Masses for the emancipation of India, wearing the currently proscribed Gandhi Caps and the like.[19] Among these was Leonard Schiff, who joined the Indian National Congress at the time and was subsequently and simultaneously an SPG missionary and secretary in the Congress secretariat during the last years of the Raj. Another was Verrier Elwin, though not on the Society's list, who, when eventually 'hounded out' of the Church by an unsympathetic Bishop of Nagpur for his public support for Gandhi, received a letter of sympathy from Cripps in Mashonaland, invoking 'the blessing of the Divine Outcaste'.[20] Cripps was an inspiration to Trevor Huddleston to 'go overseas and serve the poor'.[21] He had some support, for example from a Methodist colleague, John White, whose biography Andrews was later moved to write, and from the Society missionary at Rusape, Edgar Lloyd. Another devoted friend of his was Frank Weston, Bishop of Zanzibar, who had his own part in all this, 'storm[ing] . . . Milner in the fastnesses of the Colonial Office' in his successful campaign against forced labour in East Africa.[22] Several of the rebel missionaries found their own bishops not unsupportive, among these Lefroy of Lahore admitting that he had learned a great deal from Andrews; Foss Westcott, the Metropolitan, who signalled his own sympathy for Nehru and other Congress leaders, and spoke on Andrews's death on the text, 'Know ye not that there is a prince fallen in Israel', and Archbishop Paget who said of Cripps, 'I think I know a saint when I see one, and I just let him alone.'[23] There was, as will have been evident, something of a network amongst most of these. They had a good deal in common in addition to their opposition to empire. They all belonged to what George Orwell once called England's 'lower-upper-middle-class', and moved easily in the presence of the viceroys and governors whom they sought to influence and, eventually, see sent home. They were all from the Catholic end of the Anglican spectrum, several of them especially drawn to the spirituality of St Francis, several of them poets. Although most of them felt compelled to dissociate themselves from the Church and SPG in one way or another, no other ecclesiastical tradition 'produced holy men of quite such prophetic power'.

> Eccentric upper-class, even neurotic individualists as they were, they represented too at its greatest and freest a tradition of spiritual vision which Anglicanism seemed good at fostering. They moved out from the centre of an Establishment, powerful, Erastian, conformist, to challenge it most absolutely – and often not ineffectually – by the sheer quality of a religious commitment, love of neighbour, intellectual integrity, a flow of poetry affecting every aspect of life.[24]

Perhaps most significantly, several of them received a very specific recognition from the people whose cause they espoused, suggesting an authentic propagation of the Gospel, Andrews as *Deenabandhu*, 'friend of the poor', Elwin as *Din Sevak*, 'servant of the poor', and Cripps as *Baba Chapepa*, 'he who cares for people'.

II

'The new Tao'

On 18 November 1900, the Church of SS Peter and Paul was dedicated at Kanghwa in Korea. In its 'Korean characteristics', Bishop Corfe explained, it 'harmonized with all the other buildings in the city, overlooking them in a quiet dignity, but without any undue or conspicuous self-assertion.'[1] Kanghwa Island was the centre of the national religion and related to the founding ancestors of the Korean nation, the small, walled 'old-fashioned' Kanghwa City the ideal place from which to 'touch the population of the whole island', so the building of a traditionally wooden church using Korean traditional architecture was a bold and imaginative venture in the propagation of the Gospel. The missionary responsible was Mark Trollope, who had arrived in Seoul with Corfe at the beginning of the Anglican presence in 1890. He had mastered both Korean and classical Chinese as no other Anglican missionary had at that time, begun a study of Korean Buddhism, later published, along with his studies of Korean literature, and moved to work in Kanghwa in 1896, the first baptisms taking place the following year.

For the proposed building, a Korean who had built a number of Buddhist temples and the Kyeongbok palace in Seoul was appointed master carpenter. A church being for him a totally unfamiliar project, the continuous close dialogue required with Trollope clearly explains what was achieved. The construction was managed by Kim-Hee Jun, a catechist and later, in 1915, Korea's first Anglican priest. Kanghwa craftsmen and Chinese stonemasons completed the team. Costs were borne by SPG and the newly initiated Marriott Fund.

The church combined Buddhist, Confucian, Korean shamanist and Christian features, the basic outlines being traditionally Korean, with only the orientation and some proportions adjusted to meet the require-ments of a church, the crosses on the roof resting in Buddhist-style lotus buds, the twelve dragon heads along the edge of the roof, to protect from misfortune according to Korean tradition, twelve to represent the twelve apostles. Texts carved on the font, and in Chinese-character calligraphy on boards on the pillars, conflated Confucian wisdom with Christian doctrine, and were plainly directed at the Confucian intellec-tuals of Kanghwa. Only the six candlesticks on the altar, the piscina and, rather curiously, the doors of the building, were imported from Britain.

Worshippers removed their shoes and sat on the wooden floor, women and men separated by a curtain running the length of the nave, catechumens west of the font only. Beside the entrance gate a pipal tree was planted, sacred to Buddhism, and a pagoda tree, traditionally grown beside a Confucian worship hall.

Though there were only a handful of the people of Kanghwa baptized by 1900, the church was designed to hold 250. Trollope heard numerous expressions of local approval of the new church as it was building and over the ensuing years, at least until Japanese colonial occupation brought Korean feudalism to an end, there were 'a lot of cases' of intellectuals and the aristocratic class leading their village clan-communities to baptism in Kanghwa.

Trollope edited the Chinese and Korean texts at the Mission Press in Seoul. An early publication, *The Preaching Book about the Anglican Doc-trines*, indicates that the new 'fulfilment theology' that was winning its way in some missionary circles by this time, was doing so in Korea. It is claimed on the opening page that the intention in preaching the Gospel is not to oppose Confucianism but to complement its defects and to teach 'the new *Do* (Tao)'. Such was the rationale of the Kanghwa church.

Trollope himself later revised his objectives, in his capacity as third bishop and in the context of a modernizing country, commissioning a baroque Anglican cathedral for Seoul in 1926, with an English architect and with scarcely any concessions to Korean tradition. The approach he had initiated at Kanghwa nevertheless became normative for Korean Anglicanism until the middle of the century, while missionary appreci-ation of Korean culture was sustained with great distinction subsequently by Richard Rutt, awarded the Ta San Cultural Award of Korea in 1964 for his Korean historical, literary and social studies. Parish churches in a 'transformed Romanesque style' only began to appear in the 1990s.

Increased missionary sensitivity to indigenous culture was marked in the first half of the century, and showed up widely in architecture. In very many cases, of course, SPG's work was among the poor and in villages, with worship initially in huts and houses or under trees, moving on to very simple local church buildings using purely local materials, in such styles as, for example, in the words of Charles Johnson at Rorke's Drift, 'Early Zulu', though Cripps found a more impressive African model in the Temple at Great Zimbabwe. In early urban mission also, for example in Japan, very small gatherings of Christians also began in houses. The possibility of more elaborate facilities usually depended in the earlier stages on external funds such as the Marriott Bequest. This was accompanied in this period by more self-conscious adaptation, as for example in Burma, Sri Lanka and India, where establishment had previously made possible 'one of the more extraordinary styles of the nineteenth century, Anglo-Indian Gothic', to which English architects, Gilbert Scott, Ninian Comper, Butterfield and Bodley had all made their contributions. An early Indian venture in inculturation was St Peter's, Thanjavur, as rebuilt in 1900, but much more striking were a number of churches designed by the priest-architect, A. Coore, for village congregations in the north in the 1920s, at Ummedpur and Pak Bara in Lucknow diocese and at Mehrauli near Delhi. These were controversial initially, with the sanctuary under a Hindu temple-type roof within an open courtyard surrounded by inward-facing verandahs. Coore described them as 'Mogul and Hindu blended'. He indicated that he was responding to the desire of educated Indians 'to realise Christianity in an Indian dress'. The church-building initiative was, nevertheless, largely with the missionaries, with the exception of Azariah's cathedral, consecrated at Dornakal in 1938.[2] In Africa, the decoration of the church was often more strikingly indigenized than the building itself, though the chapel at Cyrene in Southern Rhodesia, referred to below, brought the two elements together.

Inculturation in liturgy was an obvious area of interest to SPG's missionaries, to get beyond the conditions which had disturbed C. F. Andrews in 1904. In 1933, the Society published *Worship in Other Lands: A Study of Racial Characteristics in Christian Worship*, based on an enquiry conducted by the Overseas Secretary, W. F. France and edited by H. P. Thompson. This brought together widespread and rich evidence of developments which the missionaries were either initiating or encouraging, or simply witnessing where local Christians were finding their own way in worship. In many cases, these last developments were especially evident in music and singing. Concern for Thompson's 'full Catholic tradition in worship' occasioned some odd hybridities like the adaptation of the Merbecke setting of the Holy Communion to the Burmese language by W. H. Jackson with accompanying threefold prostration as in the Buddhist tradition, or at Peking Cathedral, where the Nunc

Dimittis was set to a melody from the cry of a cigarette seller, with responses also based on street cries. There were often language difficulties in regard to liturgy. The bishop in Singapore, for example, had to be prepared to administer the rite of confirmation in up to seven languages on the one occasion. Official liturgical developments were cautious but widespread, but with more adventurous experiments by individuals. This was still largely so in a post-colonial context. A case in point was the very restrained Prayer Book revision in Ceylon, contrasted with the later 'New World Liturgy', incorporating Buddhist, Marxist and other insights, from the 'Devasarana Collective Farm' led by a Sri Lankan priest associated with the Society, Yohan Devananda.

One of the most remarkable ventures in inculturation during the period was one initiated by the UMCA missionary, W. V. Lucas, in East Africa from 1909 and Bishop of Masasi from 1926 to 1944. This was an attempt at a Christianization of *Jando*, the male initiation rite of the Makua and Yao peoples of Masasi, the first Christian version taking place in 1913.[3] Like Trollope in Kanghwa, Lucas adopted a 'fulfillment' theology, intending to show Africans that Christianity was 'the fulfill-ment for them of what . . . [had] already been adumbrated in the immemorial customs of the past', believing that this would 'do more than anything to help the church to become really indigenous', and avert the destructive individualism that so often accompanied Christian mission. This distinguished him from most missionaries, who opposed traditional initiation uncompromisingly, like the German Protestant, Julius Richter, for whom the traditional rites were nothing but 'pagan superstition and unbridled sensuality'. Like Trollope, Lucas saw it as vital to involve local people in the project, in his case 'native converts' of 'age and standing and maturity in religion' such as his closest African friend, Reuben Namalowe, and Kolumba Msigala. They helped him to see the rite of male initiation as a protracted liturgical process, and to create a Christian equivalent. Circumcision was retained, in ways that worried some UMCA doctors, and even the initiatory flogging, carried out by European and African priests, with Christian components added, litany, prayer, holy water, invocation of the saints and penitence, instruction of up to four weeks confined to a hut and culminating in the boys, shaven-headed and in new clothes, either being baptized or receiving a cross, and participating in a solemn Mass of Thanksgiving. Alongside a broader intention to turn 'the elements of paganism to the ends of Christianity', the rite was designed to stimulate a renewed sense of Christian identity, to aid 'the translation of faith into conduct'. Because, it has been suggested, no adequate theology of sexuality was available, the attempts at a Christianization of the female rite was much less successful, and 'many Christian women . . . freely consented', according to the UMCA missionary, Robin Lamburn, 'to their girls being put into the heathen rite'.[4]

Interestingly, the priest of Machombe parish, Edward Abdallah, described Lucas cheerfully participating in the first Christian *Jando* there in 1925 'in a way that no other European that I had seen in all my life'. This gave Abdallah a new vision of 'ideal community', but it was one to which few other UMCA missionaries contributed with any enthusiasm, and the successful development of the rite depended largely on its acceptance by the African clergy and congregations. Through them it became not only religiously significant, with a wide degree of acceptance, but also an important part of Masasi social and political life, though with several unpredicted ramifications. An account by a Society missionary of a *Jando* for some 150 to 200 boys in Mtandi parish in 1989 indicates a tradition well established but in need of a renewal of the Christian elements. On this occasion, the Tanzanian government required parents to provide their children with new school uniforms on the final day.[5]

Another venture in communitarian inculturation by a Society missionary took place in western India, though in a very different form. This was the creation in 1922 of a Christian ashram at Poona by J. C. Winslow, in India from 1914 to 1934. A resident community devoted to religion, the ashram had a very long history within Hinduism, with a modern revival beginning with the *Bharat Ashram* founded by the Bengali reformer, K. C. Sen, in 1872, and brought to much greater prominence with Rabindranath Tagore's *Santiniketan* in 1901 and Gandhi's *Satyagraha Ashram* in 1915. The idea of a Christian ashram originated with the ardent nationalist, S. K. Rudra, writing in *Young Men of India* in December 1910, while the first beginnings were made in 1917 in Maharashtra by a friend of Winslow, the poet Narayan Vaman Tilak, with an organization of baptized and unbaptized disciples which he called an ashram and named God's or Christ's *Darbar*. His death in 1919 brought this venture to an end. By then, two further Christian ashrams were in process of formation. One, was the *Christukula* or Family of Christ, opened at Tirupattur in South India in 1921, led by two doctors, S. Jesudason and E. Forrester-Paton, with medical care as its speciality. The other, the following year, was Winslow's *Christa Seva Sangha*, the Society of the Service of Christ (CSS).[6] Winslow insisted that the ashram should not be affiliated to any foreign mission agency, though SPG made a grant towards the ashram buildings, while Winslow's salary from the Society was converted to a monthly grant to the Sangha for the first eight years.

At its inauguration, CSS consisted of Winslow and seven young

Maratha men and women, soon to be joined by a similar number of young English men. The Sangha had two stated aims. The first was to bring together Indian and non-Indian members to 'form a spiritual family living on terms of perfect equality and fellowship, bearing witness to the world of the unity that is in Christ'. India was at this time still reeling from the British army's massacre of several hundred Indian men, women and children at Amritsar, to which this first aim was in part Winslow's response. The second was to dispense with what he called Christ's 'Western disguise', and, while affirming 'the great Catholic heritage of the Church', to develop its 'true Indian expression' in life and worship. This became one of the Sangha's most successful features, from the simple morning and evening prayers, based respectively on 'the Sanskrit *Rising Prayers* of the Hindus', and 'the compline of the Jacobite Syrians of Travancore', and including an impressive eucharistic 'Liturgy for India', based largely on oriental liturgies.[7] The Sangha concentrated in the early years on village evangelism using such indigenous means as the religious song, *kirtan*, and, at the instigation of Bishop Palmer, pastoral and evangelistic work amongst students. Winslow devoted time to writing, including a notable life of Tilak and translations of his poetry, particularly the *Christayana*. He also published *The Eucharist in India* (1920), explicating the 'Liturgy for India', with a preface by Bishop Palmer describing it as 'revolutionary and important'; two books popular in Britain, *Christian Yoga* (1923) and *The Indian Mystic* (1926), and, with his ashram colleague, Verrier Elwin, and with a preface by William Temple, *The Dawn of Indian Freedom* (1931). He also wrote a vivid and attractive account of the ashram, commissioned and published by SPG in 1930. The nationalist involvements of some of the Sangha's members have been described. The Sangha made a considerable impact during these early years, and drew admiring comments from both Gandhi and Nehru, while in 1929 C. F. Andrews described its common life as 'the very essence today of the Christian message in the East'.

The ashram, however, ran into difficulties in the early 1930s which seem to have been a demonstration of the very problem which its foundation had sought to address. It is clear that Winslow's young English colleagues increasingly dominated the Sangha, determined to change it into a Western-style religious community, in Winslow's words, 'a Western rather than an Indian pattern such as I never contemplated'. In the new pattern, finally established by majority vote in 1934, most of the original lay Indian members found themselves relegated to a Third Order, which they and Winslow regarded as a marginalizing and a demotion. The now dominant group adopted a new name, somewhat ironically the *Christa Prema Seva Sangha* (CPSS), the Society of the Love and Service of Christ, retaining the buildings and obliging Winslow, about to leave India, and a majority of the Maratha members, his original colleagues, deeply hurt at the experience, to move out and pursue their original ideals and commitment in a continuing *Christa Seva Sangha* ashram established in the village of Aundh, a few miles from Poona. The new, secessionist body, the CPSS, had a more or less continuous history to the end of the century, though the Society was only involved through the occasional participation of one or another of its missionaries. The continuing CSS functioned very successfully at Aundh for many years, becoming more or less self-sufficient, with no English members after Winslow left, occasionally attracting new members, but finally so reduced by ordination which carried one after another away into pastoral charges that the *Christa Seva Sangha* ceased to function in 1947, Shankarrao Wairagar, one of the original members, staying on at the Aundh ashram with his family until his death in 1970.

The CSS contributed to the indigenization of the Gospel through its encouragement of two Indian Christian artists, Angelo da Fonseca, a Roman Catholic who made the ashram his home from 1928 until his death about 1950, and Alfred D. Thomas, an Anglican, two of whose paintings were incorporated into the chapel in 1928, with several others reproduced in the ashram periodical, the *CSS Review*.[8]

SPG later reproduced Thomas's most important work in *The Life of Christ by an Indian Artist* in 1948. This was part of a wider programme of publishing by the Society which served both to encourage the artists concerned and to promote the idea of inculturation. The first publication in the series was *The Life of Christ by Chinese Artists*, published in 1938 and featuring the work of the group of artists around T. K. Shen at St Luke's Studio, Nanking, in the 1930s, including Hsu Chi-Hwa and Luke Chen. 'African Art and its Possibilities' had been discussed in *The East and the West* in 1927, with further consideration of African, also Chinese and Japanese art by W. V. Lucas in *The Church Overseas* in 1931. The African contribution was included in the 1939 addition to the series, *Son of Man: Pictures and Carvings by Indian, African and Chinese Artists*. The last of the sequence was *In Parables: Illustrations of the Parables of Christ by Chinese Artists*, in 1959. There were numerous reprints of these. Meanwhile, the December 1948 *Network* had featured Nobumichi Inouye's sculptured crucifix commissioned for the cathedral in Tokyo, the first piece of major Christian art executed in Japan in modern times.

SPG gave particular encouragement in this field through its sustained support of the Cyrene school founded by the Society missionary, Edward Paterson, in the Matopos in Rhodesia in 1940. The missionary significance of what he was doing in producing among young Christians at

Cyrene a remarkable new art impulse for southern Africa was recognized, and the Society provided funding, additional later missionary appointments to the school, commissioned and distributed regular duplicated news of the project, *Cyrene Papers*, commissioned two films on the artists' work and arranged a major touring exhibition of paintings and carvings in Britain in 1949.[9]

A web of associations help locate Paterson and Cyrene. While studying at the Arts and Crafts School in London, which had earlier trained Trollope's architect for Seoul Cathedral, A. S. Dixon, he was befriended by the poet Laurence Binyon, a friend also of Cripps in Rhodesia; in his *Cyrene Papers*, Paterson often quotes Cripps. He was identified for ordination by Bishop Paget, who also promoted Cyrene's first major exhibition, in Bulawayo in 1944. He trained for ordination at Grahamstown in the company of the prophetic Michael Scott. Teaching for a year at the teacher training college, Grace Dieu, before going to Cyrene, he introduced woodcarving, which was carried forward to St Faith's, Rusape, by Sr Pauline CR and Job Kekana. To Kekana, Paterson was 'one of the chosen few who illuminate the world'.

The first students were invited to Cyrene as 'an institution for the development of art in agriculture and craftsmanship', but it had a further significance. This was a commitment to break with what Paterson called the 'cultural slavery' of Christianity in Africa. They would do this through a liberating pedagogy:

> In a scripture lesson something is done to make pupils think. The missionary must sow the whole Christ . . . even if the consequence of that is that in their streaming to the light, they should refuse to subscribe to our plan for it. It is God's work to make a man good; it is our work to make him interesting to himself.

Plans from about 1948 for a Homecrafts Village for women and girls, which would challenge the mass-produced wares of 'the Kaffir Store', came to nothing. Cyrene did, however, develop a strong specialism in work with severely disabled people, uncovering often great artistic talents, as in the case of Adomech Moyo, Lazarus Kumalo and Sam Songo.

A striking feature was the chapel, richly decorated within and without, with an altarpiece of Christ as an African priest, accompanied by the martyrs Masemola and Mizeki. The *Cyrene Papers* reported in 1943,

> Our painted Chapel attracts a lot of attention as its walls slowly cover themselves in murals . . . The most recent . . . depicts a student's own

ideas on the Last Judgement . . . Our Lord is seated on a throne. He holds in His Hands an adze and a mealie-cob, and by this standard of 'What have you made and what have you grown?' He judges the world.

The freedom struggle caused much disruption to Cyrene. A photograph from the period shows two students working on an external mural, and the caption notes that as soon as they had completed their assignment they left to join the guerillas. By then, gifted alumni of Cyrene were working widely across southern and central Africa, extending a new and distinctive propagation of the Gospel.

SECTION 4

1947–2000

Introductory

The context of SPG's work changed dramatically in this period, necessitating and often determining rapid adjustments in its activities and understanding of what it was about, 'significant mutations of the organism that is the Society', as the Secretary, James Robertson, put it halfway through the period.

The period began with a celebration of the 250th anniversary on a grand scale, with episcopal envoys to the Church in every continent, reciprocal greetings from synods and assemblies in many provinces, a working model of the sailing ship *Centurion* which had taken Keith to America in 1702 sailing to ports around the British Isles, large gatherings at St Paul's Cathedral, Lambeth Palace and the Albert Hall, the dedication of new stained-glass windows in the Society Chapel commemorating the first African, Chinese, Indian and Japanese Anglican bishops and the publication amongst much more of H. P. Thompson's 750-page *Into All Lands*, hailed by *The Times Literary Supplement* as the record of 'a great religious and social movement'. Something of this grand scale continued to be reflected in the annual Albert Hall rallies until the 1970s, when they were abandoned. Lesser celebrations and commemorations took their turn, the 250th anniversary of St John's Church, Elizabeth, New Jersey, the bicentenary of Columbia University and of the Church in Tirunelveli, the diocese now rescued from its anglicized name, Bray's death commemorated in the presence of the Queen at St Botolph's, Aldgate, with a 'simple, eloquent' sermon by Dr Gareth Bennett, the centenary of the first baptisms in Nandyal and of the arrival of the West Indian Mission in the Rio Pongas, of the death of Joshua Watson, and of course many centenaries of dioceses.[1]

The Society did not, however, spend much time looking back in 1951, one aspect of the celebration being a major appeal to fund a series of projects to advance the independence of Churches. A further indication of commitment to change was involvement in the conciliar process. Despite Standing Committee's misgivings about the Society's relationship with the Conference of British Missionary Societies (CBMS), Roberts was convinced that the Society must not 'stand aloof from this ecumenical stream'.[2] Thereafter, throughout the half-century, SPG was almost invariably represented in the consultations of the ecumenical missionary process in Britain and Ireland and represented at virtually every major international ecumenical missionary gathering, from Whitby, Ontario, in 1947 to Harare, Zimbabwe, in 1999.

During the period, the Charter was twice revised. In 1956, revision facilitated the transfer of Society property to overseas Churches in the growing number of autonomous provinces. No transfer was more momentous historically than that of responsibility for Codrington College and Estates to a Codrington Trust in Barbados in 1983. The 1996 revision was to meet a requirement of the Charity Commissioners to transfer much of the responsibility of the Council to a small group of twelve trustees, elected by Council and known as the Governors, reporting to a Council including representatives of all English dioceses. Indicative of change in the Church, Governors and Council were chaired from 1997 by Canon Helen Cunliffe.

The Society and its close associates had some 700 missionaries on their lists at the beginning of the period, most of them committed to long-term work overseas; the United Society in the later 1990s had fewer than 100, most of them on short-term engagements. Hardly surprisingly, the middle years, the 1970s, saw frequent discussions on subjects like 'What is a missionary?' and 'The Image of the Missionary Society in the Parish', and Council agonized more than once over what some saw as the Society's archaic name. Missionary vocation was still under consideration in the 1990s, but now within programmes of 'reciprocal' or 'common mission'. SPG's financial position reflected change too. In spite of the very effective Home Secretaryship of John Dudley Dixon for over 30 years, the Society generally over the period had diminishing resources at its disposal.[3] The reasons for this were clear but complex, reflecting not least change in British society, including a much diminished Church of England, like all Churches throughout Europe, though the persistent commitment of parishes and individuals to SPG's work was also remarkable.

In the earlier decades, the Society and its committees were dealing in minute detail and often managerially with the affairs of Churches and institutions in largely colonial territories – land at Idaiyangudi in Tirunelveli, and a little later the sale of the palmyra topes there, and the business of the Codrington Estates on Barbados, with chaplaincies, until their transfer to the Diocese of Gibraltar in 1983, for the holiday-ing English middle classes at Rapallo, Vernet-les-Bains, Pontresina, St Moritz and the like – while in England, as patron of the benefice of Hallaton, the Society in 1951 approved a loan for a new cow-house, dairy and sterilizing room at the Glebe Farm. Further links with the past were modified as the Society handed over property in Nova Sco-tia, Connecticut and Pennsylvania as late as the 1950s. Much less of this sort of detail, especially when it related to Churches overseas, found its way on to the Society's agenda in the later decades, for most of it was by then someone else's business.

SPG was served by seven Secretaries during the half-century, the first being Basil Roberts (1944–57), former Bishop of Singapore and Principal of St Augustine's College, Canterbury, then Eric Trapp (1957–70), former Bishop of Zululand, Ian Shevill (1970–73), former Bishop of North Queensland, James Robertson (1973–83), after more than twenty years in Zambia, Humphrey Taylor (1984–91), after shorter service in Malawi, Peter Price (1992–7), after a different sort of missionary experience on a housing estate in Portsmouth, England, while in 1998 the Society set out for the twenty-first century under the Secretaryship of a former Bishop of Peshawar with significant experience in both Pakistan and inner-city Britain, Munawar Rumalshah.

12

Decolonization

On the morning of 15 August, 1947, the members, Indian and British, of the Cambridge Brotherhood in Delhi prayed at their Eucharist for their new bishop, Arabindo Nath Mukerjee, and also for the new nation that, 'at the stroke of midnight', in Nehru's moving words to India's Constituent Assembly, had awoken 'to life and freedom'. Some of the brothers then walked over to St Stephen's College to a service conducted by the principal at the raising of the national flag, and then on into the city to join the celebrating crowds. Celebration was a brief interlude in a period of communal violence, exacerbated as Hindu and Sikh refugees streamed across the frontier with the new state of Pakistan, arriving with stories of violence and murder among former neighbours, and Delhi erupted into similar horrors which were something of a foretaste of much more widespread religious conflict as the century advanced. The new government called upon Christians to help organize refugee camps, and members of the Brotherhood and staff of the College and St Stephen's Hospital took part in emergency relief programmes, distributing food among the 70,000 Muslims gathered at Humayun's Tomb and Purana Qila, the hospital dealing with huge numbers of the injured. For Doctors Morris and Roseveare at the hospital, the arrival of the first penicillin in Delhi, to them the outstanding event of the year, proved opportune. On the strength of its mediatory role, the Bishop of Nasik commented a few months later that 'the prestige of the Christian Church . . . [had] never stood so high'. This was, however, a standing difficult to sustain as the country entered upon a period of revolutionary changes which made 'the Curzon regime seem as remote as the reign of Akbar'.[1] Meanwhile, in Pakistan, many Christian agricultural workers were evicted by their new Muslim landlords and reduced to poverty and semi-slavery on the brickfields, another foretaste of oppression for the very small Christian community as the century advanced.

The inauguration of Indian independence in 1947, with that of Pakistan, Burma and Ceylon, appropriately defines the starting point for an account of the most recent phase in the Society's history, for it marks the beginning of the end of the imperial and colonial history of Britain that had provided the context for the missionary movement from Britain and Ireland from SPG's beginning. From another angle, it marked the beginning of the final stage in the emergence of what came to be known as the 'Third Church', offspring of the missionary movement from the 'Second', European Church, but embodying a Christianity predominantly of the poor, among the cultures, religions and nations of the south. Mwamba's chapter in this volume exemplifies this development in the case of Zambia. Hence, the radical adjustments to the Society's role.[2]

At the time of South Asian political independence, of course, no general decolonization was envisaged by the British government. Indeed, in Africa, there followed an intensified colonialism, with extensive new settlement of British people in southern Africa, flowing, for example, into Northern Rhodesia, as the bishop put it in 1948, 'at an almost embarrassing speed', and increased economic exploitation, represented by, for example, the disastrous Groundnut Scheme in East Africa.[3]

It was in West Africa, the Gold Coast in particular, with its relatively high proportion of educated pacemakers – teachers, clergy, doctors, lawyers, journalists and perhaps we should add the 300 students of Adisadel College who were reported by the Society as joining in the nationalist riot in 1948 – that an African freedom movement and decolonization took off first, with independence under the charismatic Nkrumah in 1957. The Church in Ghana was relatively well placed to adjust to the new situation. Standing Committee had welcomed with 'joy and gladness' the formation of a West African Province in 1951, and also the consecration of an African as Assistant Bishop of Accra the same year, 'no longer an unusual and isolated event'. The great majority of clergy at independence were nationals. That the diocese continued to be led by a non-national, Bishop Roseveare SSM, the only white leader of any large denomination, may help to explain the 1958 Report noting 'still the anti-colonial . . . feeling'. Certainly, Roseveare was soon to encounter some of the new pressures emerging in the Third World.

'Self-government on the lines of the Gold Coast' looked attractive to Africans in the Diocese of Nyasaland, the bishop noted in his report for 1951. The existing constitutional reality, with its invented tradition of Imperial Monarchy, the Church playing its part, was characterized in a picture from East Africa the following year of a memorial service for King George VI at Korogwe in Zanzibar, the District Commissioner in his uniform seated in the sanctuary for a Swahili plainsong Mass. For Central Africa the future looked no more promising, with proposals for a Central African Federation, to be dominated by settlers led by Welensky, who had 'all the making of a ruthless dictator', according to the Archbishop.[4] And yet, by 1963, Margery Perham, the deeply devout President of UMCA and 'high priest of liberal Christian enlightenment in things imperial', was able to refer in her Reith Lectures published that year to the 'astonishingly rapid emancipation since 1950 of twenty-nine states' in Africa alone, 23 of them between 1961 and 1963, and including those in which UMCA worked.[5] The Mission's reports reflect this rapidly changing situation, expressing a commitment to both an African Church and the 'teachers, civil servants, artisans, farmers and others who will help to build up a Christian civilization', as undoubtedly they did, but evidencing everywhere how easy it is to be caught out by the pace of change.

There were a number of immediate causes for the rapidity of this turnaround. One was the endless racism and repression that had always marked colonial Africa. Another was the return of tens of thousands of askaris from the Second World War, bringing back new attitudes to their villages and towns. The Groundnut Development Scheme, designed to meet a need in Britain's post-war domestic economy, also deeply affected things, most of the earmarked land being in the area of the UMCA Dioceses of Nyasaland, Masasi and Zanzibar. From 1947 for the next few years, the reports of the bishops and missionaries constantly allude to this 'invasion . . . [of] industrial civilization' and its effects, with men from the villages 'flocking in in their thousands' to the work camps, including many young men from the three dioceses. Chaplaincy to these was organized, and there is an account of a chaplain arriving one evening and a young worker running ahead of him through the camp calling 'all UMCA Christians, come and make your confession'. To one missionary, Nigel Cornwall, recalling Livingstone's quest for 'a path for commerce and Christianity', the former had at last, belatedly, arrived, with prospects for a great advance in material welfare, 'truly an entering-in of commerce on a gigantic scale such as would startle even Dr Livingstone himself'. By 1950, however, the Bishop of Masasi was writing of the project as a fiasco. 'Dumps of abandoned vehicles and deserted buildings and equipment have disfigured the countryside, but the bush is quickly reclaiming its own.' Where this large scheme failed, there were numerous others that flourished, sponsored by the Colonial Development Corporation, involving timber, tobacco and coal, and leading similarly to social upheaval, as did the 'continuous exodus of men from the villages' of the

Diocese of Nyasaland to South Africa and Rhodesia in search of work, leaving congregations, as the bishop reported in 1951, almost entirely of children, women and old men. The other UMCA diocese, Northern Rhodesia, had its own trajectory into, in the bishop's words in 1947, 'the throes of what is probably a more violent surge of development than that experienced by any other country in modern times', accentuated in this case by the large influx of British settlers, and accompanied by an intensified white racism, and an economic expansion based on copper that still in 1964 was suggesting in UMCA circles a future 'as bright as that of any country in the new Africa'.[6] Something. though, of the alienation of some UMCA missionaries from this process is glimpsed in the bishop's severe if prophetic observation in 1957 that 'the sudden and drastic fall in the price of copper should do good in calling men to turn to God and to recognize that they do not live by bread alone'.

These remarkable material changes had their political accompaniment, symbolized, for example, in the Conference of 29 Asian and African states at Bandung in 1955, and African nationalism gathered a pace throughout the 1950s that seems to have surprised almost everyone, the Bishop of Zanzibar noting of East Africa generally that 'things change almost overnight'.

As early as 1947, Bishop Frank Thorne had included in his report from Nyasaland a section on 'Africans in Government and Politics'. Noting that the death during the year of Chief Yohana Matola marked 'the closing of an era', he went on to describe how 'two societies, originally of teachers but with a much wider membership now', were meeting to discuss 'matters of public interest'. Thorne's description of the process suggests both paternalism and liberality: 'They pass their findings on to me and the District Commissioner concerned. Fortunately, after some misgivings on the part of one DC, they have met with encouragement and their voice is beginning to count.' Two years later, he reported with satisfaction the first two Africans joining the Legislative Council, Africans having previously been represented by an unofficial European, usually a missionary, nominated by the governor. The very gradualist approach suggested by this was soon to be overtaken by African impatience, issuing in 'strikes, expulsion of pupils, disturbances, breaches of the peace' and anger at the attempted 'imposition of Federation in opposition to the clearly expressed wishes of the vast majority of Africans in Nyasaland'. The return of Dr Hastings Banda in 1958, 'everywhere regarded by Africans as the Messiah who will lead them to freedom and self-government', was followed by a violently repressive state of emergency in 1959, but soon thereafter by independence. The problems for Bishop Thorne's leadership through his 25-year episcopate, boldly liberal by any standard but rarely adequate to African aspirations, led to his resignation in 1961 bearing 'all the strain of this tension', three years before Malawian independence.[7] His story is something of a classic for a period of transition, and surprisingly reminiscent of that of Bishop Lefroy in Punjab half a century earlier, and of Archbishop Clayton in South Africa.[8]

Similar sequences with variants of emphasis characterize the other UMCA dioceses through into the 1960s, Zambia and Tanzania achieving nationhood also under deeply Christian leaders, Kenneth Kaunda and Julius Nyerere, referred to with respect and admiration in missionary reports at this time. Not all were able to go as far as Bishop Russell, who, recently retired from Zanzibar after 34 years in East Africa, claimed in 1969 that the revolutionary changes were 'the reverberation of the preaching of the gospel . . . God's teaching of men and nations to stand on their own feet, and work as free men and not as needy children', though the UMCA Secretary, Broomfield, and his successor, Kingsnorth, strongly supported such an interpretation.[9] Russell belonged to the anti-colonial circles associated with Cripps in Zimbabwe and Elwin in India.

It is not surprising, however, that a certain amount of hostility to UMCA missionaries and institutions occurred during the run-up to independence. Bishop Stradling noted resentment in Masasi in 1955 at 'any relics of paternalism, however benevolent', and the people of Kanyimbi gave the diocese a jolt two years later in choosing to have a secular rather than a Christian Middle School. Equally pointed was the nationalist-ordered boycott of an ordination at Likoma in Nyasaland in 1960 (defied by members of the Mothers Union), while an experiment in community living by two European and two African priests in Northern Rhodesia in 1960 was tested by African accusations that the latter must be spies of the colonial government. Missionary support for the nationalist cause was generally very belated, if it occurred at all, but the Synod of South West Tanganyika in 1959 passed unanimously a resolution of 'sympathy with the Tanganyika African National Union's aim of self-government', Stradling being anxious to send a signal to the politicized younger generation over the heads of 'some of the older clergy and others who . . . do not take kindly to the thought of being ruled by members of their own race'.

That same year, the Nyasaland Synod, while calling upon the British government for 'a considerably increased franchise for Africans', called also upon itself for action 'to train Africans for responsibility in ecclesiastical matters'. The only possible deduction is that this extraordinarily belated attempt to move from mission to African Church was prompted by nationalism. Certainly, the UMCA had made progress in this regard in the nineteenth century, but then went into reverse in the twentieth, as the essay by Moriyama in this volume demonstrates.[10] The white bishops of the UMCA dioceses had met a group of four African bishops from CMS dioceses at a regional East African conference in 1955, but could not envisage such possibilities in their own areas. An African archdeacon was appointed in Masasi in 1959, to be followed by others in Nyasaland and South-West Tanganyika, but when bishops were appointed by African-dominated electoral colleges to Masasi in 1960 and Nyasaland and South-West Tanganyika in 1961, Englishmen – Huddleston, Arden and Poole-Hughes – were elected. This was at least partly explained in a comment of Bishop Stradling in 1960,

> We, in this diocese are much behindhand in secondary education. Only two Christians in the whole of the diocese have ever attended university, and it is only in the last three or four years that our young men have been attempting the School Certificate.

Closely related to this was the assumption that Africans, even African clergy, were incapable of functioning effectively, except perhaps liturgically and when thoroughly drilled, within European-style institutions. There are several expressions of episcopal irritation and frustration during these years at African unfamiliarity with the diocesan constitutions that the bishops themselves had only just been persuaded to introduce. There is a striking account by a missionary, Harold Wilkins, of a young woman who 'compelled attention' at the first Masasi Diocesan Conference in 1947: 'Standing with her baby on her back, and with an easy command of her subject, she spoke in beautiful Swahili about the future of African women in careers.' Much more typical is Bishop Way of Northern Rhodesia complaining of a similar conference at which 'the great majority sat mum, and were never quite sure which side they were voting on'.

A related concern lay in the way African workers had been recruited into the austerely ascetic tradition of the Mission, so that when a process of professionalization during these years began to improve financial circumstances in schools and hospitals, few were able to contemplate the increasing relative poverty of the priestly life. Much responsibility for school education passed from Church to state in the new nations, though the Church continued to make a contribution through teacher training, while in Zambia from the later 1950s many well-trained Christian teachers emerged from the Government Training College under its principal, the ex-UMCA missionary, James Robertson. Pay was much better for teachers in these new circumstances. Referring to Tanganyika's changing society in 1963, Bishop Huddleston told UMCA's General Council,

The younger generation has the world at its feet – any member of it might become a cabinet minister – and it is not going to be attracted to a priesthood which seems to them to be identified with a low academic level and an indifferent academic training, and, of course, a very low salary.

In 1968, the now United Society supported the first UMCA ordinand to go to university, while the huge dependence upon missionary clergy, almost 50 per cent of the total in the early 1960s, also began to be corrected with the introduction of auxiliary and supplementary ministries at about this time. These had been authorized by Lambeth in 1958, were introduced very effectively in Society-related Churches in India, Mauritius, New Guinea, Sabah and South Africa and eventually became a striking feature of the Central African dioceses. The Society provided some of the early trainers. By 1973, 65 out of 78 ordinands in Central Africa were preparing for the self-supporting ministry. Reversion to the earlier tradition occurred in 1990.

UMCA's final published Annual Report, in 1961, welcomed nationalism as 'a stirring of the soul of all Africa'. To its president, Margery Perham, it was, more pointedly, 'the thrust of a subject race', and she was bound to remind the Mission at the 1964 anniversary that, 'in the missions and the Church', for all the ardour and sacrifice in their history, 'it seems that the white man is still the dominant factor'. That even the Diocese of Masasi, with what Kingsnorth called its 'deadening tradition of paternalism', halved the number of its European clergy in the eighteen months up to 1965, is a measure of the speedy if belated abandonment of this dominance in response to decolonization. By then, one African diocesan bishop and four assistants had been appointed in the UMCA areas, with distinguished African leadership emerging over the next two decades, typified in Archbishops Sepeku and Ramadhani in Tanzania and Makhulu in Central Africa.[11]

Similar accounts of untidy transitions would be possible for SPG-related Churches in the West Indies, the Indian Ocean and East Asia, decolonization there more or less contemporary with or following shortly upon that just recounted. In the case of SPG, efforts to assist in the development of self-support and indigenous ministries were a marked feature of policy from well before decolonization had made much headway. Discussion in 1951 of a proposed revision of the Charter stated that 'The object of the Society is to encourage the growth of responsibility in the Church overseas.' In this spirit, Roberts made theological education and leadership training the first of what he called the 'Birthday Objectives' for the 250th Anniversary Thankoffering Fund, and a substantial part of the proceeds of the Fund went towards putting local clergy in key positions and training village leaders in India, and towards ministerial training in Borneo, Polynesia, the West Indies and South Africa. Two years later the agreements of a conference at Blackheath were being implemented, to make the training of indigenous leaders in India and the West Indies a priority over the sending of missionaries. In the case of the Far East, emphasis was upon appointing as missionaries 'those who can promote the development of indigenous leadership'. In spite of all this, the move to indigenous leadership was only slightly more impressive than in UMCA. The election of the first West Indian as assistant bishop, in Jamaica in 1947, was reported as having a remarkable effect throughout the Caribbean. India added to its indigenous bishops only very gradually after independence, and Pakistan got its first ten years after independence. A young Guyanese priest in 1971, five years after independence, suggested that 'the white expatriate clergy' posed problems to such as himself, reminding them of their 'erstwhile servitude' and undermining self-confidence by their very presence, while in the Province of the Indian Ocean in 1974, its last country about to become independent, the Report said that 'somehow the Church still smells of the mothballs of colonialism'.[12]

Anglican ecclesiastical self-government had of course partly preceded the political process, so that, for example, the Church of England in India completed its legal severance from the Church of England twenty years before Indian independence, becoming then the Church of India, Burma and Ceylon (CIBC), while Archbishop Fisher, aided by the new ease of air travel, drove through a similar process in other regions during his primacy, 1945–61, with immense energy, vision and competence. It is, however, the matter of indigenous leadership that is most suggestive for the end of colonialism. If the process was strikingly belated during the 1950s and 1960s, the course of this development through the half-century as a whole is equally striking. This is seen in attendance at the Lambeth Conferences during this period: taking the continent of Africa as illustrative, 6 per cent of bishops attending in 1948 were black, while in 1998, 93.5 per cent were. Also of interest, giving some indication of church growth under these new conditions, the total of bishops attending from Africa in this period rose from 37 to 224.

These observations indicate one aspect of the Society's recent history in particular, the rapidly changing role required in a rapidly changing situation, with questions as the Anglican Communion changed and developed as to whether indeed it still had a role. None of this, though, conveys the increasing turbulence of the world in which it had to fulfil its mandate.

13

⟡

First, Second and Third Worlds

In one region at least the Society was soon to have virtually no role at all for several decades, except in one striking and unexpected way. Destruction and appropriation of church property in the two SPG-related dioceses of Shantung and North China were reported in 1947, while, in June 1948, reporting news from the latter, the Medical SubCommittee recorded with regret the 'grave interference in the work at Tatung on account of the civil war there'. A letter from a medical missionary, Molly Moline (who had already endured internment during the Japanese occupation) reported fighting in the compound of St Agatha's Hospital, P'ing Yin, and that the Communists were now in control of the city. She gave 'an inspiring account of the courage and Christian bearing of her Chinese colleagues'.[1]

SPG records provide a vivid picture of events over the next two to three years. Many of the Chinese Christians and some of the Society's missionaries, in particular some of the women, appear to have sympathized with the ideals of the revolutionaries at this time, many years before the Cultural Revolution, and set about adapting to the emerging circumstances with imagination. Bishop T. K. Shen, for example, practised his skill as a barber on his students at the Central Theological College, Shanghai, in compliance with the official requirement to engage in 'productive work', and Hilda Holland, at a girls' school in Peiping, struggled with textbooks 'changed and taught from a different angle', and established a workroom where clothes were made for 'needy people', which led her to observe, 'If we won't take the first step, God sometimes pushes us into it'. Noting the Communists' mutual criticism meetings, she cheerily observed 'quite an Oxford Group touch'. Miss Etheldreda Fisher commented that 'There seemed no

132

irreconcilable difference between the form Communism took at Yenan and Christianity.'[2]

In early 1950, A. E. Clayton, teaching at Cheloo University, reported that they were trying to carry on their teaching in a Buddhist temple, also that there was a big increase in the numbers seeking baptism, while G. F. S. Gray's Chinese colleagues at Huachung University spent much time 'discussing the new education and politics'. Doris Brown of Tsingtao wrote in February, 'Last Sunday was the last we foreigners were able to use the Community Church', while Gray reported in April 'The pitch is gradually getting stickier', and in May that it was quickly getting 'very much stickier'.[3]

By now, with visas no longer available, SPG was cancelling missionary appointments, and missionaries were returning to Britain or moving to alternative appointments in Borneo, India, Jamaica and South Africa. On 24 September 1950, Timothy Lin was consecrated Bishop of North China with episcopal supervision also of the other Society-supported diocese, Shantung, and made a Vice-President of SPG, taking over the episcopal ministry from Bishops Scott and Wellington, two of the last five foreign bishops in the Chung Hua Sheng Kung Huei (CHSKH). The Society's funding programmes were maintained for a further year, with allocations going to the two dioceses as late as October 1951. Grants earmarked for Bishop Lin's work thereafter remained undrawn, and funds from the China Trusts were diverted to work with Chinese communities elsewhere in east and south-east Asia. One of the Society's last China contacts took the form of a beautifully inscribed scroll received to commemorate the 250th anniversary and describing SPG's work as 'a movement of liberation'.[4]

As Chinese Christianity then set out on its extraordinary pilgrimage, with its sufferings, endurance and martyrdoms, the Anglican bishops' Pastoral Letter of 5 May 1950 took issue with 'imperialism, feudalism or bureaucratic capitalism . . . as being fundamentally in opposition to the faith of the Church. The Church has ever regarded alliance with power and prestige, and the exploitation of the common people as a contradiction to the Spirit of Christ.' We get a last glimpse of Bishop Lin in 1956, when Bishop and Mrs Hall of Hong Kong visited him in Beijing, and Lin prayed with them at the Altar and Temple of Heaven. The following year he appeared in a photograph of the seventeen bishops, taken at a 'recent synod', in the January *Overseas News*. Nine years later, he was accused and denounced, and some time later died in the Cultural Revolution, though in 1980 the government sponsored a memorial meeting for him at the place where the heroes of the revolution are buried.[5]

In the *Overseas News* of March 1951, Bishop Wellington had written disapprovingly of 'a number of self-appointed, self-styled representatives of the Christian Churches' who in the previous year had met Zhou Enlai and agreed 'a so-called Christian Manifesto'. In this and in all that followed, the Society had no part, except through the theological legacy of one of its missionaries of half a century earlier, Roland Allen. That was, however, an extremely significant legacy. As the Anglican and Protestant Chinese Christians made their accommodations with the new government and system, developing the Three-Self Movement as the principal vehicle of the Churches' existence and survival, Roland Allen was 'the one non-Chinese thinker whose theological understanding of Three-Self' they referred to 'again and again'.[6]

As conditions eased in post-Mao China, SPG received a tour report from a staff member, Peter Leung, describing his meetings with members of the Three-Self Movement, and in 1982 a delegation from the Movement were guests of the British Council of Churches, among them the son of the barber Bishop Shen, himself a bishop, who was welcomed in a service of thanksgiving in the Chapel of the College of the Ascension. Also during this decade, in 1985, the Amity Foundation was established on the initiative of Bishop K. H. Ting and others. This was a new form of Christian involvement in Chinese society through educational, health and welfare work, in which foreign Christians were invited to co-operate. In terms of external funding, SPG was the lead agency, and a number of teachers were recruited annually thereafter by the Society.

An interesting sidelight on the missionaries' withdrawal from China in 1950 was an appeal to the Society, as to other missionary societies, from the British Colonial Office on behalf of the Federation of Malaya, 'for the loan of such missionaries to undertake work in the social welfare department and at rehabilitation centres under the Government, where their knowledge of the language and their humane outlook would be of particular value', an accompanying letter concluding, 'I hope you will emphasize the part that can be played in Malaya today in combatting Communism by men and women who can mix freely with the Chinese and earn their confidence.' Roberts responded cautiously, noting that 'There are certain difficulties about the proposition political and otherwise', but adding that SPG might be willing 'to encourage support of any measures which commend themselves to the Bishop of the Diocese'. What the bishop wanted, however, were theological educators, and at this the correspondence with the Colonial Office fizzled out. That Malaya did get missionaries from China at this time is evident from a comment in a letter to the Society by a later bishop, Savarimuthu, about those from CMS and the Overseas Missionary Fellowship of the China

Inland Mission. 'The diocese is plagued with internal problems created mostly by the missionaries who invaded the diocese when they were turned out of China. These extreme fundamentalists . . . do not have a right concept of Church, Sacraments and the Ministry.' It was a situation which at least helped prompt the creation of the Seminari Theoloji Malaysia.[7]

The Communist takeover of Korea, with the assistance of the USSR and China, initially most of the country, eventually about half of it, was a time of trial for what Archbishop Fisher called 'the little torn and distracted Church in Korea'.[8] At one stage in 1950, the bishop, Cecil Cooper, was allowed to visit Christians behind the Communist front line, but later in the year was himself interned, with three SPG missionaries and two Korean priests. They were in captivity for three years. When the ceasefire was declared, some Christians from the small Anglican Church and other Churches found themselves in Communist-governed North Korea, where they remained cut off from the south and from all other Christian contacts except for tenuous links with Chinese Christians. Nothing more was known of them, at least to 1999.

Reporting his Far East tour in 1952, Roberts referred to 'the ubiquitous threat of communism', and from then on and through much of the 1960s, Society reports included references to 'surging tides of communism' in south-east Asia (1951), an 'all-out attack on Christianity' in Guiana (1953) and significant Communist activity also in (for example) India, Japan, Mauritius, Mozambique, Sarawak and the West Indies. In Zanzibar many young men were going to study on scholarships in the USSR, and a Communist bookstall was set up in the shadow of the cathedral. Most Anglicans, the editor of *Central Africa* surmised in April 1964, probably looked on the Zanzibar revolution 'as a great deliverance'.

In the case of Ghana, Bishop Roseveare was briefly expelled for criticizing 'dictatorial tendencies' in the country, and in a letter to Trapp, the Secretary, there is a glimpse of his meeting with Nkrumah on his return. Full of admiration for Ghanaian progress and non-alignment, and for the president himself, he nevertheless felt that Nkrumah was under considerable strain and anxiety, perhaps fear.

> I observed a picture of Lenin in his office . . . I felt that he has moved some way towards the position in which the Church is regarded as irrelevant, if not actually a hindrance to the desired progress of Ghana. I have a feeling that he is increasingly cut off from his people and only knows what his closest advisers choose to tell him . . . Somewhere below the surface, there is a small and powerful body of men who are, I think, determined to force Ghana into Communism.[9]

Much more positive a few years later were missionary accounts of the Marxist liberation movement in Mozambique, Frelimo, those for example of Joan Antcliffe in *Lebombo Leaves* and John Paul in his *Mozambique: Memoirs of a Revolution*.[10] Bishop Cabral was also positive, according to the 1975 Report, urging support from the pulpit for the new Frelimo government. His successor, Bishop Sengulane, in 1977, insisted 'The Church is not being persecuted, it is being challenged', adding 'the Gospel is not for capitalists only, it is also for the communists – especially those who are deaf to its message.' He continued, 'I go to Frelimo meetings as a Christian leader in order to hear what the Spirit is saying to the Church.' At the same time, Bishop Sengulane robustly defied the authorities when necessary, as when an attempt was made in 1978 to prohibit administration of the sacraments to any minor under seventeen. Less ideologically concerned was Bishop Cunningham of Central Zambia, reported in the Spring 1977 *Network* welcoming China's largest overseas aid project, the 1200-mile long Tanzania-Zambia Railway as an excellent new way of linking up otherwise isolated Anglican centres, 'reminiscent of the old Railway Mission'.

The shift of economic power from Britain to the United States was little noticed in the Society until Trapp drew attention to it in a paper for Lambeth 1958, but missionary reports were picking up the new reality from their angle. Missionaries from the United States 'poured' into British Honduras from the later 1940s, 'Nazarenes, Adventists, Assembly of God . . . [the Anglicans] pestered week after week' (1956); there were also American sects in Polynesia and the Americans were 'pouring men and money' into the West Indies and Guyana (1954), and 'huge funds' into Southern Rhodesia (1959), while the growth of the Presbyterian Churches in South Korea is accompanied by references to that characteristic of Christianity under capitalist influence, 'privatized religion' (1956, 1975).

The 1953 Report referred to 'two great blocks of power'. The story of SPG and its Chinese Christian associates, and the other references above, serve to introduce this new reality, one of the most acute changes to the context of Christian mission in this period, the division of the world into two competing economic and political blocs. There was a 'First World', the capitalist option led by the USA presiding over a neocolonialism and committed to maintaining its hegemony by any means, and a 'Second World', led by the USSR and China, equally determined to develop a socialist alternative.[11] Between these two blocs, for some 45 years, a Cold War prevailed. The term 'Third World', coined in 1952, covered the largely new and decolonizing nations, dependent on the two blocs for the development to which they aspired, often trying to remain non-aligned, though many of their leaders were attracted to socialism. These new nations, stuffed with armaments by the two blocs, became the miserable arena where the blocs pursued their competing interests in over 100 major wars. Compounding the complexities, the 1950s and 1960s witnessed world economic growth at a historically unprecedented rate, making for 'the most dramatic, rapid, and profound revolution in human affairs of which history has record'.[12] This was followed by the development during the 1970s of a capitalist economic internationalism represented in vast transnational corporations and an accompanying international division of labour. Meanwhile, in the Third World the population doubled between 1950 and 1985. At the same time, much of Africa was written off by the International Monetary Fund and the World Bank, this being reflected at its most terrible in mass famines and the death of children, some 20 million per year dying of hunger and hunger-related disease. This contrasted most sharply with a United States which, with 6.3 per cent of the world's population, held some 50 per cent of its wealth. Aid agencies spoke of a holocaust of the poor. Investment was transferred initially to east and south-east Asia and parts of Latin America, leaving behind, in UN terminology, the 'least developed' nations, redesignated in the 1990s 'highly indebted'. Incomes in the richest ten countries, which were 30 times those in the poorest ten in the 1960s, were 80 times by the 1990s. Most of the Churches with which SPG was involved were located in this Third World.

Throughout the period, the Society debated in its Council and committees the issues raised as they came to attention through the reports of missionaries and Churches and in wider public debate – the question of 'Human Rights' in 1948, 'Inter-Church Aid and Missions' in 1956, collaboration with the UN 'Freedom From Hunger' campaign in 1961 and the question of 'Christians and World Development' in 1970, 'Marxism and the Gospel' in 1977, the Brandt Report (*North–South: A Programme for Survival*) in 1980 and 'Third-World Debt' in 1990 and subsequently. In addition to its traditional support for mission and Church, SPG sought to respond to the realities of the Church in this Third World in a number of ways.

The first of these was in the field of development. 'Agricultural development in rural missions' was the fifth of Roberts's 'Birthday Objectives' at the 250th anniversary, while an enthusiastic missionary at St Faith's Mission, Rusape, Southern Rhodesia, said in the 1951 Report that 'The Church finds itself mixed up with socket joints in steel tubing . . . in compost and cattle cake, because our eternal destiny is only reached after the right direction has been followed through our material environment.' This became a recurring theme in the Society. Inter-

Church Aid was emerging at this time. A discussion in Standing Committee agreed that,

> If missions were to hand over to Inter-Church Aid a section of their activities there would probably result a measure of disintegration. All missionary activities should be part of a rounded whole, satisfactorily co-ordinated. In the circumstances, it was agreed that the Society should look to Inter-Church Aid for assistance with the development of existing work and the promotion of new work.[13]

This in fact happened initially, the Society receiving funds in 1961 from I-CA to participate in the 'Freedom From Hunger' campaign in agricultural projects in Basutoland, Borneo, India, Korea, Malawi and Pakistan. This was followed by further co-operation in 1964 and 1965 with what was by then Christian Aid. 'We need their money, they need our workers', as Trapp put it at the 1965 Annual Meeting. The Society, though, was uneasy about a narrow connotation to the word 'development', 'namely works to be undertaken in underdeveloped countries for the purpose of economic advance'.[14] Individual missionaries of the Society nevertheless continued to be involved in development, their work reflecting changing and broader understandings, John Fethney in Pakistan in the 1960s, Alan Batchelor with the ecumenical Industrial Service Team in South India and the Streatfields at the Diocesan Farm in Nagpur diocese, North India.

Impressive and exemplary work in development was done in the city of Delhi by the Cambridge Brotherhood, from 1967 called the Brotherhood of the Ascended Christ, and led by Amos Rajamoney. One of the great changes in Asia, and indeed throughout the south, during this period was an exodus from the countryside and the growth of vast cities, Delhi being the fastest growing in India, from one to thirteen million inhabitants. The Brotherhood's response was a remarkable new development beyond the prestigious St Stephen's College phase of CMD's work. Rajamoney came to the Brotherhood from South India in 1967, at a time when the College was buzzing with youthful revolutionary excitement, some 30 students in the next two or three years going underground with the Marxist-Leninist party known as the Naxalites. His own response to the times, and he was aware of what was going on among the students, led him into a sustained commitment of over 30 years to the service of the poor of the city. He was supported by his older English brothers, by Indian members as they joined the community and by colleagues in other Christian institutions, St Stephen's Hospital in particular.

After starting with a priestly ministry with a colony of leprosy sufferers, but soon helping them into earning their living and their children into education, he extended his concern to some of the large 'Resettlement Colonies' into which the authorities at that time were moving people from the slums in which they were beginning to congregate in the city, and later also to a slum of 100,000 inhabitants, the Yamuna Basti. Rajamoney himself moved into a room in one of the colonies, and lived there over much of the ensuing years, often accompanied by one of the other brothers. By the mid-1980s, he had built up a team of some 50 social, community health and educational workers. In this way, the Brotherhood's work touched tens of thousands of people through a variety of public facilities, clinics, community centres and libraries, and a series of 'Deenabandhu' schools (commemorating the earlier Brotherhood member, C. F. Andrews), these latter by the 1990s educating some 2500 children, while a range of programmes was created, such as 'Child Survival' and 'Safe Motherhood', and associations such as a credit union, housing societies, a Handicapped People's Development Society, a Forum for Women's Awakening and a Youth Office. Funding came from individuals and church groups, from Indian and international agencies, including USPG. Consistently, the object was to activate the social development of people. The interreligious tradition of the former Cambridge Mission found new expresssion. To overcome initial suspicion of a Christian body assumed to be interested only in conversion, care was taken in the promotion of religious harmony, with intercommunity observance of the different religious festivals encouraged. That the colonies concerned remained almost uniquely peaceful during the widespread violence against Sikhs in Delhi in 1984, following the assassination of Prime Minister Indira Gandhi, is a measure of the success of this approach, and an indication that a new vision of community was making its way locally in the face of India's traditional, primordial understandings. A new Indian member of the Brotherhood, Solomon George, introduced new elements to the project, street theatre, and later a Hindi newspaper that he edited, while from 1992 two other Indian members, Monodeep Daniel and Sister Jothi, a Lay Companion, took on much of the considerable administrative responsibility entailed.

In the 1990s, attention was turned to the special plight and needs of children – working children, the children of pavement dwellers and slum dwellers and street children. New initiatives followed, including feeding and informal learning programmes, a home for street children, a night shelter and resettlement with families, while the Brotherhoood's attractive garden was made available for children's meetings. By now on the wider Christian scene in India, and in response to the growing marginalization of the poor as a result of advancing globalization, development generally tended to take a more politicized and communitarian form, in what became known as the Dalit movement. The Delhi Brotherhood nevertheless persevered with their long-tested and evolving understanding of development work, seen essentially as human and social development, and this continued to be their objective in the later 1990s, and was seen to be bearing fruit and worth pursuing 'with even greater determination'. In 1999, the Delhi Brotherhood Society was 'stepping into the new millennium with small yet bold initiatives', six new ones being announced that year.[15]

The second field in which the Society sought to make a contribution in the context of 'Third Worldness' was regarding health. This had, of course, been an aspect of the 'rounded whole' of mission as carried out by SPG, UMCA and CMD from their beginnings, making their contribution to the largest institutionalized international health service in the world, that of the Churches. This was, however, a diminishing aspect of the Society's work even prior to decolonization, since health, like education, was increasingly seen as a colonial government responsibility in the 1940s and 1950s. During this period much medical work was done in partnership with the colonial authorities (with additional funding from bodies like the British Empire Leprosy Relief Association and the Red Cross), but the Society, UMCA and CMD were still supporting some 50 hospitals around the world at the beginning of this period, as well as associated medical colleges and nurses' training schools, and numerous local dispensaries and clinics. In many places, at independence, Third World nations did not have the resources to take over this work completely, despite ambitions to do so, and various new Church–state partnerships were worked out, which SPG continued to support despite shrinking resources and rising costs, often in conjunction with other mission agencies and, again, with assistance from bodies like UNICEF and LEPRA. A good example of Church–state collaboration was embodied in the work of Dr James Cairns in Zambia, building up his own hospital at Katete but also establishing the Churches' Medical Association to negotiate with government, and sitting on Government Health Service committees. In some cases, of course, the state did take over completely, in China, for example, and Mozambique, while in others the local Church or the government itself had the resources to assume full responsibility, as in south-east Asia, and largely in South Africa, while in India, Bangladesh and Pakistan, wider, ecumenical support succeeded what individual mission agencies had hitherto done. At the same time, as USPG reduced its support for large and expensive medical institutions, it increased it, in line with the WHO's 'Health for All by

2000', for smaller health centres and in the relatively inexpensive but highly important field of preventative services. The Society's medical missionaries in Rhodesia had discovered the need for these in the 1970s, being shocked at the levels of 'malnutrition, ignorance and poor hygiene' that they found outside the hospitals to which they had previously confined their work.[16] Primary health care, likewise, was expanded, for example through diocesan programmes in the 1990s among tribal communities in Burma and supporting herbal pharmacies in the Diocese of Pelotas in Brazil.

A professional review by Dr Kathleen Wright in 1972 had suggested that national governments would soon be shouldering full responsibility for hospitals, but a subsequent review by Dr Peter Cox in 1984 indicated that this had not happened everywhere, and the Society made a decision in 1986 to continue to support hospitals substantially with funds and personnel in Malawi, Tanzania, Zambia and Zimbabwe. A post of Health Development Officer was created at the same time. At the end of this period, USPG support for hospitals was concentrated in nine hospitals in east and central Africa, with some help for eight others in south Asia, South Africa and Namibia. These were areas of traditional relationship, most of them marked by increasing poverty, sickness and suffering, moved on to another plane of misery by the HIV/Aids pandemic which gathered momentum in Africa during the 1980s, and in Asia in the 1990s. Critical situations often faced these institutions. For example, Mkomaindo Hospital in Tanzania was taken over in first-class condition by the government at independence but, three decades and the IMF's Structural Adjustment Programme later (a programme which relentlessly and massively increased illness), was pressed back upon the Church in an almost derelict state. Also critical was the position regarding hospitals in Malawi, the failure of government funding during the later 1990s forcing the Christian hospitals to suspend all but emergency treatment. As a Society missionary explained, 'The government . . . is trying to push all these organisations into a corner in the hope that overseas friends will bale them out.' Reports from this region throughout the 1990s indicated heroic service by local medical staff and the few medical missionaries concerned in situations of acute desperation as need so vastly outweighed resources.

A third way in which USPG sought to address 'Third Worldness' was through a modification of the overall strategy of the Society, developed during the Secretaryship of Peter Price (1992–7). Events in November 1989, the fall of the Berlin Wall and the massacre of a Jesuit community in San Salvador six days later, symbolized new circumstances which were disastrous from a Third World perspective whereby capitalism was allowed to 'once again appear . . . without a human face'. While the Third World continued to be of vital importance for the development of the First World, the greater part of its population was no longer needed, and was 'on a roller-coaster heading towards the abyss'.[17] The Society's new publication, *Together*, supported this view in a piece by Pablo Richard of Costa Rica in July 1992,

> In reality the fall of the wall was very positive, but we are aware that another gigantic wall is being constructed in the Third World to hide the reality of the poor majorities. A wall between the rich and the poor is being built so that poverty does not annoy the powerful, and the poor are obliged to die in the silence of history. A wall of silence is being built so that the rich world forgets the Third World.

Staff Tour Reports, so often an invaluable source of information, most significantly in this case Philip Wetherell's on Latin America, Martin Heath's on South Asia, Fannie Storr's and Rosemary Tucker's on Central Africa, confirmed the intensifying disastrousness. USPG's response was a new strategic plan finally approved in September 1997 which included explicit recognition of 'the special place that the poor and excluded have in God's heart', and a decision 'to relate especially to churches and others seeking to break free from poverty, oppression and exclusion'. This more explicit focus was endorsed in correspondence with the provinces with which the Society was associated.

It issued, short term, in helping launch and formally identifying with the campaign in Britain known as 'Jubilee 2000' for the cancellation of debt in the Third World. Concern for Church and people in South Africa during the 1980s had brought into play in USPG an important missionary skill, that of advocacy, and this was put to use again in regard to this new crisis. The Society, prompted by the Iona Community, had first alerted supporters to the issue, and to the biblical notion of Jubilee, in 1977.[18] It was, however, with the appointment of a retired diplomat, W. Peters, as Deputy and then Chair of Council between 1986 and 1993, that the Society began to take this up in a sustained way. As UK High Commissioner in Malawi, Peters had seen the damage the IMF, the World Bank and the Structural Adjustment Programme were doing in Africa.[19] His article, 'A Mountain of Debt', written for Christian Aid and reprinted in *Network* in April 1989, prompted the Society into a new campaign of advocacy, with the millennium providing a target date. USPG then made a grant assisting the Debt Crisis Network in launching the Jubilee 2000 Coalition. This then rapidly became a very broad-based campaign among the Churches and Christian agencies, even attracting secular allies, overcoming their unfamiliarity with the doctrine of Jubilee. Archbishop David Hope of York told a group celebrating 140 years of UMCA in the Senate House in Cambridge in 1997 that to give a new and debt-free start to over a billion people would be the '*one* millennial gesture which could set our world ablaze with real hope'. The sympathetic response of the Chancellor of the Exchequer, Gordon Brown, soon after taking office in 1997, saw the British government taking a leading role in the international community in the matter, Brown telling USPG's supporters through the Summer 1998 *Transmission*, 'If the poorest countries are to start the next millennium with realistic hopes, we must not fail.'

In a longer perspective, and more comprehensively, USPG's new strategic plan undertaken during Price's Secretaryship, and in part modelled on the ACC's 'five marks of mission', (1990) issued in a modification of all the Society's programmes, and this began to be apparent in 1998, applying to each of them in turn the notion of a preferential option for the poor.

14

⊶⫘◉⫘⊷

A new relationship

The Second World War had been a terrible trial for the Anglican Church in Japan, the NSKK, both through sharing in the nation's suffering, with the destruction of the majority of its churches and other buildings, but also through the attempt to subordinate it to the control of the Imperial government, an attempt resisted heroically by some two-thirds of the clergy and membership under the leadership of Bishop Michael Yashiro. In the aftermath, on a visit, Herbert Kelly wrote to Roberts, 'They have to begin again off the ground, just as the early Church did, a genuine Japanese Church finding its way with God and its own people.' The Society contributed funding and personnel to assist in the Church's recovery, and Bishop Yashiro was emphatic that he valued the relationship highly, 'I ask you to realise how greatly the whole of the Nippon Sei Ko Kwai has been influenced in its history by the SPG . . . In fact the whole Church here is so SPG in colour that it might be called a province of the SPG if there were such a thing.' Nevertheless, it was clear that a new relationship was now called for. This was made very clear by the NSKK's House of Bishops, and also by Leonora Lee, the only Society missionary who had remained in Japan throughout the war, when she first wrote to Roberts afterwards,

> The true Church of Japan stands victorious . . . after a colossal struggle . . . [it] has sunk down to rock bottom, has suffered intensely and been purified; she has risen strong and now stands on a lasting foundation. She is now a sister Church of the Church of England – no longer a daughter church.[1]

Articulating and implementing such a new relationship became a major concern of SPG during the second half of the century. Roberts

144

saw this from the beginning of his Secretaryship. It was confirmed for
him at the International Missionary Council (IMC) meeting at Whitby,
Ontario, in July 1947. The key statement from that meeting was entitled
'The Partnership'. This referred to 'the Partnership of the Younger and
Older Churches', though it was suggested that the terms 'older' and
'younger' rested on a 'largely obsolete' distinction. SPG's supporters were
introduced to these ideas by Henry de Candole, a consistent friend of
the Society, in a front-page article in the September 1948 *Overseas News*
entitled 'Two-Way Traffic'. De Candole underlined the progress of self-
support, self-respect and self-rule in the 'younger Churches', which the
separations of the Second World War had served to consolidate. He also
acknowleded 'the drift from . . . Christianity' experienced by the 'older
Churches', and their reversion to a 'missionary condition', illustrated by
the startling title of the recent Report, *Towards the Conversion of England*.
In these new circumstances a new relationship was called for, exemplified
in the notion of a two-way traffic of 'givers and receivers . . . alike
receiving and giving'. Echoing the title of an important new book from
the Catholic sector in Anglicanism, he suggested that this would be a
realization of the 'Common Life in the Body of Christ'.[2] He repeated
this theme the same year in a collection of essays edited by E. R. Morgan
and Roger Lloyd, *The Mission of the Anglican Communion*, the whole of
the second half of the book comprising twelve essays under the general
title, 'Giving and Receiving'. This was formalized for the Society at a
conference at Stepney in 1967, when SPG's first overall objective was
defined as 'to encourage a greater measure of mutuality' between
Churches. It was to be a quarter of a century, as colonial attitudes
lingered, before these ideas achieved anything like official recognition in
the Anglican Communion, and implementing them proved an even
more distant prospect.

Roberts' encountered the term 'partnership' in 1947 within the
conciliar process, at an ecumenical meeting, which indicates that the
search for a new relationship was widespread. Trapp came back from the
1958 meeting of the IMC in Ghana with the observation that the
majority of delegates were from the 'younger' Churches, and certainly
the character of the main conciliar body, the World Council of Churches
(WCC), itself changed markedly by the mid-1960s from being an
instrument of North Atlantic church interests to being much more
clearly a world body, with a majority of representatives thereafter from
the Churches of the south. In the same decade, various of the documents
issuing from the Second Vatican Council, itself now a more truly global,
less a merely Western forum, suggested similar changes. The same process
was also beginning within the Anglican Communion. Important steps

were represented by the Anglican Congresses of 1954 and 1963. The first, at Minneapolis, was the first representative gathering of the Communion held outside the British Isles. Roberts attended, calling it 'a bringing together in visible personal contact of the fruits of the Society's pioneer missionary labours'.[3] The second, at Toronto, is best known for being contemporaneous with the launching of the movement known as 'Mutual Responsibility and Interdependence in the Body of Christ', an attempt to develop mutuality in personnel and funding programmes throughout the Communion. Kingsnorth welcomed this at SPG's 1965 Annual Meeting as 'post-paternalist'. It certainly seemed full of promise to Bishop Goto of Japan, quoted in the July 1963 *Overseas News*,

> Formerly the giver and receiver faced each other, each ashamed, both with anxious eyes fastened on the gift. Now we are released from this, for we are to stand hand in hand facing our great missionary task.

Meanwhile, in 1960, an Executive Officer of the Anglican Communion had been appointed, initially Bishop Stephen Bayne, and a further instrument of partnership, the Anglican Consultative Council (ACC), was created, first meeting at Limuru, Kenya, in 1971. Commenting on this meeting, with 'the *majority* of delegates . . . dark-skinned', Margaret Dewey pointed out in that year's Report that 'the centre of gravity . . . (of) the Anglican Communion . . . (had) shifted', and this was 'of the utmost significance for the work of the Society'. USPG would have to make itself serviceable within the new framework that was emerging, in which older dominances and dependences would be reduced and Church speak to Church within the Communion.

Inevitably, there were misunderstandings, not least in relation to the emerging ACC. Although Dean, the second Executive Officer, had consulted mission executives including Trapp, his successor, John Howe, began by overlooking them. The Limuru meeting was intended to engage in a major reappraisal of mission in the Anglican Communion, and Trapp complained to Howe that the Society and other mission agencies were not being consulted in advance of the meeting despite their responsibility for discharging the Church of England's missionary obligation.[4] The new dynamic established by the ACC almost guaranteed a continuing edginess between it and the mission agencies, though USPG put much energy into making the relationship work.[5]

A leading development, following the Limuru meeting and formalized at the next ACC meeting at Dublin in 1973, was a process of joint consultation between Churches, known as Partners-in-Mission Consultations, the underlying principle being a willingness to open up a province to Christian 'partners' from elsewhere for an examination of its strategies, resources and needs in mission within its own area. The 1975 Report welcomed the first six of these consultations. They marked a new phase in Anglican missionary work.

> Since the planning is local, the old taunt of control from . . . a London office, is no longer possible . . . our overseas partners see themselves clearly as missionaries, and not just the objects of mission.

More than 60 of these consultations took place over the next twenty years, the Society and other mission agencies providing consultants for many of them. As they began to tail off in the later 1980s for want of adequate committed staffing in the ACC, USPG's Secretary, Taylor, pressed for a continuing relationship between the agencies and the ACC, and this took place in a Mission Issues and Strategy Advisory Group and a Mission Agencies Working Group, the latter with Third World representation and dealing with mission practicalities. More theoretical questions tended to characterize the successor body, 'Missio', in the 1990s.

The achievement of a new, 'post-paternal' relationship was a major preoccupation of the Society, particularly from the 1970s, 'The Future out of the Past', as Taylor later put it in a reflective address to Council, getting beyond the colonial pattern and seeking 'actively to help transform the colonial inheritance', to the benefit of both parties.[6] Robertson, Secretary from 1973, gave much attention to this, to realizing 'the vision behind Partnership-in-Mission', for it was very much his own vision also.[7] To Robertson, the ACC had 'had a catalytic influence on all churches organized for mission', its programmes 'real enablers in mission'.[8] He and staff colleagues had a major part in 1977 in re-drafting the guidelines for the consultations, and with evident satisfaction later remarked that they 'enshrined . . . our philosophy'.[9] Robertson was always concerned at the practical outworking of this, and regularly drew attention to programmes generated in response to a consultation. Thus, he reported to the 1977 Annual Meeting that the recent South-East Asia Consultation had led to new developments in Christian education in Sabah and Kuching, new clergy and post-baptismal training in Korea, joint working of the Philippine Independent and Episcopal Churches, personnel sharing between the Philippines and Kuching and moves towards a united seminary in West Malaysia.

USPG's concern to realize the new relationship led to the creation in 1986 of a post of Partnership Secretary, while Taylor's articulation of the

Society's role as an agency of partnership between the Churches, in a Council paper of 1986, reaffirmed the scriptural and Catholic understanding of partnership as communion. This distinguished it clearly from the approach of agencies which spoke not of Churches but of individuals as 'mission partners'.

The Society's concern also issued in a major effort to share the vision more widely in the Church of England, Taylor undertaking a round of visits to diocesan bishops and those with special responsibility for mission in the dioceses. During a six-month period in 1991–2, he visited 38 out of the 44 bishops and dioceses, in what must have been one of the most sustained visitations by a Secretary in the Society's history, explaining USPG's now settled understanding of partnership and its self-understanding as an enabler of exchange of 'the gifts which God gives to the church around the world for the sake of mission'.[10] Responses were varied. One bishop waxed nostalgic for 'UMCA elephant collecting boxes', another, well known as a supporter of the then Conservative Government, 'the one diocesan wholly and congenially at odds with the USPG strategy', believed that 'God speaks through Western capitalism'. For the most part, however, USPG's position was understood and welcomed. It was welcomed with 'excitement and deep appreciation' by Bishop Jenkins of Durham, and with enthusiasm by the two archbishops, the chief reservation being about 'a great deal of nostalgia in parishes for the old way of doing things by missionary societies . . . (and) a commitment effectively to increase dependency'.[11] To have recruited a wide degree of episcopal and diocesan support for the Society's understanding and strategy was, nevertheless, a valuable achievement.

At the same time, de Candole's proposed 'uniting in the common privilege of the bearing of the Cross' pointed to another task, that of seeking to overcome the multiple marginality of 'Third Worldness'. This required adjustments in the way the Society dealt with funding, the element most liable to disfigure the communion of Churches. Indeed, in March 1947, the year of Indian independence, *Overseas News* had carried a report of a conference of Indian Christians at the Kristu-Kula Ashram which proposed the formation of small groups in India and the West to be in touch 'for purposes of spiritual and cultural fellowship, without any financial obligations on either side'. This attractive vision could not be implemented easily in a long-established organization in which financial transfers had always been a major expression of commitment to the propagation of the Gospel. Nevertheless, the reform of the funding element in USPG's work as decolonization advanced, to expedite self-support and to express the new relationship, was especially important. The shrinking resources of the Society, combined with the deepening immiseration of the Third World, added to the complexity of the challenge.

Although the allocations of the 250th Anniversary Thankoffering Fund of 1951 were devoted to such forward-looking projects as advancing indigenous ministry, the allocations were determined in London and, indeed, as had happened from SPG's foundation, a great deal of committee time was devoted to decisions about 'grants' towards often minutely detailed schemes. 'Everything seemed to be listed, like two bicycles for here, etc.', as Robertson observed later.[12] Sometimes, of course, this procedure could be salutary: thus, a grant for a new church building in the Gold Fields Area of the Diocese of Bloemfontein was made in 1950 'on the understanding that there would be no exclusion of worshippers on grounds of race from the building'.[13] That, however, was essentially still a colonial situation.

It was in connection with South Africa, in response to the Group Areas Act, that a further step was taken towards a new relationship in finance. In order to help create new centres of church life in the new housing areas into which many people were being compulsorily moved, the Society in 1963 launched a revolving loan fund, 'Festina', which was taken up widely in South Africa. It was recognized immediately, however, as having a much wider application and, in Trapp's words to the 1964 Annual Meeting, would 'stimulate self-support and diminish the debilitating feeling of dependence' in many dioceses. 'Festina' proved a very popular resource, one that the Society was able to maintain even as income declined, with some 260 loans provided, totalling over three and a half million pounds, over the next 35 years.

Also in 1963, SPG brought its budgets as far as possible into line with the Directory of Projects created by the 'Mutual Responsibility and Interdependence' initiative. The advent of the Partners-in-Mission consultations led to further developments in the Society's funding policy, with major funds now reserved for 'Partners' Priorities', determined at the consultations. There were two broad categories, 'Continuity Funding', essentially maintenance funding, which could not easily be abandoned in the face of the North–South divide, and which a Church of England still heavily subsidized by the Church Commissioners was in no position to criticize, and 'Transformational Funding', later also 'Capability Funding', specifically aimed at increasing a Church's independence. This approach was influential at the Fourth ACC meeting in Canada in 1979.

Developments in the decision-making process were also important. The Dublin ACC had challenged the mission agencies to adopt a more consultative style. After looking, with the help of Dr Bernard Thorogood of the United Reformed Church (URC), at the brilliant transformation of the old LMS and its associated Churches into a thoroughly international Council for World Mission (CWM), the Society opted for a less ambitious but nevertheless radical step and agreed to put its mission programmes budgeting from 1981 into the hands of a group consisting of four overseas church members and four from the Church of England. The former, the overseas members, were appointed, as the 1982 Report put it, 'not to represent regional interests, but to contribute their knowledge and experience as stewards of the world Church', and included over the next few years Basil Temengong and Yong Ping Chung of Kuching, Martin Mbwana of Tanzania, Oscar Bird of Antigua, Averill White and Kortright Davis of Barbados, Winston Ndungane of South Africa and Maqbul Caleb of India, among others. The eight members at any time being people of exceptional ability, the scrutiny to which USPG's practice was exposed was salutary. Although Taylor was overruled when he pleaded initially for an overseas majority on the Group, Robertson felt able to describe the formation of the Group as 'really our biggest outward sign that we know the dangers of power, when it resides in money'. Kortright Davis observed that it was 'more than a facelift – you are going through a great rejuvenation'.[14] This Budget Group, under the robust chairmanship of Winston Ndungane, decided in 1984 to restrict maintenance funding to those Churches for which it was a matter of survival, while encouraging dioceses in the region concerned to collaborate in finding local solutions. The process was taken a step further that same year, during Taylor's secretaryship, when the entire budget of the Society was put under the control of this group, which then became the International Budget Group. With an almost impossible annual task, heroically serviced by the Financial Secretary, Michael Mason, this was discontinued as too cumbersome after the 1990 meeting.

Thereafter, the 'consultative style' of relationship was formalized anew in what were called Provincial Consultations. These brought small USPG staff teams, usually with a Council member also, into residential consultation with bishops and others from a province, the watchword being 'open relationships', the objective, 'to assist USPG in representing the realities of your situation to the churches in Britain and Ireland, enable you to understand and reflect with us on the realities of USPG's situation within the church in Britain and Ireland . . . [and] develop the opportunities for interchange between us.' The first such consultation was with the Igreja Episcopal Anglicana do Brasil in March 1995, and subsequently they involved the Provinces of Tanzania, also 1995, Southern Africa in 1996, Central Africa in 1998 and the West Indies in 1999. These proved helpful to the Society, and undoubtedly served the needs of individual provinces, which spoke warmly of them. The ACC's observer at the West Indies consultation, David Hamid, described it as 'a demonstration of *koinonia*'.

How effective the Society has in fact been in its effort to transform the colonial inheritance and take sensitive account of the huge and often terrible economic changes in the past half-century will be difficult to evaluate, but this introductory account points to a serious and sustained commitment to think and act responsibly. Failure abounds, as suggested in Kingsnorth's account of how, following a Partners-in-Mission Consultation in Africa in the 1970s, two English bishops from the province concerned immediately set off 'cap-in-hand to Canada and America' on behalf of their own dioceses.[15] While a mission agency supplied with shrinking resources by the Church could be of little economic significance among the injustices of the second half of the twentieth century, adjustments which served to affirm the integrity of Churches in the Third World may perhaps in the long run prove to have been of greater significance.

15

The Society's missionaries

The period from 1947 saw many interesting new developments in self-propagation by virtually all the Churches associated with SPG. Some of these were entirely independent and unsupported initiatives by individuals, often hard to discern, like the creation of a worshipping house church by a handful of mineworkers in a Copperbelt town in Zambia. There were also, of course, many more organized ventures, some with an earlier history, like those in Tirunelveli, which had a 'Native Association for the Propagation of the Gospel' from 1861, provided missionaries through the Society to coolie communities in several British colonial settlements and had established the National Missionary Society and the Indian Missionary Society early in the twentieth century. Tirunelveli continued to produce mission-minded leaders in this period, like Christopher Duraisingh, Director of the WCC's Commission on World Mission and Evangelism (CWME) or, within the Tamil dispersion, a bishop in West Malaysia, Savarimuthu, and at home in India leaders such as Patrick Joseph, whose Friends Missionary Prayer Band was in 1999 leading 'the largest conversion movement in the history of the country'.[1] Similarly, the NSKK, which had provided a first catechist in Korea in 1880 seven years after SPG had begun work in Japan, developed its own work in Bangladesh. Sea Dayaks in 1957 initiated a mission among the Dusons of North Borneo, while the Sabah Anglican Inland Mission was established in 1958 and made a significant evangelizing impact over the coming decades. We also get a glimpse of something spontaneous happening among the Sea Dayaks of Sarawak themselves, with an overstretched missionary remarking in the 1959 Report of isolated groups that 'the most that one can do for them apart from an occasional visit is to leave them the Scriptures and Prayer Books and to choose someone to lead them in prayers and worship'. The Report of fifteen years later reported the area as witnessing an 'explosion . . . [with] thousands of new Christians'. In other regions, long-established self-propagating structures continued to function. Thus, the 1974 Report noted that over the previous twenty years, the Melanesian Brotherhood had sent 125 missionaries to other South Pacific countries.

Despite the growing resourcefulness of local Churches in pursuing their own mission, SPG continued throughout the period to support the appointment of missionaries, though striking changes took place in this regard. In the 1950s, SPG, UMCA and CMD had some 700 listed missionaries, recruiting about 40 new men and women annually. Then, as in so many other respects, the 1960s saw a remarkable development, perhaps reflecting the new vision granted to the world and the Churches by the Ecumenical Council, Vatican II, or something of the urgency and aspiration expressed in the UN's Development Decade. At the time of Lambeth 1958, the Society under its new Secretary, Trapp, had brought 50 of the attending bishops together in regional groups. These drew attention to 'nationalisms, resurgent religions, industrial revolutions, new alignments of power, new demands regarding standards of living, an explosion of population'. The expulsion of missionaries from China, and other 'closing doors' added their own urgency. All this led Dewi Morgan, editor of the subsequent Report, to conclude (in a phrase that the prophetic Barbara Ward was to use a few years later) that this was 'a hinge moment in history'.[2] With this in mind, SPG then took an initiative among the eleven recognized missionary societies to launch a joint appeal to all incumbents of the Church of England, a 'call to evangelise the world on a scale . . . never before . . . attempted'. Trapp explained that in spite of the growing numbers of lay and ordained nationals serving in their Churches, there was no sign of any abatement in the requests for missionaries, while the tendency to serve for shorter periods also increased the demand. Backed up by a prayer campaign, a 'Budget of Opportunity' and the encouragement of parishes to focus their concern through a new 'Projects' scheme, the appeal was unprecedentedly successful in the Society, and throughout the 1960s over 100 new listed missionaries were recruited every year, a total of 135 in 1963, the largest number in any one year of SPG's history. Most of these were from England, with a handful also from Ireland, Scotland and Wales, and mostly clergy, the second largest group being medical, the third teachers, though with a shrinking number of single women recruited. Quite the largest number went to central and southern Africa, then the Caribbean, initially a large number to India also. By 1967, there were over 900 missionaries on the Society's list, with some 850 at the end of the decade.

Where this period of recruitment differed from earlier ones was that it was clearly post-colonial in the acknowledged need for missionaries willing to adapt to changed circumstances. The November 1962 *Overseas News* carried a message from the General Secretary of the All Africa Council of Churches, David M'Timkulu,

> The kind of missionary that is now wanted is not the man [*sic*] who has come to do something for the Africans . . . but . . . to work as a co-equal with his fellows in the field . . . a worker in the Church of Christ, just like any other worker who may be African by descent.

This was a theme taken up by the NSKK in 1966, suggesting that their sense of a new beginning after the war had not been fully realized. A consultation set up in Tokyo on 'The Role of the Missionary' sought to establish a view of the missionary as a team member.

In the early 1970s, recruiting began to decline, with an average of about twenty new missionaries per year by 1980, while by then the total on the list had dropped to 300. The Society agreed with the CPSA in 1988 that most of USPG's approximately 40 missionaries working there should be transferred to the local payroll, leaving sixteen on the Society's list for South Africa in 1999. In the 1990s, a target of ten new recruits per year was proposed, though it proved difficult to reach, while the total missionary list in 1999, including spouses and all categories of appointment, but also including in a notable development thirteen teachers in China under the Amity programme, was 86. The most obvious explanation for this trend was, of course, the growing independence and resourcefulness of the Churches of the south in the post-colonial context, with the decline of the Churches in Britain the other side of the coin.

A further factor had been what the Society in 1972 called 'Closed Doors', whereby governments of newly independent countries imposed restrictions and bans on the entry of foreign missionaries. In the case of China, the ban was complete, with no work permits after 1948, and from 1966 the same had applied to Burma (which also restricted the travel of its own Christian nationals outside the country); during the 1970s, East Malaysia, with 'some religious persecution' under an Islamic government, was expelling some missionaries and making entry very difficult; increasing difficulty was also being experienced, especially for new appointments, in India, where, on top of a generalized post-colonial reaction, high levels of graduate unemployment were a further reason for not admitting foreigners to work there, another argument against admitting British missionaries stemming from Indian reactions to news of racial discrimination experienced by Asians in Britain; work permits were now demanded also for Sarawak, Singapore and West Malaysia, later for Japan also. In other countries, political turbulence was a factor, specifically at this time in Bangladesh, while in South Africa the position was 'variable and unpredictable . . . [with] expulsions . . . often made quite suddenly for obscure reasons', and of course for reasons less obscure.[3]

There was also the proposal, originating among some Africans at the 1972 CWME conference at Bangkok, for a moratorium, in the sense of a pause in the receiving of money and personnel, in order to break a persisting tendency to paternalism and dependency. USPG took this seriously, sending Kingsnorth to a conference in Geneva on the subject in February 1975, and interviewing for the September *Network* the newly appointed Dean of Johannesburg, Desmond Tutu, who explained,

> It is not that the Church in Africa wants to have nothing to do with missionaries and missionary societies. It is an attempt by the Church in Africa to find answers to questions like: 'What *is* the Church in Africa? Does it have an identity? Is it going to be always a dependent Church? Is it likely to develop its own style?' This is a moratorium *for* mission, not *of* mission.

This had been Kingsnorth's message from Geneva, too, though he pointed out that moratorium was irrelevant to one of his areas of greatest concern as a former UMCA missionary, grass-roots Christianity in Africa, which no longer depended on personnel and money from overseas. Meanwhile, however, as Council had been told in December 1974, requests for missionaries from bishops in many areas were growing in volume and often in urgency.

Just as significant for the work of USPG, in consequence, was the report presented to Council in February 1974 by a working party led by John Leake and including Desmond Tutu, at that time still working in London, on 'Calling and Sending'. This pointed out that requests were increasing for short-term appointments. It also observed that, although the number of missionaries being sent was declining, the quality of the people required was critical, since the difficulties they faced were increasing. For missionaries in post for some years, in the same way, new challenges arose.

A case in point was John Dorman, who had first gone from a parish in the English Lake District to work in the Amerindian interior of Guyana in 1957. Accounts of his earlier years in his 15,000 square-mile parish give a somewhat timeless sense of the pioneer missionary in a remote place. 'Old-style missionary?' he asked in his report of 1966,

> Yes, and on his way to an old-style mission task, the planning of a new station among an unevangelised group of Carib Indians. Most people assume that such an assignment is as extinct as the dodo; but in a few days . . . we shall have to start making decisions there, such as confronted missions elsewhere a century or more ago.

The decisions were in relation to his discovery of the 'Alleluia Dance' religion of the Awakaio people, an indigenous Christian tradition which over the next few years he sought to bring into relationship with the wider Church. Dorman's picture of 'incredible beauty of scenery, idyllic days spent in little villages of the gentlest people in the world, nights on sparkling rivers in the moonlight, or in a swaying hammock listening to the hunting jaguar and the baboon', could not last for ever, and by the 1970s there were guerillas and saboteurs to avoid, and the physical and social disruption caused by large hydroelectric schemes and in the 1980s the tragic degradation of the tribal people through the incursions of alluvial mining. Of course, there were some gains, such as local air services, so that the hard days walking over the mountains and some of the long river journeys were over, but his report of 1989 summarized some of the new problems: at the local government centre, Kamarang, 'shops, with discos and jukeboxes round the clock . . . video-shows . . . drink and "girls" . . . brawls, broken-bottle fights and drug-pushing. The large majority one meets there are villagers, formerly courteous and dignified, but now broken and degraded.' Dorman's later years in Guyana saw the creation of the Alan Knight Centre, with USPG missionaries training an Amerindian clergy, while Dorman himself, before finally returning to Britain in 1998 after some 40 years as a missionary, became involved in social surveys of the emerging situation and in encouraging the Church which he and others had built up to engage in action to ameliorate the effects of rapid social change, 'before the irretrievable destruction of yet another hidden people, in the New World that Christian Europe has shared out among its people since Columbus'.[4]

A further example of the new circumstances faced by the Society's missionaries in the post-colonial and Third World is that of Ronald Wynne, an older missionary who, after long service in India and then the West Indies, offered himself for new work in primary evangelism in Africa, which he began in 1970. Botswana in the 1970s was coping with large numbers of refugees from Rhodesia, South Africa, Lesotho,

Namibia, Uganda and Angola. The Hambukushu amongst whom Wynne was sent to work at Etsha in Botswana were typical victims of their time, having fled from the chaos of Angola as the Portuguese colonial army sought to suppress the Angolan Marxist freedom fighters. After painstaking preparatory years which led to Bible translation and an English–Mbukushu dictionary, and relying on the guidance of Hambukushu helpers, Thakusheka and Paghulus, he led some four hundred people in village groups to baptism and the eucharistic life in a deeply inculturated Church. 'I have never come upon a place like Etsha,' commented the Archbishop of Central Africa, 'it is quite bewildering. There you are confronted by a New Testament situation.'[5] It was also, however, a twentieth-century situation, with Wynne insisting on working ecumenically, answerable to the Botswana Council of Churches, in involving refugees from a decolonizing and Cold War situation, and in the collapse of the old tribal ties, with many of the men becoming migrant workers in the South African mines.

The greatly changed circumstances in which Society missionaries worked was often understood and experienced especially acutely by women missionaries. In India in 1969, Joan Barker, working in a tribal area of the Diocese of Chota Nagpur in north India, protested at the survival of the missionary bungalow in its alienating if dilapidated grandeur, herself, until her murder in 1976, choosing to live in a mud hut, innocent of sanitation, on a diet of rice, lentils and vegetables. In a society like that of Pakistan, where modernity was undermined by a conservative Islamization, Christian women had to face a choice between being invisible and being insulted, and for a missionary like Judith Ware who had to travel about the Diocese of Lahore as a Christian education adviser, there was in this sense no choice. Amongst the very poor, however, as she herself noted in the October 1988 *Network*, 'sisterhood may be more important than creed', and this became a watchword for some very creative work among poor women both Muslim and Christian by missionaries such as Ruth Musgrave and Mukti Barton in Bangladesh.

The long-term 'career missionary' continued to be a feature of the Society throughout the period, though, as we have seen, in rapidly dwindling numbers. Society publications from the 1960s and through into the 1990s recorded the retirement or death of numerous missionaries who had worked in overseas Churches, many for 30 or 40, some for 50 or 60 years. Some stayed on, like Robin Lamburn, chaplain to leprosy patients in Tanzania, in 1985 awarded the Albert Schweitzer International Prize after 55 years there. New personnel programmes emerged during the later decades of the century which in some respects replaced this older pattern, so that the Society reported '209 people moved in nine programmes' in 1993. Two of these nine should be mentioned here.

The smallest though not necessarily the least significant was a series of what were called 'South to South' appointments in which the sending and receiving Churches in the south were the principal partners, but in which USPG had an enabling role. An early example was the Society's support in the 1970s for a nurse, Mirl Trim, who went from Trinidad to work in Tanzania, and Venice Guntley from Jamaica serving on the staff of Lusaka Cathedral, Zambia, while in 1989 Henry Fergusson, a layman from Sierra Leone, went to be secretary to the Diocese of Southern Malawi. Fergusson saw his appointment as 'relevant to the catholicity of God's church on earth and in keeping with the missionary history of Sierra Leone'.[6] In 1999 there were three appointments maintaining this relevance, with Arun John and family from north India bringing his experience of interfaith work to South Africa, Solomon and Diana Nkesiga from Uganda working with the unemployed and Aids sufferers, also in South Africa, and Glauce do Nascimento from Brazil working with children, young people and women in Mozambique.

In 1983, recognizing both a new need in some overseas Churches and also new vocational possibilities and limitations in Britain, the Society launched a scheme, 'Skills in Action', later 'Special Skills', to fill short-term needs for qualified people willing to work for one or two years in a voluntary capacity. The initial posts were for teachers, nurses, a college chaplain, an accountant to set up a diocesan system and train a local successor, and a curacy in Yokohama. In the first two years of the scheme 25 people were recruited, and numbers remained relatively high into the 1990s.

USPG made many adjustments during this period, but the huge change in a role as central and traditional as the sending of missionaries marks as little else does the end of one era and the beginning of another.

16

⋯⇌⇐⋯

The Society, the societies and the Church of England

Speaking at the Society's Annual Meeting in 1964, Trapp drew attention to the more than 80 missionary agencies of the Church of England, the officially recognized eleven missionary societies, some 60 diocesan associations, the Church Army and Mothers Union and ten religious communities, all involved in work overseas. He suggested that this multiplicity of agencies did not serve the best interests of the Church, and that what was needed was a drawing together of these wherever possible.

Official dissatisfaction with the diversity of the mission agencies went back far into the nineteenth century, and was renewed at the Lambeth Conference of 1920, but by and large the societies seem to have preferred their separate existences, and even guarded them jealously, the UMCA Council, for example, in 1939, greeting news of a likely overture from SPG with 'alarm and despondency and a fair amount of determined disapproval'.[1] The official Church view was voiced again in 1949 when the Church Assembly's Missionary Council published a Report under the title 'Growing Together', though the Society's *The East and the West* the following April called it a 'timid' document. Lambeth 1958, as we have seen, spurred the eleven societies into co-operating in a successful joint fund-raising appeal to the Church of England for the 'Budget of Opportunity', but generally separateness held firm until the 1960s. Prompted by a consultation organized by the Anglican Executive Officer, Stephen Bayne, in 1963, what was by now the Missionary and Ecumenical Council of the Church Assembly, under the energetic leadership of David Paton, launched the following year 'A Scheme of Co-operation' between the eleven missionary societies and the Council. Its inauguration evoked characteristic responses. John Taylor of CMS welcomed it on

159

the grounds that it would 'eliminate all vestiges of competition . . . avoiding duplication . . . while preserving the independence of the separate voluntary associations'. The Society's Standing Committee affirmed that SPG and UMCA regarded this as 'only a first step towards . . . unification'.[2] Perhaps its most important achievement was the establishment of a regular meeting of the missionary society Secretaries, convened by Paton. Paton asked Trapp to lead off at the first meeting because he had 'been right through the discussion as no other General Secretary'.[3] Trapp suggested 31 areas for co-operation. This gathering over the coming years enabled a good deal of work together, most significantly a further joint appeal under the title 'No small change', and an associated joint visitation of the dioceses in 1971–2.

By the time of the Scheme of Co-operation, however, there were other developments. To Trapp at the 1964 Annual Meeting, 'a modicum of consultation and co-operation in matters peripheral' was not enough. For one thing, the Church overseas was asking for more co-ordination in England. The formation of new provinces had sharpened the issue, the necessity for these to confer for example with both SPG and UMCA in Central Africa, or with CMS, BCMS and UMCA in East Africa, complicated their work and made it harder to develop provincial coherence, while the six UMCA dioceses by now belonged to three separate provinces of the African Church. These overseas Churches, and north India also, were 'pleading for "Church-to-Church" relationships', and the unification of the societies would be a step towards this. There was also pressure for amalgamation from within English parishes, not least among SPG and UMCA supporters. At this particular point, progress was achieved. Almost immediately after taking over as General Secretary of UMCA, Kingsnorth had pointed out in the April 1962 *Central Africa* that the union of 'CMS' and 'UMCA' dioceses in the new Province of East Africa was working well with a valuable interaction of traditions, and making the case for UMCA to share 'a lot of technical staff and facilities with SPG and CMS' in England. Though CMS did not respond, Trapp and Kingsnorth clearly saw eye to eye, and on 18 July 1963 their governing bodies passed resolutions recommending amalgamation. At the same time, their press release announced that they would be ready to begin similar conversations with any other missionary agency of the Church of England. A meeting of the Primates and Metropolitans of the Anglican Communion on the eve of the Anglican Congress in Toronto a few months later welcomed the initiative, bestowing, as Trapp put it, 'a pan-Anglican benediction on our aspirations and our toil'.[4] This toil had its reward when the two societies were amalgamated on 1 January 1965 as the United Society for the Propagation of the Gospel, with Trapp as Secretary and Kingsnorth as Deputy, the inauguration celebrated with a Eucharist in Westminster Abbey beside Livingstone's grave.[5]

The merger no doubt simplified the relationships of the Central and East African Provinces, for the UMCA was still a very significant presence in six dioceses, and SPG also had work in the region; it simplified also the work of parish treasurers in Britain. Administrative costs were reduced and this showed in the accounts for a year or two. What else changed? Interestingly, the cultic language of the UMCA publications for their English constituency, 'the offering of the Holy Sacrifice . . . Missal . . . Pontifical High Mass' and the like did not carry over into *Network* in its new format as the monthly publication of the United Society, and there were indications of UMCA supporters who felt the draught, though it is also the case that much of this tradition in Africa itself, particularly the older disciplinary system of the mission, with its terminology of 'hearers' and 'anointed catechumens', its 'Christians living out of grace' and 'lesser excommunications' had been disappearing in a torrent of social change by the mid-1950s. Evidently, though, some also felt the draught in Africa. The Community of the Sacred Passion let it be known that since the merger they did not feel that they 'belonged' as they had in UMCA, perhaps suggesting their failure to recognize the colonial era ending.[6] This all reflects the fact, though, that the merger was of a Society that drew its strength from its sense of being the Church of England in mission, and a Mission with narrower and more exclusive enthusiasms. It was, nevertheless, a case of two missionary societies broadly in the Catholic tradition, which had managed some co-operation virtually from the inception of UMCA, coming together in response to a changing African reality. None of the deeper fissures in the life of the Church of England were involved, and that reality could therefore be addressed relatively easily.

This last point would also serve to explain the amalgamation which soon followed, bringing the Cambridge Mission to Delhi into the United Society, with a Eucharist to celebrate the event in the USPG chapel on 15 January 1968, for CMD's official publications had always described it as 'in association with SPG', its office had long been in the Tufton Street building and its members saw themselves as 'Liberal Catholic' in ethos and theology. While a very small operation, its distinguished dialogical, educational and medical record, its religious communities and its radical new venture in urban mission, just at this time beginning to take shape, were assets that enriched the United Society, while a Cambridge Committee for Christian Work in Delhi helped to sustain interest and support, and to feed missiological insights back into the Churches in Britain.

A number of other, small bodies were engaged in exploring amalgamation at this time, with varying degrees of success. Somewhat similar to CMD, and with a similar long association with SPG, the Dublin University Mission to Chota Nagpur, after a strikingly brisk and sensible negotiation in which it was recognized that it had 'probably completed the task it first set out to do', entered an amalgamation on similar terms in 1971.[7] The Oxford Mission to Calcutta decided to wind up its London office in 1969, and the Society offered its services to its dwindling administration, though this never amounted to much. The Australian Board of Missions had suggested through Paton in 1965 that the United Society approach both the New Guinea and Melanesian Missions with an eye to amalgamation, but neither agreed to this. In Melanesia, the bishop clearly wished for a merger, as did some missionaries, including one who prayed 'that one day the Melanesian Mission will be taken over by USPG and we shall begin to be put on the C. of E. map', but supporters in England preferred to retain their separate identity.[8] A further initiative by the Society in 1975 led to an invitation to be represented on the committee of the Korean Mission, later the Korean Mission Partnership, but this did not lead to an actual merger.

Despite the success represented in the Society's becoming the 'United Society', a merger with CMS continued to elude those in both Societies who sought it. The question was addressed 'time and time again' as Trapp put it in 1967, with a further major exploration of possibilities in the 1970s, and another in the 1980s, and informal probings in the 1990s, these being almost invariably initiated by the Society.[9] Of course, there were continuous instances of good collaboration, for example when Trapp agreed to represent CMS on a visit to Japan in April 1959 and Warren the Society on another in the November, Trapp welcoming the opportunity 'to stress . . . [their] fellowship in the overseas work of the Church'.[10] There was similar collaboration later over attendance at Partners-in-Mission consultations. During the 1960s, the uneasy relationship between Trapp and John Taylor was the most noticeable feature, and the source of a series of small explosions. Undoubtedly, the Society's role was misrepresented in CMS publications at this time.[11] The next endeavour was a working party of the two societies set up by Shevill during his brief tenure of the Secretaryship. Something of a stranger to the English scene, Shevill suggested to the 1972 Annual Meeting that 'the existence of two great missionary organizations of the same Church in the same country serving the same God and the same world, can surely not be tolerated indefinitely either by the Church abroad or the Church at home'. The Working Party was chaired by Paton and ran from 1973 to 1976. By 1975, Robertson was acknowledging that merger was 'a non-starter from the CMS view-point'. As the final report put it, 'It . . . [was] mutually recognised that there is a stronger yearning for integration within the councils and committees of USPG than is apparent in CMS', and so 'no major insight emerged which could have provided the propulsive power for take-off into structural unity'.[12]

Pressures for significant change were nevertheless now at work. These concerned the relation of the societies to the Church of England. This particular issue had a very long history, going back to proposals in 1869 for Mission Boards for the Convocations.[13] These were established in 1884 and 1889 respectively, being succeeded in 1921 by a Missionary Council of the Church Assembly. Getting a fruitful relation of Church and societies was always the challenge, with a major effort cut short in 1939 by the outbreak of war and resumed in 1946 on the energetic initiative of the Council's General Secretary, McLeod Campbell. At this point, Roberts made it clear that 'the Society would not be a detached and subordinate servant but also an experienced and responsible partner', for what was being sought was what in fact SPG was 'according to its Charter, the authoritative instrument of the Church for the direction of missionary strategy'.[14] The process was undoubtedly then nudged forward by the development of the ACC. Thus, John Taylor of CMS returned from the Limuru meeting persuaded that 'either this would be the last swansong of dying Societies . . . with . . . [their] outdated Victorian image . . . or the start of a new stage . . . Limuru could mark an important potential step forward in the relationship between churches and the corporate agencies.'[15] The problem in this relationship, as Robertson put it in 1975, was that while the societies as a group were in fact operationally an organ of the mission of the Church of England, nevertheless the Synod had only a tenuous way of authorizing them to speak in the name of the Church. Both Church and societies needed 'a *metanoia* leading to a new relationship in which the Societies would receive the commissioning they needed from the Synodical structures, and the Church would recognize them as being the arm it needed in relation to the younger churches'.[16] The working party set up that same year, chaired by Professor Norman Anderson, and with Robertson playing a leading part, brought much of this about, the final report in 1977 leading on to the formation in 1978 of the Partnership for World Mission (PWM). This brought the societies and the Church together into a continuing working relationship, consolidated in the reforms of the Church of England's infrastructure in 1988. Robertson described PWM as offering 'a more coherent and cohesive form of organisation for mission by the Church of England', and one in which the overseas partners of the Church of England would see the societies as 'a living bridgehead with the whole church in Britain'.[17]

The creation of the PWM made possible a first and only English Partners-in-Mission consultation, in 1981. Indeed, it was only pressure from partner Churches overseas and the mission agencies in PWM that stirred the Church of England to have a consultation at all.

Four other strands to this story need to be mentioned. First, there was USPG's work at the level of the diocese in England. Here, the Society's 'yearning for integration' led to the abandonment of separate representation by an Area Secretary when opportunity arose, and to sharing with the diocese in the appointment of a 'Diocesan Officer for Mission' or a 'World Mission Officer'. This happened in the Diocese of Ely (1969), though it did not last here, and also Lichfield (1985) and Worcester (1989). Almost invariably, the Society had to strike out alone in these initiatives, other societies being unwilling to move in this direction. If they had been, the integration of mission and Church in England would have been immeasurably strengthened. The great success of the Lichfield scheme showed what was possible in this regard.

Related to this was the question of USPG's representation in Wales, which arose in 1984. Humphrey Taylor, introducing himself on his appointment as Secretary to the Archbishop, explained that the Society's self-perception was 'as an arm of the Church obliged by Anglican polity in England and Wales to be a voluntary Society, rather than being voluntary on principle'. In his reply, and after conferring with the other Welsh bishops, the Archbishop asked whether there was 'any prospect of joint representation of CMS and USPG in Wales?'. Subsequent correspondence makes clear that CMS was standing by separate representation.[18]

About a third of the older Diocesan Associations, whereby an English diocese sustained interest in and support for a particular overseas diocese, and which the Society had often, if rather reluctantly, helped to administer, were closed down from the 1960s, while about half of those remaining in the 1990s had become associate members of the PWM. Replacing many of them, 'companion links' between a diocese of the Church of England and a diocese elsewhere began to be made from the 1960s, and almost all English dioceses had such a link by the 1990s. Some of these were useful in strengthening bonds of friendship, mutual learning and support, but many others tended to engender quite appalling new versions of old dominances and dependences. In several cases it seemed as if the British Empire was resurrecting. From the mid-1970s, concern was expressed in the Society at this latter tendency, while in 1985 Taylor used a meeting with diocesan bishops to offer USPG's experience and skills in the development of these relationships, an offer subsequently taken up in a variety of ways, and to promote PWM's guidelines for companion relationships, of which the bishops appeared not to have heard. The random way in which these links were being formed continued to concern Taylor, who saw the matter bordering on the chaotic in the later 1980s, despite the best efforts of the PWM.

A development which served to support convergence arose unexpectedly from a decision of the Society in the 1980s to sell its valuable property in Westminster, find more modest accommodation and in the process release a large capital sum which would help counteract the serious shrinkage of income and 'facilitate a move forward into the 21st century in good heart'. In November 1983, Council, endorsing a proposal to move outside the London area, proposed that PWM partners should be consulted on possibly relocating together. The eventual outcome was unexpected and in almost every way remarkably satisfactory. USPG remained in London, which had a number of obvious advantages for such an organization, and moved 'Under One Roof', to give the project its name, to share the headquarters building of CMS in Waterloo, and was followed by the ACC and, immensely significantly, by the office of PWM. HM Queen Elizabeth II opened the newly named Partnership House on 30 October 1987. Interestingly, a proposal on these lines had first circulated in the Society 120 years earlier.[19] Nevertheless, in the perspective of the two societies' long incapacity to merge, this looked to many like a minor miracle. It allowed for a great deal of collaboration between the two societies subsequently. The next, informal explorations for a merger, in 1995–6, threw up the almost predictable mix of goodwill and resentment, and the long-standing fissure in the Church of England held firm, but at least it was now endured under one roof.

In 1946, Max Warren, the Secretary of CMS, had published a pamphlet, 'Iona and Rome', characterizing two strands in the life and mission of the Church of England, the one stressing 'inspired spontaneity working through voluntary associations', the other 'the need for centralized direction . . . to consolidate the ground already gained'. Roberts, from his Catholic perspective always looking for 'a trustful partnership . . . [the] integration of complementary gifts and values . . . [and a] synthesis of visions and functions', did not think this distinction was necessarily for all time.[20] Warren, nevertheless made a point that proved significant for the Society. The 'tension between "Iona" and "Rome"', he suggested functioned in the Anglican Communion 'as a real reserve of power' and provided 'the best hope of her surviving the other more disruptive tensions in her life'. Certainly, disruptive tensions were active as Warren was writing, in connection with the South India scheme of union, and they loomed large again as the century advanced, in the question of the ordination of women from the 1980s and regarding homosexuality and the clergy, the cause of great agitation at the 1998 Lambeth Conference. The Society, as we shall see, pursued in spite of great pressures a policy over South India that undoubtedly in time overcame potent disruptive tensions, though there was a price to pay. This was also the case regarding the ordination of women, when USPG judged it impossible to take a position for or against because it sought to be an agent of partnership between provinces which ordained women and provinces which did not. This might be said to have contributed to that 'reserve of power' in a small way, though it was misrepresented in a leaflet of the 'Traditional Anglican Communion' in 1989. This lost the Society some support, and subsequently the Church Union began to promote a small agency called 'Mission Direct' which appealed to an element among the Society's supporters. Among the governors in the 1990s there was some concern to repair the bridges damaged in that controversy, which would certainly have vindicated Warren's suggestion. The appointment in 1999 of Michael Houghton, a former missionary of the Society, tutor at the College of the Ascension and Council member, as a Provincial Episcopal Visitor, had raised hopes in this regard, only to be deferred by his tragic death. Regarding the controversy over homosexuality and the clergy, an attempt was made prior to Lambeth 1998 by one of the most exercised episcopal protagonists to recruit the Society's staff and their CMS colleagues in the Centre for Anglican Communion Studies at Selly Oak into the debate, but they rejected this.[21] In this case the reason was that there were other issues of much greater missionary importance to most of the staff and students at Selly Oak. By declining to major on the topic, nevertheless, the Centre was in a position to promote valuable occasional consideration of it in which widely divergent views were explored in a climate of mutual respect.

If the Society's Catholic instinct, its 'yearning for integration', had periodically during this half-century seemed to set it in contestation with CMS, though not on this last issue, the Partnership for World Mission and its visible expression in the new cohabitation in Partnership House provided a valuable interim fulfilment of that yearning. At the same time, there was much to suggest that the circumstances which forced USPG to operate as a voluntary society in Britain and Ireland were not likely to change quickly, while Warren's perception of 'the Missionary Societies of the Church . . . [as] the true safeguard and citadel of the spirit of "Iona"' prompts the suggestion that the Society underestimated a creativity which it, along with CMS, continued to exercise.

17

✦⟺○⟺✦

The College of the Ascension

The College of the Ascension during the earlier years of this period continued in its role of training women missionaries, with an additional handful of women from Africa and Asia coming for courses and, from the 1950s, a handful of men candidates taking advantage of the Selly Oak resources, under the direction of a male Warden but not living in the College. A few men continued to go to Kelham and Lee Abbey, most to St Augustine's College, Canterbury, the Society continuing to have a substantial interest there until the mid-1960s.

By then the College of the Ascension had gone through the first of a series of developments reflecting changing circumstances and policy and which set it on course for an increasingly pivotal role in the work of the Society. Change was signalled by a correspondence initiated by Archbishop Clayton of Cape Town in 1950, who wrote to Roberts that the Society's newer women missionaries did not seem to have the sense of vocation of earlier generations and seemed less willing to adapt to 'levels of simplicity proper to a missionary sent to a poor and primitive people'. Roberts solicited the staff's views and stood up for the College. The Principal, Laura Jackson, was committed to promoting 'Franciscan standards of living', but explained that many candidates now came from non-Christian homes, their grasp of 'basic Christian virtues' less secure. In the words of the Warden, P. N. F. Young, inability to 'stick it out' seemed to be 'a real trend'.[1] The sense of an increasingly inappropriate training was then reflected in a routine inspection report in May 1963. The students were 'intense', relying on a 'terribly stodgy' fiction library, the only hobby evident 'some polite embroidery in the common-room after supper'. Much more seriously, the order and discipline of the College, against which 'no word of criticism or revolt' was ever heard, imposed 'a limitation of their personal decisiveness'. This criticism led Trapp to institute a review by a friend of the Society, Susanna Hodson. Published in March 1964, this confirmed the need for change. There were social factors, particularly earlier marriage in Britain reducing the number of younger women offering for long-term mission service, while co-education was becoming the rule rather than the exception. In addition, for many of the increasing number of 'nationals', principally men, coming to Britain for further training, the ecumenical climate of Selly Oak would be beneficial, while their presence would enrich the College as a place of missionary preparation. The changed situation overseas, 'the awakening to self-conscious nationhood of the countries of the "younger" churches', called for a more deliberate formation of mission candidates in 'humility [and] a willingness to be identified with the hopes and aspirations of those among whom they live'. The report recommended that the College become co-educational, with a Priest-Principal, though with a woman staff member also, 'responsible for the ordered decencies of life'.

The College in its new, mixed form, opened in Autumn 1965, with Leonard Schiff, a former missionary, as principal. The concern to sensitize mission candidates to the 'hopes and aspirations' of the new nations was evident in his appointment, for while a missionary he had been a member of the Indian National Congress during the final years of the freedom struggle in India. Among the mission candidates were three married couples with young children. Also admitted were two German Lutheran mission trainees and an African Presbyterian, pointing forward to what were to become two striking features of the College in the later decades of the century, its ecumenical and international membership.

The climate of change raised hopes that CMS, with plans to move their missionary preparation to Selly Oak, might support the idea of a single Anglican missionary college and Council in 1968 went so far as to propose that if necessary, to realize this, 'the College of the Ascension should become a CMS institution to which the USPG would be entitled to send missionary candidates for training'.[2] CMS regretted that the existing College building would not be suitable for their needs, though eventual joint training was tentatively proposed.

This latter, joint training, came a good deal nearer with the decision that same year to provide a new central building at Selly Oak, thanks to Quaker and Cadbury munificence, with provision for a Centre for Training in Christian Mission, towards the cost of which USPG and other interested mission agencies contributed. CMS came in on this joint endeavour on moving its training to its own new college, Crowther Hall. Shared educational facilities at Selly Oak had always been important, but were now greatly enhanced, with increasing opportunities for members of the mission colleges to study together in a series of centres and departments. As the decades passed, these increasingly reflected the post-colonial world, relating to the study of the world religions, new religious movements and the Christian partnership of black and white people in Britain, with other centres and courses intended to meet the needs of increasing numbers of students coming from non-Western Churches – development, cross-cultural communication, English language, church education and management, Third World theologies, women's studies and conflict resolution. At the heart of this from 1973 was the Centre for Training in Christian Mission. This was led by a Dean of Mission, initially David Lyon of the Church of Scotland, previously a missionary in India, the Centre also sharing with Birmingham University its distinguished Professors of Mission. From 1976 it was known as the Department of Mission, and then in the 1990s as the School of Mission and World Christianity. The increasing participation of members of non-Western Churches was initially met with a determination on the part of the Dean of Mission in the 1970s, Dr Ian Fraser, to resist the demand for conventional academic qualifications, concerned that this might alienate students from the poor Churches from which they came. Under a new Dean of Mission, however, Dr Marcella Hoesl, a Roman Catholic and a Maryknoll Missioner, the growing need of non-Western Churches for academically qualified personnel was recognized. This led to a developing relationship with Birmingham University from the 1980s and an expansion of opportunities for postgraduate study and research, with, by 1995, most of the University Theology Department's research being done at Selly Oak in what had become a centre of exceptional quality.

The entire Selly Oak interaction, as it developed from the 1960s, with several hundred men and women of never less than 60 nationalities, and ecumenical in both the ecclesiastical and the wider sense, living and studying together, created an ideal context for the development of USPG's college.

Developments within the College had followed from the new beginning of 1965. The principal in 1970, Frank Weston, welcomed Bishop John Sadiq of the CNI who combined a tutorial with a missionary role in Britain at large. The immediate successor to Sadiq was the Roman Catholic scholar, Adrian Hastings, a part-time tutor at the College while working on a study of marriage in Africa for Lambeth 1978. From 1986, staff from non-Western Churches were an invariable feature of the College. Fellowships further enriched its work, the early ones in the 1980s being largely provided *ad hoc* to assist senior people needing a temporary respite from, for example, Nicaragua, Sri Lanka and South Africa, but bringing experience of great value into the College's life, while a regular annual fellowship was instituted from 1994.

A further development originated in 1968, just a year after the closure of the short-lived Central College of the Anglican Communion at St Augustine's, Canterbury. Bishop Dean, the Anglican Executive Officer, raised with Trapp the idea that the College of the Ascension might be developed into 'a kind of Central College', utilizing the St Augustine's endowments and other trust funds. A few months later, Trapp took this up with Archbishop Michael Ramsey and Dean's successor, John Howe. Trapp drew attention to the increasing variety of the College community, not least with increasing numbers coming from overseas dioceses, and to the formation of the Centre for Training in Christian Mission, all of which, he suggested, might well 'be of interest . . . throughout the Anglican Communion'. Bishop Howe agreed.[3] Though largely lacking participants from the Anglican Churches of the USA, Canada, Australia and New Zealand, major participants at Canterbury, this did gradually come about thereafter. 1972 was something of a landmark, with a first enquiry from the Bishop of Grahamstown regarding 'opportunities for . . . some of our potential leaders to have the opportunity to live, preferably for at least a year outside the claustrophobic atmosphere of our country'. In 1976, this became one of the CPSA's major Partners-in-Mission priorities, and the first eight of these potential leaders, all priests, seven of them black, and not only from Grahamstown but more widely from the province, arrived in Britain in September 1978.[4] A large number from South Africa came to the College as bursars over the next two decades. Also in 1972, Shevill told the Bishop of Rangoon that, though he realized that the oppressed Church in Burma was not likely to be able to make immediate use of the facility, Sabah and other dioceses were making use of the College for a 'period of orientation and training' for prospective bishops.[5] In fact, the Province of Burma did get two very creative lay workers, Wilfred Aung La Tun and Edward Saw Marks, to the College later. Also in 1972, in the light of these new developments, the Society appointed an Overseas Students Secretary, Gillian Court. With such encouragements, a new block of flats at the College was dedicated by the Archbishop in October 1974, with generous funding provided by the Swedish Lutheran Church, whose missionary candidates were now regular users of the College.

The changing nature of the College's usefulness was not always immediately recognized. Thus, the marked decline in missionary candidates led the 1976 Council to question the College's future. This decline persisted through the 1980s, with occasional terms in which there were no new missionary trainees. Fresh factors, however, were making the College if anything increasingly significant, certainly continuingly relevant to much of the Anglican Communion. The number of students being sent from overseas was increasing, with a Bursaries Programme established in 1979 as 'a way of helping partner churches to strengthen their own resources by providing various types of training . . . for their members', some 24 bursars being funded by the Society in 1977, 55 by 1981.[6] Approximately a third of the students at the College throughout the 1980s and 1990s were Society Bursars, including a number of spouses coming usually for part of the year, with a succession of holders of the residual St Augustine's scholarships also. These Bursars, John Davies suggested to the June 1977 Council, 'probably . . . [represented] the most important contribution which USPG (and Britain as a whole) . . . [could] now make to the world-church'.

The College community was increasingly diverse, some 45 students of never less than twenty nationalities by the 1980s, Roman Catholic, Oriental, Orthodox and Reformed, as well as Anglican, and with the occasional Hindu or Muslim also, all living, worshipping and studying together, and bringing with them the joys and sorrows of their home situations and a rich cultural variety which was encouraged not least liturgically, so that life in the College was an educational event in itself for all who entered it. 'Every day,' it was observed, 'brought some new story or insight from the world Church', and in a sense all the College members were educating each other.[7] This had a particular significance for missionary candidates, USPG's own and others from Churches, chiefly Lutheran, who were preparing for work outside Europe, for Council in May 1970 had recognized, in discussing 'A Missionary in the 1970s', the 'necessity of training men and women for a situation of weakness and not of strength', what the Dean of Mission later called 'a "new era" of missionary attitudes', for which their minority situation in such a mixed community was an ideal preparation.[8] The experience was, of course, no less significant to participants from the Third World, often from still discrete societies and communities. Others from within the Society also started coming to the College, groups preparing for the Experience Exchange Programme and for Root Groups, and also new Area Secretaries on appointment.

Supremely perhaps in the 1980s, the travail of the Church in South Africa at a time of intensifying struggle there, reinforced by the concerns of other students from Southern Africa, from Angola, Botswana, Mozambique, Swaziland, Zambia and Zimbabwe, and a regular group recruited by the Namibian liberation movement, SWAPO, meant that the issues and the joys and sorrows associated with that situation were often uppermost in the community's mind and prayers. Other situations also, however, loomed large from time to time, international and interreligious conflict in South and East Asia, and famine in other parts of Africa, for example. There was also the richness of the cultural exchange, with its periodic and salutary misunderstandings, including those relating to gender, all of which added to the educational value of College community life. Speaking at the November 1982 meeting of the Board of Governors on behalf of the Common Room, the Ven. David Banda of Malawi thanked the Society for the opportunity not of coming to Britain but of coming to the College of the Ascension and sharing in the experience of USPG's 'bringing the universe together at one point'.[9]

A further development in the 1980s arose from an observation of the principal, Daniel O'Connor, that the Church of England was missing the experience to which Banda had alluded and the opportunity to learn from world Christianity as represented at Selly Oak. This was addressed temporarily by a new modular programme which attracted short-term participants from the British Churches, but in a longer perspective through a strategic review, culminating in the September 1988 Council's recognition that the College's development was 'a key plank' in USPG's forward strategic thinking, both in this regard and others, including development with CMS of some sort of study centre for the Anglican Communion. This led to a decision to add a new educational wing to the College buildings, with appropriate additional staff, the costs to be underwritten by the sale of the Westminster premises, but to be recovered by an appeal. Though the latter failed, the new wing was completed and dedicated by John Habgood, Archbishop of York, on 7 November 1991.

Under Andrew Wingate, principal from 1990, a more extensive programme of short courses was initiated for individuals and groups from British Churches, supported by grants from the General Synod and also, as a joint endeavour with the CMS, the establishment of a Centre for Anglican Communion Studies. Of course, in a wider sense, as Humphrey Taylor indicated, this latter was work the Society was 'already doing with Anglicans who . . . [came] to Selly Oak', but here the aim was more focused, 'to study aspects of contemporary Anglicanism', and explicitly, in the words of the initial curriculum, 'to explore *Anglicanism as a living tradition*'.[10] Scholarships were established by the two Societies and with some of the St Augustine's endowments. The Centre was opened on 1 December 1992 by a former Principal of Crowther Hall, Simon Barrington-Ward, Bishop of Coventry, with an inaugural speech by Kenneth Cragg, the last Principal of St Augustine's. The programme was the responsibility jointly of the Principals of Crowther Hall and the College, with Bishop A. C. Dumper, formerly a Society missionary in

Singapore, as Honorary Tutor. By 1997 the course, now called 'Anglicans, Ecumenism and Mission', was an accredited element of the MA in Mission Studies and a recognized sphere for doctoral research in Birmingham University, and was enrolling some 24 students annually from around the Anglican Communion. In that year also, the Centre ran two short courses for British and Irish bishops in preparation for the 1998 Lambeth Conference. Two other developments included a working relationship with a similar centre being set up at Virginia Seminary, with a similar prospect of others in Africa and Asia under consideration, and the publication to coincide with Lambeth 1998, with a Foreword by Archbishop Carey, of *Anglicanism: A Global Communion*, essays related to the contextualization of Anglicanism.

Another development of the 1990s reflected both the ecumenical aspiration of the current interchurch process, and also the recognition that in economic terms there was by then one mission college too many in the Selly Oak federation. This was felt most strongly by the Methodist Church, whose Kingsmead College was closed in 1993, with an initiative for a united college taken more or less simultaneously by Wingate and the Principal of Kingsmead, the Trinidadian theologian, George Mulrain. With the agreement of Council and the Conference of the Methodist Church, the United College of the Ascension was inaugurated on 1st October 1996. The presence on this occasion of the Archbishop of Canterbury, George Carey, and the President of the Methodist Conference, Nigel Collinson, underlined the significance of the occasion as their two Churches continued, in many respects not very successfully, to search for common ground, the Archbishop expressing the hope that 'our two Churches will catch up some day'. In 1999, the third remaining mission college, St Andrew's Hall, which had been supported by the Baptists, the URC and the CWM, became a solely Baptist institution alongside Crowther Hall and the United College of the Ascension. In the latter, commitment at the level of day-to-day life and worship made for a positive ecumenical expression, while the union brought welcome funds to build new staff houses, and an enhanced staff. The federal structures, however, proved increasingly unsustainable during the 1990s, and by 1999 the mission agencies remaining at Selly Oak were searching for new ways to continue their collaboration. They were challenged by the suggestion of the Professor of Mission, Werner Ustorf, that the phase of training that Selly Oak had so significantly offered for Third World Churches was coming to an end, and by his vision, in 'the era of an interlinked and transforming World Christianity' of 'a centre for high-profile research, teaching and learning in . . . [the fields of] de-occidentalization and modernity, generating a special knowledge'.[11]

18

⋯≈◯⋐⋯

Ecumenism, theology and Third World theologies

A series of theological issues occupied the Society during the period, none more persistently in the early years than those around how to relate to the Church of South India, inaugurated on 27 September 1947, a month after Indian independence. The Society provided the first Moderator in Michael Hollis, one of its former missionaries at Nazareth in Tirunelveli, Bishop of Madras from 1941 and one of the Anglican negotiators. The inauguration was reported in the December *Overseas News* by Cordelia Hollis. She described the preliminary retreat, conducted by another Society missionary, Herbert Pakenham-Walsh, another earlier negotiator, who had worked in India for more than 50 years, originally with the Dublin University Mission, later becoming Bishop of Assam. She then gave an account of the inauguration itself. 'The *Te Deum* can never have been sung with a greater sense of thankfulness for what God has done.' The majority of Society missionaries, 23 of them, identified fully with the CSI, but a minority of nine either left or functioned by agreement in a semi-detached mode.

Although in one sense the debate was over at that point, entombed so far as the Society was concerned in 25 heavy and, Trapp later warned, 'highly . . . inflammatory' files, in another it had 26 years to run.[1] The continuing debate was over the extent to which the Church of England, and other Churches of the Anglican Communion, could be in communion with a Church which had embraced the historic episcopate but included from its inauguration a number of ministers not episcopally ordained. The problem, indeed, was not SPG's but the Church's. The Society, in the context of a continuing deep division in the Church of England, and indeed among its own supporters, chose to 'pronounce no judgement . . . and await the judgement of the Church of England'.[2] It was a situation such as that envisaged by Max Warren the previous year in his 'Iona and Rome' paper as an important and creative opportunity for a voluntary society, though how creative the Society was is less easy to determine. It was certainly required to walk a razor's edge. Whenever Provost Noel Hopkins of Wakefield, the long-experienced editor of the *Quarterly Intercession Paper*, invited the Society's supporters to pray for the CSI, he knew he would get protesting letters.[3] Archbishop Fisher had, nevertheless, given the process a constructive launch. The Charter did not allow SPG to use its General Fund to support dioceses not part of the Anglican Communion. The Archbishop proposed the establishment of a Special Fund to enable those who wished to give continued support to the Church in South India. Roberts implemented this, and was remembered at his death in 1957 for his eirenic handling of the problem and for achieving, for example, virtual unanimity in moving the Standing Committee to easier relations with the CSI in 1955. This latter position was based on the fact that the Church of England by then accorded the status of 'true bishops, priests and deacons in the Church of God' to those who had been consecrated or ordained in the CSI since its inauguration in 1947. SPG nevertheless had to endure continuing mis-understanding and to absorb continuing hostility. Trapp, for example, was told, by some English supporters that the Society's transfer of properties to the CSI following the revision of the Charter in 1956 was 'a . . . [concession] to schism', encouraging a 'break-away from the Catholic Church'. At the same time, he was surprised on a visit to South India in early 1960 to discover that people like Hollis, the Moderator, felt that SPG had 'delivered a body blow' to the Church at its inception. This was also the view of a later Bishop of Madras, Lesslie Newbigin, in his autobiography, who nevertheless in a letter quoted in *Overseas News* in January 1957 appealed to the Society to increase both its Special Fund and the supply of missionaries representing its 'tradition of churchman-ship'. Regarding this latter point, Trapp, in answer to a query from Archbishop Ramsey in 1963, explained that five South Indian dioceses were currently asking SPG for priests, and he assumed that this was a request for 'a "Catholic" contribution . . . for they know the sort of person the Society is likely to recruit'. Ramsey was 'glad that SPG . . . [was] still giving so much service to CSI'.[4] As the Church of England gradually shed its objections, the Society's support for the CSI broadened, and when Council in December 1973 agreed to follow Archbishop Ramsey's advice to make its financial support a charge on the General Fund, 'the decision was greeted with thankfulness and joy'. Ramsey, writing to Robertson after the meeting, called it 'a happy ending to a long and troubled story'.[5]

A particular problem arose in the case of the Archdeaconry of Nandyal in the Diocese of Dornakal. While the diocese as a whole under the ecumenically committed Bishop Azariah had voted to participate in the CSI, the extensive archdeaconry, previously known as the SPG Telugu Mission, made up almost entirely of people from the most oppressed levels of Indian society, for whom baptism had been a profound liberation, stood aside and declared themselves to be 'The Orthodox SPG Telugu Union', or, in the Society's terminology, 'Continuing Anglicans'. Undoubtedly, the Society's acquiescence in the Church of England's judgement in 1947 was interpreted in Nandyal as the Society's own judgement on the union plan, and as such the final word. This unquestioning dependence on the supposed views of their original liberators was reinforced by other, decidedly non-theological factors, to do with property and land, so important, as their bishop later explained, to 'the hitherto oppressed and deprived'. Long-standing rivalries between groups and individuals also came into play. An episcopal observer complained to Roberts in 1947 of an 'unscrupulous and violent campaign that is being carried out in the name of SPG'.[6] In consequence, Nandyal stayed on in the Anglican Communion, initially as an archdeaconry and, from 1963, as a diocese of the Church of India, Pakistan, Burma and Ceylon. In 1970, however, it became a diocese of the CNI, the North India Plan of Union being acceptable to the Anglican Communion from its inauguration, and at last in July 1975 entered the CSI, with firmly 'Catholic' liturgical features and adherence to the CIPBC Prayer Book, which often baffled some of the CSI's more 'Protestant' members. It is clear that throughout this long process the Church in Nandyal was seen by some Society supporters in England as a principled and heroic minority, 'the loyal Anglican congregations', 'steadfast Anglicans'. The Society stood by it, Roberts and a delegation visiting in 1952, Council sending greetings and good wishes on the entry into CSI and continuing generous funding until 1984.

Such doctrinal and theological issues as were relevant in this sequence were, or were thought to be, those of 'the mother Society'.[7] The Nandyal Church nevertheless did, in the 1980s, witness a remarkable cultural renaissance, a flowering in congregations all over the diocese of Telugu lyrics, under the inspiration of Bishop Devapriam. A popular theological vitality, in other words, found expression alongside a deep and dependent concern for doctrinal orthodoxy.

At about this time, the Society's long, persevering and often painful witness to the threefold ministry and the historic episcopate found corroboration in the WCC agreements on ministry embodied in the 'Lima text' of 1982.

After the South Indian union, ecumenical issues did not have the same inflammatory quality in the Society. This was partly because the ecumenical climate improved markedly with Vatican II, and with Lambeth 1958 urging Anglicans into union negotiation. A front-page feature by Jonathan Graham CR in the August 1960 *Overseas News* commemorating the Edinburgh 1910 World Missionary Conference called for the quest for unity to be given absolute priority. Also, of course, in the post-colonial context, church life and mission were becoming much more clearly matters of local decision. Reports throughout the 1960s in particular were full of accounts of high levels of local co-operation with both Roman Catholic and Protestant Churches in many parts of Africa and South Asia in particular.

⋅→≡◎⊜≂⋅

The question of the theology of mission had exercised individuals and groups in the Society in earlier periods, for example in *Essays Catholic and Missionary* of 1928. In 1948, E. R. Morgan and Roger Lloyd edited a further collection, *The Mission of the Anglican Communion*. Most of the contributors, including five Asian and African, were connected with the Society. Starting with an explication of a church-centred theology of mission, that of a Louvain Jesuit, Pierre Charles, the main part of the book launches into the partnership theme and looks at aspects of 'the need of "give and take" in the life of the Body', the theme which was to recur so persistently in the Society during this period.

Kingdom-centred reflection on mission, however, inevitably advanced during such turbulent years, and most of the issues were aired and many of the leading books and reports reviewed in *Overseas News* and *Network*. Shevill's brief Secretaryship was the occasion of a formal consideration of some of the issues by the Society in the early 1970s. Shevill, a political conservative, was uneasy with what he felt was the radical stance of USPG on a wide range of issues, a view shared by a good number of letter writers to *Network*, and he wanted what he called in his autobiography 'a clarification of the Gospel we were propagating'. Uncomfortable also with the trend of thought in the WCC, particularly as enunciated at the 1968 Uppsala Assembly, where 'humanization in Christ' seemed to be superseding a more traditional understanding of salvation, he invited the June 1972 Council to approve the conservative Lutheran riposte to Uppsala, the 'Frankfurt Declaration', which he actually read out to the Council. Council declared that this 'did not represent the Society's position', and set up a working party consisting of George Braund, Lorna Kendall, Kenneth Sansbury, Douglas Webster and Frank Weston. In December, Council declared the working party's theology of mission too radical, and Bishop Sansbury was invited to try on his own. His paper, 'The Meaning of Mission', presented to the June 1974 Council, dealt with five main issues. First, it declared, 'We make our own the Affirmation on Salvation Today', an allusion to the liberation theme which had emerged as the dominant motif in ecumenical thought on mission at the 1973 CWME meeting at Bangkok, a refinement of but no declension from the position of Uppsala. Second, a stress on the doctrine of the incarnation, 'God has entered into our human condition in its greatness and its misery to restore us to himself'. Third, continuing the kingdom focus, 'there can be no clouding of the goal of justice and freedom and human dignity: on that USPG cannot be neutral'. Fourth, relating the Church to this, 'the Church is called to be the prototype of the new humanity'. Fifth, 'the Spirit of God has indeed been active in the religious traditions of other lands'. Sansbury's paper was well received by Council. By then Shevill had departed, but his discomfort had elicited a useful formulation of a contemporary theology of mission. Discussing the public perception of the Society with Robertson on his arrival as successor to Shevill, Kingsnorth said that he thought that *Network*, despite the views of Shevill and many readers, was balanced but had 'a Gospel edge'. At a time of strong conflict of opinion in the Church, he suggested, USPG was inevitably 'caught in the crossfire . . . for example in reactions to our posters, to *Network*, to our association with the BCC', but the staff were convinced that the Society could not contract out of such debate.[8]

A third area of interest for the Society which emerged in the later decades concerned the new 'Third World theologies' then emerging. Of course, attempts to express the Gospel in different cultural contexts had always happened, and many USPG missionaries had encouraged this, not least in the first half of the twentieth century. Theologies of the Third World, however, were a new development beginning in the 1970s, rooting the Gospel in the realities of social and economic marginalization and in the struggles of the marginalized for freedom and dignity. In a sense, much of the earlier artwork encouraged and sponsored by the Society and its missionaries was related to this development in that it gave a voice to the voiceless. The very act of installing carved wooden panels by Job Kekana of St Faith's Mission, Rusape, Southern Rhodesia, on the pulpit of Johannesburg Cathedral in 1947 had something of this character. On the other hand, indications of what was becoming of Cyrene in the references in the Autumn 1976 *Network* to 'the growing market for African art' and to tourists looking for 'mementoes of genuine

African workmanship' pointed in a different direction. It was with the knowledge of God among the many victims of the globalized market that Third World theology was concerned. The term thus comprehended not merely the poor in the South and their search for liberation, but black people in Europe and the USA, tribal peoples including those in developed societies such as Japan, women almost everywhere and those who were prepared to identify with these groups. It was this new, sharper definition which provoked Shevill, in his autobiography, alongside expressions of admiration for Portuguese colonial rule in Mozambique, to describe Black Theology as 'one of the bi-products of African violence in the religious field'. This was a very different interpretation from that which Andrew Walls shared with the 1974 Staff Conference, when he said, 'the only theology worth bothering about now is Third World Theology'. Kingsnorth, also, in the 1975 Report was supportive, 'Many cosy Christians just do not want to hear the voice of the young churches . . . they sound strident, they sound radical; they speak of justice and human rights more than, say, sacraments and family life.' They were, however, 'our partners in mission'. While he saw Black and Liberation Theologies as 'temporary stops on the way to a truly Catholic theology', they were necessary developments, 'the break-up of that tight, compact, all-answers-within theology of a few generations ago – the theology we taught, for example, in Central Africa in a comprehensive catechism with 270 questions and answers'.

USPG sought periodically to share the new insights of Third World Christians through its publications, though these tended to be refracted through a Western lens, in, for example, a compendium of liturgical resources, *Let All the World . . .* of 1990, and an impressive study resource published jointly with CMS and the Methodist Church, *The Christ we Share*, in 1999.

The Society's most significant involvement in and contribution to this development, and avoiding much of that refraction, was at Selly Oak. At the May 1989 meeting of the Board of Governors of the College, a student representative, Charles Thomas, Asian but working in Africa, told the Board that he had only discovered Third World theologies on coming to Selly Oak. The theological teaching he had encountered in both India and Zambia had been no different from that generally available in Western academic institutions and Churches. A theology taking as its starting point the poverty, culture and religious pluralism of the Third World, however, was something new to him. In this Selly Oak was at that time developing a new strength. A Lectureship in Third World Theologies had been established in 1984, initially by the CWM, but subsequently supported by USPG and all the sponsoring mission agencies, the first lecturer being a Roman Catholic bishop, Patrick Kalilombe of Malawi. In 1986, the Society appointed R. S. Sugirtharajah, a Sri Lankan Methodist, at that time teaching the New Testament at Serampore, as a Tutor at the College, and in 1989 he succeeded Kalilombe as Lecturer, subsequently Senior Lecturer in Third World Theologies. His teaching, starting while he was college tutor, proved very influential, introduced many Selly Oak students to this striking development in Christianity and also attracted substantial numbers of research students. Sugirtharajah also developed a wider ministry, publishing, in addition to his own work in Asian biblical hermeneutics, a series of collections of essays by Third World biblical scholars, most of these collections appearing initially from the publishing house of the Catholic Missionary Society of America, and with titles such as *Voices from the Margin* (1991), *Asian Faces of Jesus* (1993), *The Post-Colonial Bible* (1998) and the apochal *Dictionary of Third World Theologies* (2000). In his Introduction to the first of these, he pointed out that a *Dictionary of Biblical Interpretation* published in London the previous year had not carried a single entry by an Asian, Latin American or black scholar. His collections have included contributions from biblical scholars, both women and men, and 'people's readings' from, to mention only the two editions of *Voices from the Margin*, Argentina, Brazil, Cameroun, China, Costa Rica, Hong Kong, India, Indonesia, Japan, Malawi, Malaysia, Nicaragua, Pakistan, the Philippines, the Solomon Islands, South Africa, South Korea, Sri Lanka, Thailand, Trinidad and Tobago, and Zimbabwe, and a Palestinian in Israel and black and Native American scholars in the USA. These publications have served to give Third World scholars a platform for their adventurous and mould-breaking biblical explorations, to share more popular rereadings of Scripture and to challenge the universalizing presuppositions of biblical scholarship in the West. Though the Society's role was nothing more than to provide something of an initial launching pad and some funding to this development, such an enabling role was at this stage in mission history precisely one of the more useful tasks available to a missionary society.

19

⤙❖⤚

Religions and dialogue

One of the earliest effects of the Church Assembly report of 1949, 'Growing Together', was the formation of the Church Assembly Muslim Council, with Kenneth Cragg as its Secretary. *Overseas News* in May 1950 welcomed this development. While it was necessary to learn from past mistakes, through centres of Islamic studies such as the Henry Martyn Institute in India, for which SPG had been providing funds and a member of staff from its inception in the 1930s, the writer judged that Muslims were 'prepared to listen to the message of the Redeemer' because Jesus Christ was 'the one bridge by which they can cross over the abyss created by the impact of Westernization on the East'.

Other responses to that impact, however, soon began to appear. In the 1958 Report, Trapp observed that missionaries were reporting an 'awakening of the ancient religions'. Two years later, SPG's Teachers' Conference turned, with the help of Cragg and its own missionary, George Appleton, to 'the challenge of resurgent religions', while the Association of Missionary Candidates' conference the same year was on 'Christ and the World's Religions'. The February 1960 *Overseas News* sought to put these in context, quoting Hendrik Kraemer,

> For the first time since Constantine's victory of A.D. 312 . . . the Christian Church is heading towards a real and spiritual encounter with the great non-Christian religions – because the younger Churches live among them and also because the interdependence of the whole world forces the fact of their existence upon us and challenges the Church to manifest in new terms its own spiritual and intellectual integrity.

181

The Society returned to the issue in the following year's Teachers' Conference, this time on 'The Challenge of Islam', and in 1962 carried a full front-page review by a staff member, Hans Ollman, of David Brown's *The Way of the Prophet*. Reports of an Islamic resurgence occur in numerous missionary reports in the 1950s and early 1960s from Pakistan, Singapore, Malaysia, Borneo and East, Central, West and South Africa. The causes of the resurgence of Islam and other world religions and their politicization no doubt owed much to colonialism and to the Christian missionary movement of the previous two centuries, but, in addition, in what was observable from the 1950s on, religion was now functioning as a source of identity for the new nations. Nevertheless, at that time the forces of modernity looked set to prevail. In the 1960s the secularizing process seemed to many Christian observers (Cragg, with his deep knowledge of Islam, was an exception) to be irresistible, so that Harvey Cox identified versions of 'The Secular City' in every continent, and Bishop Ah Mya told the Society that he was studying Cox's book of that title (and John Robinson's *Honest to God*) with the other denominational leaders in Buddhist Burma. The resistance that religious identity provided against alien, Western and Westernizing forces was in this perspective underestimated, and probably represents a further phase of this resurgence. Nothing illustrated this more graphically than the Iranian Revolution of 1979, 'the *eighth* major battle that . . . Muslim . . . [Iran] had embarked on [since 1872] to defend its sovereignty against mercantile and military exploiters from the West'.[1] This became a powerful source of inspiration to the impoverished majority of Muslims in many other countries, to the extent that, with the end of the Cold War in 1989, Samuel Huntington of Harvard, but also associated with the State Department of the USA, proposed in a landmark article in the journal *Foreign Affairs* in 1993 that there were indications of a new 'clash of civilizations' on the basis of religion.

The relationship with people of other faiths became a major issue for the Churches worldwide from the 1950s, with, initially, post-colonial attitudes of conciliation and dialogue reflected in the discussions at Lambeth 1958, in the documents of Vatican II and in the WCC. A sense of the increasing dangers surrounding the issue was reflected in Pope John Paul II's invitation to religious leaders of many of the major communities to observe the World Day of Prayer for Peace at Assisi in October 1986, and in the WCC's transferring and elevating the dialogue question to an 'Office of Inter-Religious Relations' at the very core of the structure of the Council in 1991. In the same year, and indicative of how immigration had changed the religious make-up of the population in Britain, as it had across Europe, the Church of England's House of

Bishops was asking itself a question it had never asked before, how bishops could promote good interfaith relations in their dioceses.

From that 1950 observation in *Overseas News*, the Society sought to respond to these new issues, although, in fact, in over half of the overseas dioceses with which it was associated, according to the 1968 Report, they were not new, with the majority population adherents of other faiths, so that for the local Christians and many of the missionaries a daily encounter, evangelism and dialogue had always been a part of life. In the Seychelles and Mauritius, for example, the Church was neighbour to an indigenous religion, and to Chinese and Indian religions brought by indentured labourers and others, so that mission there had always had a dialogical dimension. In UMCA areas, likewise, although scholarly interest in African traditional religion was rare, missionaries like Godfrey Dale (UMCA 1899–1925) took a serious and scholarly interest in Islam.

New attitudes, nevertheless, were being called for widely. In Zanzibar, 'the shrine and fountainhead of our Holy Faith in East Africa', there was concern in 1950 that, with the cathedral bookshop closing and the printing press out of date, a very small staff was left to cope with 'Muslims highly educated from the secular point of view'. When the new bishop arrived at Kilwa Masoko in 1952, this chief Islamic centre in the diocese was described as 'stagnating under the shadow of Islam'. It was 'a prophetic note for a new episcopate that the first offering of the Holy Sacrifice' should be there and, perhaps the time had come 'to raise the evangelists' banner once again among our teeming thousands of Muslims'.[2] The bishop himself, however, in the UMCA *Review* two years later was using the word 'dialogue', and speaking approvingly of one of his staff for his 'many Muslim friends'. In the September 1964 *Review*, the General Secretary, Broomfield, observed that 'the old method of argumentative controversy with Muslims' had 'seldom produced any results', and he claimed that 'a very different approach', such as the dialogical one embodied in Kenneth Cragg's recently published *The Dome and the Rock*, was now needed. On the ground there were other evidences of dialogue. Bishop Neil Russell of Zanzibar, after the revolution, observed that 'in our witness to the priority of God and his kingdom, we find ourselves shoulder to shoulder with our Muslim brethren'. Nation-building was also proving to be a catalyst for 'a new charity between Christians and Muslims' elsewhere in Tanzania and in parts of Malawi.[3] A similarly conciliatory approach was advocated among the Chinese of Singapore by the assistant bishop, Ronald Koh. Missionary 'superiority', he claimed, 'and mere condemnation of other religions' had hardened the hearts of many against Christianity. They were to harden them again, in the 1980s, when the Charismatic Movement entered that diocese. For Koh, though, only 'love, humility, patience plus a deep sympathy and understanding' were appropriate.[4] The very different circumstances of Malaysia after independence in 1957, with its restrictive religious clauses, called for its own distinctive approach. The fact that both the first and second bishops of the Diocese of West Malaysia, Koh and Savarimuthu, received at the hands of the nation's Muslim rulers the highest national honour, with the title 'Tan Sri', in 1968 and 1980 respectively, is some indication of the approach they took. In 1990, in *A Malaysian Theology of Muhibbah* (goodwill), the theologian and priest Batumalai, closely associated with the Society, sought to advocate goodwill as the correct Christian response to resurgent religions.

Such conciliatory approaches did not always commend themselves to local Churches. In many parts of India, the language of conciliation and dialogue was necessarily subordinate to concerns for liberation and justice, the great proportion of Christians being from the outcaste and tribal communities. They had been victims of centuries of what the outcaste Bishop Devapriam of Nandyal called in 1985 'caste terror', and from the mid-1980s, as Hindu fundamentalism grew, were intentionally designating themselves 'Dalits', the broken people, in a new political movement. There also, however, a new dialogue began to develop in the early 1990s, pioneered by the General Secretary of the Indian SPCK, James Massey, of Dalit Christians with ex-outcaste neo-Buddhists. These are indications in only a few areas of both changing approaches to people of other faiths during this past 50 years, and the vitality of the issue.

From the 1952 IMC conference at Willingen, a new and more broadly based era in interfaith relations was opening. New study centres 'for the re-appraisal of the main non-Christian religions' began to be established under ecumenical auspices following this conference. The Society contributed funding and sometimes personnel for these in Burma, South India and Ceylon, and similarly, from the 1970s, for the Islam in Africa Project.

SPG's position is well illustrated in the account of the two 1960 conferences in the March *Overseas News*. The leading role of Cragg and Appleton, the latter by this time well known for his sympathetic approach to Buddhism, learned from 'the gentle, tolerant Buddhists of Burma', and exemplified in his *Glad Encounter: Jesus Christ and the Living Faiths of Men* of 1959, set the tone.[5] The conference was also distinguished by talks from adherents of the religion they expounded. The two-page report of these conferences carried quotations from William Temple, Charles Raven, Temple Gairdner and Paul Tillich, all supportive of an inclusivist stance, not least in Raven's suggestion that to find points of contact in the teachings of other traditions was 'to magnify Christ's glory'. The next issue carried a piece by the elderly but sprightly evangelist of St Stephen's Hospital, Delhi, Alice Milward, quoting approvingly the inclusivist views of Raimundo Pannikar, his *Unknown Christ of Hinduism* not yet published.

In Selly Oak, there were a series of new initiatives. The long-standing work in Islamic studies was consolidated in 1976 in a Centre for the Study of Islam and Christian–Muslim Relations, with both staff and students from both communities. This was a postgraduate research department of the University of Birmingham from the beginning. A smaller centre relating to Judaism, and another dealing with New Religious Movements had shorter existences for want of funds, but encouraged significant study and research during the 1980s. The Multi-Faith Resource Unit, which also flourished during the 1980s, picked up many of the new questions facing people as a result of the settlement of religious communities largely new to Britain. A Centre for the Study of Christianity and Asian Religions was founded in 1999. In most of these new initiatives, members of the staff of the College of the Ascension were involved in one way and another, in teaching and management, and many of the Society's students from around the world were able to make use of and contribute to this assembly of resources.

Inevitably, the new questions arising for the Church in Britain from its increasingly plural society were often on the agenda of the Society. The overall situation was characterized in the 1978 Report,

> The presence of large Muslim, Sikh and Hindu communities in Great Britain, and the impact of so excellent a TV series as the BBC's *The Long Search*, encourage a climate, not just of tolerance of other faiths, but of sympathy for the view that all religions are equally the way to the Truth.

The writer went on to ask 'Can there still be a place for a United Society for the Propagation of the Gospel?' The anonymous author drew an affirmative answer from an inclusivist exposition by John Taylor, former Secretary of CMS. Other less general questions also arose for the Society, the question of 'interfaith worship' (1967, 1979, 1991), the use of church properties by other faith communities (1972), the conduct of the Decade of Evangelism (1990). The reply to a query on the first of these, to the effect that 'we accept others in these situations, without compromising our belief in the unique Lordship of Christ', appears to sum up the position of the Society, though there was often lively debate on the subject. When the second question was under consideration, Shevill was inclined to support the view (citing what he claimed was 'unanimous

Indian Christian opinion') that 'when a church is no longer required it is best for it to be demolished and the site sold'. This saddened a former missionary in Pakistan, John Fethney, who recalled 'the goodwill of the large majority of Muslims' he had encountered in Pakistan and how, when he was building a church there, 'individual Muslims would gladly make considerable donations to the building fund', while 'a number of Christian congregations . . . [had] the use of what were formerly Sikh places of worship'. He suggested that in Britain 'inherited . . . redundant fabric . . . [had] for many Christians . . . obscured the substance of the Gospel, and that Asian Muslims living in their midst, far from being a threat . . . [might] prove to be the catalysts who will help them to rediscover it'.[6] Not all missionary messages were in this vein. Rodney Hunter wrote from Malawi in 1987 of 'the country . . . being filled with mosques and a new, educated, and highly articulate and aggressive class of Muslims . . . emerging'. It was 'not very helpful to think in terms of a "wider ecumenism"', and his understanding of Christ was 'incompatible with the secular humanist vision of a multi-faith democracy'. Another view was put by the Bishop of Guildford who told the General Committee that 'The oecumene was becoming a multi-religious, multi-cultural global village . . . [and this was] coming to this country'.[7]

Hunter was quoted when Roger Hooker, one of CMS's very gifted inter-faith specialists and a lifelong missionary in India and Birmingham, was invited to address the June 1987 Council on 'The Way Inter-faith Issues Confront a Missionary Society'. Hooker himself commended an inclusive position in the CMS tradition of Max Warren and John Taylor. He urged the Society to rediscover its own history, for, if it was anything like CMS, there would be, along with 'the dark side', a long and positive encounter with people of other faiths waiting to be reasserted, going back far behind the 1950s, when the current phase had begun. Returning to the issue in 1990, Daniel O'Connor, Principal of the College of the Ascension, reminded Council of USPG's history and of the classical theology of mission and dialogue, demanding both openness and conviction, that was part of the inheritance from the Cambridge Mission to Delhi.[8] Just as much of the distinctive character of UMCA had been largely lost in the merger with SPG, however, so that of the CMD seemed never to have registered within the United Society, and had to be reinvented. There had been, however, as we have seen, plenty of evidence of a not dissimilar inclusivism, and this position was reinforced when the two Synod nominees at the 1993 Council criticized USPG as, in the words of a *Church of England Newspaper* reporter eager to traduce the Society, 'sliding towards syncretism'.[9] Council affirmed that it had no other position than that of the Church, expressed in the inclusivist statement of the 1988 Lambeth Conference. This position was given a fuller exposition by Andrew Wingate, now Principal of the College. He had helped the Doctrine Commission of the General Synod prepare the chapter on 'Christ and World Faiths' in their 1993 Report, *The Mystery of Salvation*, and he explicated this for supporters of the Society in the April 1994 *Thinking Mission*, entitled 'The Uniqueness of Christ in a Multi-Faith World'.

Perhaps the chief way in which CMD's specific charism had effect in Britain was through the Westcott Lectures, endowed by William Teape. These provided from 1955 for a yearly exchange of lecturers between India and Britain, lecturing at St Stephen's College, Delhi and Cambridge respectively (the lectures usually being published subsequently) on themes in the relationship of Hinduism and Christianity. The theme prescribed, 'The Upanishads in the Catholic Church', was not always strictly observed, but the lectures – from well before the term 'dialogue' entered the missiological vocabulary – offered a range of Christian thinkers an occasion to share and develop their reflections on interreligious questions. From India scholars such as P. D. Devanandan, Raimundo Pannikar, Nalini Devadas, S. J. Samartha, James Stuart, Aloysius Pieris and Sara Grant were among the lecturers, and from Britain, among others, Ninian Smart, R. C. Zaehner, Stephen Neill, Geoffrey Parrinder, John Hick, Daniel O'Connor, Roger Hooker, Julius Lipner, Ursula King and Keith Ward. The 'Lent Term Dialogues' at Cambridge, also benefiting from Teape's foresight, were another aspect of this.

In 1984, the Secretary received a letter from the Islamic Friendship Society of Khartoum. Interspersed with Quranic quotations, it said, 'Brothers, we understand that your organization is dedicated to spreading the cult of Christianity in other parts of the world. The Holy Quran instructs us to warn unbelievers before destroying them . . . etc.'[10] Coming from Sudan, where Christians and Muslims were in protracted armed conflict, it was a reminder that the context of interfaith relations and dialogue was increasingly problematic. USPG's decision to appoint as Secretary in 1999 Bishop Munawar Rumalshah, with an unusually rich and broad experience in interracial and interreligious relations, both in Pakistan and Britain, including an eirenic ministry in the religiously plural parish of St George's, Southall, in London, and the testing leadership of the small Christian community confronted by violent Muslim hostility in the Diocese of Peshawar, was indicative of a concern to continue to develop the Society's usefulness in a particularly challenging aspect of mission.

20

Regional issues: Latin America

The Society had had a long involvement in Guyana in South America, but that in Latin America had been restricted to supporting chaplaincy for limited periods, for example to people of Welsh origin in the Pampas in Argentina earlier in the twentieth century. Lambeth 1958, however, described it as 'the neglected continent . . . so far as the Anglican Communion . . . [was] concerned', and, with 'vast masses . . . [owing] no allegiance to the Roman Catholic Church, and . . . a prey to materialism or to distorted forms of the Christian faith', suggested it offered a challenge and opportunity to the Communion as 'a great field of evangelistic work'. Over the next few years, Australian, Canadian and United States Anglicans responded and began new work in Peru, Venezuela, and Colombia and Ecuador respectively. USPG deliberated during 1966 but the devaluation of 1967 ruled out new work at this time. Lambeth 1968 returned to the subject. It was by now a time of widespread revolutionary ferment, not least in Latin America, where the United States and its client military élites were reaping a turbulent but in the longer term ineffectual whirlwind. Che Guevara had been killed in Bolivia the year before the Conference, guerilla warfare was being taken into the cities in Brazil, Uruguay and Argentina, though a short-lived democratic interlude under Salvador Allende was about to be achieved in Chile. The Lambeth bishops saw the 'rapid social, economic, political and religious changes' creating a situation in which the Anglican Churches must make their 'unique and full contribution'. This time the Society did respond. At the May 1969 Council, after conferring with the South American Missionary Society (SAMS), Trapp presented a paper on 'Latin America and USPG', listing a number of good reasons for getting involved: he mentions the context in terms of population growth and urbanization, but ecclesiastical matters predominate. Both the newly autonomous Province of Brazil and the Diocese of Argentina and Eastern South America with the Falkland Islands had been asking for closer links with the Church in Britain through USPG, some Roman Catholic hierarchies after Vatican II were thought to be ready for a measure of ecumenical co-operation, to which the Society might be suited, and some of the fast-growing Evangelical and Pentecostal Churches were becoming aware of their need of a well-trained ministry, a task in which, again, there might be a place for USPG alongside SAMS. Trapp acknowledged that, relative to the huge Roman Catholic presence, anything USPG could do would be minute, a matter, perhaps, of 'humbly and unobtrusively identifying ourselves with the work of other Christians and helping it to grow'. Council responded positively, and asked the staff to pursue the matter, in consultation with the Methodist Missionary Society (MMS) and SAMS.

While consultation with SAMS continued throughout this episode, the critical stage which Church of England–Methodist union negotiations had reached were particularly significant to Trapp, and he immediately asked G. T. Eddy, his opposite number in MMS,

> whether there was any possibility of our working together . . . on a small but imaginative ecumenical venture of some kind in Latin America . . . regardless of whether our respective churches decide to move forward into Stage I – though of course, if they do so decide, a joint enterprise of our two Societies (and maybe others) in some part of the world would be a splendid way of marking the event.

Alternatively, it could be 'an appropriate act of penitence and reparation, and a way of ensuring that some of the mutual goodwill engendered lately is preserved'.[1] MMS was enthusiastic, though the Anglican–Methodist negotiations did indeed come to nothing. The Church of England rejected the proposals at a Synod at which the union in North India was welcomed, prompting Metropolitan Lakdasa de Mel to observe that the Church of England was 'ready to unite to the last Indian'. The two societies, however, carried through their collaboration over the next six years remarkably smoothly. The problems were to occur elsewhere.

There followed eighteen months of extensive enquiry, in Britain, Europe and North America, and correspondence with Anglican, Methodist and Roman Catholic leaders in Latin America. SAMS was helpful, among other things sponsoring a consultation. Most of those consulted during this period were encouraging. Philip Potter, for example, at the WCC, wrote in November 1969 to say that they were all excited by this prospect because of their 'concern to promote Joint Action for Mission wherever possible'. In early 1971, a delegation of four, the Secretary of each society, by now Shevill for USPG, with George Braund, and H. O. Morton for MMS, with Betty Pares, spent three weeks visiting church leaders in Brazil, Argentina, Bolivia, Peru, Ecuador and Colombia. Shevill gives a somewhat flippant account in his autobiography. For example,

> On my first night in Rio, I preached in a vast Pentecostalist tabernacle . . . about Lent, and they clapped, and then Harry Morton told them about the Methodist contribution to British Socialism, which they seemed to find equally fascinating.[2]

His dissent as, in his terms, a 'conservative' from the 'liberal' thinking of people like Morton must have made him an uncomfortable inheritor of the project. More significant, perhaps, were the questionings of three Latin Americans whom the delegation met, Emilio Castro, Orlando Costas and Luís Gonzales, who expressed 'a great fear of disguised colonialism'. At many points on their tour, however, but particularly in Buenos Aires, the delegation met with encouragement, though it was often from expatriates, including the Anglican bishop in Buenos Aires, Cyril Tucker, who, it was suggested, did not have 'a clue about what such people . . . [as Castro and his colleagues] were talking about', but saw this simply as an opportunity to strengthen the Anglican witness in Argentina.[3] A memorandum by Andrew Kirk, a SAMS theologian in Buenos Aires, echoed the hesitations of Castro and others. The project 'would represent a negation of indigenous principles. Latin Americans financially supported from outside to work a project originally conceived abroad would propagate the image of cultural and ecclesiastical dependence which the Latin American Churches slowly and painfully . . . [were] striving to break free from'. It was particularly unfortunate from the point of view of the Anglican Church in Argentina, with its almost exclusively upper and middle-class Anglo-Argentine membership 'in a position of transition from a culturally homogeneous and isolated position' to, it was hoped, 'an integrated, heterogeneous structure'. The sponsoring bodies would be well-advised to 'wait . . . until the Church has become truly Argentine'.

Despite these misgivings, but presumably because of episcopal enthusiasm, that of Tucker and also the local Methodist bishop, Gattinoni, plans were then developed to locate the project in Buenos Aires. In mid-1971, the Society launched a financial appeal, with an educational accompaniment. This latter included a striking audio-visual presentation,

'Something More Important than God', which must have appalled the 'conservative' Shevill. It was marked by a fierce analysis of the social, political and economic oppression of the majority in the continent, a sympathetic presentation of the views of Marxists and other revolutionaries, of Archbishop Helder Câmara of Brazil and Father Camillo Torres, the Colombian priest-turned-guerilla, killed in 1966, and quotations also from the recently held Medellín Conference of Latin American Bishops (1968), which had effectively launched the theology of liberation and on which the Peruvian theologian Gustavo Gutierrez (his *Theology of Liberation* yet to be published) had been so influential. The Society's supporting parishes can rarely have been challenged by such an arresting presentation of a contemporary mission issue. It had a wider circulation, too. Julian Filochowski of the Catholic Institute of International Relations took and showed it on a tour of Latin and Central America, and wrote to its chief maker in the Society, Joan Bloodworth, that the response had been that it was 'the best thing that had been written on the continent by outsiders and they were astounded that it was produced in England'.[4]

The next stage was to decide what form the project was to take. For this, the basic document was a paper by Morton, dated January 1972, with the bold title, 'Pro Vita Humana'. The project was 'as concerned with the unity of mankind as the unity of the Church'. Though small, it ought to be 'significant'. Morton envisaged the formation of 'an Ecumenical Theological Community', largely Latin American but with British participants from the two societies, with Roman Catholic members, women and men, a team which might hope to win its way as a service to the Churches in the continent by the quality of its study and reflection, but with an impact on the British Churches also. Morton recognized that this was at a remove from the procedures of the liberation theology then evolving, and liable to be seen as 'academic and parasitic' by comparison, but it would, he insisted, 'serve the poor best by a life of prayer, study, dialogue and thoughtful reflection'. While his vision was never fully embraced by the Argentine Anglican and Methodist Churches, and indeed never clearly introduced to them by their leadership, both bishops secured authorization from their synodical bodies formally to invite the two societies, in June 1972, to participate in what was now to be called the 'Anglican–Methodist Project in Latin America' (AMPLA).

Further serious weakness in the project became evident at the next stage, that of reception of Morton's vision in Buenos Aires, and its translation into a practical programme. The Advisory Group established there was of competent but very busy people, most of them frequently absent from the group meetings, and they were being asked to collaborate with a Staff Working Group in London with a rapidly shifting membership, manifestly impatient and careless of the fundamental principle that this must, despite its origins, be allowed to become a Latin American project with minority British participation. There were various areas of confusion. With regard to recruitment, for example, there was little co-ordination, the group in London going ahead and recruiting two English Methodist couples, called Hopkin and Roberts respectively, ahead of the Buenos Aires Group's establishing the Argentine side of the team, though the latter did then identify a Methodist couple, called Sabanes, and a part-time Roman Catholic participant, Sister Orfilia, though she withdrew before all the British participants had arrived. Despite a long and rather desperate search, USPG failed to find a suitable and willing candidate for the team. It was a time of runaway inflation in Argentina, and the societies found themselves solely responsible for funding, increasing the 'colonial' look of the project. There was also confusion as to where authority lay, and over aims.

When the Hopkins and Roberts arrived, in April and September 1974 respectively, they found Carlos Sabanes working at proposals for an initial programme, but in every other respect were deeply discouraged. A letter from Miguel Bonino, the Argentine Methodist theologian, to a friend in Britain indicates that practical and pastoral care for them was very poor, and no one seemed willing to take any responsibility, and it was not surprising that they showed signs of serious culture shock.[5] They quickly developed their own critique of the project. It was not rooted in the Latin American soil. 'AMPLA at present is like a Christmas Tree', John Roberts wrote, 'ornamental and superficially admirable but it has no roots and is incapable of growing or producing seeds of life', while John Hopkin asked 'How can we avoid the charge of "theological imperialism" in bringing the ideas, the money and personnel from outside?'[6] Before the year was out, both had submitted their resignations and, the Argentine 'partners' never having been more than reactive, the project was to all intents and purposes at an end, the Advisory Group in Buenos Aires formally recommending its suspension on 12 March 1975.

There was possibly some truth in Shevill's subsequent rueful obervation in his autobiography that the money expended on the project might have been better spent in enabling the hard-pressed little Anglican Church there to do what they were already doing a little better. His successor, Robertson, was left with little to do at the British end beyond ensuring that the project was wound up with grace. A review was instituted of all that had taken place, with a report published in February 1976. Michael Hardy, a dissenting member of the Society staff on this topic, pre-empted the review with a memorandum, playing on the words of the imperialistic song 'Land of hope and glory' in its title, 'AMPLA still and AMPLA shall thy bounds be set', though he added a question mark. The report, written by Betty Pares of MMS, was carefully documented and very thorough. Recognizing that the quest had been for something new, the process had involved old and unreconstructed methods which could not succeed and had no right to succeed. On 28 March, Kirk wrote to George Braund, commending 'the incredible honesty with which the apparent failure of the scheme has been faced . . . no recriminations, no self-justifications, no despair, just a sober and very clear assessment'.

Subsequently, from the later 1970s, USPG developed a modest but effective association with the Anglican Church in Latin America, in Argentina, Brazil and Uruguay, some of this in collaboration with CMS and the Scottish Episcopal Church. Less ambitious and introduced without fanfare, this involved a number of women and men in sacrificial ministries in the cities and favelas of the continent, and broadened the partnership of the Church there with the Church in Britain and Ireland.

21

⋆⟶⊜⟵⋆

Regional issues: Southern Africa

The Society's substantial involvement with the Church of the Province of Southern Africa (CPSA) ensured that the momentous struggle through which the people of South Africa went during this period was on the Society's agenda almost continuously. In the earlier days, the dilemmas of the liberal conscience characterized SPG's involvement.

Reports from the huge locations being established around Johannesburg in the 1930s, including those of Society missionaries belonging to the Community of the Resurrection and Dorothy Maud at her Ekutuleni or 'House of Peace' in Sophiatown, and curtailment of the franchise by means of the Native Bills of 1935, had alerted the Society. Then, following the Second World War, racially based legislation, initially the Mixed Marriage and Immorality Acts of 1949 and 1950, stirred consciences in Britain, and in response the Society issued in October 1950 a report on 'Race Relations in South Africa', in which racial discrimination was condemned without qualification. This started a train of responses. Roberts sent copies to the South African bishops with a covering letter explaining,

> A point has been reached at which it was difficult to restrain the outraged feelings of responsible Christians in this country, and I hope that we have succeeded in relieving our consciences without damaging your cause.[1]

The episcopal response was to ask people in the Church of England to keep out of such matters. However, the South African situation now deteriorated rapidly with further legislation, on Suppression of Communism (1950), Separate Representation of Voters (1951), Public Safety, and Criminal Law Amendment (1953), and in a letter to the *Church Times* on 10 July 1953, Trevor Huddleston CR urged people in Britain to disregard the request of the South African bishops. Geoffrey Clayton, the Archbishop of Cape Town, then intervened in a letter to Roberts, saying that the South African government was wrong, but the Church was not yet muzzled, and he feared that Huddleston's militancy would unite white South Africans behind the government, and that protest in Britain would do the same, and he urged SPG not to be part of it, a view supported by Archbishop Fisher, who told Roberts that Huddleston was 'one of those unwise people who rush wildly into a controversial attitude'.[2] It is clear that a South Africa advisory group in the Society also took this view, but by now Roberts was plainly deeply concerned at developments 'alien to the Gospel', and set the Society to scrutinize its policy and practice for anything that supported these, and had a major part in drafting an updated version of 'Race Relations in South Africa', which, despite the advisory group's refusal to endorse it, was published in the April 1954 *Overseas News*.

Throughout these years, the Society's funding, beyond staple support of missionaries and medical and educational work, was directed to, for example, the South African Institute of Race Relations and the building of a chapel for Beda Hall at the South African Native College, Fort Hare, this being the only place where African ordinands could do a university course. A much greater funding contribution followed the Bantu Education Act of 1954 of the new Prime Minister, Hendrik Verwoerd, which used the educational system to reinforce racial oppression. Initially, SPG found itself caught between the proactive and radical response of Bishop Ambrose Reeves of Johannesburg who, supported by the Community of the Resurrection and the Society of the Sacred Mission, closed his schools, and the more reactive response of Clayton and the other bishops, who leased theirs to the government, thus enabling children to remain at school, albeit in religionless schools which reinforced apartheid. Reeves launched an appeal in Britain in conjunction with Christian Action and the Africa Bureau to alleviate the educational crisis in his own diocese, but was persuaded by Dixon, the Home Secretary, that it should be subsumed within a South Africa Emergency Appeal to sustain religious education in all the dioceses. This was launched by SPG in November 1954. The *Church Times* supported the appeal with their main front-page article on 26 November, 'A challenge to the conscience of all Church people', and *Picture Post* carried two weekly six-page articles in support. The Society provided an exhibition, 'A People Apart', to tour Britain, and issued as its Lent Book for 1955 *The Church Serves South Africa*. The campaign was not helped by the Bishop of Kimberley and Kuruman who, speaking at an SPG meeting in Oxford, assured his audience that 'all the ministers of the Union Government . . . [were] good men', though Raymond Raynes CR set the record straight, explaining that 'many of them . . . [were not] good'. Despite such confusions, and despite an equally urgent overlapping appeal for the Church in the West Indies, the South Africa Appeal was exceptionally successful, raising nearly £45,000 in four months. Alan Paton wrote of the generosity of the Church of England through the Society rising 'to extraordinary heights', the debt of the Church in South Africa to SPG throughout the Church's history being 'hard to overestimate'.[3]

In 1956, shortly before his death, Roberts wrote to Archbishop Clayton to thank him on the Society's behalf for establishing, with Bishop Reeves' support, the Treason Trial Defence Fund. Though a prophetic streak had been evident in Clayton as early as 1938, when he adumbrated the possibility of civil disobedience in a charge to the Johannesburg Synod, it was his resolute resistance to the Native Laws Amendment Bill in 1957 and, shortly before his own death, his announcement to Verwoerd that he and the other bishops could not obey this law, that marked a new stage in the witness of the Church, or of that part of it prepared to side with the oppressed. Noting this legislation, SPG in July formed a special group, including Huddleston, now back in Britain, to review policy. One immediate outcome was Trapp's request to the new Archbishop of Cape Town, Joost de Blank, to keep SPG 'fully informed of events as they unfold . . . [to assist] our work in this country', while a slightly later outcome, a grant to a Churches Relief Fund set up in the year of the Sharpeville massacre and following disturbances in Cape Town also, was interpreted by de Blank as 'an act of solidarity on the part of the Church in Britain'.[4] Here are two related aspects of the Society's role as it developed during this new stage, that of funding significant work in South Africa against apartheid, and that of advocacy in Britain for the Church and people there. In this latter task, *Network*, not least under the later editorship of Tony Rich- mond, a former editor of the *Cape Herald*, played a major part, this advocacy being a way of sustaining the solidarity between the Churches in Britain and South Africa that de Blank so valued.

The next substantial oppressive legislation came with the Group Areas Act. Trapp flew out to South Africa to consult the bishops in July 1962 as to how SPG should respond. The outcome was a substan- tial grant to build churches and priests' houses in the new areas into which people were being removed and, to consolidate this, the launch- ing of the Festina revolving loan scheme. To inform and secure support for these moves, an exhibition toured Britain in 1964, entitled 'For I am a man.'

The Society's chief concern through into the 1970s was with related issues in Namibia and Southern Rhodesia, though the violence of the South African government against its people intensified, dramatized in the appearance of police with their dogs driving protesters out of Cape Town Cathedral in 1972, but chiefly endured, of course, in such atrocities as the massacre at Soweto in 1976, in the endless pressure upon the black community and in enforced resettlement, illustrated in USPG's filmstrip presentation, 'The Promised Land'. A number of Society missionaries, Michael Broadbent, Colin Davidson and John Davies among others, were deported or denied re-entry in the earlier 1970s, the government 'seeking to be rid of the middle echelons of Christian leaders', often branded in the Orwellian official terminology as 'spiritual terrorists'.[5] At his first Council meeting in December 1973, Robertson observed that the CPSA was 'undergoing a passion of the highest order'. His time as Secretary witnessed USPG's deepening friendship with Desmond Tutu, initially in London working for the WCC, and a member of Council from 1972, but returning to South Africa as Dean of Johannesburg in 1975, and rising rapidly by way of the Diocese of Lesotho, the South African Council of Churches and the Diocese of Johannesburg to the Archbishopric of Cape Town eleven years later.

With the major British banks investing in South Africa, Britain having of course long been the leading economic supporter of the regime, a major concern of USPG over the next few years was with the stewardship of its own funds, some of which were handled by Barclays Bank. The matter first came before Council in December 1973, at which time an advisory unit was being set up by the BCC, which Finance Committee was instructed to consult, but little happened at this time. The matter came up again at the June 1980 Council, and the outcome was a dialogue with a senior management group of Barclays. USPG found Barclays' South African counterpart open to change, and 'one of the most enlightened employers' in South Africa, willing to finance new black-owned businesses and to encourage partnerships between black and white businessmen.[6] In a report to Council the following year, Robertson described this dialogue as 'looking for cracks in the economic structure of apartheid'. The case for disinvestment, however, grew stronger over the next few years and, after Taylor's visit to South Africa in May 1986, Council agreed on 11 June that it had become imperative as 'the only remaining peaceful means of achieving . . . fundamental change'.[7] At the same time, USPG pressed the British government to support sanctions. The official replies in subliterate letters from the

Foreign Office were, in the Society's judgement 'seriously inadequate', for the latter's policy was 'obviously designed to evade and indefinitely postpone decisive action to end the apartheid system'.[8]

Meanwhile, there were other aspects to the Society's concern. In October 1982, in order to review the relationship with the province, specifically in regard to the Bursaries Programme and Mission Personnel, and more generally 'to sustain and renew . . . understanding and affection', three members of USPG's staff, Geoffrey Cleaver, Roger Symon and Humphrey Taylor, visited the province, going to fifteen dioceses and meeting some 300 individuals and twenty groups, from parish groups to the Provincial Standing Committee. Their joint report published in February 1983 disclosed the admiration they felt for 'one of the major provinces of our communion, strong in numbers, rich in talent, efficiently led, active in evangelism, powerful in stewardship, deeply involved in social concern . . . to be compared favourably with any other province we know'. One of their strongest impressions, however, was of the Church's persistent reinforcement of 'the *status quo* of which . . . [it was] part', and also of

> the intense and deeply felt anger of a great many . . . at the pattern of leadership and government in the CPSA. Despite the black majority (80%) in its church membership, of seventeen diocesan bishops in the Province, only six were black.

Over this, of course, USPG had no control, beyond a decision to reduce the number of missionaries it seemed right to support. The report suggested that 'the vocation of the Society [was] to sustain a close and persistent partnership with the Province', and this was formalized in fresh agreements in 1988.

Certainly this close and persistent partnership was attempted over the next few years, in many respects the most terrible, 'the situation of death', as the Preface to *The Kairos Document* of 1985 put it.[9] At a time when news out of South Africa was gravely distorted by official disinformation and marked by a 'concerted virulence' against Bishop Tutu, Taylor saw that 'communicating information from South Africa, fostering awareness of events there, and keeping in touch with people under pressure' was a major task for the Society, and there was a constant stream of letters and phone calls in both directions to realize this.[10] Reliable information on such matters as the detention of clergy, even of whole congregations, the threats and actual violence against bishops and the firebombing of their homes by the agents of the regime made USPG by mid-1985 a respected source of information to the British media. The following year the Society helped to establish the South Africa Crisis Information Group to improve this service. Also in 1985, following a phone call to say that the Suffragan Bishop of Johannesburg, Simeon Nkoane CR, a man of 'conspicuous holiness and gentleness', was in danger, the Society was instrumental in a hurried visit to South Africa by the Archbishop of Canterbury's representative, the Bishop of Lichfield, Keith Sutton, who publicly identified himself with Nkoane at a large funeral gathering at Kwa Thema.[11] In the year following, USPG inaugurated a 'Crisis Links' scheme whereby parishes in South Africa and in Britain were enabled to link up in prayer and exchange of information, 'to encourage contact as the crisis . . . [deepened]'.[12] That same year, taking advice from a South African priest in Britain, Barney Pittyana, a former friend and colleague of the Black Consciousness leader, Steve Biko, the Society did much preparatory briefing, accompanied by a prominent exhibition at Church House, for a major debate at the July General Synod on the urgent need to establish as peacefully as possible 'a new South Africa' which would be 'non-racial, democratic, participatory and just'. Also in 1986, Taylor and Symon helped Archbishop Runcie prepare his sermon and accompanied him to the enthronement of Desmond Tutu as Archbishop of Cape Town. Despite the importance of the event, 'a portent of hope . . . [exemplifying the] transformation of the English-speaking churches . . . into a vital spiritual vanguard of the black-led struggle', they were the only clergy of the Church of England present, alongside a large group from the USA.[13]

Throughout these years, a number of indications reached USPG that the Church in South Africa was in fact divided on the official provincial priority of opposition to apartheid. The Suffragan Bishop of Dunwich, for example, brought back evidence of this after a visit and meeting with Beyers Naude of the South African Council of Churches in 1985. He found a number of white bishops of the Province at best complacent about the situation, and there were indications that others of them did not wish to support the Society in its role of advocate. A member of Council, after a visit while the Charismatic Movement was in full spate, observed that the Church was 'at its best a magnificent small sign of the Kingdom – at its worst a glittering betrayal of that Kingdom as it sticks with a purely "spiritual" message'. If the force of events was indeed changing the quality of the Church's witness so that it was 'moving to the status of a "confessing church"', as Peter Lee of Johannesburg suggested to Symon in 1986, like other such, the confessing part was not the whole.[14]

Indications such as these had made the process of Tutu's election to the archbishopric the more surprising. While the process was expected to be bitter and long drawn out, it went 'smoothly and easily . . . a remarkable occasion, with a palpable sense of the Spirit's presence'. At the subsequent enthronement Taylor presented the Archbishop with a copy of Pascoe's history of the Society as 'an expression of our gladness at being in partnership with the CPSA under your Primacy'. On the same visit Roger and Daphne Symon were briefly detained by the state authorities, a reminder that nothing had as yet changed. Indeed, the Archbishop's own experience of the subsequent and last few years of apartheid was of arrest and detention, house searches and abuse. He expressed his gratitude for the Society's continuing support, 'We know we are not alone . . . we are grateful for your share in this', his letter to Taylor continuing characteristically, 'We are certain . . . we shall all be free, black and white together.'[15] Gratitude was also evident in a December 1988 letter of the Provincial Executive Officer, Winston Ndungane, to Taylor, saying that the Archbishop wished to honour him with a Provincial Canonry for his association with the province and his 'inestimable contribution towards its life and work'. The Archbishop elaborated after the event, 'We were honouring you in your own right and also because of USPG.'[16]

While in Cape Town in July 1989, Taylor was told by an adviser of the Archbishop, a former banker, that sanctions were working and their desired outcome was imminent. The British Ambassador to South Africa, on the other hand, and no doubt echoing official British hopes, told Symon, now working at Lambeth, that Nelson Mandela would not be released 'for some time', because 'it would definitely set the glacier moving'. It began to move on 12 February 1990, Bishop David Russell of Grahamstown writing to Taylor that Mandela was 'about to be released in an hour's time'.[17] The Society's sense, however, of the necessity to maintain its 'close and persistent partnership' with the province until and indeed after apartheid was dismantled, was sustained into the 1990s, inaugurated with a letter of 13 February 1990 to the *Church Times* in support of a vigil of prayer in Westminster Abbey, to be attended by Archbishop Runcie on 26 February, followed by a lobby of Parliament the next day.

USPG's role, perhaps its most creative for the propagation of the Gospel in the second half of the century, was not primarily about personnel or funding, though these played a part, but about advocacy, the promotion of 'understanding and affection', in which the Church of the Province clearly judged the Society to have made a worthwhile contribution.

--=◦◦=--

In addition to the dramatic events in Church and state in South Africa itself during this period, all neighbouring countries were deeply affected. In all of them, the Society and the Churches it supported were deeply engaged.

Namibia, as a mandated territory under South Africa, was subject to the most direct oppression, this intensifying as its own resistance under the South West African People's Organization gathered strength from the 1960s. The founder of SWAPO in 1959, Toivo Ya Toivo, was an alumnus of the Society-funded St Mary's School, Odibo (and later, for sixteen years, of the prison on Robben Island), and the Anglican Church was the first to emerge as a political force, in spite of its small membership of about 60,000, though soon to be followed by the Lutheran and Roman Catholic Churches. While a number of Society missionaries and in succession three white Bishops of Damaraland – as the diocese was then known – were deported, and the white diocesan secretary imprisoned, it was, of course the black members of the Church, women and men, including many of the clergy, who bore the brunt of South Africa's reign of terror, in the form of detention, flogging, torture and murder. USPG's involvement took a variety of forms, in addition to the support of missionaries and substantial funding, including, at one stage, Namibian clergy stipends. Thus, in regard to advocacy, the Bishop-in-exile in the earlier 1970s, Colin Winter, acknowledged the Society as, 'always, right from the beginning, my strongest supporter', and did much to enable him to continue to champion the Namibian cause from outside the country as well as help sustain the life of his diocese.[18] Also in the matter of advocacy, USPG helped bring a Namibian delegation, including Archdeacon Shilongo, to Britain in 1976, and provided significant information for a debate in the General Synod in London in February that same year, which, in the face of what *The Daily Telegraph* of 25 February admiringly called 'the lone dissenting voice' of Edward Norman, passed a motion strongly supporting the people and Churches of Namibia, and promoting a national appeal sponsored by the Society. Support was also provided through the Bursaries Programme, enabling a number of clergy and others to study at the College of the Ascension, among them Erastus Haikali, Chaplain to SWAPO members in exile in Angola and Zambia, and Charles Kadhikwa, who discerned his vocation to the priesthood while under torture for three months at the hands of the South African authorities. The College also hosted a series of annual groups of young exiles selected by SWAPO for training as teachers, funded by the British Council, Anne Spence, Tutor at the College being seconded to their course. The consecration of James Kauluma, another alumnus of St Mary's, Odibo, as bishop, in Westminster Abbey on 15

January 1978, the first consecration there of a bishop of a fully autonomous Church of the Anglican Communion, was a very Anglican recognition of a bravely witnessing Church. A visit by a Society missionary, David Bruno, Dean of Windhoek, to the war-torn areas of northern Namibia in 1986, found St Mary's Mission reduced to ruins by the South African forces. In 1989 the Society responded to a request of Bishop Kauluma and provided a large grant towards its rebuilding. Bruno had also found the Church in northern Namibia strongly growing, and eagerly anticipating the national independence finally secured in 1990.

The liberation of Zimbabwe from settler-domination in 1980 was a very different story from the perspective of the Church, for, despite some bold attempts by some of USPG's missionaries to create multiracial congregations, and projects such as the Clutton-Brocks' venture in rural development at Rusape, generally the tens of thousands of white Anglicans dominated the hundreds of thousands of black Anglicans, controlled church finance and neutralized or co-opted some of the clergy into the all-pervasive racist system, in so many respects like that of South Africa. Among the Church's white leaders, only Kenneth Skelton, Bishop of Matabeleland from 1962 to 1970, consistently and unambiguously opposed settler power, though his position was strongly supported by many of the clergy and of course by black church leaders such as the Suffragan Bishops Patrick Murindagomo and Peter Hatendi.[19] The Society began to respond seriously to the emerging situation in 1965. Although SPG's Report had referred admiringly to Arthur Shearly Cripps at the time of his death in 1955, staff were still involving themselves in such events as the Rhodes centennial celebrations in Bulawayo in 1963. A sermon by Bishop Skelton in 1964, challenging the impending Unilateral Declaration of Independence, a sermon which initiated six lonely years of prophecy, helps date this new response. It was followed by John Kingsnorth's warning to the Society in February 1965 of the 'African distaste for a Church apparently closely allied to the ruling white Government'.[20] In that same year, the Society made a book grant for detainees, and supported Archbishop Ramsey's call for the British government to end the illegal regime, if necessary by force. Thereafter, USPG consistently advocated change. This was done in the face of aggressive opposition even from some of its own missionaries in the Rhodesian Christian Group, led by A. R. Lewis, who was intruded as Rector of Rusape to supplant the Clutton-Brocks. Lewis was removed from USPG's list in 1976 for his identification with the illegal settler regime, although, despite his continuing virulent public attacks on the Society, assistance continued with his National Insurance contributions in Britain. The Society worked in close association with the CBMS and the BCC, for example in moving a resolution at the 1979 Annual General Meeting of Shell BP on oil supplies to Rhodesia, while much attention was given to providing, as in the case of South Africa, reliable information both to people in Britain, including Synod members in 1978, and also to church people in Rhodesia kept in ignorance by censorship – 'information as a prelude to mission understanding', as Robertson put it at the 1979 Annual Meeting. USPG was represented at the independence celebrations in April 1980 by Skelton, now Bishop of Lichfield, who the following year, as Chair of Council, welcomed Peter Hatendi, now Bishop of Mashonaland, to the June meeting. Hatendi spoke of the challenge in a new nation 'for the Church to be made new'. In this task USPG sought to share, Robertson the following year telling his former colleague, the now Prime Minister, Robert Mugabe, of special Society grants that had already been made, including a large increase in the Bursaries allocation, and a number of specialist missionary appointments.

The three independent nations surrounded by South Africa, Botswana, Lesotho and Swaziland, were all at one time and another during these years pressurized economically, politically and militarily, and the Anglican Church in all three assumed heavy responsibility, as in the case of Bishop Philip Mokuku attempting to reconcile armed factions in Lesotho after a coup in 1986. There was also the care of refugees, chiefly from South Africa but also from Mozambique after South African terrorist disruption began there around 1982. A Society missionary, John Osmers, grand-nephew of another Society champion of the oppressed, C. F. Andrews, was injured along with an Indian and three African colleagues, Osmers losing a hand, by a parcel bomb while working among refugees in Maseru in 1979.

The South African effect was most intense and widespread, however, in Mozambique, with some 700,000 killed at the hands of Renamo, the terrorist organization funded and armed by South Africa. The January 1986 *Network* described the two dioceses of Maputo and Niassa as 'chronically affected', a situation persisting into 1990, when Bishop Sengulane rang Taylor to report another priest, Absalom Dende, killed in an ambush. The bishop played an outstanding part in reaching the reconciliation of 1994, being described as 'Peacemaker *Extraordinaire*'.[21] Beyond the Province, Malawi took in 800,000 refugees from Mozambique, the Church being much involved in their care. Only with the beginning of the end of the apartheid state in 1990 could the Church throughout Southern Africa hope to work under less violent circumstances.

22

⟿ ◉ ⟸

Regional issues: the United Kingdom and Ireland

At the beginning of the period, SPG supporters in Britain and Ireland had been reminded that 'the conversion of England' was on the agenda of the Church, but there was little in the Society's business at that time that took account of this.

The issue which first brought a shift in practice was that of immigration to Britain from the Indian subcontinent, the Caribbean and Africa from 1948 and increasing through the 1950s and 1960s, bringing eventually some 3 million new citizens to the country, a process slowed through increasingly restrictive legislation from the 1960s. Anti–immigrant riots in London in 1958 and 1961 raised awareness of the issue, the latter prompting Warren of CMS to support such legislation in a letter to *The Times*. Trapp declined to sign the letter, 'to keep . . . [himself] free of "taint" in West Indian eyes'.[1] The Church's concern with immigration, which was initially pastoral and evangelistic, but subsequently also included calls for racial justice, was reflected in the formation in the 1950s of an Immigrants Group within the Overseas Council of the Church Assembly, made up of representatives of all the main Anglican mission agencies and chaired by a former Society missionary, George Appleton. Trapp took a keen interest on behalf of SPG. The Society was also represented in the BCC's slightly later emerging work in this field. Among contributions to the former group, SPG took responsibility in 1957 for the initial funding (out of its annual grant to Jamaica) for a Jamaican priest, Roy Campbell, as first Chaplain to West Indians settled in the London area, and subsequently for his successor, Canon John Hay. The West Indians certainly needed encouragement; small and unfriendly English congregations creating 'a shock that would have shaken the Pope if he were a West Indian', as one young Barbadian put it in *Overseas*

204

News.[2] The Society also took its own initiatives. Thus, the meetings in four regional groupings convened during the summer of 1958 with 50 of the bishops attending the Lambeth Conference were used to elicit advice on serving the needs of immigrants from their regions. A minute of the meeting with bishops from India and Pakistan stressed that the care of immigrants was the task of the Church of England, not of missionary societies. This was a recurring point made by the Society over the next few years, while repeatedly pressing the Church to accept this responsibility. A further case in point was at a meeting convened by SPG in February 1962 for representatives of eighteen English dioceses with significant concentrations of settlers from the West Indies, when Trapp declined to accept a co-ordinating role for the Society in what was, or should be 'the concern of the whole church'.[3] Council in November 1969 explicitly recognized the issue of immigrants as an aspect of 'Mission in Six Continents', but continued with this insistence. The role of ex-missionaries, nevertheless, was recognized by the BCC in 1969 as potentially constructive, and in fact already from the early 1960s a former Society missionary in Korea, Paul Burrough, was developing a pioneering ministry in the Diocese of Birmingham, living in a caravan and 'wandering round' among the parishes in which West Indians lived. He was succeeded by another Society ex-missionary, though not as a caravaner, Leonard Schiff, who left 'the shelter of the College [of the Ascension, of which he was Principal] for the confused and very turbulent world of race relations' in 1969.[4] That same year, USPG reviewed its personnel resources in the form of returned missionaries, and organized regional gatherings to secure their interest, making names available to the BCC which was at that time forming a Unit for Community Relations. The Society's Area Secretaries also got involved, a group of seven of them in the Midlands, for example, that same year convening a meeting with parish clergy including the Rural Deans of Wolverhampton and Smethwick, where racism was being dangerously and violently politicized. The Rector of Wolverhampton explained that the MP, Enoch Powell, a communicant member of his congregation, notorious for his hostility to immigration, 'saw himself as a man of destiny . . . bent on saving the nation', and that the congregation was deeply divided on race issues. Again, the Society was invited to get more fully involved, and again the challenge was pressed back upon the Churches.[5]

One of the Area Secretaries at the meeting in Wolverhampton had described race as 'the most pressing social problem of our time'. USPG clearly attempted a catalytic role in promoting this aspect of the mission of the Church of England, and, in relating it to other Churches of the

Anglican Communion, provided an illustration of the role of an agent of partnership before the theory had been much enunciated. The Society's subsequent involvement, after the 1960s, was initially relatively slight, Council in November 1970 declaring its reluctance to divert further funds to this work from the still financially struggling Churches in Asia, Africa and the Caribbean. By now, however, the BCC and, later, diocesan Boards of Social Responsibility, were beginning to assume responsibilities in this field. USPG did, however, from 1979 contribute as a major funder of the Community and Race Relations Unit of the BCC, and, with CMS, to funding the Church of England's first Race Relations Field Officer from 1981, and also to support for the formation of the Simon of Cyrene Theological Institute in London in 1989 to help black people towards ordination. Racism continued to characterize much of British society and its institutions, driving the discriminated-against to form a National Civil Rights Movement in 1999, while the Church of England proved a reluctant learner, General Synod in 1999 still talking about an 'action plan'.

On a somewhat related issue, the welfare of overseas students, the Society made financial loans and contributions from as early as 1951, jointly funding with CMS the new William Temple House in Earls Court, and championing their cause when the government raised fees drastically in the 1980s.

With an eye to Britain as a mission field, the Society joined with the other mission agencies and some of the partner Churches in pressing for an English Partners-in-Mission consultation, and for Third World voices to be heard there. The Chair of Council, Bishop Skelton, thought the Church in southern Africa might be able to advise on leadership in a situation of national economic, political and moral confusion, and on problems of racism and the needs of alienated young black people, while there was much to learn from the European Churches, 'coping with precisely the same difficulties'. He was concerned, though, 'to get away from the sentimental attitude which leads us to deceive ourselves into thinking that what we really need is a team of first-generation Christians from the "younger churches" to galvanise us into evangelism . . . Our problems . . . in the developed post-Christian world . . . are vastly more complicated than, for instance, Rhodesia's – or at least their issues are clearer than ours.'[6] The Society had high expectations of the consultation when it was at last agreed to hold it in 1980, and certainly over the longer term it advanced some of the organizational changes which USPG wanted to see. It is not clear in what other ways it advanced the mission of the Church. The report, in which the Society's Deputy Secretary, John Kingsnorth, had a leading editorial hand, picked up for its title a phrase from Ezekiel to which the external consultants had alluded, *To a Rebellious House*, and said, 'What is new ... is the persistent voice coming through the "message" of fellow-Christians of other lands and other traditions, whose main impressions were of wide-open opportunity and of sad failure to seize it.'

The Society also supported some of the Church of England's own internally generated initiatives for mission. Thus, in response to Archbishop Coggan's 'Call to the Nation' in 1974, Robertson launched a prayer project called 'Praying the News'. The Society also sought to engage constructively with the Nationwide Initiative in Evangelism, launched in 1979, and with the Church of England's response to the 1988 Lambeth call for a Decade of Evangelism, though in neither case did this lead to significant, practical programmes. The Society did nevertheless initiate a number of its own programmes from the 1970s directed at the British scene.

The first of these was a poster campaign, masterminded by one of the more radical of the London staff, Joan Bloodworth, assisted by Neil Taylor. This was a successor to the Society's Parish Picture Service, and posters were published periodically from 1972 to 1987. These combined striking photographic images from around the world with equally striking texts from a wide variety of sources, presenting the Gospel in contemporary terms, and providing largely implicit Christian comment and questions about the predicament of people and society. They broke new ground both in their avoidance of the pedestrian and their subtle but sharp challenge. They aroused a good deal of protest, explicitly in one case from 'darkest Norfolk', and particularly from clergy with a low view of the intelligence and perception of their parishioners. They evoked growing admiration also, and were widely used in parish education, and also beyond conventional church circles. They proved effective beyond Britain, a teacher writing from Bulawayo that 'the idea of a radical, forceful religion was a new one to many young people', while they proved also a 'most effective means of communication' to the large numbers who passed through Calcutta Cathedral under the prophetic leadership of Canon Subir Biswas. They were, however, produced primarily to propagate the Gospel in Britain, and the animated and increasingly positive response mark them out as a successful contribution on the part of the Society.

Amongst much more, the posters sought to arouse a response among Christians to the desecration of the environment by this time becoming increasingly apparent, and a concern of the Churches ecumenically from the WCC's Vancouver Assembly discussion on the 'integrity of creation' in 1983. This was reinforced by USPG's audio-visual presentation published in 1989 on the insights of Native Americans, including statements ascribed to Chief Seattle, on humanity's relationship with the earth. The Society's new strategy agreed during the mid-1990s took this concern further with budgetary support for dioceses and provinces taking up environmental issues.

Virtually all the mainline Churches and mission agencies began during this period to bring people from partner Churches as missionaries to Britain, though usually on a very short-term basis. USPG's first endeavour of this sort was to bring Bishop John Sadiq on his early retirement in 1970 from the Diocese of Nagpur to be what the Church of North India described as 'Missionary Bishop of the CNI in the UK'. This was a two-year appointment, the Bishop and Mrs Sadiq being based at the College of the Ascension and travelling about Britain to speak and listen. As an outsider he detected little sense of a missionary Church in Britain. Mission in 'the truest and deepest sense' was 'peripheral to an average churchman', and 'the collection bag rather than the towel and basin still . . . [remained] the symbol of missionary interest'.[7] USPG later arranged a visit by Bishop Dinis Sengulane of Lebombo and a group of others during six weeks of public meetings in the autumn of 1986, with the title 'Walking on Water' to acknowledge the courageous faith of the Church in Mozambique, and the 'Lichfield Pilgrimage' in 1988, involving a number of bishops in Britain for the Lambeth Conference, but these were closer to the older-style rallies at the Albert Hall than new ways of propagating the Gospel in Britain. Much closer to this aim was the way in which the Bursary Programme was shaped in the 1980s, parish attachments around Birmingham being arranged for bursars from overseas studying at the College of the Ascension, with visits also to parishes and deaneries further afield during vacations. The considerable experience and ministerial skills of bursars were in this way put at the service of local churches, and this often proved an enriching experience for a parish. Thus, Julius and Flora Murombedzi from Zimbabwe brought to their placement in 1982 new insights on marriage, motherhood and bereavement counselling, together with an image of black leadership otherwise hardly conceivable in a Birmingham parish at that time.[8]

The notion of exchange of personnel, with the Churches in Britain and Ireland as receivers as well as givers, was formalized in 1992 in an 'International Visitors' Programme' with a modest budget. A series of groups and individuals were invited for short visits in what might be best termed a consultancy role. Thus, five younger church leaders, from Guyana, Malaysia, Mauritius, South Africa and Zimbabwe, all former bursars at the College of the Ascension, came in 1993 as a mission team 'to challenge and assist the "mother church"', visiting the Dioceses of Lincoln, Manchester and Salisbury in a breathless and demanding month.[9] Subsequently, there was a similar visit to Southwell, Bristol and Northern Ireland, and others included groups of women from South India and Korea, with individuals also invited from Zambia and Brazil to explain the impact of international debt on their country and community, and a priest from Malawi, James Tengatenga, to speak at a UMCA 140th-year commemoration and meet church groups. Some of these visits were under the joint auspices of USPG, CMS and the Methodist Church. While one of the earliest such visitors, Archdeacon Batumalai of Malaysia, thought he saw a new realization of the Society's foundation text, 'Come over and help us', there is very limited evidence that the Churches in Britain and Ireland were voicing such a request. An evaluation of one of these visitations in Southwell Diocese in 1997 included the complaint that 'Our Vicar kept telling people . . . [the visitors] were "here to learn about English church life" – no mention of what we could learn from . . . [them]', while on a visit to Witney in Oxford Diocese in the same year, Tengatenga concluded, 'no one wants to know', though he had more fruitful encounters elsewhere, including Westcott House, Cambridge. There were other encouragements, like the Korean women's visit in 1997, which proved in Liverpool Diocese 'an important event for us, widening perspectives . . . taking our Christian foundation seriously'. Despite many discouragements, initial evaluation of the programme encouraged the Society to persevere.

Other programmes were also developed to propagate the Gospel in Britain, three in the 1970s, chiefly aiming to attract young people into mission. The first of these was Christians Aware, started in 1977. This grew out of the Association of Missionary Candidates which had originated in the 1950s with an overseas orientation, but, as Christians Aware, took on also a concern for mission in Britain. Led initially by Primrose Cooper, later by Barbara Butler, this association was only loosely linked to USPG and tried to reach 'beyond the Society's boundaries'. Seeking to be international and ecumenical, Christians Aware drew together mostly young people into its lively programme of conferences, work camps and the like on radical themes, and provided opportunities for exchange with like-minded groups in Africa and Asia. Its slightly maverick organizational style made for a continuingly awkward relationship with the Society, and after some ten years it launched out into full independence, although continuing through the 1990s to share in lively events with the Society.

Also in 1977, the Society's youth department established Root Groups, to provide young people aged between 18 and 30 an opportunity to live and work together in a parish for a year. At a time when young people were increasingly disaffected with the Church, these proved, under the guidance through the 1980s of Gabrielle Grace and Derek Hanscombe, to be a demanding and effective way of deepening Christian experience while serving a local church and community, often in the more challenging housing estates and where adventurous ministries were being attempted. Participants largely supported themselves, sometimes from their unemployment benefit or the casual work that a member of the group might pick up, and with help from the receiving parish. By 1982, eight groups were functioning, including one in Scotland on one of Edinburgh's most desolate housing schemes, the first in Wales, in the Rhondda Valley, and the first ecumenical group, a joint Anglican–Baptist–Methodist project in Grimsby, while every diocese of the Church of England had asked to have a group. The location of some of the groups in what were known as Urban Priority Areas, as Taylor indicated to Council in 1986, was a direct, practical contribution to the mission of the Church called for in the Archbishops' 1985 report, *Faith in the City*. The impact upon a parish and community was often significant, while many of the young people matured in faith through the experience, some going on into formal ministry, others into education and social work. The adoption of the scheme in the Episcopal Church of the USA in 1985 suggests that the Society had found an effective new instrument for mission. Overseas participants were recruited under the Bursaries programme to join groups in Britain from the early 1990s. Despite continuing requests from parishes, and despite the Methodist Church becoming full participants in 1996, recruiting young people in Britain was becoming increasingly difficult. A major factor beside the disaffection referred to was the financial difficulty confronting students in tertiary education, previously a principal source of recruits, but now often faced with a large debt at the end of their studies. Only two groups were functioning in 1998–9, and the programme ran out of recruits and was closed in August 1999.

The Experience Exchange Programme was established in 1979 for 'committed Christians wanting to learn from the Church in another country', who would be given a placement, usually in a church institution, for six to twelve months, like the newly qualified English doctor in a Bangalore hospital 'doing a bit of everything' in 1982. Costs were shared by the participant, the receiving Church and USPG. The age range was 18 to 65, and while the majority of participants initially were young people, in what was known as the 'gap year' in relation to tertiary education, older people increasingly participated, like the redundant engineer who went to teach electronics in a Zambian church institution for a year, and the increasing number of people who were taking early retirement from the 1980s. Partly for this reason, the programme continued to expand through the 1980s and 90s, with 25 participants in 1998 and 30 in 1999. Because participants had to raise much of the cost themselves, the very different circumstances of the Third World meant that 'Reverse EEPs' occurred only rarely, though in 1981 a Chinese youth worker in Sabah, Victor Leong, and in 1982 a young Tanzanian leprosy worker, Peter Asmani, spent 6 months in placements in Britain. A few participants moved from this programme to further work with the Society, like Judith Crouch, who graduated from an EEP experience to a Special Skills post in Brazil. The programme provided useful links with dioceses and institutions in North and South India after many of the Society's relationships there had been lost in the more impersonal connections with the two Synods. This programme also became joint with the Methodist Church in 1996, while also during the 1990s applications began to be received from Roman Catholics and Baptists. Participants often made a worthwhile contribution during their placement, and brought significant experience of the world Church back with them to Britain and Ireland.

Another element in the Society's activities that came to be seen as contributory to mission in Britain and Ireland was the work of the Area Secretaries distributed about the dioceses of England, Ireland and Wales. Of course, they had no such role in the earliest years of this period, being the Society's representatives solely to promote interest in overseas missionary work, known as missionary education, in order to encourage financial support and recruit missionaries. Their frequent involvement, however, in areas of immigration brought several into an active role, helping and challenging churches in Britain with their own missionary obligations in regard to both racial and other-faiths issues. Subsequently, they were given responsibility for the vacation placements of overseas bursars. They also assumed some responsibility for any Root Group in their area. A survey by Bishop Skelton in 1987–8 reaffirmed the significance of the Area Secretaries for mission in Britain. A painful decision, however, was reached in a financial crisis in 1992 to declare all the Area Secretaries redundant and put the Society's regional representation in the care of a much smaller team of some fourteen Field Workers for England, Ireland and Wales. With such a small team, representation of the Society was, inevitably, a more exclusive responsibility. Where, however, good collaboration with diocesan officers for mission and evangelism made it possible and where local volunteers were available, successors to the earlier supporters' organization, The Friends of USPG, to sustain a close relationship with parishes and deaneries, mission in

Britain and Ireland was taken for granted as a continuing part of the Field Workers' role. A special responsibility was the promotion of the Jubilee 2000 campaign regarding world debt.

The Society had been established three centuries earlier to, among other things, re-evangelize the Church in America. As the Tercentenary approached, with increasing numbers throughout Britain and Ireland abandoning the Christian faith in favour of a frenetic consumerism, the urgency of a re-evangelization, and one which comprehended a transformation of the Christianity of Britain and Ireland like that going on in the south, was only too evident.

⤙⟶◉⟵⤚

The Society prepared for the Tercentenary with measured thankfulness. The 1990s had seen USPG still remarkably well supported by individuals and the Churches' generally small congregations throughout Britain and Ireland, with wider relationships proving renewable through the Provincial Consultations, and the beginnings of a fuller internationalization of the staff. Involvement in the Jubilee 2000 campaign was helping USPG's supporters to confront one of the great, global injustices of the age. A series of small but well-directed interventions had kept the Society near the cutting edge. For example, in 1993, USPG and CMS together had initiated and funded a consultation of participants from ten African provinces on African culture and Anglican liturgy, supporting 'the African Church's struggle to reclaim her liturgical genius'. Thus, also, during the years 1996–8, the Society provided a scientist-theologian, who had previously directed the Church and Society work of the WCC, to lecture and conduct seminars on environmental and ecological questions in the Church of North India. Also, from 1997, the Society was renewing its assistance in the educational, health care and church-planting endeavours of the Karens in Burma and in exile across the Thai border, victims of an ethnic cleansing 'as bad as anything seen . . . in Europe or Africa', the only agency supporting them from both inside and outside their homeland.[10]

With Queen Elizabeth II as Royal Patron of the Tercentenary, the Society would have the encouragement of a devoted and enduring Christian example and would also establish continuities with its beginnings and history. A pilgrimage would also span the history, starting in Thomas Bray's parish of Sheldon, now adjacent to the airport in the fringes of one of Britain's most pluralistic cities, Birmingham, and culminating in London in a eucharist in St Paul's Cathedral surrounded by the temples of the city's globalizing market-makers, and where Bray had preached before a group of early missionaries about apostolic charity.

Other plans included a travelling exhibition, with a computer kiosk for a virtual journey with USPG around the world, and events in other provinces of the Anglican Communion, including a conference of American and Canadian historians in Toronto. Plans were developing to help people in a group of dioceses in south-west England to look at personal vocation, and for an international conference called 'Venture Fourth' to discern the new directions called for in the Society's fourth century.

Samuel Wilberforce had concluded that the eighteenth and nine-teenth-century Society had been an 'Angel of Mercy' within 'a godless colonization'. Whether in an equally godless globalization the Society had continued to be such an angel is best left to the judgement of others. What was increasingly clear as USPG approached the third millennium and its fourth century was the emerging context of mission. All that that great Christian prophet of the past half-century, Barbara Ward, had indicated was inescapably present, the biosphere of our inheritance and the technosphere of our achievement in deepening conflict, while two of its most significant historians wrote of a crisis in all humanity's social and economic systems, and planetary conditions making for 'the very hardest of times'.[11] It looked to be a testing context for the propagation of the Gospel.

Epilogue: a Church in mission

We started with a missionary, we conclude with a Church in mission.[1]

Bengal had been, in the words of the poet Ezra Pound, 'sung into a nation' by its own great poet, Rabindranath Tagore, early in the century, but then, on Britain's withdrawal and division of the subcontinent in 1947, much of it became a colony again, and one of the world's largest Muslim societies, East Pakistan. Only with its war of independence in 1971 did Bangladesh begin to find its way as a nation. Initially a secular, socialist democracy, then with an Islamic military government, the 1990s saw a more moderate Islamic government in place. The war of independence had effectively finished off the country's largest cash crop, jute, increasingly supplanted by the West's synthetic fibres, leaving it the world's poorest country and also, over time, one of the most heavily indebted. Cyclones in the Bay of Bengal routinely shatter its coastal areas and, while quality work is being done on flood control, reckless deforestation in Nepal and north-east India brings to its vast Ganga-Meghna-Brahmaputra river system an annual peril of floods for its crowded, impoverished population.

The Church of Bangladesh came into being with independence, uniting a small Presbyterian community and the former Anglican Diocese of Dhaka under Bishop Blair, son of SPG-missionary parents, getting its first Bengali bishop, Barnabas Dwijen Mondal, in 1975. Bishop Mondal writes,

> The atmosphere has not been conducive to the upliftment of minorities. We have not been called on to play our part in the life of the nation. We have often been left alone, the remnant of foreign rule. However, all the odds have not overtaken us and the Church has not

become some inward-looking ghetto. Our efforts have been to become faithful under God. The Church is there to share the self-giving love of Jesus Christ in full solidarity with the people, living close to them.[2]

The Church now comprises some 2500 families, in two dioceses under Bishops Mondal and Baroi, a powerless and 'microscopic minority'. They are a 5 per cent minority alongside the relatively large Baptist and Roman Catholic Churches, but all these together are not much less of a microscopic minority, approximately one-third of a million, predominantly from among the country's oppressed tribal peoples, amidst 130 million Muslims. It is a striking illustration of the observation that 'Christians everywhere live in a diaspora', in so many places 'the little flock'.[3] The Church of Bangladesh is essentially a Church of the poor, a few living in the towns and cities, the majority a rural Church of subsistence farmers, fishermen and day-labourers. To build up the Church there has been a deliberate effort to provide education and training for one child from each poorer church family. Because it is such a Church, its workers, including its handful of missionary co-workers, including the Society's five in 2000, are called to live 'close to the poor . . . [as] real friends and . . . [with] a simple life-style', bearing in mind that 'the poor around us can teach us much'. In the words of one missionary, 'Actions must be simple. Costs must be low. Staff must be ordinary. We want a movement in which people find each other and the meaning of who they are. Prayer is focal. Teaching is central.'[4]

In response to frequent hostility from Muslim militants, the mission emphasis is upon 'a servant ministry' through a Social Development Programme. This is co-ordinated by David Mazumdar, a College of the Ascension alumnus, and aims 'to build communities and break down barriers'. Through it, the Church shares in one of Bangladesh's most successful endeavours, development. With its particular communitarian aim, the Programme's staff of more than 700 includes some 140 Muslims and 85 Hindus alongside their Christian colleagues, seeking to overcome a colonial past in which Muslims and Hindus were merely 'our targets of evangelism', and which 'never helped build communities of love'. The Programme is sustained externally by 'generous resource sharing from various partners especially by the USPG', and internally by a worshipping community with a penchant for Catholic ritual, copious incense and the music and songs of Rabindranath.

In renewed international relationships, 'oneness in a common mission . . . sharing resources, both human and financial, and global concerns, among churches as equal partners', the Church of Bangladesh has found 'new confidence and self-respect'. What remains essential, though, is 'costly discipleship and . . . a community of faith in its own situation', aspiring to the Gospel ideal of becoming 'an insignificant but essential item, something like salt'. Bishop Mondal concludes his short history of the Church of Bangladesh, 'May God in his grace make us the salt of the earth.'

Notes

Reference to the Society's own archives, either at Rhodes House, Oxford, or Partnership House, London, are indicated by [ ]. References to C. F. Pascoe, (1901) *Two Hundred Years of the SPG*, London, and to H. P. Thompson, (1951) *Into All Lands*, London, are given as Pascoe and Thompson respectively. Fuller details on publications since 1950 are in the Select Bibliography.

Prologue

1. Information on Gordon comes from *Bulloch's Roll*, a (slightly inaccurate) unpublished compendium in the Royal Society.
2. P. Gordon, *Geography Anatomiz'd*, London, edition of 1699 – edition of 1693 not seen. Gordon's computation is the same as Bray's in his 1697 sermon, which follows 'the learned Herebord' of Leiden (1614–61).
3. Latourette is thus a century out in suggesting that Carey was the first Anglo-Saxon Protestant to make global proposals for mission – K. S. Latourette (1941) *A History of the Expansion of Christianity*, London, Vol. IV, p. 68.
4. [Appx. B.6].
5. G. Keith (1706) *A Journal of Travels from New Hampshire . . .*, London, p. 1; [Gordon to Secretary A. I. Letter XII]; [Col. L. Morris to Archdeacon Beveridge, 3 Sept. 1702, A.I. no.45].

Chapter 1

1. Henry VII's charter granted to John Cabot. For the theological justification provided by, for example, Jeremy Taylor, see Blackburn (1997), p. 249.

2. Anniversary Sermon, 1707; the Acts text had previously been used on the seal of the Massachusetts Bay Colony, designed in 1629.
3. See Clark (1985), and Nockles (1994), especially Ch. 1, 'Church and state: the politics of High Churchmanship'.
4. [Committee for Receiving Proposals, 31.3.1702]
5. [Journal, 27.3.1702]; for Royal Letters, Pascoe, pp. 823–5.
6. For the instructions as given to the Governor of New York and New Jersey in 1703, Pascoe, p. 60; [Journal, 27.2.1702].
7. This helps to explain the comparatively low income of the Society – apart from that raised through Royal Letters, and parliamentary grants – beside that of other mission agencies in the nineteenth century, and makes comparisons with them largely meaningless.
8. For links with Francke, Halle and continental pietist mission, see Ward (1999), *passim*.
9. Woolverton (1984), p. 88.
10. For the colonists use of I Samuel 15.3, see Bosch (1991), p. 275. This theme was taken up 250 years later by a Native American writer, Warrior (Dec. 1989).
11. Sermons of 1711, 1731.
12. Sermons of 1770, 1771.
13. Hinderaker (July 1996).
14. E. Settle (1711) *A Pindaric Poem on the Propagation of the Gospel in Foreign Parts*, London.
15. D. Humphreys (1730) *An Historical Account of the Incorporated SPG*, Downing, pp. 24, 254, 35, 356.
16. A series of studies by F. J. Klingberg and his associates deals with the Society as a humanitarian force during the period. See also McCulloch (1950).
17. Bennett (1958), *passim*.
18. See the Dedication in Boehm's 1709 English translation of the letters of Ziegenbalg and Plutschau, Pascoe, pp. 471–2; also Singh (1999).

Chapter 2

1. T. Bray (1699) *Bibliotheca Catechetica*, quoted in Thompson (1954), p. 103. All other quotations in this chapter, unless otherwise stated, are from Thompson (1954).
2. T. Bray (1727) *Missionalia: or, a Collection of Missionary Pieces Relating to the Conversion of the Heathen, both the African Negroes and American Indians*, London, p. 1. The British Library edition of this is bound with Bray's (1729) *Directorium Missionarium*, London, with excerpts from Thomas à Jesu, etc. in the latter.
3. Sardar *et. al.* (1993), *passim*.
4. *Missionalia*, p. 1.

5. *Ibid.* All subsequent quotations in this section are from this collection, except the last, which is from Thompson (1954), p. 65.
6. See the request of 1765 quoted in F. J. Klingberg (1940) *Anglican Humanism in Colonial New York*, Freeport, p. 248. For Native American horticulturalists, see Axtell (1981), p. xvii.
7. Axtell (1985), Ch. 7, 'Reduce Them to Civility'.

Chapter 3

1. [E. Clarke to J. Braithwaite, 25.6.1797, C]; Report, 1712, pp. 67–8.
2. [Journal, 15.3.1706]; D. Humphreys (1730), *An Historical Account*, p. 69.
3. Examples quoted from Bolton (1982). See especially Chapter 5, 'The Character of the Clergy'.
4. T. Bray, *Missionalia*; Thompson (1954), p. 89.
5. *Ibid.*, p. 63.
6. Calam (1971), pp. 104, 107.
7. For a twentieth-century application, see the Standing Committee's correspondence with the Synod of Irish Bishops in 1901, 'The Society represents the whole Church . . . It refuses to be a tribunal, believing that private tribunals are tyrannies', Report 1901.
8. Bentley (Apr.–June 1966); H. and C. Schneider (eds) (1929) *Samuel Johnson, President of King's College: His Career and Writings*, New York, Vol. 1, pp. 424–30.
9. [Journal. Appx A, 1701–1810, p. 21].
10. Prefix to *Apostolick Charity*, p. 4.
11. Figures for the earlier period are given in Nelson (1962), p. 43; later figures from Pascoe.
12. [Abstract of Proceedings, 1792].
13. [App. to Journal, B.50]; Clement (1973), p. 32.
14. [Journal, xxii, 363].
15. [Journal xvii–xxvi]; Thompson, p. 531.

Chapter 4

1. Quoted in Raboteau (1978), p. 96.
2. [Commissioners for Trade and Plantations to Archbishop of Canterbury, 25.10.1700; Appx. to Journal A.5].
3. [B.xxi.13 ff].
4. This passage is based largely on Bolton (1982).
5. [Le Jau to Secretary, 2.12.1706. A.III].
6. [Le Jau to Secretary, 15.9.1708, A.IV]; Lambeth, Fulham MSS, S. Carolina no.10.

7. Anderson (1997), p. 312.
8. [Andrews to Secretary, 9.3.1713, A.18.143; Ogilvie to Secretary, 25.12.1755, Journal 13, pp. 182–5]
9. Quoted Raboteau (1978), p. 99.
10. Bishop of London, 'To the Masters and Mistresses of Families in the English Plantations Abroad' (1727), quotes I Corinthians 7.20, 24.
11. J. B. E. Thompson, 'The Secretaries of the SPG, Part II', *Mission Field* (Sept. 1938).
12. Quoted Bolton (1982), p. 104.
13. Raboteau (1978), pp. 118,116; Frey and Wood (1998), p. 72.
14. [B.V.19.49].
15. Blackburn (1997), pp. 260, 345.
16. 1802, Bishop of Chichester; 1811, Bishop of Carlisle.
17. Letters of 26 Jan. and 3 Mar. 1760, quoted in J. H. Bennett (1958), p. 88.
18. *Ibid.*, p. vii; F. J. Klingberg (ed.) (1949) *Codrington Chronicle: An Experiment in Anglican Altruism on a Barbados Plantation, 1710–1834*, Berkeley, p. 10.
19. [T. Moore to Secretary, 13.11.1705, A.II]; Humphreys (1730) *op.cit.*, p. 22.
20. Letter 27 Oct. 1755 in H. and C. Schneider (eds) (1929) *op.cit.*, Vol. I, p. 225.
21. D. Humphreys, *op.cit., passim.*
22. F. J. Klingberg (1943) 'Contributions of the SPG to the American Way of Life', *Historical Magazine of the Protestant Episcopal Church*, XII.
23. For Smith, see Woolverton (1984), Ch. 9, 'The Enlightenment, Education and Politics'.
24. Bridenbaugh (1962), *passim.*
25. [A.13: 144–5]; Humphreys, *op.cit.*, pp. 3, 37, 148–9.
26. Mills (1978), p. 39, and Lambert (1999), pp. 206–12.
27. Bultmann (1950), p. 65.
28. Humphreys, *op. cit.*
29. Quoted in Bolton (1982), p. 35.
30. [W. F. France, Overseas Secretary, 'Report of the Selly Oak Conference 22–25 July 1946', 98.110].
31. Lewis (1996), pp. 4–5.
32. Cf. the Bishop of Long Island at a Missionary Conference prior to Lambeth 1878, quoted in Pascoe, p. 84.

Chapter 5

1. Hobsbawm (1968), p. 13.
2. *Mission Field*, Jan. 1856.
3. Hereafter in Section 2, unless otherwise stated, missionaries' and bishops' reports, and statements of the Society, are quoted from the annual Report.
4. Tatz (1999), *passim.*
5. Foucault (1991), p. 125.

6. Report, 1827; Report, 1851.
7. Pascoe, p. xvi; 151st Anniversary Sermon, 1852.
8. Pascoe, p. xvi; Bishop Blomfield, Anniversary Sermon, 1827.
9. 'an epoch-making year in the history of Missions'; E. Stock (1899) *History of the Church Missionary Society*, London, I, p. 57.
10. Ray (July–Dec. 1964), pp. 83–9.

Chapter 6

1. Nockles (1994), *passim*, and Webster (1954). They were also known as the Clapton Sect, both names in distinction from the core group of CMS founders, the Clapham Sect.
2. J. B. E. Thompson, (Sept. 1938), *op.cit.*, p. 303.
3. Middleton to the Secretary, 16.11.1818.
4. From the Hackney Phalanx's mouthpiece, *The British Critic*, 1817, quoted in Webster (1954), p. 30.
5. Stanley (1979); G. A. Selwyn (1855) *The Work of Christ: Four Sermons . . .*, Cambridge, pp. 44–5.
6. Prime Minister Gladstone, snatching 'a few moments from the crowd and pressure of other very different, most imperious events', was moving a Resolution for enhanced support of the Society at the 1867 Anniversary Meeting – 1867 Report.
7. White (1968), p. 59. See also W. F. France (1941) *The Overseas Episcopate: Centenary History of the Colonial Bishoprics Fund 1841–1941*, London.
8. Quoted White (1968), p. 1.
9. Report, 1897. For a fuller account, see Jacob (1997).
10. Cnattingius (1952), p. 232. See also Yates (1978).
11. Stanley (1979), p. 101.
12. Maughan (1995), p. 40.
13. Froude, but Newman also saw the missionary diocese as a 'refuge' for disaffected Tractarians; White (1968), pp. 42–3; see also Rowell (1983), p. 166, and, for a penetrating interpretation of Anglo-Catholic missiology, Jeffery (1980), pp. 119–36.
14. Report, 1880, 1891.
15. S. K. Rudra (April 1914), *St Stephen's College Magazine*.
16. Report, 1848.
17. A. M. Oakley (1998) 'St Augustine's Theological College, Canterbury: the training of missionaries', Canterbury (typescript).
18. Grafe (1990), p. 205.
19. The missionary at St Matthew's, Keiskamma Hoek, in the Diocese of Grahamstown one Sunday in 1860 noted that everyone had been reclothed and 'there was not a blanket to be seen'.
20. For this development, see Bowie, *et. al.* (1993).

Chapter 7

1. *Mission Field*, May 1862; F. Boatright, (Apr. 1948), 'Anglican Backwater', *The East and the West*.
2. Quoted Clark (1985) p. 216.
3. Wilson (1968), pp. 11, 216.
4. Only the Archbishop of Canterbury's intervention, at Inglis' request, got things on to a better footing; Jacob (1997), pp. 77–8.
5. e.g. Carrington (1963).
6. Report, 1857.
7. [M.vi.221].
8. *Mission Field*, May, Nov. 1856.
9. *Ibid.*, June 1862.
10. Quoted in Davidson (Dec. 1990), p. 177.
11. H. W. Tucker (1879) *Memoir of the Life and Episcopate of G. A. Selwyn*, Vol. II, London, p. 48.
12. Davidson (Dec. 1990), p. 181.
13. Hodgson (July 1987); Ngewu (1998), pp. 77–8.
14. Chilton (1993), *passim*.
15. *Mission Field*, Oct. 1870.
16. Labode (1993), pp. 126–44.
17. On the Baptists and Roy, see Hollenweger (1976), pp. 23–7; Sugirtharajah (1998), pp. 29–53.
18. Singh (Jan.–Feb. 1982).
19. Webster (1976), p. 188; even the rightly revered William Carey was close to the imperial system, working for the East India Company at Fort William College on an official salary that was, by Indian standards, astronomical – Dharmaraj (1993), pp. 54–5.
20. For a modern interpretation of the Society's work as Dalit liberation, see Jayakumar (1998).
21. Bennett (1950), p. 29.
22. Goodridge (1981), pp. 91, 88.
23. J. Mitchinson, Ramsden Sermon, 1883.
24. Sands (1998), p. 88; Davis (1983).
25. *Mission Field*, Mar. 1856.
26. Titus (1983).

Chapter 8

1. See Pascoe, pp. 800–13.
2. *Mission Field*, Feb. 1856.
3. This account is based on Young (1981), and Amaladass and Young (1995),

with a few details from the *Dictionary of National Biography* entry 'Mill, William Hodge', and Spear (1970), pp. 177–88.

4. Quoted in Amaladass and Young (1995), p. 32.
5. Report, 1832.
6. Letters to Secretary, 7.10.1846; 14.2.1849.
7. Paul (1961), p. 245; cf. Paradkar (1969). Nilakantha was on the Society's list 1868–70, and also later worked in parishes supported by the Society.
8. Quoted in Philip (1982), p. 67, on which this account is largely based, and from which, unless otherwise stated, quotations are taken.
9. Quoted in Copley (1997), p. 224.
10. Copley (1997), p. 226.
11. Baago (1969), pp. 1–7.
12. Jayakumar (1999), pp. 136–7, 161.
13. Quotations on Caldwell, unless otherwise stated, are from Ravindiran (Jan. 1996).
14. Shirai (1999), p. 63 (this and other passages translated by Jerome Moriyama).
15. Shirai (1999), p. 304.
16. This account is based largely on Guy (1983) and Parsons (1997), pp. 135–75.
17. M. Jarrett-Kerr, quoted in Parsons (1997), p. 169.
18. Report, 1871.
19. Jacob (1997), Ch. 5.
20. See key texts for a reassessment: Guy (1983); and Parsons (1997).
21. Hastings (1994), p. 256. For Hastings, the other intellectual prince, with Colenso, was Livingstone. See also Pato (1989), pp. 159–76.

Chapter 9

1. Pascoe, p. 341e; Hodgson (13–17 Jan. 1997), p. 5.
2. *Ibid., passim.*
3. In his farewell address at the time of his retirement in 1928, Davidson said the Society was 'intended to be, had always been intended to be, and had the right insistently to claim to be the official Society', while he told Walter France, the Overseas Secretary, 'personally and privately . . . [that the SPG was] the Archbishop's Society through which he . . . [could] act officially'. ['Report of Selly Oak Conference, 22–25 July 1946', p. 9].
4. J. A. Hobson (1902) *Imperialism: A Study*, London, pp. 196, 198, 202–3; J. C. Bannerjie, (Sept. 1904) 'The future of Christianity in India', *Hindustan Review*.
5. Thompson, p. 584.
6. Ranger (1973), pp. 1–26, including Ranger's account of how the missionaries' 'narrow view of the missionary task' frustrated Msigala's efforts (p. 22).
7. *Central Africa*, Dec. 1937, quoted *ibid.*, p. 24.
8. Iliffe (1973), p. 69.
9. This leading role has been maintained, a survey indicating that more than

half of India's ten leading tertiary colleges in 1998 were Christian foundations, St Stephen's leading all others on every criterion; see Thapa (6 July
1998).

10. Jayakumar (1998), p. 190.
11. For CMS, see Williams (1990); for UMCA, see Moriyama's essay in this
    volume and Moriyama (1984).
12. Caldwell was accused by the leader of this movement, J. Thomas, of
    throwing 'every imaginable obstacle in the way'. Correspondence included
    with 1866 Report.
13. [Acheson-Williams to Montgomery, 3.5.1910, Letters Received].
14. Thompson, p. 559; [Lefroy memorandum, Jan. 1907, File 'Principal of St
    Stephen's College' CMD papers].
15. Weller (1971), p. 42; Harper (1991), p. 219; H. H. Montgomery (1902)
    Foreign Missions, London, p. 35.
16. Millington (1993), p. 28.
17. S. A. C. Ghose, (May 1907) 'The Indian nation and Christianity', *Student
    Movement*.
18. Harper (1991) p. 148.
19. V. Elwin, Circular Letter, 29.8.1937, Elwin Papers, India Office Library and
    Records (IOLR), British Library.
20. Sundkler (1954), p. 59; quoted in J. McLeod Campbell (1946) *Christian
    History in the Making*, London, p. 313.
21. Sundkler (1954), p. 51. Unless otherwise stated, all subsequent information
    is from Sundkler.
22. Quoted in White (1992–3), p. 36.
23. Millington (1996), p. 100.

Chapter 10

1. Kiernan (1972), p. xxxiii.
2. Ch'en (1960).
3. See Allen (1995); and Talltorp (1988).
4. *Cornhill Magazine*, Nov., Dec. 1900, Feb. 1901; Allen (1901) *The Siege of the
   Peking Legations*, London; *Church Missionary Review*, June 1927; *Guardian*,
   July 1902.
5. See, for example, ['Some autobiographical notes and ruminations', written
   when Allen was 75, Allen Papers, Box 8].
6. Report, Christmas 1902.
7. Paper read at JCMA Conference, Manchester, 11/12 Nov. 1903; Report,
   Christmas 1902; the fullest account is in the Epilogue to his (1912) *Missionary
   Methods: St Paul's or Ours?*, London.
8. Leaflet 'The Anglican Mission at Yung Ch'ing, North China', 20 Feb 1903.
9. As in note 5.
10. *Living Church*, 26 Jan. 1929.

11. *Pilgrim*, July 1926; letter to *The Daily Telegraph*, 12 July 1922.
12. C. H. Robinson (1915) *History of Christian Missions*, Edinburgh, pp. 10–17; letter of 17.4.1912, quoted in Harper (1991), p. 197; *Delhi Mission News*, Oct. 1917.
13. Cripps commends Allen's books in 'Missionary Heroes and Heroines: Notes on the G. F. S. Kalendar for 1928'.
14. 'C. F. Andrews of India', dated 1934 and included as an envoi in B. Chaturvedi and M. Sykes (1949) *Charles Freer Andrews: A Narrative*, London.
15. *Church Times*, 16 Dec. 1910; C. F. Andrews (1908) *North India*, London, p. 160.
16. For a fuller account of this ten years, with sources for the quotations, see O'Connor (1990).
17. Tinker (1979), p. 143.
18. Paton (1996).
19. For Winslow and his ashram, see O'Connor (1993).
20. For Cripps, see Guha (1999) and O'Connor (1993).
21. Guha (1999), p. 332.
22. Steere (1973), p. 95.
23. Steere (1973), pp. 95, 125.
24. Hastings (1986), p. 94, referring particularly to Andrews and Cripps.

Chapter 11

1. *Morning Calm*, February 1900. This and all other quotations on Kanghwa, and on Seoul Cathedral, are taken from Lee (1998).
2. Butler (1986), p. 95; *Delhi*, April, July 1927.
3. Lucas published his main paper on this as 'The Christian Approach to Non-Christian Customs' in E. R. Morgan (ed.) (1928) *Essays Catholic and Missionary*, London, pp. 115–51, and later as a small book (1950) *Christianity and Native Rites*, London. The following account is based on this and Ranger (1972), pp. 221–51.
4. Ranger (1972), pp. 239, 247.
5. Robertson (1990), pp. 27–31.
6. The main account is the Society publication, J. C. Winslow (1930) *Christa Seva Sangha*, London; see also Barbara Noreen CSMV (1994).
7. This found its way into the Supplement to the CIPBC Book of Common Prayer of 1960.
8. For an appraisal of their work see Taylor (1975).
9. See Walker (1985), which is based to a great extent on Paterson's cyclostyled *Cyrene Papers*, produced for and distributed by the Society between 1940 and 1953. For the Cyrene students' use of the distinctive landscape as a setting for the events of the Bible, see Ranger (1999), pp. 55–6.

Section 4 – Introductory

1. [Robertson at AGM, 1980].
2. [Roberts's draft circular letter to overseas bishops, 1945, H.9]; [Report of visit to USA and Canada, 1950, H.10].
3. The annual income at 1900, 1910, etc., through to 1990, with an averaging of 1997 and 1998 (with a third column giving figures at 1900 values: factors taken from the table of English consumer prices published by Global Financial Data, figures prepared by David Richman):

1900	£178,396	(178,396)
1910	211,419	(211,419)
1920	342,540	(131,411)
1930	387,320	(301,958)
1940	275,635	(174,067)
1950	378,744	(119,325)
1960	671,567	(148,441)
1970	1,096,316	(159,575)
1980	2,243,040	(89,686)
1990	4,913,282	(105,710)
1997/8	5,580,958	(96,307)

Chapter 12

1. *Overseas News*, Nov. 49; Annual Report, 1954.
2. See Buhlmann (1976).
3. UMCA Annual Report, 1948.
4. For the Korogwe picture, cf. Ranger (1983); [Archbishop of Central Africa to Archbishop of Canterbury, 14.11.57, H.7].
5. Hastings (1986), p. 433; Perham (1964), p. 18.
6. All quotations throughout this account of UMCA are from UMCA Annual Reports and *Central Africa*.
7. For a perceptive Malawian account, see Tengatenga (1996).
8. For Lefroy, see Cox (1994).
9. Report, 1969.
10. This pattern was repeated in the CMS in West Africa; Williams (1990), *passim*.
11. [Kingsnorth confidential report, 18.3.65, TF.199].
12. All quotations in this paragraph from Standing Committee minutes (SC) and Report.

Chapter 13

1. [SC, 3.6.48].
2. *Overseas News*, Apr., June, Dec. 1949.
3. *Overseas News*, Feb., May 1950; for Gray [H.20, reports of 30.4.50, 28.5.50].
4. Report, 1952.
5. For further details, see Whyte (1988).
6. Wickeri (1988), p. 39; Whyte in Paton (1996), p. 36; Bishop K. H. Ting describes Allen as at the 'head' of this 'school of missiological thinking', *ibid.*, p. x. A 'Manifesto of the Church' published at the inauguration of the National Christian Council at Shanghai in 1922 seems to have been the launch pad for the Chinese adoption of these ideas – see Lin (Jan. 1998), pp. 14–15.
7. [Roberts's circular, 9.10.50, and Roberts to H. E. Sir Henry Gurney, 17.10.50, H.20]; [Savarimuthu to Thistle, 18.10.74, TF. 2557].
8. [Fisher to Roberts, 29.6.51, H.19].
9. [Roseveare to Trapp, Dec. 1962, TF. 283].
10. Harmondsworth, 1975.
11. See Nelson-Pallmeyer (1989).
12. Hobsbawm (1994), p. 286.
13. [11.10.56].
14. [General Committee, 4.2.70].
15. Typescript James Stuart, 'The Story of the Delhi Brotherhood'; 22nd Annual Report, 1998–9.
16. Report, 1976.
17. Hinkelammert (July–Aug. 1990).
18. Graeme Brown, 'Jubilee' *Network*, Spring 1977.
19. Dent and Peters (1999).

Chapter 14

1. [Kelly to Roberts, 23.4.46; Yashiro to Roberts, 9.12.50; Lee to Roberts, 18.9.45, H.19].
2. By L. S. Thornton CR, and published London, 1941.
3. [Roberts's paper for SC, 14.10.54, H.11].
4. [Trapp to Howe, 1.1.70, TF. 3436].
5. The mission agencies were not even invited to Lambeth 1988, though they were back in strength at Lambeth 1998.
6. [Council, June 1991].
7. [Report to AGM, 1977, TF. 1987].
8. [Robertson, 'Dublin to Trinidad', 2.1.76, TF. 663].
9. [Mission Programmes Budget Group, 26.5.81, TF. 3484].

10. *Thinking Mission*, 7 July 1991.
11. [95.115].
12. [Mission Programmes Budget Group, 26.5.81, TF. 3484].
13. [SC, 2.2.50].
14. *Network*, Autumn 1983.
15. ['African Tour Report', Council, Dec. 1976].

Chapter 15

1. Jayakumar (1999), p. 190; for the dispersion, see Sargent (1962).
2. Ward and Dubos (1972), p. 47.
3. ['Closed Doors', 18.1.72, TF. 199].
4. *Network*, Apr. 1989.
5. Wynne (1985), p. 75.
6. *Network*, Apr. 1990.

Chapter 16

1. *Network*, Dec. 1970.
2. CMS Members' Bulletin, 47, July 1964; [SC, 9.4.64].
3. [Minutes, 25.9.63, H.15].
4. [Sec's files, Apr. 1964, TF. 1994].
5. The Railway Mission followed after a brief negotiation; see Roden (1999).
6. [19.7.66, TF. 1975].
7. [20.8.69, TF. 1994].
8. [17.6.66, 29.10.70, 17.12.70, 18.1.72, TF. 1994].
9. [27.6.67, TF. 1994].
10. [Warren to Trapp, 22.5.58; Trapp to Warren, 29.5.58, H.9].
11. [Trapp statement on Taylor's 'Mission starts at home', 16.2.65, TF. 1994].
12. [SC, 26.6.75]; [1.3.76, TF. 2009].
13. For the early years, see Clark (1999).
14. [Roberts's paper for Warlingham Staff Conference, 29.10.46; Conference Report, H.21].
15. [17.3.71, TF. 297].
16. [17.2.75, TF. 663].
17. [Report to Annual Meeting, 1977, TF. 1987].
18. [5.6.84, 8.11.84, Acc.95.115–Wales].
19. Report, 1867.
20. [Roberts's first report to SC, 7.12.44, H. 24].
21. [College/CEFACS file – Sinclair to Wingate and Chapman, 3.4.96].

Chapter 17

1. [Clayton to Roberts, 21.3.50; Jackson to Roberts, 19.4.50; Young to Roberts, 11.4.50; Roberts to Clayton, 18.1.51, H.16].
2. [SC, 11.7.1968].
3. [2.1.69, TF. 1975]; [27.5.69, TF. 2025]; [30.5.69, TF. 3436].
4. [Bp of Grahamstown to Earl of March, 30.11.72, TF. 663]; [J. D. Davies's memo to Robertson, 6.8.75, TF. 1998].
5. [Shevill to Bp of Rangoon, 4.1.72, TF. 2026].
6. [SC, 15.3.82].
7. Davies (1983), p. x.
8. [SC, 13.6.80].
9. [SC, 19.11.82].
10. College files, Taylor to Archbishop of Indian Ocean, 17.6.91; Curriculum, 29.5.92.
11. [W. Ustorf, 'World Christianity and Current Trends in Missiology', 22 Mar. 1992, 96.150].

Chapter 18

1. [Memorandum, 23.1.58, TF. 995]. Unless otherwise stated, references in this section are to this file and [TF. 994].
2. [SC, 8.5.47].
3. [Hopkins to Roberts, 13.8.56, H.6].
4. [Trapp to Ramsey, 29.11.63; Ramsey to Trapp, 2.12.63; TF. 2025].
5. [Ramsey to Robertson, 14.2.73, TF. 2025].
6. [Devapriam to Taylor, 31.7.86, TF. 4080]; Elliott to Roberts, 22.11.47, quoted Millington (1993), p. 90.
7. *Ibid.*, pp. 74, 76, 108.
8. [Kingsnorth memos, 3.1.74, 21.11.73, TF. 1832].

Chapter 19

1. A. Pieris, in Fabella and Torres (1983), p. 192.
2. *Central Africa*, 1.50, 2.53.
3. *Overseas News*, Nov. 65, Apr. 66.
4. *Overseas News*, July 58.
5. Appleton (1990), p. 37.
6. [2.72, TF. 663].
7. [Council Paper, 6.87, TF. 3484]; [General Committee, 23.4.80].
8. [D. O'Connor, 'USPG and the "Other Faiths/Inter-Faith" Issues', Council, June 1990].

9. *Church of England Newspaper*, 18 and 25.6.93; for Bp Skelton's correction, 2.7.93.
10. [8.6.84, TF. 3484].

Chapter 20

1. [Report, 'Anglican Methodist Project in Latin America', Feb. 1976, TF. 969]; [Trapp to Eddy, 16.7.69, TF. 277]. Except where othewise stated, all references in this section are to this report, or to papers in these files and [TF. 968].
2. Shevill (1988), p. 54.
3. [Braund to Sulston, 27.2.72, TF. 968].
4. [Filochowski to Bloodworth, 27.3.75, TF. 968].
5. [Bonino to Webb, 27.12.74, TF. 968].
6. [Roberts, 'Personal Reflections', Nov. 74; Hopkin to Braund and Pares, 2.12.74, TF. 968].

Chapter 21

1. [Roberts to South African bishops, 11.10.51, H.21].
2. [Clayton to Roberts, 1.8.53; Fisher to Roberts, 11.10.53, H.21].
3. *The Isis*, 16.2.55; Paton (1974), pp. 258–9.
4. [Trapp to de Blank, 13.11.57; de Blank to Trapp, 29.3.60, TF. 729].
5. [Report, Colin Davidson to Overseas Committee, 16.3.71, H.169].
6. [M. J. Mason to N. I. Kerr, 25.8.86, TF. 957].
7. [H. V. Taylor to Society supporters, 6.86, TF. 3212].
8. [H. V. Taylor to Bishop of Grahamstown, 24.3.88, 94.046]; [O. Tambo to G. Howe 31.7.86, TF. 957].
9. Kairos (1985), Preface to the 1st edition.
10. [Memo A. Richmond to H. V. Taylor 14.2.86, TF. 3212]; Council, June 1986.
11. [H. V. Taylor to Bishop of Lichfield, 6.9.85, TF. 3212]; [see also Bishop Nkoane to R. Symon, 5.2.85, TF. 3212].
12. [R. Symon to J. Ruston, 16.2.87, TF. 957].
13. De Gruchy (1997), p. 155.
14. [Memo R. Symon to H. V. Taylor, 10.7.85; memo A. Richmond to R. Symon 14.8.85, TF. 3212]; [R. Acworth to H. V. Taylor, 28.6.89, 94.046]; [note R. Symon, 10.7.86, TF. 957].
15. [P. B. Hinchcliff to H. V. Taylor, 1.8.86, TF. 957]; [Archbishop of Cape Town to H. V. Taylor, 8.3.88, 94.046].
16. [W. N. Ndungane to H. V. Taylor, 20.12.88; Archbishop of Cape Town to H. V. Taylor, 12.6.89, 94.046].

17. [Memo R. Symon to H. V. Taylor, 1.8.89, 94.046]; [Bishop of Grahams-town to Taylor, 12.2.90, 95.115].
18. [Trapp to Winter (quoting Winter), 5.11.69, TF. 1998].
19. For a careful analysis, see Lapsley (1986).
20. [Kingsnorth confidential report, 18.3.65, TF. 199].
21. Article with this title, McVeigh (April 1999).

Chapter 22

1. [Trapp to Warren, 28.9.61, H. 9].
2. *Overseas News*, Nov. 1957.
3. [Report of 18 May 1962 conference, TF. 141].
4. [Schiff to Wheatley, 28.1.70, TF. 141].
5. [Report, 29.6.69, TF. 1141].
6. [Skelton to Arnold, 1.3.76, TF. 663].
7. [Council Paper, 'See Christ and be Christ', Dec. 1972].
8. On the Church and black people in Birmingham, see Wilkinson (1993), partially funded by USPG.
9. Report by S. Keegan von Allmen, 1985; other refs, file 'International Visitors' Programme'.
10. Hodgson (Advent 1993); D. L. Gosling; [A. G. Bacon, Report on the current situation on and near the border between Burma and Thailand, 14 July 1997].
11. E. J. Hobsbawm, *Le Monde Diplomatique*, Dec. 1999; A. Hastings, *The Tablet*, 8 Jan. 2000.

Epilogue

1. Quotations, unless otherwise stated, are from Bishop B. D. Mondal's 'History of the Church of Bangladesh' (typescript), 2 Sept. 1998.
2. [Quoted in M. Heath, Tour Report, 1996].
3. K. Rahner (1981) 'Perspectives on pastoral ministry in the future', *Diakonia*, Vienna.
4. Dr Edric Baker, annual report, 1997–8.

PART 2

Perspectives

I

⋯⇒◉⇐⋯

Anglican mission among the Mohawk

OWANAH ANDERSON

White, frothy wild flowers, known as Queen Anne's lace, border a
narrow roadway in the quiet valley of the Mohawk River in upstate
New York. This valley was once the ancestral home of the Mohawk,
the eastern-most peoples of the all-powerful Iroquois Confederacy. At
the outskirts of the near-deserted village of Fort Hunter, 44 miles upriver
from Albany, ancient birch trees shade an old two-storey limestone
dwelling, the home of Anglican missionaries in the early 1700s, during
the reign of Queen Anne. Today the old rectory stands as a solitary
monument to mark the Church of England's first missionizing efforts
among American Indians within the later United States.[1]

The rectory had been home to the first and last resident missionaries
sent by the Society to minister to the Mohawks and live among them.
In 1712, fresh from London, William Andrews wearily trudged up from
Albany on 'a rough Indian path filled with rocks and fallen trees' to take
up residence, and, just before Christmas 1770, John Stuart, tall, comely
and Philadelphia-born, moved in. Shortly afterwards, Stuart welcomed
in the old rectory history's best-known Mohawk chief and churchman,
Thayendanegea, better known as Captain Joseph Brant. Then in his mid-
twenties, with eminence and esteem yet ahead, Brant was grieving over
the death of his beloved first wife, Peggie. During the long winter
months of 1772–73, Brant and Stuart toiled together in the rectory to
translate the Prayer Book into the Mohawk language.

While the Mohawk mission was not the first Anglican evangelizing
effort, it was the most sustained. Royal Charters authorizing English
settlements in the New World all bore mandates to share the Gospel
with the 'savages along the shore'.[2] Beyond the baptism of the celebrity
convert, Pocahontas, at the Jamestown Colony in 1611, history records

scant Anglican evangelizing of Native Americans prior to the work among the Mohawks in the New York Colony.[3]

Centuries before white contact, the Iroquois had established under the 'Great Tree of Peace' a league for mutual defence wherein each nation retained its identity, dialect and territory, within a vast domain, stretching from the Hudson River through the valley of the Mohawk River to the Great Lakes and south into present-day Pennsylvania. In addition to the Mohawk, original member nations of the Iroquois Confederacy were the Oneida, Onondaga, Cayuga and Seneca, later also the Tuscarora.

The Iroquois domain was strategically crucial in the persisting rivalry between the French and English. By the mid-1600s, French Jesuits had netted some 2000 converts deep within the forests of the Iroquois. To counteract French ecclesiastical colonizing, the English colonial authorities sent a request to London in 1703 for Anglican missionaries who would live among the Indians to promote religion and also better the interests of England.[4]

The year following, SPG sent Thoroughgood Moor to the Mohawks. Despite eager expectations, Moor would never live among the Mohawks, residing instead in Albany, visiting them only occasionally. Within a year, disillusioned, he resigned. He complained that the behaviour of the colonists gave Indians a sad notion of Christianity. His report to the Society concluded that the Indians 'waste away & have done so ever since our arrival amongst them like Snow against the Sun . . . very probably forty years hence there will scarce be an Indian seen'.[5]

The Mohawk mission was temporarily abandoned except for an occasional visit from Albany clergy. Indeed, mission was only intermittent until the American Revolution drove the Mohawks and their Anglican clergy into permanent exile.

In 1710, four Iroquois *sachems* (chiefs) were taken to London and had an audience with Queen Anne. The chiefs took London by storm. They were driven about in coaches, had their portraits painted by Verelst, were written about by Steele and Addison. The chiefs were presented in formal ceremony at St James's Palace; on cue, they expressed their distrust of the French, against whom they were preparing war, and reminded the Queen of an earlier promise of military assistance, adding through their interpreter,

> Since we were in Covenant with our Great Queen's Children, we have had some knowledge of the Saviour of the World, and have often been opportuned by the French Priests . . . but ever esteemed them as men of Falsehood, but if our Great Queen would send some to Instruct us, they should find a most hearty Welcome.

The Queen promptly promised £400 to underwrite two missionaries and an interpreter, a fort, a chapel and a house for the missionaries.

By August of 1712 the Queen Anne Chapel was completed at Fort Hunter on the Mohawk River. The log chapel was 10 feet high and 24 feet square with garret and cellar, surrounded by a 150 feet square fort. The rectory was built nearby on higher ground.

Queen Anne designated this a Royal Chapel and sent linen and altar plate, the communion plate inscribed:

> The Gift of Her Majesty Anne, By grace of God, Queen, of Great Britain, France and Ireland and of her Plantations in North America, to her Indian Chapell of the Mohawks.[6]

It arrived in the autumn of 1712, brought by the new resident missionary, William Andrews. He reported to the Society being received 'with an abundance of joy . . . every one bidding me welcome'. Andrews' reports provide a clear glimpse of community life in Fort Hunter:

> I cannot give an exact account of the number of adults but am informed around 260 . . . they have a great many children . . . there are seldom above half the Indians at home together . . . always going and coming. Their Chief Town, or Castle as it is called, stands by the Fort, consisting of 40 or 50 homes . . . their houses are made of mats and bark of trees together with poles about 3 or 4 yards high. Another chief town of about 20 or 30 houses [Canajoharie] is some three or four and twenty miles distant. They have several other little towns.[7]

Andrews reports 'Extream coldness and deep Snows', and summers tormented by 'flyes and muschetoes . . . and danger of being stung with the Snakes . . . Especially the Rattle Snake'. Alcohol consumption was the major social ill and he criticized the Dutch traders for bringing barrels of rum into the village.

Despite flies, mosquitoes and snakes, Andrews shortly learned the Mohawk language, translated the Lord's Prayer and Creed and set about translating the Prayer Book. He opened a school and taught children in their own language though he admitted to providing inducements.

His Mohawk flock proved difficult for the sensitive young missionary. Some argued that baptism was all that was required to make anyone a good Christian, and they did not need to come to his services after baptism. One man, whom Andrews had excommunicated for 'drunkenness, sabbath-breaking, cruelty in biting off a prisoner's ears and other offenses', threatened to shoot the missionary. In the fall of 1718 Andrews requested transfer. It would be eight years before the Mohawks had another resident missionary. Meanwhile, Society clergy journeyed from Albany, in summer by boat, in winter over rough forest paths, to minister to the Mohawks.

The face of the Mohawk valley was rapidly changing. The early 1700s saw a rush of German Protestant refugees from the Rhineland Palatinate. With the blessings of Queen Anne, 1710 brought 3000 'high Dutch' who had sought refuge in England but were dispatched instead to the Mohawk River valley. The Mohawks bitterly complained about European encroachment, but to little effect, and more settlers poured on to the ancestral homeland.

Nevertheless, a turning-point in Mohawk conversion came in 1735 when SPG appointed Henry Barclay to Fort Hunter. Native to the region and a Yale graduate, Barclay evangelized with fervour. He opened a school which soon had 40 students, and a catechetical school to train adults as lay readers. He acquired a horse and began regular visits to Canajoharie, the 'upper castle', twenty miles upriver.

Few Mohawks remain unbaptized

Being too young for ordination, Barclay came first as a catechist, journeying to England two years later for ordination. Upon his return he began a lasting translation of the Book of Common Prayer and set about rebuilding the dilapidated Queen Anne Chapel. A 'neat stone church' was completed in 1741. Under Barclay's tutelage two Christian *sachems*, Daniel and Cornelius, were trained as schoolmasters. Within six years Barclay reported that only a few of the Mohawk remained unbaptized.

Of particular interest, Barclay records that on 18 July 1741, Peter *Tehonwagkwangeraghkwa* and his wife, Margaret, presented two young children for baptism. These children would appear to be older siblings of the man known as Captain Joseph Brant, indubitably the best-known Indian in the annals of the Society.

Barclay's work among the Mohawks ended in 1746 when he departed to the prestigious post of Rector of Trinity Church, New York. The Society's mission to the Mohawks was again temporarily abandoned.

In 1750, a protégé of Barclay's, John Ogilvie, arrived to be resident missionary, recently ordained but already knowledgeable in the Mohawk language having studied under Barclay. His first reports to SPG express discouragement upon finding the Mohawks 'universally degenerated . . .

entirely given up to Drunkeness'. However, his subsequent reports indicate a decrease in alcohol consumption. Ogilvie trained Mohawk readers to conduct divine worship and function as schoolmasters. Several of his trainees appear prominently in the annals of the Mohawk mission, including Abraham and Petrus Paulus.

It was in this period that the French and Indian War of 1755–62 was fought to determine control of what is now the eastern United States. Though the Mohawks fought as loyal allies of Britain, they did not receive the rewards of victory. Instead, settlers arrived in ever-increasing numbers occupying Mohawk land.

It was in this period that a dynamic young Irishman, William Johnson, arrived as a trader and was appointed the Crown's Indian Commissioner for the Colony of New York. His record in the French wars earned him a baronetcy and his fair treatment of the Indians earned him their unparalleled respect.

In 1763 Ogilvie moved to Trinity Church as assistant curate. Though he had spent considerable time away from the Mohawk mission on military duty in Canada, he had continued an active oversight. Between the years 1763 and 1770 a series of 'interim' clergy took care of the mission.

At this time, the Canajoharie Mohawks set about raising £100 toward building a chapel. Sir William contributed the rest. Just up the hill from Joseph Brant's house, it was a handsome little chapel in which the Mohawks took pride. A staunch Anglican, Sir William cast about for clergy to serve the Mohawk mission, including attempting to recruit Samuel Seabury, later the first bishop of the Protestant Episcopal Church of the United States of America.

Joseph Brant, Loyalist

The best known eighteenth-century American Indian, Joseph Brant lived and died loyal to the Crown and the Church of England. He was a younger brother of the bright and lively Molly Brant, loyal consort of Sir William Johnson. Molly (baptized Mary) was born around 1736 and at 23 came into Johnson's household, where she was eventually recognized as the lady of the manor, running a huge household of slaves and servants. While it was reported that she and Sir William were eventually legally wed, first in Mohawk ceremony, later in the Anglican chapel at Fort Hunter, no record of the marriage survives. The couple had at least nine children. Molly, often referred to as the 'brown Lady Johnson', was described as an able hostess, helping Sir William entertain a stream of white and Indian guests at Johnson Hall, the stately white manor house built in 1763.

Several years younger than the high-spirited Molly, Joseph or *Thay-endanegea* was born in 1742 along the Ohio River when his parents were on one of their periodic hunting excursions. His mother, Margaret, after her first husband, Peter, had died, had married a man named Brant who was related to the renowned 'King Hendrick', one of the Mohawk *sachems* of the 1710 delegation to Queen Anne.

Joseph was baptized at the Mohawk settlement of Canajoharie. He probably attended the mission school taught by Petrus Paul, and at 15 joined a force of some 400 Indians under Sir William to battle against the French. The young warrior saw his first action at Ticonderoga at the head of Lake Champlain.

Young Joseph saw action in several engagements, ending up with the victorious English forces in Montreal in 1759, with a silver medal for good conduct. An officer whom he met in the war commended Joseph to Eleazar Wheelock, founder of the Moor's Charity Indian School in Connecticut. With Sir William's approval, Joseph, accompanied by two other young Mohawks, joined Wheelock's school. His English was poor when he arrived but he grasped the language quickly, learning from a white minister whom he taught the Mohawk language in exchange.

During Joseph's two years at Wheelock's school, he 'inclined toward becoming a minister'. His mentor and benefactor, Sir William, approved. At the end of the two years, Joseph's sister Molly summoned him home. Sir William's health was failing, and he needed him. The Ottawa chief, Pontiac, had fomented a widespread uprising among tribes of the west. As Commissioner of Indian Affairs, Sir William was bound to intercede before the uprising engulfed all the Iroquois nations.

During the weeks that followed, Joseph rushed away on various assignments for Sir William, his diplomacy shortly leading to Pontiac's capitulation. Meanwhile, the ailing old Irish statesman masterminded the Proclamation of 1763, establishing the crest of the Appalachian Mountains as the boundary between the colonies and the Indians. It prohibited whites from settling west of the mountains. The agreement was disregarded; settlers continued to pour over the Appalachian passes.

As a full-grown man, Joseph was almost six feet tall, good looking, with a wide infectious smile. At 23, he was sent by Sir William to Oquaga. There he met a pretty Oneida girl called Peggie, daughter of Isaac, the Christian religious leader of the village. After a brief courtship, they were married on 22 July 1765 at Canajoharie in an Anglican ceremony conducted by Theophilus Chamberlain, a new missionary at Albany. Shortly thereafter, Joseph was employed as an interpreter at Fort

Ontario. It was here that their son, Isaac, was born. Soon, however, for reasons unexplained, Joseph brought his young family back to Canajoharie where he engaged increasingly in social justice issues, steadily developing a new role as a Mohawk leader. Their second child, Christina, was born in 1769.

John Stuart, missionary

The Mohawk's next resident missionary arrived just before Christmas 1770. He was John Stuart, a 30-year-old six-feet-tall scholar of unblemished character. The earnest young man, who had just returned from the perilous voyage to England for his ordination, preached his first sermon on Christmas Day at the new church at Canajoharie. On Christmas afternoon he visited the nearby home of Joseph Brant and was saddened to observe that Joseph's beautiful Peggie was dying of consumption. Within a year, Stuart would console young Joseph grieving at the death of his wife, and again years later console Captain Brant, the renowned tribal leader and British warrior, in his bitterness following the American Revolution.

After Peggie's death, Joseph moved into the rectory at Fort Hunter where he and Stuart began the translation of St Mark and the Anglican liturgy. Periodically for the rest of his life, Joseph was involved in translation, eventually learning Greek to perfect the translation of Mark's Gospel into his language.

A single incident occurred in the winter of 1772–3 in which the warm relationship between Joseph and Stuart may have been tested. Joseph asked Stuart to officiate at his wedding to Susanna, a half-sister of Peggie. Joseph explained tribal custom of a sister taking a deceased wife's place especially where there were children to raise. Stuart refused to officiate, citing Anglican prohibition. Joseph sought out another Society missionary, John Jacob Oël, who served the Schenectady Anglicans. There were no children of this marriage and Susanna also died of consumption within a few years.

Rebel Drums on the Mohawk

Sir William, who influenced the Iroquois nations to fight with the British in the protracted French and English clashes along their colonial borders, died on the eve of the American Revolution. When the Revolution came, the British again sought the assistance of the Iroquois; the Continental Congress sought their neutrality. When the question came to the

Council of the League, a decision was ultimately left to each nation. In the course of the war, the Oneida and Tuscaroras joined the colonists, being eventually allowed to retain their ancestral lands, though enduring much encroachment. The Mohawk, Onondaga, Cayuga and Seneca all adopted the King's cause, and Brant lived out his life in exile from the ancestral Mohawk homeland for his allegiance to King and Crown.

Meanwhile in 1776 he had been sent to England to resolve land disputes between the Mohawks and encroaching white settlements along the Mohawk River. In London Brant had been quite the sensation. Romney painted his portrait. He was presented to King George III (though he eluded kissing the king's hand). The King conferred the salaried rank of captain. His negotiations were successful. During his sojourn, however, earth-shaking events had occurred in America! Soon the land settlement would be irrelevant; the Mohawks would be chased from the Mohawk valley by the colonial army and the Oneidas.

Arriving back at British-held Staten Island, the young Mohawk must have gazed across the bay at New York City, then in rebel hands. Within the past three weeks the thirteen colonies had formally declared their independence and his Anglican clergy friends were at peril.

Captain Brant, who had served the British well in the French and Indian War, offered his services to the British under General Howe. In the late summer of 1776, he distinguished himself in the Battle of Long Island. Subsequently, the British command granted his request to slip through the American lines in disguise to return to the Iroquois. At the end of his dangerous three-week journey, he was given a hero's welcome at Oquaga where he had left his two young children. Brant rallied the Iroquois warriors to take up the King's cause.

Iroquois bloodshed followed. The colonists confiscated Johnson Hall at the beginning of the war, dispossessing Molly who fled to her old home at Canajoharie where she took up trading and continued to encourage the Mohawk to support the Crown. Indeed, the 'brown Lady Johnson' was a Tory spy, managing throughout the conflict to get strategic messages through to her brother. Her advance warning of a rebel troop movement in August 1777 accounted for his major victory in a ravine near the Oneida village of Oriskany.

Vengeance followed quickly. In the early autumn of 1777, rebel colonists, escorted by a band of Oneida, swept down the Mohawk valley and raided Molly's Canajoharie home. She escaped with her children to the Cayugas, departing so hastily that she left behind all her treasured finery. The entire Canajoharie village was plundered; livestock driven away; corn and other food supplies carted off. Canajoharie was burned to the ground as its residents fled for their lives.

Most of the Canajoharie Mohawks fled westward to Niagara, which by winter was overflowing with 3000 Iroquois refugees. British officials described the dismal refugees as 'lounging about or getting drunk or helping themselves to traders' merchandise or cattle'. Soon everybody was undernourished and suffering with malaria and dysentery. Molly Brant, in the role of 'brown Lady Johnson', was welcomed to the ramshackle old fort as peacekeeper between the dejected refugees and indignant British officials.

The Fort Hunter Mohawks fared no better than their Canajoharie neighbours. In addition to food supplies and livestock, the colonists seized wagons, sleighs and farm implements, furniture and even glass windows. They confiscated the church property and turned the beautiful little chapel into a tavern. A keg of rum was stored in the reading desk. Later the chapel was used as a stable. Just before the raid, Stuart and some of his faithful flock buried the Queen Anne communion silver.

Led by their chief, John Deseronto, the Fort Hunter Mohawks fled north and eventually reached Lachine, Quebec, where they stayed about a year awaiting word of their fate.

John Stuart, the missionary, continued reading prayers for the King until patriots placed him under house arrest for three long years in Schenectady. There he was abused and taunted by the populace and fined. Denied permission to teach to support himself and his family, they experienced great hardship. Like many other Anglican clergy families, they eventually migrated to Canada in a prisoner exchange.

Captain Brant emerged as the undisputed war chief of the Mohawks, leading raids of British loyalists and Iroquois war parties across the backcountry that he knew so well. Dubbed 'Monster Brant' by the colonials, he distinguished himself again and again in battle. Colonel Daniel Claus, Deputy Superintendent of Indians and a member of the Society, wrote to the Secretary from Montreal in June 1778:

> The Mohawk Chief Joseph Brant that was in London in 1776 has since his return to his country and nation proved and distinguished himself as the most loyal and firmly attached friend to his majesty's cause and interest . . . most active chieftain in the last campaign . . . he attacked the rebel post called Cherry Valley in Tryon County and cut off a party of upwards of 300 entirely. Though he is a thorough Indian born, he allows no cruelties in his exploits; his proficiency in Christianity is amazing and incomparable, he has acquired the English language so perfectly that he is the best interpreter . . . and has translated a great part of the New Testament.

Again a widower, Captain Brant married Catharine Crogan in 1779 in a civil ceremony at Fort Niagara. She was 20, he 36. A niece of *Tekanihoga*, titular head of the Mohawks, Catharine's father was George Crogan, an Irish trader who served as a deputy to Sir William Johnson. A handsome tall woman, in her old age Catharine was called the 'old Indian queen'. The couple had seven children.

Abandoned by the British

When the war finally ended, the Iroquois were the major losers. The Treaty of Paris overlooked the Indians entirely. An incredulous Captain Brant said, 'The English have sold the Indians to Congress.' England relinquished all teritorial claims, ignoring both ally and enemy, and thus the ancient country of the Iroquois was included in the boundary granted to the Americans.

Captain Brant hastened to Sir Frederick Haldimand, the Governor General of Canada, recalling a prior promise to the Mohawks that they would be compensated for their losses in the war. Haldimand agreed first to convey a tract for the now homeless Indian nations on the Bay of Quinté, on the north-east edge of Lake Ontario. Though desolate and fog-shrouded, the area had a certain appeal as the birthplace of *Deganawida*, the Peacemaker who in Iroquois tradition had made the peace among the five nations that allowed them to form a Confederation. Some, especially the quarrelsome Senecas, opposed the Quinté location, as too distant from 'the home of the ancestors from far beyond earliest traditions', but John Deseronto and his band of Fort Hunter Mohawks were to settle there permanently.

In May 1784 Haldimand agreed to purchase from the Missisauga Indians a 1200 square-mile tract of land on the Grand River west of Fort Niagara in southern Ontario. Within a year 1843 expatriate Indians would be living there under the chieftainship of Brant. Émigrés included not only Mohawk and other nations of the Iroquois but also displaced Delaware, Nanticoke, Totele and a few Creek and Cherokee.

Still driven to demand the English government indemnify loyal Mohawks for lost homes and possessions, Brant set sail again for England. Arriving on 1 December 1784, it was reported that 'Colonel Joseph Brant, the celebrated King of the Mohawks', had arrived. As with his visit a decade previously, Brant was quite the celebrity. He made friends with the Prince of Wales and had several audiences with King George III. He went to balls and accompanied the Prince of Wales to 'lurid and unlikely places of entertainment'. Boswell wrote about him. Stuart painted his portrait. His negotiations at the highest level netted the Mohawks £15,000 in compensation for war losses along with almost £1500 for himself and his sister Molly to recompense for Canajoharie land and other properties.

During his London visit, Brant supervised a new edition of the Prayer Book and Psalms in the Mohawk language to which he added his own translation of St Mark's Gospel. Printed on alternate pages in English and the Mohawk language, the new edition was published by SPG in 1787 under royal patronage. The frontispiece depicts an interior of a chapel in which the king and queen are handing out copies of the Prayer Book to assembled Indians.

Re-establishing the Anglican Mohawk Church

Gentle John Stuart had endured grave hardships while the colonists held him under house arrest in Schenectady. When finally released in 1781 and allowed to go to Canada, he was reunited briefly with the Fort Hunter Mohawk refugees. The missionary was elated to find that a Mohawk whom he had trained had continued to read services regularly during the four-year exile. His former flock welcomed him with joy and an unusual display of affection. Stuart's first report on arriving in Canada informed the Society that the 'plate belonging to the Mohawk Chapel is yet safe; as also the furniture of the reading-desk and communion table. The pulpit covering was stolen when the Church was plundered.'[8]

The Mohawks volunteered to build a house for the missionary so that he could live among them as formerly, but such was not to be. John Stuart would never again be assigned wholly to the Mohawks though he remained their spiritual overseer for the rest of his life. His first assignment upon arriving in Canada was as chaplain to the regiment of Sir John Johnson, son and heir of Sir William.

Despite the demands of the growing white population, Stuart reported to the Society that he had, within the year 1784, baptized 104 Mohawks. He had also engaged an Indian schoolmaster for the Quinté Bay Reserve. Aso in 1784, Stuart set out on a journey to visit loyalist settlements all along the north side of Lake Ontario. On 18 June, he reached Niagara, to which a large number of homeless Mohawks had flocked in 1777. Earlier reports from *sachem* Aaron Hill, Joseph Brant's son-in-law, to the Society had acknowledged receipt of 25 Prayer Books. Hill assured the Society that 'Christianity is upheld among us here'. Little else is recorded of the spiritual welfare of the despondent Niagara refugees over the first seven long years of their exile. On that June morning when Stuart reached Niagara, he preached first to the garrison, then rode horseback nine miles westward to the Mohawk village where he preached and baptized 78 children and five adults. The unnamed Indian who had continued to read prayers on Sunday had instructed them well. The Society's Report noted:

> It was very affecting to Mr Stuart to see those affectionate people from whom he had been separated for more than seven years assembled in a decent commodious Church, erected principally by themselves, with the greatest seeming devotion and becoming gravity. Even the windows were crowded with those who could not find room within the walls. The concourse of Indians on this occasion was unusually great, owing to the Oneidas, Cayugas and Onondagas being settled in the vicinity. Before Mr Stuart left their Village, he afterwards baptized at different times, 24 children and married six couples.

This unnamed church, located nine miles west of Niagara, would appear to be the first Indian Anglican church in Canada.[9]

1785 found Stuart assigned to Cataraqui, later called Kingston. His reports indicate he frequently made the 42-mile journey, usually by boat, to the Mohawk congregation at the Bay of Quinté, which went by various names including Tyonderoga and Deseranto. Again and again the Mohawks pleaded unsuccessfully for a resident missionary.

In his reports Stuart informed SPG that the Tyonderoga Mohawks were 'busy in building houses and laying the foundations for their new village'. The schoolhouse was almost finished and 'must ere now be ready for reception of the Masters and Scholars'. By 1785 the settlement was making preparations for building a church.

Farewell journey

John Stuart journeyed to the Grand River to deliver the Queen Anne silver to the Six Nations Reserve in the spring of 1788.[10] Accompanied by his oldest Mohawk friend, Joseph Brant, Stuart made a nine-day boat trip across Lake Ontario from Kingston. The two rode horseback the last 25 miles to the village of Brantford, named in honour of the now ageing warrior, statesman and churchman. Stuart preached, baptized 65 and married three couples at the new St Paul's Church, and wrote:

> The Mohawk Village is pleasantly situated on a small but deep river. The church is about 60 feet in length & 25 in breadth . . . built with

squared logs and boarded on the outside and painted . . . with a handsome steeple & bell, a pulpit, reading-desk & Communion-table with pleasant pews.[11]

Joseph and fifteen Mohawks escorted Stuart back to Niagara and bidding him farewell urged that he visit again. Such would not happen. It would be Stuart's first and final visit to the Grand River Reserve. Though he would never again minister exclusively to the Mohawks, for the remainder of his long life Stuart continued an interest in the people he had first served. A year after his Brantford visit, Bishop Charles Inglis appointed him Commissary in Upper Canada and by the year 1803 five other missionaries had been appointed under Stuart's supervision. He died on 15 August 1811, aged 71, and was buried at St George's Cathedral, Kingston.

Also buried at Kingston was the sprightly Molly Brant who had died on 15 April 1796. Her grave is unmarked. Molly, the 'brown Lady Johnson', remained as loyal as her brother to the English cause and in recognition of her services to the King, British officials had built Molly a home in Kingston, and provided her with a yearly pension of £100. As an old woman, she was glimpsed sitting in her pew in St Paul's Church, 'appearing very devout and attentive to the sermon'. The Canadian government issued a commemorative postage stamp honouring Molly Brant 190 years after her death.

Joseph Brant died at 65 on 24 November 1807 at his estate at Burlington Bay on Lake Ontario, some 40 miles north of the growing township of Brantford. The old Mohawk church bell tolled continuously for 24 hours across the mourning valley of the Grand River.

He had supped with royalty. He had raised his hatchet in gory wars. He had been praised by some and castigated as 'the monster Brant' by others, experiencing moments of both exhilaration and dispiriting defeat. Even today, nearly 200 years after his death, Joseph Brant remains an enigma. One certainty stands out. He stayed unflaggingly loyal to Church and Crown.

His final resting place is an imposing stone tomb in the churchyard of the old Mohawk church at Brantford. His remains were tenderly borne there from Burlington Bay many years after his death on strong brown shoulders of young Mohawk men.

⤜●⤛

Dr Owanah Anderson is a member of the Choctaw Nation of Oklahoma. She was on the staff of the Presiding Bishop of the Episcopal Church of the USA for fourteen years as Officer for Native American Ministry.

Notes

1. It was among us, the indigenous peoples of the Americas, that evangelizing efforts began that evolved into the worldwide Anglican Communion.
2. W. Perry (1885) *History of the American Episcopal Church 1587–1883*, Boston, I. 35.
3. Anderson (1988), p. 17.
4. While the Jesuits had been living among us in the most primitive dwellings for generations, early Society documents specify that 'our missionaries must have distinct houses ... which must be Pallisaded ... moreover, they cannot subsist without two servants to attend each Missionary'.
5. J. W. Lydekker (1938) *The Faithful Mohawks*, London, p. 22.
6. This historic treasure is still preserved in Mohawk chapels at Tyenderoga and Brantford, Ontario. Queen Anne sent a second set of communion plate to the Onondaga people when a second mission was proposed. However, the Onondaga Nation has never yet received it. It reposes still at St Peter's Church, Albany.
7. Lydekker, *op.cit.*, p. 37.
8. *Ibid.*, p. 174.
9. Both the later constructed churches on the Grand River and at the Bay of Quinté claim that distinction.
10. The Mohawk congregation were still using the Queen Anne silver in 1994 – Anderson (1998), p. 25.
11. Lydekker, *op.cit.*, p. 186.

2

⤙⇒◯⇐⤚

Concurrence without compliance: SPG and the Barbadian plantations, 1710–1834

NOEL TITUS

In 1710 the infant Society suddenly found itself the beneficiary of two sugar plantations in Barbados. These were the gift of Christopher Codrington, who had enjoyed an outstanding civil and military career before retiring from the post of Governor-General of the Leeward Islands. The purpose of the benefaction was twofold. First, the trustees were charged with the responsibility of establishing a missionary college with professors under a monastic rule. Second, the trustees were to ensure the maintenance on the plantations of three hundred slaves, who were to enjoy the benefit of medical attention and religious instruction. This slave population was to provide the labour for the two plantations, the produce to provide the financial base for the projected college.

On 18 August 1710, SPG's General Committee took note of the death of Christopher Codrington and of this remarkable benefaction. Subsequently, the Society received from a confidant of Codrington, William Gordon, a letter explaining the intentions of the testator, to maintain monks and missionaries 'for the conversion of Negroes and Indians'. The plan also required three visitors, whose duties would be to visit the colonies, keep the Society informed of the state of Christianity in each and advise about the best means of advancing 'Religion and Piety'. Part of this was impracticable, the Church of England having abandoned monasticism during the Reformation. In any case, when Gordon mentioned Codrington's association with a Jesuit in developing his plan, he was unwittingly damning that aspect of it. The other aspect, the undertaking of missions to the enslaved population in Barbados and other colonies, was another matter. All it required was sufficient people with the necessary zeal to implement it. Our questions are, did the

Society commit itself to this object of the testator, and did it impart to its agents any sense of commitment to the task?

The first significant reference to the benefaction came in the Anniversary Sermon of 1711, preached by the Bishop of St Asaph, William Fleetwood. With a text on Paul's mission to the Gentiles, Fleetwood stressed the duty of every Christian to preach the Gospel, acknowledging the duty to preach to the colonial slaves, and reflecting on certain erroneous views on the part of the slave owners. The first of these was that slaves became free by baptism. Fleetwood observed that there was no slavery in England, and that this was not detrimental to the country. It was better, he believed, to pay for one's pleasures and conveniences than to have them 'cheaply at the expense of so much misery, such cruelty and hard treatment of men, as good as ourselves, and at the hazard of their souls'. Yet, arguing that people were not free of obligations by becoming Christians, he opted only for such freedom as could be reconciled with trade and the nation's interest, 'tho' a little perhaps abated'.

The second view on which he commented was that the slave owners would have to treat their slaves less harshly after baptism if they were not to lose them ultimately. Fleetwood urged that Christianity commanded mercy and compassion towards all. To deal harshly with the slaves was to disobey Christ. On these grounds, he urged slave owners to be true to their religion by their physical treatment of the slaves.

The third misconception to which he referred was that after baptism the owners could not sell their slaves. In response Fleetwood offered the strange opinion that Christ would prefer them to be sold rather than be slaves of sin. Let the soul be free from sin and the hand from unrighteousness, he reasoned, and Christ would not care 'how the Body is encumbered with its Weights, nor how those Hands are worn with Bonds and Labours'. He concluded that if they could be sold before they were baptized, the Laws of Christ would not deprive the owners of that property after baptism.

Referring specifically to the Codrington plantations, Fleetwood asserted that if all other slaves remained infidels, 'ours alone must needs be Christians'. They must be instructed and baptized, and thus SPG would preach by example. They would be treated as Christians, while being useful and hard-working servants, the two things being reconcilable. 'The Servants of this Society shall be, assuredly, the Lord's Free Men, whatever else their Condition shall be in this World.'

This remarkable sermon provided a strong endorsement of slavery, rather than a critique of the system, and proposed no method of dealing with the Codrington plantations beyond a desire to convert the slaves to

Christianity. It constituted an acceptance of the state of slavery and a commitment to operate within it. In this, it created a framework for discussion of the bequest which was to stand for many years. More than fifty years later, for example, the 1766 Anniversary Sermon, by William Warburton, Bishop of Gloucester, would follow similar lines. It would vary only in specifying SPG as innocent partakers of 'the fruits of this iniquitous traffic'. And it would describe the Codrington bequest as intending to compensate for the 'violations of the Laws of nature and humanity'. It would represent the Society as well placed by God to be 'honoured Instruments of producing Good'.

In accepting the gift, SPG recognized the benefactor's intention to have a college 'as a Seminary of Missionaries to be dispersed throughout the Plantations'. Given the criticisms of the Roman Church and the Jesuits in some of its Anniversary Sermons, support for a Jesuit-inspired programme would have been miraculous. While monks were an impossibility in eighteenth-century Anglicanism, aggressive and well-planned mission was not. Codrington wanted a vibrant, missionary Church, and attached that dream to what he foresaw as a vibrant, missionary Society. SPG went along with the view that a grammar school should be erected to educate the sons of the planters. Yet there was a trickle of untrained persons going to England for ordination while the college was not being used 'as a Seminary of Missionaries'. This suggests that the Society had temporarily shelved the wider missionary aspect of the bequest, despite one of the institution's first students, Richard Harris, travelling to England in 1760 for ordination.

Discounting Codrington's priority of missionary work among the colonies, the Society's attention was directed to the plantations and the slaves who constituted the labour force. All final decisions regarding these were made by SPG's General Committee, with a Barbados Committee to review financial and other reports from Codrington and to advise the General Committee. The Society also established in Barbados a group of attorneys with general oversight of the estates, responsibility for ensuring that the Society's policies were carried out and authority to appoint officials to transact the Society's business.

It is somewhat ironical to find the Archbishops of Canterbury and York, the Bishops of London, Durham and other dioceses presiding over the meetings of the two committees in London. The business before them concerned the minutiae of plantation management, the sale of sugar, inventories of plantation stock and similar mundane matters. The minutes of the committees read, for the most part, like the minutes of any business dealing with matters of a similar nature. Tragically, they do not reflect qualms about slavery or discussions of its morality. Rather than give leadership in what was a critical issue, SPG remained quiet and merely sought to ensure a process of catechizing and the regular production of sugar. What the Quakers and the Clapham Sect were able to do towards the end of the century, the Society had the capacity to do if it had so desired.

Given its location in London, SPG was necessarily dependent on others in Barbados. This dependence would prove a major problem in the attempt at distance management. Critical to this were the Society's attorneys. These were planters who were knowledgeable about Barbadian affairs, as well as local clergy. This group met at intervals on the estates, inspected the crop, the slaves and the accounts, and reported regularly to the Society. Equally critical to SPG's mandate were those appointed as catechists or chaplains, with responsibility for giving religious instruction to the slaves, according to guidelines set by the Society.

Operation of the plantations

It was some time before the Society got a satisfactory picture of the state of things on the plantations. Nevertheless, in approaching its task, the General Committee asked the Secretary to instruct the overseers to relieve the slaves of work on Sundays to facilitate their religious instruction. For that purpose also, the Society ordered the slaves to be free for their private tasks on Saturday afternoons. While this policy was said to be in operation by 1714, it would be changed in the course of time. We need to remember also that, however much those on Barbados expressed their willingness to observe SPG's instructions, conflicting reports from year to year raise questions as to whether they ever did.

A major concern of the Society was that clause of the will which required the maintenance of three hundred slaves on the plantations at all times. This would prove to be SPG's most intractable problem, not being realized until the second decade of the nineteenth century. At the outset it was found that the plantations had less than three hundred slaves at the time of Codrington's death. In the years following, until increases were reported in 1817 and 1818, the plantations regularly showed an annual decline in its labour force. So it was that the attorneys routinely recommended that SPG authorize the purchase of more slaves, or sought retrospective approval for this. The Society frequently approved or ordered the purchase of slaves during the eighteenth century, and yet the financial reports from the estates regularly showed disbursements for the hiring of additional slaves. These accounts were passed without comment by the Barbados and General Committees. In 1766 the Society had purchased the Henley plantation on the recommendation of its attorneys, at a time when Codrington had merely 181 slaves. When the 149 Henley slaves were transferred to the Codrington plantations the following year, the total of slaves on the estates was 336. Decline set in again from 1768 when the aggregate was 327, and by 1776, notwithstanding natural births, there was an aggregate of 301 slaves. While natural deaths could have caused decline, the rapidity with which the slave population declined is striking.

The first expression of concern over this came in 1770, following a review of plantation stock. The London meeting directed that 'every kind of humane treatment' should be shown to the slaves, with proper care taken of their families, especially of young children and child-bearing women. In addition, it urged the attorneys to co-operate with James Butcher and Michael Mashart, Master of the College and Usher/Catechist respectively, in this matter. The meeting of February 1771 heard from the attorneys that slaves were the support of every plantation, and that masters would prefer increase to decrease. To that end they needed to be 'well fed, regularly clothed, and moderately worked'. The attorneys promised to remind the manager of those things. This is as close as one gets to a confession that those in authority were not complying with the principles of humane treatment enunciated by the Society. Yet, surprisingly, there was no reprimand or attempt to investigate the working of the system.

In 1778 a letter was sent to the Society by a clergyman under the pseudonym 'John Codrington English', complaining about inhumane treatment at Codrington. Charging that the manager had 'the most unlimited power of any in this Island', he accused him of selling the ground provisions 'for the supposed advantage of the unfortunate slaves' while actually enriching himself at the Society's expense. He also accused the manager of overworking the slaves for the entertainment of himself and his friends, and urged SPG to inquire into these matters before it was too late.[1] Not only was there no Society comment on the letter, but there seems to have been no inquiry either. Yet the Society had received this letter during a period when its own anxiety had been aroused about the continuing steady decline in numbers. Its inaction under the circumstances is inexplicable.

In February 1779, the Anniversary Meeting noted the decrease over several years. No mention was made of the pseudonymous letter, the Meeting merely instructing the attorneys to purchase additional slaves in order to maintain the required level. Coming after the acquisition of slaves from the Henley plantation, a stronger statement was called for. The following year the Society expressed its inability to purchase more slaves because of its own indebtedness. General Committee commented in February 1779, however:

> It cannot be too strongly recommended to the manager, to pay the strictest attention to the Negroes, with regard to a mild and humane conduct towards them, of which some Judgement may be made by the Increase or Decrease of them.

Given its principle of humane treatment, this oblique comment sounds rather lame. SPG had resources to send someone out to investigate conditions at first hand. This it never did throughout the period of slavery; and this impaired its ability to deal with matters as it should have done.

In its meeting of December 1781, General Committee acknowledged the receipt of a letter from one of its attorneys, Sir Philip Gibbes. Gibbes reported that the slaves were in good condition, reflecting the 'great care and mild treatment of them' by the new manager, Downes. In December 1789 the Committee received a letter from Sir John Gay Alleyne expressing reservations about a subsequent manager, Barrow, and concern that Barrow's management appeared 'disadvantageous on the principles of humanity to the poor slaves'. Yet this George Barrow enjoyed a long tenure as manager of the Society's estates. Here were two clear representations on the issue brought to its attention and seeming to bear out the pseudonymous report of 1778. Neither, however, evoked any comment from SPG. Either the Society was not as committed as it ought to have been, or it failed to grasp the destructive nature of plantation slavery. It appears also to have failed to grasp the fact that slavery could not be ameliorated, and that no argument could justify such a system. It was thus set on a path of real difficulty and embarrassment, and seemed unable or unwilling to change its course.

While overwork might have been partly responsible for the reduction of the slave population, another largely unrecognized cause was the practice of discarding slaves who could no longer work productively. Though there is not much about this in SPG's records, there are some disturbing references. The matter first arose at two meetings of the Barbados Committee in 1716. On 18 May the manager, John Smalridge, sought the approval of the Society for the disposal of 'refuse Negroes' from the plantations as had been done during the time of General Codrington. According to Smalridge such persons were sent to Barbuda, and that was 'an advantage to the Plantation and eased them of a Burthen and charge'. The Barbados Committee recommended to General Committee that the Society should renew its application regarding Barbuda.

In a later meeting, on 26 May, a letter from Smalridge expressed the hope that the Society had secured its interests in Barbuda as thus 'the Plantation may be purged of such Negroes as are Burthensome to it'. When that request was repeated in January and December 1718, the Society ordered the slaves in question be shipped and sold. A similar order was issued at the meeting of 17 November 1721. Quite apart from itself contributing to the reduction of the slave population, the Society had thereby endorsed the inhumane policy of disposing of the 'refuse Negroes as being useless and disadvantageous', as the manager repeatedly described them. Even worse than the policy, though, was the perception of the slaves as 'refuse'. SPG had adopted the conclusion of its manager and therefore could not enforce a policy of humanity.

By the time the process of slave amelioration got under way in 1823, SPG had litttle idea what was really taking place on its plantations. For example, as early as 1792 the Society had instructed the manager to have hospitals built to care for the sick slaves. The attorneys and the manager successfully evaded this responsibility until 1805. In that year construction was in progress on the upper plantation, but not on the lower as the Society had also instructed. Presumably the latter was never built; certainly there was never any reference to it. By 1819 the Society approved the manager's intention to convert the hospital on the upper plantation into a chapel, and to construct a new hospital. The conversion was never effected because the hospital was blown down in a storm in 1819, with no record of it ever being rebuilt, though a new chapel was erected later.

Punishment was another area for which information is not clear. The amelioration programme of the early 1820s required each plantation to keep a register of all punishments. As late as November 1828, the Society discovered that no register had ever been kept on the Codrington plantations. The explanation given was that there were very few crimes on the plantations, and these were cases of praedial larceny. There is no way of determining whether such larceny on these and other plantations was linked to the inadequate provision of food for the slaves. It is quite likely that it was. A meeting on the estates in September 1829 ordered that a register of punishments be kept, though it is not clear that this was complied with. The use of the whip, and the practice of carrying it as a badge of authority, are mired in uncertainty. The abolition of this emblem of authority, and the substitution of punishment inflicted in the presence of a credible witness, had long been required by the Colonial Office. In November 1828 it was reported that the driver had resumed carrying the whip because the slaves were proving unco-operative. The manager, Foster Clarke, reported that the practice had been suspended some three years previously; but the report suggests that it was resumed when the Codrington authorities thought fit. By 1830, the Bishop of Barbados reported that the whip was no longer being carried by the driver, but his only evidence was that he did not see it being carried. That the driver could dispense with it during the Bishop's visit never entered the latter's mind. This uncertainty as to actual practice makes it dangerous to make categorical statements on the matter.

The instruction of the slaves

In accepting the Codrington plantations, SPG found itself cast in the role of slave owner. Quite apart from the stigma attached to such a role, the Society was committed to demonstrating that Christianity and slavery were not incompatible. The attempt to demonstrate this presupposed a community of interest on the part of all concerned. As events revealed, this did not exist. For one thing, Barbadian planters and others had considered the scheme quixotic, and their opposition exerted considerable pressure on successive attorneys and managers. The latter's failure to resist local pressure with any degree of consistency suggests a lack of conviction. Local planter opposition did not decline over time, and serious efforts at amelioration were not pursued until the arrival of William Hart Coleridge, the first Bishop of Barbados, in 1824.

Critical to the success of the programme were the catechists and chaplains. Their task was to instruct the slaves in the tenets of Christianity, preliminary to demonstrating the compatibility of that religion with slavery. In the early years the undertaking suffered from frequent changes in personnel, partly as a result of deaths. The succession of catechists, and the lack of enthusiasm which they displayed in the early years, suggest that very little could have been done. The first chaplain, Joseph Holt, did not stay long, leaving on the grounds of poor health. There is no evidence that Holt exerted himself to instruct the slaves on the plantations, as he had been appointed to do, or was active in looking after their medical needs. Three others who followed Holt died in quick succession, and the office remained vacant from 1717 to 1726.

The first catechist to survive any reasonable time was Thomas Wilkie, who served from 1726 to 1733. Wilkie does not appear to have been an energetic representative of SPG, for in 1730 it sought certificates from three local rectors concerning his preparation of the slaves for baptism, his sobriety and diligence. It was more than a year before the Society was satisfied with the certificates supplied, having expressed its displeasure with the original ones. These certificates had merely shown that Wilkie had been active among the slaves on the plantations, but stopped short of suggesting that he was diligent. The first substantial report from the plantations was that issued by Wilkie's successor, Samson Smirk, in December 1740. This indicated that there were 65 baptized slaves – 17 men, 23 women, 17 boys and 8 girls. It is not clear how many of those baptized had been presented by Smirk since he was reporting in his seventh year. Smirk's report suggests no great exertion on his part. The adults attended every Sunday morning, and the children daily. However, the plantations being short of labour, he explained, they could not attend more often. With respect to the 'heathen Negroes', their lack of facility with English hindered their instruction and baptism.

In 1743 the Society introduced a change, combining the office of catechist with the duties of usher or assistant master of the school. The new usher was now 'charged with the Instruction of the Negroes, instead of the Catechist', and this was reinforced by orders subsequently sent to the college stipulating instruction on Sunday afternoons.[2] No reason was given for this change. Perhaps SPG was not satisfied with the service Smirk had rendered before leaving. The following year the post was vacant, and manager Abel Alleyne filled the breach, claiming that he had done better in five months with the slaves than the catechist had done. The arrival in June 1745 of Thomas Rotherham and Joseph Bewsher as master and usher/catechist respectively, seemed to herald improvements. Bewsher, however, was unable to instruct the slaves since they were only available when his services were required in the school. He put their instruction in the hands of two young boys whom he supervised, though he indicated his willingness to instruct the new acquisitions as soon as they had acquired sufficient English.

SPG was not being well served by its catechists and chaplains, and its remoteness made effective supervision impossible. They seem often to have been doing little more than the minimum. Two of them, Falcon and Hodgson, expressed inability to make any headway with the field slaves. Falcon's only explanation was that there were 'many very great, and too frequently insuperable impediments in such undertakings'. Hodgson similarly reported being able to instruct only the house slaves, who, 'being more civilized than the rest are proportionately more capable of comprehending the plainer principles of our Religion'. Regarding his inability to instruct the field slaves, there was an unanswered question about their availability. In addition, Hodgson had a purely negative view of the field slaves. They had no ideas save those forced on them by necessity, or such barbarity as they had brought with them. He also disapproved of their constant mixing with new arrivals, which meant that he was always having to begin afresh. The Society, apart from generally lamenting Hodgson's report, merely added, 'we trust in God that their perseverance will be rewarded with better success'.[3]

There was a succession of short-term catechists before Michael Mashart took office in 1769. A letter from James Butcher, the Master of the College at the time, to SPG early in his tenure showed him completely negative about the slaves, whom he considered 'unteachable' because of their 'perverse and untractable dispositions'. In his view, plantation work was inimical to efforts at religious instruction, rendering the latter a waste of time. For once, the Society was strong in expressing surprise at his attitude, and demanded his compliance with their instructions. One year later the demand had to be repeated, Butcher and Mashart being directed to pay strict attention to the instruction of the slaves. By the end of 1773 both men had gone. This state of affairs continued under Henry Husbands.

In the year 1795, a new Master, William Thomas, outlined an expanded programme for the instruction of the slaves on the plantations. This included teaching them to read, so far as time and plantation demands allowed. In February 1795, he assured SPG,

> no attention shall be wanting in him to carry the instructions of the Society into execution, as far as can be done consistently with the opportunities that can be spared both by the Negroes & himself, & compatibly with the arrangements, the oeconomy & discipline, the habits, prejudices, & above all, the ignorance of that race of people.

His intentions appear good, but it was all so conditional. SPG, for its part, ordered that all slaves over four years of age were to be taught to read, and that a woman should be appointed to head the school. This latter instruction had not been carried into effect some months later, and an attorney of the Society commented that little progress had been made with instructing the slaves since the time of the Rotherham brothers in the later 1740s. It was a shocking revelation, and suggests that the claims often made were not reliable. It prompted stronger demands by the Society, reinforcing the call for a woman to teach those between four and eight years of age, and insisting on the slaves being taught daily rather than only once per week. In November 1796, the demand for women teachers had to be repeated.

In 1797, a new president or head of the college was appointed, Mark Nicholson, though it is not clear that this was cause and effect. Women teachers were now appointed. The college at this time seemed to have functioned without the usher/catechist for some time, the post remaining vacant until 1801, when Nicholson recruited William Harte, well known later for his sympathetic ministry.[4] Instruction was frequently interrupted by the demands of the plantations. By 1806 Harte was gone. There had in the mean time been general compliance with respect to the school, but significant differences were noticeable. Schooling was done only two hours daily, and children began at six and continued until ten or twelve.

1819 brought significant change with the appointment of John Pinder as chaplain and catechist. The latter office now seems to have been separated from that of usher. Pinder was restricted in that he and the governors were required to frame regulations for the religious and moral instruction of the slaves 'without interfering with the cultivation of the estates'. Pinder's zeal and discretion were noted by Nicholson, who also believed that his being Barbadian would make him acceptable in the island. Pinder himself felt that the initial reaction of the slaves was favourable towards him, an impression subsequently confirmed by his successor, John Packer, who spoke of the high esteem in which they had held him.

That Pinder was energetic is clear from the records, though certain aspects of his work were not in accord with the objectives of the Society. One of these was the omission of writing and arithmetic from the school programme. His explanation indicates that he shared planter prejudices. After all, Nicholson did describe him as the son of someone of distinction in the island, and he later spoke of giving instruction on his father's plantation. According to Pinder, the slaves would not benefit from writing or arithmetic; besides, if able to write, they might be imposed on by persons ill-disposed towards the community.

Another aspect of his work that caused tension concerned the promotion of marriage among the slaves. From the beginning of his tenure, Pinder seems to have been fearful of this. He confessed to not knowing how to act because of the difficulties associated with the marriage of slaves, even though he considered it beneficial. His decision to proceed with caution determined his course over the next few years. While promising to promote marriage, Pinder expressed concern about the moral dangers to which the parties might be exposed if separated by sale, the novelty of sentiment for them of not changing husband or wife, the lack of example from the free coloureds and those in social classes above the slaves. While promising to promote the cause, Pinder was willing to wait until the disadvantages he perceived had been removed, and others had set the example he considered necessary. It seemed a rather long time to wait. Pinder was in something of a dilemma here. He was expected to follow SPG's requirements, but saw pastoral difficulties in doing so.

Pressing the marriage issue further, SPG was willing to consider incentives for those who married, and sought the views of both manager and chaplain. When the manager laid before the governors of the college the Society's desire to know what more could be done to encourage marriage, they declared that nothing more was feasible. They noted that in some places those in common-law unions were given a house, and hinted at the possibility of something similar when the houses on the upper plantation were completed. SPG and the manager were not in agreement on the matter. The chaplain thought that the slaves were unlikely to abandon their polygamous relationships, notwithstanding the inducements. He represented the manager, Foster Clarke, as preferring indulgences 'as the recompense of virtuous conduct after marriage, [rather] than as an invitation to seek the solemnity'.[5] Clarke further promised to relieve from labour any mother who had borne six children in wedlock. The likelihood of finding such mothers was of course very slight, since slaves coming forward for marriage were usually elderly. The rate of live births being low, this goal likewise might have been long in the achieving.

Marriages began to increase under the chaplaincy of John Packer, who succeeded Pinder in 1827. The number of slave couples being married averaged about two per year. In April 1829, General Committee expressed concern about the paucity of marriages, and asked the Bishop of Barbados for a report. In a letter of 2 July 1830, the bishop reported that the original allowance of one day off per week for married women was not satisfactory. He indicated that a change to every morning throughout the year had proved more acceptable. This, of course, did not explain the paucity of marriages. At the time of his writing, the bishop should have received from the Society a letter of 25 April 1830 directing that slaves married and continuing to live together should get a day off weekly. There was no compliance here with SPG's directives, but the Society did not make it an issue. Marriages continued slowly and regularly, but many served merely to formalize existing common-law relationships.

As emancipation drew closer, the Society issued a statement on 21 January 1831 attempting to clarify its position. Arguing that the current directors were not to be blamed for SPG's involvement in slavery, the statement made a number of interesting observations. The choices before them had been, first, to relinquish the trust, in which case the cause of religion and humanity would not have been served; second, to enfranchise the slaves, in which case the level of suffering from a sudden emancipation would have been greater than any previously witnessed; third, to make provision for their gradual emancipation and, by the introduction of free labour, 'afford an example which may lead to the abolition of Slavery without danger to life and property'. The Society had adopted this last option believing that holding property in slaves might confer benefits on the slaves and lead to their ultimate freedom. The Society had been able to use the benefaction to demonstrate the susceptibility of the slaves to religion, to overcome their resistance to marriage and to show planters how to proceed to emancipation without destruction of their property.

These were specious arguments. The record of the Society on the Codrington plantations does not suggest that all was done that might have been for the slaves. The statement contained all the arguments characteristic of West Indian slave owners, and showed that SPG was close in thought to those they sought to influence. This was the continuing dilemma that the organization faced. But perhaps the greatest problem was that the Society spent so much effort agitating for the appointment of bishops in the West Indies and America, when it was as well placed to agitate for the abolition of both the slave trade and slavery. That it consciously chose to do neither is not to its credit. The Society was not so zealous for the welfare of the slaves that it was prepared to push its agents too far. Its remoteness from the scene made its supervision superficial, and its agents were able to do as they wished, with no sanctions against them.

⋅⇒◎⇐⋅

Dr Noel Titus is Principal of Codrington College and a Canon of St Michael's Cathedral, Barbados. He has published extensively on religious and church history in the Caribbean.

Notes

1. J. C. English to Dr J. Hind, Barbados, 20 July 1778.
2. General Committee Minutes (GCM), 16 Mar. 1743.
3. GCM, 24 Feb. 1758; 21 Nov. 1760.
4. Harte was brought before the Court of Grand Sessions in 1827 for refusing to discriminate between black and white in administering the sacrament.
5. Pinder to Secretary, 22 Jan. 1819.

3

~⋗⟫⟩◉⟨⟪⋖~

Parsons and pedagogues: the SPG adventure in American education[1]

JOHN CALAM

Educating the SPG

Among eighteenth-century religious associations aiming to extend Christianity, the Society showed remarkable perseverance. Its proponent Thomas Bray visited Maryland for two months as the Bishop of London's Commissary, and drafted a bill for church establishment there. Returning to England, he secured political ratification of his efforts, followed by a royal charter designed to prevent encroachments on Church of England ambitions in 'Plantacons, Colonies and Factories beyond the Seas'.

Unswerving in its purpose, the 1701 Charter provoked a variety of responses as to implementation. Once home, Bray had stressed provision of colonial libraries. The Lords Commissioners of Trade and Plantations emphasized the military and economic advantages of missionary intervention among Native Americans. Others saw acquisition of tribal languages as crucial. Influential American Anglicans added their perspectives. For instance, New England Governor Joseph Dudley's demographic estimates helped inform Society strategy. New York Governor Lord Cornbury requested that he and his peers be regularly advised of Society policy lest they unknowingly interfered with the conduct of SPG servants. Colonel Lewis Morris of New Jersey declared that top colonial officials should be 'firm Churchmen'. In the mean time, Westchester landowner Caleb Heathcote called for Society-sponsored churches and schools accountable to a resident colonial bishop.

With a view to acquiring direct appraisal of the colonial scene, SPG also dispatched to America three experienced envoys. One was George Keith, sometime Presbyterian and Quaker. By then he considered Quakers the major obstruction to Church establishment abroad but believed New England Dissenters could be brought over given a trained, solvent Anglican missionary force. But he was shocked by 'theological deviations' at Harvard College. The antidote, he felt sure, was sending a president and fellows from Oxford and Cambridge to assume administrative and academic control there. Keith's contemporary John Talbot reassured the Society of its wisdom in strengthening ties with colonial governors. He also added Native American conversion, rural circuit riding and adequate missionary stipends as priority issues. The third emissary, Gideon Johnston, commented on church welfare in South Carolina. That colony, he said, was fever-ridden, in debt, fond of spontaneity in sermon and prayer and given to electing ministers by vestry or congregational vote – a practice calling in his opinion for summary erasure.

Technically, SPG's Charter augured well for the Society's undertaking, instigating a functional bureaucracy and attracting support from authoritative church, political and financial interests. For two notable reasons, however, it experienced insuperable difficulties. First, younger clergy of rising fortune were prone to remaining in the promotional stream of things at home. Mostly, just those for whom the missionary voyage abroad was a necessity of conscience or subsistence chose to go. Not surprisingly many of these risked adverse conditions including hazards to life, health, dignity and reputation. Second, through its anniversary sermons and journals, the Society broadcast critical accounts of America. These prompted Nonconformist countercharges of distortion. In one such rebuttal, Cotton Mather explained how his antecedents came to America to enjoy self-rule – a notion foreign to the Society. Taking issue with perspectives like this, SPG arrived at an uncomplimentary opinion of colonists whose democratic preferences ran contrary to its own message of church and empire orthodoxy. Its image of stubborn, unyielding, inferior Americans was to drain three-quarters of a century of Society educational energy.

Educating Queen Anne's America

An examination of the Society's rules, journals, abstracts and sermons confirms that by 1713, major policies were in place. These called for instructing colonial parishioners, Native Americans and slaves and their sacramental incorporation, as well as providing formal schooling adjusted from bare literacy to Latin and mathematics, depending on locale. Vital to the process were missionaries and schoolmasters. The former were to be ordained ministers holding university degrees. Some of the latter were well educated but lacked degrees. Others were Oxford or Cambridge graduates. Naturally, both callings required sober, prudent men of good reputation. Whatever their qualities though, many suffered disappointment abroad, few so profoundly as missionary John Urmston.

Translated in 1711 from Essex, England, to Chowan River, North Carolina, Urmston inherited a vast circuit over bad roads and dilapidated bridges penetrating an area 70 miles square. 'Hoggs and Cattle' occupied remote church buildings. His Society allowance of £30 per annum fell short, he complained, of providing a worthy living. Yet 'to Digg a Garden [and] Raise Beans, Peas, etc.' struck him as unseemly. Nor was North Carolina establishment legislation initially of much help. Intoxication, Urmston claimed, interfered with vestry meetings. Financially embarrassed, vestries were forced to employ readers rather than ministers. What began as honourable negotiations over schoolmasters' stipends degenerated into haggling over sums impossible to collect. Worse, local opinion that church servants had no place in vestry constantly offended him.[2]

Considered together, Urmston's letters supply an arresting commentary on men striving to reconcile set instructions with unanticipated threats to personal and professional integrity. In this respect, schoolmasters were worst off. Granted, some enjoyed the patronage of town mayors or colonial governors. Not so others. Though destitute, Joseph Robinson never obtained the teaching post for which he petitioned. On Staten Island, Benjamin Drewitt and Simon Brown endured their classrooms for one and four years respectively. Francis Williamson held out a year or so, Thomas Potts a year and Benjamin Millar just two. Although they commanded better stipends, Society parsons shared with pedagogues many similar frustrations including physical danger. George Keith narrowly escaped when a squall snapped the Portsmouth ferry mainmast. In Mohawk territory, William Andrews braved mosquitoes, floods, snowdrifts and nights in the forest. Gideon Johnston was marooned twelve days on an island off Charleston, rescued, then drowned eight years later.

Whereas certain Society servants strove to propagate Anglican Christianity among a white colonial population, others accepted the challenge of Christianizing Native Americans. In so doing, they encountered two nagging problems. One was their inability to speak Indian languages.[3] The other was that Indian leaders did not match Society paradigms. They were not kings. Nor were they children. They appeared less concerned than SPG over alleged Jesuit wiles. Their thirst for letters and Christianity proved less keen than expected. Moreover, they were orators in their own right as well as sensitive to economic and political power struggles thrust upon them by European intransigence. Impeded from reaching Native Americans via their chiefs, SPG parsons and pedagogues pursued alternative avenues of approach. They brought Indians to English outposts, an arrangement meeting with little success. Or they sent Society missionaries into Indian-speaking regions. A case in point was William Andrews' arrival in 1712 among New York Mohawks. Unfamiliar with their language, Andrews brought along certain translated works, but relied on Dutch interpreters for oral instruction. These performed miracles of double translation from English to Dutch to Mohawk and back. But the system proved cumbersome. As well, the lure of provisions for which pupils needed neither to trade nor hunt eventually wore off. Discouraged, in 1719 Andrews withdrew.

Unlike the nomadic Native American, the African slave was a captive pupil. Even so, educating slaves in America was a politically delicate matter. Middle and southern colonies had enacted legislation stating a Christian slave was still a slave. Aware of these laws, French Huguenot convert and Society catechist Elias Neau none the less opened a cate-chetical school in New York City. By 1705, he was providing evening religious instruction for eighteen men and 28 women. But when the rumour spread that baptismal candidature was the first step to freedom, slave owners ensured his class shrank to a mere dozen. The rumour proving false, enrolment doubled its initial figure. Then, following a black uprising in 1712, citizens already cool toward Neau maligned his school and implicated his students. For some time thereafter, attendance assumed its previous modest level. This tension between Christian duty and slaveholder prerogative seemed imperfectly understood in London. As anniversary sermons contended again and again, Christian education of the proprietary black should have been less difficult than that of the travelling aboriginal. In America, though, no amount of colonial legisla-tion or SPG earnestness allayed a deep-seated American fear of slavery disturbed even by minimal literacy.

Lessons in print, 1714–63

Between 1714 and 1763, Society expenditure on printed works for overseas distribution rose from £3119 to £5344, impressive sums in those days. As the Charter made clear, the purpose of these readings was to persuade colonial inhabitants of the benefits of Anglican Christianity. Here was no small task, given changing conditions of colonial life including development of a multiplicity of professions and crafts, accu-mulation of wealth through trade and proliferation of religious sects.

Together, such trends undercut the assumption in England of colonial subservience, prompting SPG to augment its propaganda campaign.

Anniversary sermons provided one means. These rehearsed a mercantile theory of economics, a political order based on loyalty to the Crown and a colonial social structure based on rigid class divisions. Society abstracts discussed news from overseas, especially numerical assessment of missions abroad. To the American reader, however, they could be provocative. Nonconformists were not amused at accounts of preferential treatment afforded Society emissaries ranging from free ferry rides to advantages before the law. To these perspectives from London, SPG parsons in America added their thoughts unaffected, it seemed, by growing diversification of colonial life. They reminded colonials about the divine right of kings and warned citizens that they 'meddle not with them that are given to change'. They urged dependence on England and obedience to royalty 'according to . . . [their] Several Stations'.[4] In sermons celebrating peace with France, Cambridge, Massachusetts, missionary East Apthorp not only extended his benediction to George III, the nobility and the magistracy, but also endorsed agriculture and simple commerce as ideal for general colonial employment. His analysis could not but satisfy church establishment interests, principally those of British merchants and manufacturers.

As well as sermons and abstracts intended to advance Anglicanism abroad, the Society generated historical publications. A major early work was the Secretary, David Humphreys', *An Historical Account of the Incorporated Society for the Propagation of the Gospel in Foreign Parts* (1730). In subsequent years, what proved exceptional about this book was the durability of its central contention that SPG brought civilization to a barbarous land by a process of direct cultural transfer. In the jargon of his time and associates Humphreys told of a mission among impudent sectaries, vile ringleaders, wild Indians, subjugated Negroes, colonists lacking common humanity and decency and those negligent of all religion. No less blunt was James MacSparran's *America Dissected, in Sundry Letters from a Clergyman there* (1753). Society parson at Narragansett, MacSparran filled many pages enumerating the benefits to England of its American colonies, in particular their value as sound investments, suppliers of timber for shipbuilding and repair and frontier buffers in time of war. Eventual attainment of colonial church establishment he took for granted, regardless of New England opposition and lukewarm practice elsewhere. Provisions for higher learning he considered slender and the proliferation of small colleges unlikely to garner rich endowments or achieve academic standards commensurate with those of Oxford or Cambridge. In his opinion a few colonies passed muster as to moral fortitude. The worst of them, he charged, attracted the very sweepings of London's streets.

Besides sermons, abstracts and histories, SPG distributed printed material with more direct bearing on its endeavours in America. Priority items were Bibles and liturgical pieces in English, French, Low Dutch, German and both Narragansett and Mohawk tongues. Other books addressed such temporal concerns as envying one's betters, profanity, gambling, factionalism and drunkenness. As for the ideal community, the anonymous author of *The Husbandman's Manual* defined it in the traditional imagery of the beehive. William Beverage's *The Church Catechism Explained*, White Kennett's *The Christian Scholar* and Richard Allestree's *The Whole Duty of Man* likewise offered advice on instructing children, establishing charity schools and resignation to one's lot as the key to serenity and civic order. From the colonial – especially the colonial dissentient – point of view, however, the sum of Society printed works with their blend of royalist supremacy, condescension for colonial ways and Anglican ecclesiastical imperialism occasioned resistance to Society inroads, particularly the tendency of SPG rationalists to look upon America as guarantor of Old World power and ease. American Dissenters like Noah Hobart and Jonathan Mayhew respectively warned of High Church designs in their *Ministers of the Gospel* (1747) and *Discourse Concerning Unlimited Submission* (1750). As they did so, Boston and New York newspapers became battlegrounds for encouraging or resisting an American episcopate.

Classrooms for the colonies

Though the functional boundaries of Society schoolmasters, catechists and missionaries overlapped, schoolmasters trod the bottom rungs of the hierarchical ladder. The purpose of their labour was plain enough – instructing and disposing pupils to believe and live as Christians. To this end, students learned to read the Bible and memorized the Church catechism. They also acquired such skills as writing, calculating and good manners. Since changing circumstances dissuaded SPG from subsidizing a colonial network of permanent school buildings, the 65 Society pedagogues active in America between 1714 and 1763 got by with what was available. Some like William Forster at Westchester enjoyed in 1726 a comfortable winter in new premises seating 60 scholars. More often teachers held classes in their own houses or in rented chambers that, according to locality and season, were frequently too hot or too cold.

Ideally, Society pedagogues were expected to teach three dozen or more pupils, accepting Dissenters' children to keep the numbers up. Five hours of school in winter, six in summer, constituted an average day. In *Notitia Scholastica* (official reports), schoolmen made reference to 'effective and rapid teaching', implying concentration on one pursuit for a substantial length of time. From Westchester, New York, Forster reported the parson's son to be in grammar, six others in arithmetic 'whereof one in Practise three in Reduction one in Multiplication . .' and seventeen in spelling and reading.[5] Teaching method was logical. Rowland Jones of Chester, Pennsylvania, described children memorizing words in increasing order of syllabification from one to eight. They likewise read the Testaments from simple to more complex passages 'so making of 'em perfect in the Vowels Consonants and Diphthongs'.[6]

Despite instances of cultural adaptation and job satisfaction showing up in the records, Society schoolmasters appear to have been particularly susceptible to professional frustration. Some of this stemmed from stipends as low as £5 per annum, which they considered slender, turning to supplementary occupations such as farming, clerking, even surgery. At other times, far more complex issues led to their downfall. Upon his arrival at Burlington, New Jersey, in 1714, Rowland Ellis feared a Quaker plot. Local inhabitants questioned the validity of his licence. Since there existed no colonial bishop 'to suppress such irregularities', and Governor Robert Hunter himself countenanced Quakerism 'as well as Christianity', Ellis was slow to start. At length, objecting to receiving Quaker children and demanding Quaker teachers be disallowed, he landed himself in political trouble. In 1719 his outcries found their way into Society abstracts widely circulated in the colonies. Burlington Quakers secured copies and were aghast at what they read. Even Burlington churchwardens were sympathetic to Quaker interests and so informed their schoolteacher. Thus censured, Jones restricted subsequent comments to classroom affairs. In 1739, however, Elizabethtown SPG missionary Edward Vaughan accused him of 'Notorious Neglect of Duty'. Ellis complained to the Society, but to no avail. Over his protestations, it dismissed him.[7]

Whether British expatriate or native colonial, the Society pedagogue had reason to feel squeezed between Society expectations and local religious, cultural and political conditions. Much of this pressure arose from the fact that church hierarchy yielded at times to colonial redefinition or outright disregard. Occupied with their own parochial duties, the Bishop of London's Commissaries, Gideon Johnston, Alexander Garden or William Vesey, seemed to catch up with pedagogical misdeeds only when they burgeoned into full-blown political crises. Society missionaries considered schoolmasters as subordinates who relieved them from the tedium of readying parishioners for public catechizing. As for security against rivals, an earlier shortage of qualified men, growing appreciation for formal schooling in New England and elsewhere and growing reluctance on the part of colonial governors in time of war to concern themselves with relative trivia such as teaching licences, together eradicated church teaching monopolies in mid-century America. An SPG pedagogue thus endured at best a physically and emotionally demanding occupation, at worst a socially humiliating marginal subsistence. Perhaps he read *The Husbandman's Manual* with its allegorical reference to bees, 'the meanest doing their Duty, with as much Chearfulness as the greatest'. By the time of the French cession in Canada, though, colonial America was no apiary.

Learning and loyalty

'No aspect of the American Revolution', wrote Carl Bridenbaugh, 'holds more fascination than the adjusting, part conscious and part unconscious, of the [American] colonists' view of their past to meet the requirements of the changing social and political conditions of the age.' This 'usable past' – reconstructed through such works as Edward Johnson's *Wonder Working Providence* . . . (1650), Cotton Mather's *Magnalia Christi Americana* (1702) and Daniel Neal's *History of the Puritans* (1720) – was, Bridenbaugh argued, wrought on the Puritan premiss that arrival in the New World constituted the preordained culmination of an 'historical process'.[8] Indeed, during the last two decades of its American educational adventure, SPG witnessed assertive colonials mapping out a usable future often radically different from the one the Society had in mind. In his *Common Sense* (1776), for instance, Thomas Paine argued the absurdity of the monarchy. Thomas Jefferson's *Bill for the More General Diffusion of Knowledge* (1779) proposed basic instruction for all and advanced education for the gifted, to be repaid through public service. And Charles Turner's *Discourse* (1783) prophesied that even the masses could be brought to wisdom. Their views were aided by a variety of flourishing institutions. These included at least 70 bookshops in Philadelphia and as many elsewhere before 1776; lending libraries in principal cities prior to 1774; over 4000 titles from American printing presses between 1761 and 1776; nineteen newspapers in circulation over the same period; and in 1765 an American Academy of Science – renamed the American Philosophical Association – which in 1769 elected Benjamin Franklin as its first president.

By means of its propaganda from the early 1760s onward, the Society continued to conceive of an America out of tune with these expressions of colonial destiny. From the pulpit at London's St Mary-le-Bow, bishops preached repetitively about filial duty, fidelity to the Crown, Native American trade and military alliance, and dishonest, jealous colonists grown morally soft on freethinking, irreligion and greed. Not surprisingly, Society parsons and pedagogues in America trod with greater care than their episcopal superiors installed with relative comfort in their British dioceses. In a speech to the American Philosophical Society in 1773 for instance, William Smith made a case for differences of opinion and freedom of discussion. After Lexington and Concord in 1775, however, Society servants in America were pressed to favour one political cause or the other. Some had little choice. Obliged in 1775 to preach before a congregation of colonial riflemen, Daniel Batwell conceded that the Continental Congress was motivated not by disloyalty but by the desire to preserve long-established privileges. Nevertheless, by far the greater proportion of Society parsons abroad developed in their principal statements pro-British sentiments and church establishment apologies inimical to American patriots whatever their religious affiliation. In New England, where Jonathan Mayhew contended SPG had misinterpreted its own Charter, their task was particularly hard. Society missionary East Apthorp claimed that some discretion in its interpretation was permissible, but to little avail. Elsewhere, Anglican missionaries recapitulated time-tried theories of divine rights and defined civil liberty as service to God through conscientious subjection to law and government. In *An Alarm to the Legislature* (1775), Samuel Seabury deplored colonists who affronted the British Parliament, nation and king, confused freedom with sedition and mistook liberty for rebellion. More boldly stated yet was *The True Interest of America . . .* (1776) attributed to Charles Inglis. Refusal to submit, he predicted, would bring upon America confusion, dispossession, closure of peace negotiations, restoration of Canada to France, even the subdivision of the colonies among various European powers – in short, ruination.

While Society parsons did their utmost to rally a flagging cause, Society pedagogues struggled in face of mounting criticism to manage their faltering schools. Most, however, were unable to hang on. Fewer British-born teachers risked the dangerous Atlantic crossing during hostilities. And diminishing numbers of colonial-raised schoolmen dared admit to SPG connection. Not infrequently out of touch with the persistence of local ambitions or the cross-currents of resentment threatening their work, they gradually vanished from the scene. Within a decade revolutionary combats ceased, marking the final salary remittance to the last Society preceptor within United States territory. Thenceforth,

Americans would receive their lessons in loyalty from other teachers or, in some cases, from the same teachers with new outlooks on American politics, culture and Christianity.

Parsons and pedagogues

In 1701, the Society had reason for optimism. Its historical roots were firmly set. At home it enjoyed invaluable political connections. Abroad, it merited the attention of colonial governors. Under its auspices hundreds of parsons and scores of pedagogues eventually served Anglican interests in colonial America. Thanks to its efforts, congregations heard sermons, pupils of all ages learned to read, blacks memorized prayers and Native Americans received a smattering of letters. Its mood was humanitarian. If it condoned slavery, it was a more considerate bondage it had in mind. If it abetted traders, in the main Native American exploitation was reduced. What was missing was a colonial bishop. Its requests notwithstanding, the Society never persuaded Britain's government to allow one.

Thus left to fend for themselves, Society envoys confronted America with misgivings. Often uncertain of their commissions, they provided London headquarters with a picture of American conditions less deliberately distorted than inadvertently coloured by the frustrations of a nebulous charge. Society pedagogues found much unusual about their schools, pupils, parents and buildings. Society parsons appeared embarrassed by less rigid social divisions than those they were used to. Custom, for instance, dictated they live with a degree of refinement; but modest stipends ruled out pretence. Habit suggested they avoid manual labour; yet necessity sometimes decreed dirty hands. Interestingly enough, colonial-born Society servants depicted colonial existence every bit as critically as did their counterparts born in Britain. In correspondence to the Secretary, they lamented the scarcity of books, unsteady school attendance, drain on schools by competing local or itinerant teachers, fragmentation of effort among concurrent jobs, never-ending struggle for accommodation, rampant illiteracy, shortcomings of colonial colleges and their own incipient poverty. Most persistent of such observations, however, was the near-axiomatic supposition of general colonial inferiority.

During the five middle decades of its American adventure, churchmen who published theories of empire on either side of the Atlantic came up with more sophisticated versions of the proper relation of colony to mother country. Anniversary sermonists and abstract compilers unhesitatingly proposed personal or national dividends as just returns for

British investment abroad, and urged those reaping profits to lend financial support to SPG. Society historians also listed colonial natural resources as inducements for subsidizing missionary interests. Clerical, military and political observers added their strategic interests in a hinterland beyond colonial settlement. Upon these foundations, the Society attempted to raise an educational structure designed to house its recurring thesis of colonial obedience. Its authors belaboured the concept of duty – metaphorically through reference to astronomical or natural laws; systematically via endorsing parliamentary prerogatives, royal authority and the power of magistrates.

What marked the declining years of the SPG adventure in American education was not, however, the refinement or modification let alone the retraction of set beliefs in a closed society. Rather it was the persistence of these ideas and their resultant fragility in face of jolting contrary opinions. At last convinced of the hopelessness of its educational commitment abroad, in 1783 the Society withdrew. Some of its servants returned to Britain. Others joined the Loyalist procession to Upper and Lower Canada, the Canadian Maritimes and the West Indies. A few stood fast to serve a disestablished American Episcopal Church. On its part, SPG turned to Canada, the West Indies and Africa to continue work so abruptly interrupted in the new American republic.

At this last juncture, it was not atheists, infidels or 'divers Romish Priests' but dynamic Christian Nonconformists and Low Church latitudinarians that thwarted the Society's endeavours in America. Indeed, a quarter century before the revolution itself, clerics like Jonathan Mayhew and Noah Hobart had shown there was nothing inconsistent about being at once an American Dissenter and a good citizen. Yet here was a proposition the Society seemed incapable of accepting. With all the power at its disposal, it delivered an unchanging message of colonial subservience, never quite grasping throughout the eighteenth century the infinite variety of American opposition to such a premiss. While American Episcopalians later referred with gratitude to their origins in the Society's work, Americans generally may recognize in these limitations a contribution to their eventual political dissociation with Britain.

***

Dr John Calam was born in England but has spent most of his life in education in Canada and the USA. After working at McGill and Columbia Universities, he is now Professor Emeritus in the University of British Columbia's Faculty of Education.

Notes

For fuller annotation, see Calam (1971), from which this essay has been abstracted with the permission of the publisher, Columbia University Press.

1. The Society dispatched its servants into often unknown territory where it met unanticipated challenges. It also prompted both personal and institutional financial risks. These are the traditional components of adventure. The enterprise was educational in the sense that the Society promulgated its values not only in schools but as well through all other means at its disposal.
2. [J. Urmston to Secretary, 7 July 1711, *SPG Letter Books*, A.7, pp. 366, 372, 375].
3. A notable exception was Henry Barclay, in 1736 appointed Society missionary to the Mohawk and Albany.
4. A. Brown (1746), *The Folly and Perjury of the Rebellion in Scotland Display'd*, Boston; H. Carver (1763), *The Great Blessing of Stable Times*, Boston.
5. [W. Forster to Secretary, 3 Nov. 1717, *SPG Letter Books*, A.12, p. 364].
6. [R. Jones to Secretary, 17 June 1730, *ibid.*, A.23, pp. 159–64].
7. [R. Ellis to Secretary, 8 Oct. 1715, *ibid.*, A.XI, p. 264]; [E. Vaughan to Secretary, 29 May 1739, *ibid.*, B.VII, no. 158].
8. Bridenbaugh (1962), pp. 171, 172–8.

4

-◈-〓◉〓-◈-

The SPG and the impact of conversion in nineteenth-century Tirunelveli

VINCENT KUMARADOSS

In the nineteenth century Protestant missionaries in southern Tamil Nadu in India largely concentrated their energies on winning converts and establishing churches. As zealous messengers of the Christian faith, they deployed various means to gain adherents to the faith and enable them to sustain themselves within the fold of the Church. The interaction between the missionaries and the indigenous people among whom they worked, was, however, complex, setting in motion unpredicted consequences. In this chapter I attempt to trace the complex story of how conversion to Christianity by lower castes – in this case, the Shanar converts of Tirunelveli region ('Tinnevelly' in the British period) – was animated by both spiritual and temporal desires. In other words, it tells the story of how the missionary spiritual labour had to come to terms with the temporal issues – in particular the structure of power mediated by caste – grounded in the local cultural milieu.

Conversion in Tirunelveli

In Tirunelveli the number of upper-caste – Vellala – converts to Christianity, who preferred the new faith chiefly on spiritual grounds, was always small. With traditional caste and other privileges in the indigenous order, their conversion to Christianity meant the loss of these privileges, their social status and family ties. They also faced persecution and economic deprivation. 'The penalty paid for becoming a Christian . . . [was], in the case of the . . . [upper castes], the loss of everything.'[1] However, entry into the fold of their new faith secured them a privileged space within the Church. They had been the missionaries' earliest targets,

were celebrated as prized catches and were counted on for the further-
ance of the Gospel. As collaborators in the missionary venture, they were
expected to guide others to Christianity and consolidate the infrastructure
of the missionary enterprise. Acting as catalysts in the growth of the
Church, they gained leadership as catechists, preachers and pastors in the
newly founded churches. Subsequent generations of upper-caste Christians were to derive still further benefits from conversion through access
to Western education, which enabled them to occupy high positions not
only in the Church but also in the secular domain.[2] The recognition
accorded them and their early domination in the Church led to the
perpetuation of upper-caste privileges within the Church.

Two kinds of conversion

Until about 1840, most catechists in the churches of Tirunelveli were
upper-caste Vellalars trained at Tanjore. These Vellalar converts treated
the lower-caste Shanar and Paraiyar converts as inferior because both the
latter groups were considered outcastes in the traditional caste hierarchy.[3]
Even the Vellalar catechists treated the Shanar converts with 'contempt,
. . . disrespect . . . [and] aversion', while 'exalting their own superior
position'.[4] C. T. Rhenius, a well-known missionary in this region, had
to close a seminary for some time because the Vellalars were unwilling
to be trained with Shanars and Paraiyars.

Contrasted with the conversion of upper-caste individuals, lower-
caste conversions were characteristically conversions of single-caste
groups and were motivated not merely by spiritual quest but also by a
desire to challenge upper-caste authority in the indigenous society. By
embracing Christianity, the lower-caste converts defied the old order
and questioned traditional caste-based practices such as sanctions against
using public thoroughfares and wells, entering market places and courts,
wearing jewellery and even covering women's breasts with an 'upper
cloth'. Traditionally denied education, access to education in mission
schools and colleges was an added attraction for them. This is clearly
seen in the story of the conversion of the Shanars in Tirunelveli. They
accepted Christianity on their own spiritual and material terms rather
than as passive objects of the missionary project.

Shanar conversion to Christianity

Among the localities where Protestant missions made a profound and impressive impact, none has been more conspicuous than Tirunelveli. For SPG's missionaries, the Tirunelveli conversions were a great numerical success, extensively referred to in the Society's literature during the nineteenth century.[5] Characteristically, a later missionary presented Tirunelveli as a site where 'the greatest success' was achieved, despite being one of the 'most difficult' terrains to conquer in the 'whole world'.[6] Thus, the 1847 Report:

> The proportion of the inhabitants of Tirunelveli who have embraced Christianity is larger than that of any other province in India. In many places entire villages have renounced their idols, and the movement in favour of Christianity is extending from village to village, and from caste to caste. In every district in the province, churches and schools, and, missionary houses and model villages are rising apace, testimonies of the church's faith in expecting to possess the entire field.

The beginnings of the new faith in Tirunelveli at the turn of the eighteenth century were attributed to the spadework done by Lutheran missionaries stemming from Tanjore. The faint stirrings it produced subsequently gained new adherents to Christianity from 'all kinds or castes of Hindus' ranging from the small group of upper-caste Brahmins, Vellalars and others to the lowest, Shanars – later known as Nadars – Pallars and Pariars.[7]

The honour of raising Christianity among the Shanars is rightly ascribed to a Vellalar catechist and leading figure, Satyanadhan, and his most notable assistant, David, the first Shanar catechist. Appointed in 1796, David was actively involved in the extension and consolidation of the early breakthrough among the Shanars. Conversion subsequently swept into the Christian fold a high proportion of these poor, illiterate, despised and oppressed Shanars, whose flocking into the Church, wave after wave, was of crucial importance for the missionary labour in Tirunelveli and the history of Protestant Christianity in India as a whole.[8] For the August 1893 *Mission Field*, it 'verified . . . the saying . . . "The poor have the Gospel preached to them"'.

In terms of sheer numbers, the lower-caste Shanar converts outnumbered all others in Tirunelveli, the famous and popular Society missionary at Nazareth, Margoschis observing that by the 1890s, out of a hundred thousand native Christians, ninety thousand were Shanars.[9] At one stage, the Shanars' 'popular movements' had become so famous and the 'staple of the Christianity of Tinnevelly' that terms such as 'Shanar Christianity', 'Shanar Gospel' and 'Shanar mission' were coined and gained currency, typifying the success of this missionary endeavour.[10]

Christian villages

The Christian message preached by the SPG missionaries through the selective interpretation of the Bible struck deep chords. Quoting extensively from the Old Testament, especially from the books of Exodus, Joshua and Judges, God's power and authority over the 'people' was exalted. Emphasis on God's mighty hand in the liberation of the people of Israel from the Pharaohs, after 'five centuries of oppression', fed the aspirations of the oppressed Shanars. Their appropriation of this message found its most obvious expression in the construction of the Shanar convert as descendant of the 'Lost Tribe of Israel'. Identifying with the Israelites' liberation guided by Jehovah, the Shanar converts imbibed and appropriated the doctrine of a powerful god who would look after their 'worldly as well as spiritual prosperity' and protect and bless them if they remained loyal and steadfast despite persecution.[11] Such perceptions became a powerful resource in the hands of the Shanar converts both to constitute a community of themselves and to contest their oppression by the upper castes. Christianity was a weapon of emancipation to them. It raised their status: they were now worshippers of the powerful 'new god' presented by the missionaries and colonizers who had defeated the rulers of the region, their local persecutors and oppressors.[12]

There were clear early indications that the Shanar converts were no longer willing to submit meekly to the coercion of the upper castes and would fight for what they considered the rights and privileges which they had first legitimized in their expression of corporate life through the 'new faith'. A section of the earliest Shanar converts, with the active involvement of David the catechist, tried to resolve the local violent persecution by migrating in 1799 and establishing Mudalur, 'First Town', the first of a series of Christian colonies that served as 'Towns of refuge' for the converts.[13]

Mudalur, the first Christian colony in Tirunelveli which 'owed its existence solely to Christians', was a trendsetter, its very name 'intended to express the converts' hope of many other Christian towns yet to come'.[14] Following the Mudalur pattern, a number of Christian villages such as Jerusalem, Samaria, Bethany, Bethlehem and Nazareth came into existence. Nurtured by the Christian missionaries, the Christian village pattern took deep root. These efforts had their precedent in earlier initiatives of Rhenius,

> He collected his converts wherever he could into Christian villages, but he was on the whole remarkably successful in avoiding the . . . pauperizing dependence on the missionary for everything . . . He formed societies among the Christians . . . for such purposes as the support of the church, of widows and orphans, and for Christian literature. No doubt the fact that the . . . [Shanars] already held a position of some economic independence was a great help here, but Rhenius may be given the credit for encouraging and not depressing initiative. The Christians in Tinnevelly never seem to have looked upon the missionary as merely a milch cow for their benefit.[15]

Subsequent missionaries nurtured the Christian settlements, and these became the nerve centres of the two chief missions that laboured in Tirunelveli district – SPG and CMS. They entered Tirunelveli pursuing their courses independently and agreed their separate spheres of labour. The work of SPG was confined to selected villages of a smaller region in the south-west around Nazareth and the region of 'great Nadar concentration' in the south-east.[16] The Society was successful in attracting here a number of missionaries of great distinction, including some former Lutherans, D. Rosen and A. F. Caemmerer, also A. Margoschis, R. Caldwell, who became bishop, G. U. Pope, J. A. Sharrock and numerous others. These played a pivotal role in the rise of new and prosperous Christian villages – overwhelmingly of Shanars – in the arid and sandy regions of southern Tirunelveli. The prosperity of such Christian settlements as Nazareth, Idyangudi and Sawyerpuram led to the mushroom growth of Christian villages under missionary patronage.

Created on a new concept with church, school and other supportive structures as the chief components and visible symbols of the new order, these Christian villages thrived under the guidance of missionary authority and the supervision of local catechist-teachers. Describing their striking features, Caldwell wrote:

> When a Tinnevelly village embraces Christianity, it immediately forms itself almost as a matter of course . . . into a Christian Municipality, and authorises its headmen to exercise a general superintendence over the congregation, and, in conjunction with the native teacher or catechist, to carry into effect the Missionary's views. Even in those cases where only a portion of a village becomes Christian, and that not the most influential portion, it forms itself,

not only in ecclessiastical and educational matters, but even in the greater number of social matters, into a new municipality, and generally manages to maintain its independence.

The headman, often the elder in the congregation, not only settled 'civil and social disputes' in the village, but also ensured 'obedience' to 'Christian rules' and 'Church discipline'. He was held responsible for the converts' regular attendance at church and school and for the 'collection of contributions for religious and charitable purposes'. His power was exercised under the supervision of the European missionary who was the final arbiter or rather 'universal ruler and divider' in case of controversies and appeals. These villages were treated by the missionaries as emblematic statements about the Church's civilizing mission. To quote Caldwell again,

> In passing from village to village you can tell, without asking a question, which village is Christian, and which is heathen. You can distinguish the Christian village by such signs as these – the straight-ness and regularity of the streets, the superior construction and neatness and cleanness of the cottages, the double row of tulip-trees or cocoanut palms, planted along each street for ornament as well as for shade, and the air of humble respectability which everywhere meets your view – all so different from the filth and indecency, the disorder and neglect, which assure the visitor that a village is heathen. You notice also, as you pass through, a marked difference in the people themselves especially in the women. The Christian women are more decently attired and more intelligent looking than their heathen sisters . . . villages which have held fast and valued the Christianity they received, have risen, sometimes in the first gener-ation, always in the second, to the enjoyment of greater prosperity and comfort, and to a higher position in the social scale, than any heathen village of the same caste.[17]

In order to help the converts overcome the problem of scarcity of water supply, wells and tanks were built. The Mudalur tank was provided by the mission and supplied by a channel maintained by mission, government and the people who were dependent on it, enabling the converts to cultivate rice, vegetables and fruits. Similarly in Nazareth, the Caemmerer Tank and wells made possible the cultivation of corn and millet. Irrigation of sandy tracts, the planting of coconut and other fruit trees and several other agricultural experiments increased the agricultural prospects, giving the converts economic gains. Consequently 'barren spots' in the 'barren wilderness' were converted into 'oases of prosperity'.[18]

For Shanar Christians the new village settlements sounded the death knell of the discrimination and disabilities under which they had long suffered. The Christian village boundaries ceased to be the lines of social demarcation or distinction; they became simply lines of protection and emancipation. Incorporating the traditional municipal system, the converts became autonomous in conducting their affairs without interference from the traditional indigenous élite.

Recasting caste

The creation of Christian villages as the exclusive domain of the converts enabled them to safeguard themselves against upper-caste assaults, and also freed them from the traditionally wielded power of the indigenous élite. Social boundaries were redrawn. They could evade the payment of discriminatory taxes imposed on them and refuse to yield to the forced labour demanded of them. Resistance was displaced from a vulnerable to a more protected site. Significantly, the new Christian settlements reinforced in a peculiar fashion the consciousness of caste exclusivity: Christian Shanars virtually formed a 'caste by themselves' and occupied all together one great locality, so that 'they could act almost as if they were not a caste at all'.[19]

In this context, while members of the Anglican Church, the Shanar converts combined the elements of Christianity with aspects of their cultural past, retaining caste and also their traditional occupations. Caste exclusiveness perpetuated in the Christian settlements led to the building up of 'caste Churches'. The Shanar converts retained caste without reservation or 'abhorrence', and 'Nadar' was a title in common use amongst them.[20] Missionaries such as Margoschis, who recognized the inevitability of Christianity being interwoven with the Shanar caste, tacitly approved the prevalence of caste sentiments among the Shanar Christians. This contributed to the perception that Christianity was compatible with caste, and that Shanar could accept the new religious tradition and keep caste too.

In the ambience of the Church and the exclusive Christian villages, no stigma was attached to the traditional Shanar occupation of toddy-tapping, considered to be polluting in the indigenous caste hierarchy. In fact, the Church was symbolically identified with the palmyra palm, 'Christianity and the palmyra' appearing to have flourished together. It was observed, 'Where the palmyra abounds, there Christian congregations and schools abound also; and where the palmyra disappears, there the signs of Christian progress are rarely seen'.[21] In Idyangudi a special service was conducted annually from 1858 on 6 January to inaugurate the climbing season. This date was carefully chosen for more than one reason. It coincided with the feast of Epiphany in the Christian calendar celebrating the announcement of the birth of Christ to the Magi. Further, the date preceded the annual indigenous Hindu festival of Pongal, thus defying the belief that commencement of the climbing season before Pongal was inauspicious, bringing misfortune and loss to the climber's family. It was a grand occasion for the Shanar converts, both during and after the service, with 'prayers that the tree might yield its fruit, and the climbers' foot might not slide'.[22] Customarily, the Shanar convert placed the devices used in climbing palmyra trees on the altar during the service. The festival came to an end with a Shanar *panayeri* (climber) climbing the nearest palmyra carrying an *arival* (sickle), and the exchange of greetings. Thus, aided by such liturgical incorporations, the palmyra became a symbol of dignity affirmed by the missionaries, and the Shanar converts of the first generation could continue their traditional occupation without inhibitions.

The convert's early quest for justice even found militant expression as David raised a 'club wielding force' to counter the persecution of converts and to protect their lives and property. In defiance of the orders of his 'superiors', Satyanadhan and Gericke, but with the support of a sympathetic friend, a merchant called Sawyer, David's force of young Shanar converts took the offensive, going about 'from place to place redressing the wrongs of the native Christians by force'. His daring acts were a morale booster to the converts who hailed him as the 'Lion of Mudalur' for his dauntless deeds. After his premature death in the year 1806 at the age of 31, which local tradition attributed to poisoning by his enemies, David came to be known as the first martyr among the Shanar Christians and the first seed of the Tirunelveli Church.[23]

Anything within the Church that affronted the dignity to their caste was met with protest and withdrawal. In 1886, at the Sawyerpuram mission, the catechist David Arulappen of the Pallar caste used the term *Ilappajathi* to indicate that the Shanars occupied an inferior position somewhere between the upper and lower castes. This expression annoyed the Shanar converts and they complained to the missionaries. Arulappen had to apologize to the congregation though he protested that he had not intended to wound the caste pride of the Shanar converts. The Shanars refused to accept his apology, declared that they could not accept 'catechists of any caste not equal or higher than their own', and withdrew from the Church.[24]

The upper castes who increasingly resorted to coercive action against the Shanar Christian villages were forced to accept the new situation, which was reinforced by the missionary appeal to British officials, who then extended protection to these oppressed people. The Tirunelveli Shanars showed an increased preference for Christianity when the British defeated their chief local persecutors, the Maravar landlords.

Despite such dependence on the Western missionaries, they refused to accept any move by the missionaries which slighted them in terms of caste. For instance, Robert Caldwell's book, *The Tinnevelly Shanars* (1849), which appeared insulting in supporting the missionary opinion that the Shanars were a despised community, was vehemently criticized. The Shanar Christians were mobilized to rally against the book. Though the Church empowered the converts in the indigenous society, their position within the Church in relation to the Western missionaries was often one of marginality. This led to confrontations. Perhaps the best illustration is the complex saga of Sattampillai. Encountering heavy-handed missionary authority, Sattampillai, a Shanar catechist well versed in theology, chose to move out of the Anglican Church and to found the Hindu–Christian Church of Lord Jesus in 1857. Sattampillai established the new Church to subvert European missionary authority. Interestingly, he developed a substantive critique of Western Christianity as corrupt and inauthentic. Simultaneously, he appropriated elements of Judaism for his own Church and represented it as the restoration of an original and purer form of Christianity. This both delegitimized Western Christianity and denied missionaries their authority; and also invested the adherents of the Hindu Christian Church with a superior identity.[25]

Thus, Shanar converts were successful in negotiating their inferiorization within and outside the Church. In this, their considerable numbers were a help.

> The most distinctive feature of the situation in Tirunelveli was the great numerical predominance of the Shanars everywhere. This fore-shadowed an entirely new aspect of the caste question – the dominance of the Tinnevelly church by the Shanars, or as they preferred to be called, Nadars, which was was evident in the next decade (1870s).

Simultaneously, the Shanar catechists trained at local seminaries multiplied rapidly, the catechists in Tirunelveli gradually becoming almost exclusively Shanar. By the end of the nineteenth century, nearly 'nine-tenths of the native clergy' were, as they were now known, Nadars.[26]

After gaining a dominant position in the Church, the Shanars strove to bring in Panikers, Pallars, Pariars and other castes, and carried the

Gospel to other places, a measure affirming their new-found identity and recognition. Thus the neo-converts enjoyed their new-found freedom to the extent of preaching their new faith and winning new converts to the Church. Evangelizing societies were launched, supported entirely by funds raised from converts in order to maintain their own 'catechist and other subordinate agency'.[27] Evangelists were engaged by these societies to preach the Gospel not only in Tirunelveli district but also in other parts of the presidency, and even in Ceylon and Mauritius.[28] A major project was the formation of the Indian Missionary Society in 1903, the first of its kind in India, crossing denominational, caste and geographical boundaries. A wide range of voluntary and welfare societies were organized on a self-supporting system to buttress the growing needs of both Christian and non-Christian communities. Funds poured in from the Shanar converts with 'increasing readiness and cheerfulness' to manage local religious charitable societies. The liberality of the Shanar converts' contributions to the Church became proverbial, with missionary accounts drawing attention to this.[29]

Through these developments, the Shanar Christians of Tirunelveli came to occupy key positions in most of the Protestant Churches all over Tamil Nadu in the earlier twentieth century. When the Church of South India was inaugurated in 1947, Lesslie Newbigin observed that 'all major posts in the Mission institutions and all the places in the governing bodies of the Church were held by people of one caste only, the Nadars of Tinnevelly'.

> The spectacular growth of this community under missionary leadership in the nineteenth country had produced an abundance of educated men and women who were available for service in the (later) missionary work of other churches in the rest of Tamil Nadu. They had great gifts of intelligence and hard work, and they were also a close knit community of families interlocked by marriage. It was easy and natural for them to monopolize all the higher posts and to create an atmosphere of accepted opinion that the local Christian products of more recent evangelism among the outcaste communities were 'not yet fitted for higher responsibility'.[30]

Advancement in the secular domain

The missionaries were also instrumental in advancing the economic independence of the Shanar converts. For example, trade prospects in palmyra products received an impetus from improved transport and communications which the missionaries negotiated with government. New roads, a railway line and a postal service were provided for Nazareth, linking it with other towns and cities.[31] A weekly market was started in 1872 at Nazareth and loans were advanced by the missionaries which were a great boon to Shanar Christians involved in business. Other Christian villages like Idyangudi and Mudalur, Sawyerpuram and Mukuperi also benefited from missionary initiatives. Such facilities encouraged the Shanar Christians to take to trade, initially in a small way, as a means of livelihood.

Gradually Shanar Christian merchants moved with their commodities to distant places and became an enterprising business group. Those from Nazareth and Mudalur carried jaggery (unrefined brown sugar) and other items to Tirunelveli, Madurai, Virudhupatti, Trichy and Tanjore, and established their own trading centres. Shanar Christians from Idyangudi involved in petty business turned to wholesale business and established trade links with Tuticorin, the developing port town. The 'barrenness of soil', scarcity of rain, failure of crops and inability to make a 'sufficient living' also contributed, driving a good number of Shanar Christians from Mudalur and Nazareth to go over to Ceylon to trade and earn their living in the 1890s.[32] They organized a community credit fund in Ceylon for mutual help, and this was still working well 50 years later, with contributions from about 300 Christian traders in all parts of Ceylon.

For the converts, however, this was not the end of the road. Gradually, the Shanar converts of their own accord gave up their traditional occupation and moved into various spheres that moderniza-tion was opening up. These changes were the effect, to a considerable degree, of the 'Protestant ethic' propagated among the Shanar converts by the Church. As Caldwell put it,

> The changes that have already taken place are a good omen for the future, especially seeing that they have been carried into effect by the people themselves, of their own accord, and at their own expense and are directly the results of Christian influences. Christianity has given people higher ideas of their capabilities and duties . . . it has taught them self-respect, and some degree of self-reliance . . . it has made them more enterprising, more energetic; it has knocked off the fetters wherewith their intellects were bound, and bid them go forth free; and thus it has opened before them an unlimited prospect of progress and improvement.[33]

The other important factor aiding the advancement of Shanar Chris-tians in the secular domain was missionary education. This was undoubtedly introduced as an integral part of the evangelization process, with teaching of the Bible and knowledge of Christianity as the chief accompaniments of such education.[34] The educational system of SPG in Tirunelveli included primary schools, boarding schools, seminaries, industrial schools, orphanages and colleges. While the important Society mission bases such as Nazareth, Idyangudi, Sawyerpuram had a greater share of these institutions, one of the distinctive features of SPG in South India was that primary schools were started wherever they had gained a foothold – 'always in Christian villages' and wherever they had 'an opening and funds to work with in non-Christian villages'.[35] Schools in general, particularly boarding schools and seminaries, imparted Christian education to the converts with a view to their future usefulness in the Church as mission agents, catechists and wives of catechists, schoolteachers or Bible women.

The educational efforts of the Society were used by the converts, however, for their own social and economic benefit, with only a limited number of those trained at mission schools and seminaries serving as church workers. There was no prospect of employment for the educated Christians in government service because of the hostility of European officials, and because 'all the posts were monopolised by the Hindus'. In 1840 a government order was passed so that Christians might be employed in public services, but little came of this as 'the only Christians employed in public services in 1846 were 12 sweepers and one writer'.[36] Under these circumstances, the 'literate Shanar converts' sought fresh avenues of employment. They 'drifted to towns and cities and even to Madras by the 1840s', occupying the area adjacent to George Town (Black Town) known as 'Tirunelveli settlement' where 'some of them became even more independent and prosperous'.[37]

The opening up of coffee and tea plantations in South India, Ceylon and Malaya in the nineteenth century provided employment as fieldworkers, clerks and conductors for Shanar Christians with the commercially valuable English knowledge learnt in the mission schools. With a steady flow of income they achieved a measure of economic stability. Regular remittances to their homes led to the building of better houses and to the expansion of the church establishments. Some of them returned home with savings and became petty traders and cultivators, improving their business and cultural pursuits. A few became extraordinarily successful planters, as the stories of A. V. Thomas, P. D. Devasahayam and P. P. Joseph illustrate. Within 'the Shanar planting group, one individual who stood head and shoulders' above all the others was A. V. Thomas. Hailing from Caldwell's village, Idyangudi, and educated only up to the school level, he emerged as the doyen of the tea industry, becoming the second Indian president of the United Planters' Association of Southern India (1953–54). From humble origins, he became the owner of 'an enormous enterprise encompassing various production units and wide trading networks'.[38] He made liberal provision to aid the schools at Idayangudi and the general development of this village, and donated a large sum to construct the AVT Hostel at Sarah Tucker College.

During the second half of the nineteenth century, 'hundreds of these Christian Shanars migrated . . . as soldiers, labourers, railway clerks, and petty Government officials . . . not only to other parts of South India, but to Ceylon, Burma, and Malaya'. The largest number of educated Shanar migrants have been Christians rather than Hindus, earning 'decent salaries . . . in several walks of life'. Among the succeeding generation, an appreciable number has become distinguished and affluent 'land owners, traders, entrepreneurs, advocates, physicians, engineers, teachers and Government officials'. Discussing the effects of conversion on the Shanars, Dettman notes, 'There is not a single avenue of service, private or public, in which the Nadars are not found, not only in these districts [Madura, Ramnad and Tirunelveli] and other parts of India, but also in the globe wherever the Tamil Christians are found.'[39]

Such was the effect of missionary-sponsored mobilization on the Shanar converts who previously, in the indigenous structure, had no scope or opportunity whatsoever to gain access even to formal education. Their transformation was amazing. From toddy-tappers living in the *teris*, the barren and sandy palmyra tracts, and suffering severe social disabilities and economic deprivation, the subjects of even Caldwell's derisive portrayal in his book emerged as 'one of the earliest groups who rose from social lowliness to occupy places formerly reserved for Brahmins'.[40]

Conclusion

The saga of the Shanar converts in Tirunelveli indicates that spirituality cannot have a disembodied existence outside the social universe of the converts. Often the engagement of the converts to reconstitute their social universe was resented by the clergy. For instance, commenting on such tendencies, a local priest observed, 'Many of our native Christians are wanting in spiritual life, very slow in spiritual growth, and are in consequence apt to slide away from the faith when they are put in trouble. Many of them expect only temporal prosperity and success by joining Christianity. They look to the mission as a means of giving them worldly influence and support in time of trouble.'[41] Such attitudes gave rise to the derogatory category of 'rice Christians' in the missionary discourse.

However, such attitudes were more than offset by a more complex culturally grounded notion of spirituality deployed by other missionaries. In the context of Tirunelveli, such a nuanced understanding was embodied in several of them. For instance, Caldwell, a missionary of unparalleled importance in the region, could openly endorse the presence of both spiritual and temporal desires in the converts' agenda:

> In the greater number of instances the conversions that have taken place have been the result, not of spiritual motives alone, but a combination of motives, partly spiritual and partly secular, the spiritual motives predominating in some instances over the secular, in others the secular predominating over the spiritual.

What is more, in accommodating the needs of the poor, lower-caste converts, he could work with an expanded notion of spirituality. More influential than material help from the missionary were the converts' expectations 'of being at all times kindly inquired after and spoken to' in a ministry 'governed by principles of Christian justice'. Experience of this sort conferred 'indirect benefits' whereby they felt that they were 'men' and, as such, 'capable of advancement'.[42]

It is precisely such sensitivity on the part of the missionaries – a product of dialogue and contestation between the local converts and the missionaries functioning in a culturally alien context – which resulted in a steadfast community of Christians from among the Shanars of nineteenth-century Tirunelveli.

⊷═◉═⊷

Dr Vincent Kumaradoss teaches Medieval and Modern Indian History in Madras Christian College, Chennai. He has published extensively on the history of Christianity in South India.

Notes

I am grateful to M. S. S. Pandian for his comments on a draft of this paper, and to the Institute of Development Alternatives, Chennai, for intellectual support.

1. J. Mullens (1854) *Missions in South India*, London, p. 110.
2. For the Vellala converts, *Report*, 1866; also R. Caldwell (1857) *Lectures on the Tinnevelly Missions*, London [Caldwell, *Lectures*]; D. A. Christadoss (1980) *Caldwell Athiatcher*, Danishpet; Grafe (1990).

3. Jayakumar (1998), p. 112.
4. R. Caldwell (1881) *Records of the Early History of the Tinnevelly Mission of the SPCK and SPG*, Madras, pp. 58–9 [Caldwell, *Records*].
5. Report, 1853; *Mission Field*, Apr. 1889; Apr. 1895.
6. J. A. Sharrock (1910) *South Indian Missions: Containing Glimpses into the Lives and Customs of the Tamil People*, London, p. 3.
7. *Mission Field*, Aug. 1893.
8. For full details, Jayakumar (1998).
9. A. Margoschis (Oct. 1893) 'Christianity and caste', *The Indian Church Quarterly Review*.
10. J. Mullens (1854) *Missions*, pp. 100–16; Caldwell, *Lectures*.
11. Jayakumar (1998), p. 172; R. L. Hardgrave (1969) *The Nadars of Tamilnad*, Bombay, pp. 80, 87.
12. Grafe (1990), pp. 94–5, 220–1.
13. Caldwell, *Records*, p. 61; Devapackiam (1963), pp. 131–8.
14. Caldwell, *Records*, p. 61.
15. Gibbs (Sept. 1965).
16. Hardgrave, *The Nadars*, p. 46.
17. Caldwell, *Lectures*, pp. 68, 116.
18. Caldwell, *Records*, pp. 242, 239; *Mission Field*, May 1892; Christadoss (1950), p. 82.
19. Mullens, *Missions*, p. 110.
20. Margoschis, 'Christianity and caste'.
21. Caldwell, *Lectures*, p. 31.
22. *Ibid.*, p. 37.
23. Caldwell, *Records*, p. 101; Christadoss (1976), pp. 55–6; Devapackiam (1963), p. 87.
24. Hardgrave, *The Nadars*, pp. 71–2.
25. Kumaradoss (Jan. 1996).
26. Gibbs (1972), p. 249; Margoschis, 'Christianity and caste', p. 547.
27. Report, 1855, p. cxi.
28. Report, 1880, p. 39.
29. Caldwell, *Lectures*, pp. 85, 119; Sundkler (1954), pp. 30–1.
30. Newbigin (1985), p. 59.
31. D. A. Christadoss (n.d.) *Canon Arthur Margoschis Aiyar*, Palamcottah.
32. *Madras Diocesan Record*, July 1892, pp. 127, 129.
33. Caldwell, *Lectures*, p. 117.
34. 'Among the gods', *Mission Field*, Nov. 1895.
35. J. A. Sharrock, (July 1886) 'Distinctive features of the missionary work of the SPG in South India', *Harvest Field*.
36. J. S. Ponniah et al. (1938) *The Christian Community of Madura, Ramnad and Tirunelveli*, Madura, p. 39.
37. Frykenberg (1978), p. 205.
38. P. E. Baak (1977) *Plantation, Production and Political Power*, New Delhi, pp. 85–6, 162.

39. Dettman (1967), p. 21; Ponniah, *The Christian Community*, pp. 39, 40.
40. Grafe (1990), p. 84.
41. *Mission Field*, May 1892, p. 165.
42. Caldwell, *Lectures*, pp. 75–6, 76–7.

5

·✦·══◯══·✦·

Supporting a colonial bishop and patriot: William Grant Broughton and the Society

GEORGE P. SHAW

The enigma of William Grant Broughton is this: today he is little remembered, whereas in his own day he was honoured in both hemispheres. Joshua Watson praised him greatly as his favourite bishop. He was written up as a mission hero. The *Annual Register*'s obituary ran as long as any duke's. His English associates arranged for his burial in the nave of Canterbury Cathedral, the first such burial since Cardinal Pole's. Clearly, Broughton excited the admiration of his British contemporaries, many of whom were associated with the SPG.

In Australia, the outcome was similar. For a quarter of a century, Broughton's slight figure, with his distinct limp, was a visible and much debated part of Sydney's early colonial life. He arrived in 1829 and died in 1853 while abroad on church business and still in office. He was the senior ecclesiastical officer in New South Wales, progressing from archdeacon to Bishop of Australia, then Bishop of Sydney and Metropolitan of Australasia. He was, too, for most of his colonial career a civil officer serving on the Executive and Legislative Councils. Broughton served Church and state with distinction. As the colony's Chief Justice put it upon hearing of his death,

> There was not one great object for the promotion of civilization and special advancement in the colony with which he was not connected; there was not one effort to raise its name in the estimation of the world with which his name was not identified . . . Out of his Church, indeed, he knew no sect, no party, and his whole efforts were for the common good; and if ever there was a patriot, in the best and highest sense of the word, that patriot, in the colony of New South Wales, was Bishop Broughton.[1]

None of this is remembered today. Blame partly falls on the Diocese of Sydney's peculiar century-long ambition to become a citadel of puritan evangelical Protestantism. Broughton, an uncompromising High Churchman, was an aberration in an otherwise acceptable line of evangelical clerics dating back to the foundation chaplains, Johnston, Marsden and Cowper. To preserve its evangelical pedigree the diocese excised Broughton from its memory.

This neglect by his natural defenders has allowed the civil historians to toy with Broughton's reputation. They portray him as a leading protagonist for all those undemocratic privileges imposed by English authority on colonial society and which colonists had progressively to dismantle to create Australia's much-boasted egalitarian democracy. Broughton was identified with a short-lived privileged colonial society and marginalized from Australia's future.

Manning Clark, doyen of Australian nationalist historians, once contemplated correcting this. He wrote, in the planning stages of his second volume, 'In the second period I hope to make Broughton and Lang central figures.'[2] It never happened. His second and third volumes rarely mention Broughton, and only as a villain deserving of a mocking farewell.[3]

This dismissal of Broughton in civil histories is justified by a simpleton's logic. It asserts that since Australia was founded in the slipstream of the Enlightenment and the Industrial Revolution it was shaped by the sceptical and materialist values of those transforming events. Religion survived, but in Australia it could be no more than an entertainment, nor church leaders any more than actors in a futile drama. The true architects of Australia's bold new experiment in egalitarian democracy were modern men inspired by 'the chance to lavish on each other the love previous generations had given to God'.[4]

The truth is otherwise. Broughton's episcopate ensured that the Judaeo-Christian tradition took root in Australia. As a consequence, Australian history is a far more complex case of the contest between the Judaeo-Christian tradition and its secular rivals than civil histories admit. Broughton foresaw such a conflict, and his episcopate is best evaluated as an attempt to put in place a strategy for all future contingencies. He explained and discussed his strategy with the SPG from 1835 onwards, at a time when Australia was not one of the Society's missions, and won its backing. The tie was always more between Broughton and the SPG than between Australia and the SPG.

To understand what turned Broughton to the Society, it is necessary to know the conditions of his appointment. He accepted the Archdeaconry of New South Wales under auspicious conditions. The King-in-

Council had recently established a Church and Schools Corporation, to be lavishly endowed with revenue from Crown lands, for the expansion of churches, schools and colleges throughout the Australian settlements. Broughton, as executive director of this Corporation, believed his task was to steer the colonial Church of England to its guaranteed future.

While Broughton was still en route to Sydney, the Corporation was suspended, never to be effectively revived. A sympathetic British Tory government counselled patience whilst it searched for alternative funding, leaving Broughton meanwhile dependent on modest colonial-treasury grants which inhibited expansion. It was a subsequent Whig government which resolved the issue, authorizing a new governor, its own appointee, to do as much or as little as he liked in support of religion and education provided it cost the British government nothing and did not soak up funds better used in the management of the convicts. The foremost aim of the Whigs of the 1830s was to shift the cost of the convict system from the British to the colonial treasury.

Broughton lobbied the new governor against making the latter a priority at the expense of the former. He argued that 40 years of transportation had created a population of ex-convicts disinclined towards supporting religion and not naturally inclined to self-regulation. Intervention in support of religion was essential if a civil society was to emerge. Though the past support given to religion by the civil authorities had been far from adequate, the outcome had been beneficial in the level of self-regulation evident in the beginnings of a civil order. Broughton cautioned the governor, Richard Bourke, not to equate this with a rebirth of a religious temperament in the community, and called on him to expand government support until there was a sound civil order based on Judaeo-Christian principles and a general acceptance of self-regulation.

Bourke, an Anglo-Irishman, acquiesced on two conditions. Firstly, the major denominations were to share around the government grants in proportion to their membership. Secondly, there were to be no more denominational primary schools, but a single system of civil schools with a religious curriculum of the type acceptable to Protestant and Roman Catholic church leaders in Dublin. The ideal outcome would be a Judaeo-Christian but non-sectarian civil order.

Broughton rebelled. He saw government grants for the maintenance of Anglicanism frozen while Roman Catholics and Presbyterians received catch-up funds. Even worse was the prospect of surrendering Anglican schools to the new-fangled Irish religious curriculum. This Broughton considered a desperate compromise, winding up England's least successful attempt at propagating British Protestantism abroad. Why shackle the bad outcome of an old Irish venture on to a new Australian venture with an entirely different destiny? Broughton stood firm against the governor.

Broughton had arrived in 1829 believing the King-in-Council had charged him with responsibility for invigorating the emerging colonial civil order with churches and schools supportive of traditional British Protestant culture. Instead, by 1833 he found himself battling to defend the very idea that traditional British Protestant culture had any special place in the colonial civil order.

Broughton soon discovered that rhetorical opposition in Sydney produced no extra funding, so he applied for leave to intervene in London. The governor clearly wanted him out of the colony, but not in London where he might do mischief. Archbishop Howley intervened, and Broughton sailed for London late in 1834. His mission was to snatch back a primacy for Anglicanism in the colonial civil order.

Fortuitously, Canterbury was home to Broughton's in-laws, and he made his base there. Soon he met with Howley and joined the Archbishop and the Duke of Wellington, his former patron, at a public function where *The Times* reported his saying that 'he had been placed at the head of Christianity in a land where education was unknown and it was part of his duty to attempt the removal of difficulties produced by the absence of an establishment for inculcating religious and general knowledge'.[5] *The Times* advertised his mission.

Howley supported but also trimmed his mission. The Archbishop believed as firmly as did Broughton that the Church of England should enjoy an exclusive relationship with the state but such an arrangement was no longer available to the Church of England let alone in a new colony. Howley tutored Broughton in the art of compromise, advising him to settle for the best arrangement he could negotiate in London and leave nothing to be settled by a contest in the colony.

Broughton changed direction. He asked the Colonial Office to guarantee him two things: a religious subsidy which never fell below the £9200 currently being paid; and that all existing Church of England schools become church property, along with £1000 a year towards their upkeep. In effect, Broughton offered to take responsibility for the Church's future expansion provided the colonial government maintained the foundations already there.

This did not impress the Colonial Office. It preferred to have the colonists themselves settle their religious and colonial affairs, but it offered Broughton a bishopric for added status in dealing with the colonial government.

For Broughton this was the most feared outcome. He played for time and turned his thoughts to how he might provide for the future expansion of the colony's churches and schools. Someone, possibly H. H. Norris or J. E. N. Molesworth, close associates of Joshua Watson in the Hackney Phalanx, suggested he approach SPG. Hitherto, the Society had largely bypassed Australia, arguing that its penal purposes identified it as a British government responsibility.

Broughton put a simple case to SPG. He pointed out that each year Britain poured 4600 of its unwanted thieves, brawlers and prostitutes into Australia and had the gall to tax Australians for their reformation. Was not this topsy-turvy? Ought not those who lived in England in added security also contribute to the task? 'So far as the Government and people of this country are concerned,' he said, 'these crowds of offenders are cast forth upon the shores of New South Wales without the slightest concern being displayed whether they and their posterity from want of religious ordinances degenerate into heathens and pagans.'[6]

SPG capitulated, and drew Australia into its fraternity. The Society voted Broughton £1000 for new churches, and the SPCK followed up with £3000 for new schools. The Society also invited Broughton to use its organization to recruit a lobby of English supporters. It was also through SPG's many contacts that Broughton was introduced to the thought of the Tractarians, which enlarged his understanding of ecclesiastical authority. Broughton began to understand for the first time how he might be a bishop in a civil society which repudiated the English Reformation settlement and where the notion of Royal Supremacy was bankrupt. He dropped all opposition to becoming bishop on unfavourable terms. 'It was the conviction,' he said, 'that if I declined no one else could take up the matter in an instant so as to be prepared to carry it on as I might do, which decided me upon coming back.'[7]

Broughton's episcopate stretched from June 1836 to February 1853. These were sixteen years of spectacular expansion. What began as the Diocese of Australia in 1836 was four dioceses by 1853 – Sydney, Tasmania, Newcastle and Melbourne. Sydney, where Broughton concentrated his effort, expanded from twelve parishes in 1836 to 38 by 1853. At least 40 priests joined the diocese, and by the mid-1840s Broughton had a theological college, St James, up and running for training local ordinands.

The SPG vitally influenced this expansion, largely through Broughton's ingenious handling of the funds the Society channelled into Australia. Immediately after his return, he set up a Diocesan Committee of the SPG to raise funds locally for church and school expansion. He wanted to capitalize on a local enthusiasm for Sydney's elevation to a bishopric, and cash in on a rivalry with Rome which had also made Sydney its Australian bishopric. More significant than either of these were the new Church Acts which removed the special status of the Church of England and offered religious subsidies to other religious denominations. Broughton formally protested the passage of these Acts, then marvelled at his good fortune. Never had he so much money. He encouraged local gifts by offering £ for £ subsidies from the SPG funds, then applied to the government to match that again under the terms of the Church Acts, thus turning a £1 local gift into £4 towards a nominated project. So much money fell into Broughton's hand that within a year of his return he had 40 projects under way and the foundation stone for St Andrew's Cathedral in place. Little wonder the Colonial Office considered the Church Acts a hasty extravagance! By 1840 government subsidies were limited to £30,000 annually, of which two-thirds went to the Anglican Church. Broughton's sole reason for remaining a member of the Executive Council after resigning from the Legislative Council in 1843 was to protect his share of religious subsidies from revision.

The SPG also took over from the Colonial Office responsibility for recruiting colonial clergy. The Colonial Office appointees had fallen into two categories: those trained in missionary colleges and directed to the Australian colonies; and those with a university education who, more often than not, were in disfavour at home or else were looking for an escape route, often from creditors. The former were compliant, the latter often testy. Even so, Broughton emphasized that 'a mere parochial clergy will not suffice', and pressed the Society to find him university men.[8] He needed recruits who could live on £150 a year and who had a talent for moderate controversy to combat Rome and liberalism. The type, he said, were to be found at Oxford rather than Cambridge, and were well schooled in Mr Newman's principles of ecclesiastical authority. Broughton put in an order immediately he returned for fifteen such recruits and, if SPG jibbed at the request, Broughton assured the Society that the list of donors suggested that there was plenty of goodwill towards the diocese at Oxford.

The Society found a few star recruits, but by and large the outcome was disappointing. Broughton found young recruits fresh from university quite ambitious and impatient for advancement; the older recruits were often men searching for a fresh start but too loaded with past disappointments to cope with the hardships of colonial life. By the early 1840s, Broughton supported Edward Coleridge's proposal for a special college at Oxford to train non-graduate clergy for settlements like Australia which were not mission fields but had special needs. When the English bishops sank that proposal – though it was soon to be raised as St Augustine's College, Canterbury – Broughton asked SPG to recruit young men for training in Australia. Any loss in 'fine scholarship', he said, would be 'more than corrected by the experience of living and learning in the environment in which they would work'.[9] The Society approved, and SPCK contributed £3000 towards a building for a local theological college. Broughton intended the college to grow into a university college (to be called Pembroke Hall), and an appeal by Edward Coleridge for books from Oxford colleges gave the diocese a fine theological library.

Early in the 1840s the Society was drawn into the process of subdividing Broughton's diocese. The matter was officially in the hands of a London committee which originally acted without consulting him. Broughton did not like its recommendations to create new dioceses at Port Philip (Melbourne) and Adelaide, and sought the intervention of SPG to put his case for a new diocese north of Sydney at Newcastle and another south-west of Sydney in the Manero (Canberra). He dismissed Adelaide as premature and thought Port Philip could be reached with ease by ship whereas the Manero was a difficult journey away. The Society secured Newcastle for Broughton, but not the Manero. Approval, however, did not flower into appointments. The Colonial Office insisted that each new diocese have a £30,000 endowment fund. Broughton asked the SPG to search for conscientious curates with private incomes of £600 annually. He also told the Society to inform Gladstone at the Colonial Office that he would donate half his salary towards new bishoprics to get action. Gladstone was impressed, took a quarter, £500, and pushed forward with the dioceses of Melbourne and Newcastle. A friendship began between bishop and statesman which had profound consequences for later attempts by colonial dioceses to reform their ecclesiastical government.

The creation of these new dioceses sapped SPG's treasury, and in the late 1840s the Society gave Broughton notice to move towards self-sufficiency. By then Broughton was plotting another role for the Society in Australian religious affairs. He welcomed the multiplication of dioceses, but did not want to see this issue in a diversity of policies which might weaken the impact of religion on the civil order. To forestall that outcome, Broughton put to Selwyn, in New Zealand, his bold thoughts on the restoration of synodical government.

Broughton's readiness for so radical a development indicated that he had dumped the Royal Supremacy from his thinking. Two incidents had finally converted him. The moment he advised the Colonial Office of his intention to appoint an archdeacon to assist him, and named a candidate, James Stephen urged the Crown to intervene and claim the right of nomination to this and all other senior ecclesiastical offices in the colony. Then, in a startling and unannounced intervention in 1846, the colonial Legislative Council debated whether to transfer from the bishop to Lay Trustees control of clerical stipends, and to have the civil Supreme Court arbitrate any dispute. This meant that funds raised by SPG would pass directly under the control of laymen and a civil court. Broughton had no forewarning of this legislative debate. Despite a hasty appeal from the bar of the Council, the proposal sank only on a technicality. Its revival remained a threat. Clearly, to Broughton, the Royal Supremacy amounted to mischievous intervention without any accompanying benefits. The *Tracts for the Times* directed him to a more ancient form of ecclesiastical government, and his mind blossomed with thoughts of self-governing diocesan, provincial and patriarchal synods free from the British Crown and colonial parliaments.

Broughton was quick to acknowledge that each diocese must incorporate the laity into its government, for it would be their contributions, not the Crown's, which built the future Church. He wanted the bishops in a provincial synod to decide matters of doctrine, discipline and liturgy to be followed uniformly throughout Australasia. He also wanted all the future dioceses of the Pacific and South-East Asia, from Singapore to Hong Kong, to collaborate as they inevitably adjusted the traditions of Canterbury to the needs of another hemisphere. Broughton foresaw that the future unity of Anglicanism would be a dialogue with Canterbury, not an imitation of it. He also foresaw Anglicanism as a collection of patriarchates, Australasia one, America another. However visionary the outcome, he believed it was timely to begin pushing for changes in this direction. 'The time is good for *Recommendation*,' he told his fellow bishops, 'so that *when* state fetters drop off (as they must ere long) we may be found *in possession* of a system of acting.'[10]

Selwyn responded vigorously with ideas of his own, and from the dialogue came the momentous occasion of 1850 when the six bishops of Australasia met in Sydney.

Two far-reaching decisions came from their meeting. An Australian Board of Missions was founded on a pledge to recruit native evangelists for a renewed ministry to the Aborigines and Pacific Islanders. 'Time has not passed without effort,' Broughton declared, 'but it has passed without fruit.'[11] In fact, effort, but not concern, had eluded Broughton. He wrote about the Aborigines for government, and attended several inquiries, but he directed his limited resources almost exclusively to a ministry among free-settlers. He once said of the Aborigines, 'Within a very limited period those who are very much in contact with Europeans will be utterly extinct.'[12] He was equally pessimistic about convicts. 'I cannot venture to hope that the exertion of any individual, even if an angel, could effect any very general reformation . . . in those receptacles of the worst of Criminals.'[13] Broughton was pre-eminently the pastor of the free-settler. By 1850 convicts were rarely seen, but the Aborigines were very visible. The Australian Board of Missions reflected a renewed concern.

The other far-reaching decision was an agreement to revive synodical government in each diocese and to form a Province of Australasia. Broughton turned to the SPG to secure the necessary legislation in the House of Commons. He envisaged a simple Bill authorizing colonial dioceses to form synods and, having done so, to forego recourse to English ecclesiastical courts. The Society assembled the necessary talent, and Gladstone took the Bill into the House of Commons. Unbeknown to Broughton, the Bill allowed an appellate jurisdiction to the Arch-bishop of Canterbury, which undermined his vision of an autonomous Province of Australasia. The Bill failed. The government would not object to colonial legislatures passing such a Bill, but it did not want any debate in England which might encourage an expectation of English synods. Broughton feared what a colonial legislature might do with such a Bill.

Broughton hoped to convert Gladstone's failure into a better Bill where appellate jurisdiction resided with the bishops collectively in a Provincial Synod, not with the Archbishop of Canterbury. Unfortu-nately, delay afforded more opportunity for local debate producing as many models for synods as there were dioceses. Moreover, the laity aggressively demanded equality with the clergy in all matters, and some clergy (and one bishop), fearing a Tractarian bias among the Australasian bishops, supported the Archbishop of Canterbury's appellate authority.

The SPG, aware of a wider interest in synods by this time, brought a number of bishops to London in 1853 to draft a model synod and confront the Archbishop of Canterbury to secure his support. The Society chose Broughton to chair the group, which met once before he died suddenly in the February. The group soon lost direction, and a decade of confusion delayed real progress.

Broughton's concern was the proper government of the Anglican Church abroad where the Royal Supremacy had collapsed. Gladstone extended Broughton his patronage believing the colonial experiment would benefit English bishops when they too confronted a defunct Royal Supremacy. Broughton's tomb in Canterbury's nave was his English memorial for devotion to the good ordering of the Anglican Communion generally. After his funeral, a group met in the Chapter House to consider funding the completion of St Andrew's Cathedral as an Australian memorial. The proposal died immediately it was noted that colonists had access to the new wealth of the Australian goldfields to complete their own cathedral.

This fair prediction was Broughton's just memorial. He had left behind a Church expanded and comprehensive and able to meet the great demands accompanying the transformation of Australia. After 1850 no one lived beyond the reach of a religious ministry. The alliance forged between the Society and Broughton was fundamental to this expansion.

Since the late 1830s Australia has had a great many Churches and much religion. It has lacked, though, and still lacks, a tradition of theological scholarship essential for its Christian renewal. Broughton foresaw this need and planned a Pembroke Hall for tertiary studies and a theological canonry for St Andrew's Cathedral to meet it. Pastoral priorities confounded both proposals. The greater enemy, however, was the colonial ideal, adumbrated in the 1830s and entrenched in the 1870s, of Australia becoming a model non-sectarian state – that is, a state where theological discourse had no place in any debate on the civil order. To help achieve this, the study of theology was banned from the University of Sydney in the 1850s, establishing a precedent for all universities established over the next century. This reduced the Judaeo-Christian tradition in the Australian civil order to a religious sentimentality. Broughton foresaw this possibility. His expectation was that a self-governing Anglican Church in Australia would recover the integrity to challenge the myth of non-sectarianism, which he equated with an abandonment of a vital Christian faith. Anglicanism in Australia may yet recover his vision. Meanwhile, his tomb in Canterbury Cathedral is a reminder that his contemporaries, especially those in the SPG, understood well his mission.

⊷⊜⊷

Dr George Shaw is a priest in the Diocese of Queensland, and was Reader and Director of the Australian Studies Centre in the University of Queensland. He published a major study of Bishop Broughton in 1978.

Notes

1. Shaw (1978), p. 278.
2. S. Davies (ed.) (1996) *Dear Kathleen, Dear Manning. The Correspondence of Manning Clark and Kathleen Fitzpatrick 1949–1990*, Carlton, 1996, p. 15.
3. C. M. H. Clark (6 vols, 1964–1998) *A History of Australia*, Carlton, Vol.3, p. 457.

4. Clark (1998), Vol. 6, p. 500.
5. Shaw (1978), p. 88.
6. Shaw (1978), p. 85.
7. Shaw (1978), p. 99.
8. Shaw (1978), p. 116.
9. Shaw (1978), p. 187.
10. Shaw (1978), p. 241, quoted from Perry's *Diary 1850*, pp. 6–7.
11. Shaw (1978), p. 239.
12. Shaw (1978), p. 93.
13. Shaw (1978), p. 99.

6

Anglican tradition and mission: sources for mission methodology in the nineteenth-century Pacific

SARA SOHMER

Given the hegemony of the 'Christianize and Civilize' formula emphasized in historical treatments of the nineteenth-century missionary movement, this might well be the last place where one would expect to find indigenous cultures ascribed worth and value. But ethnocentrism and cultural insensitivity never constituted the *only* responses of European culture in its interaction with the strange and the different. The Victorian missionary movement encompassed individuals capable not only of recognizing the inherent value of indigenous culture but also of accommodating the Christian message to its needs.

Both historians and Victorian observers of the British missionary effort have pointed to the prominence of this pattern of recognition, validation and accommodation among three missions with ties to the High Church traditions of the Church of England: the Universities' Mission to Central Africa (founded 1858), the Anglican Mission to Papua (founded 1894) and the Melanesian Mission (founded 1849). All three received support from SPG at their inception and for specific needs subsequently. While none of them could claim to be overwhelmingly successful in terms of numbers converted, they sustained an active, organized presence in Africa and the Pacific until the post-colonial era and provided the foundation for independent Churches of continuing vitality. This chapter will examine the rather unexpected ways the leadership of one of these, the Melanesian Mission, mined both traditional Anglican theology and the distinctive Anglican vision of the historic Church that evolved in the first half of the nineteenth century for the intellectual and spiritual resources to sustain its particular vision. This Anglican context supported the commitment to Christianize largely without any concomitant obligation to 'civilize'.

The Melanesian Mission

The Melanesian Mission served the Solomon Islands, portions of the New Hebrides and other smaller island groups in the south-west Pacific from the initial exploratory voyages of its founder, George Augustus Selwyn (1809–78) until the inauguration of the Church of Melanesia as an autonomous province of the Anglican Communion in 1975. The common thread in commentary on the Mission is a recognition of its distinctive, culturally accommodating approach to evangelization.[1] But where in the Victorian world could one expect to find the origins of this unique perspective? For those who served the Mission, the source of the Mission's distinctiveness was readily apparent; everything stemmed from the perceptions of the founders. Certainly, Selwyn's understanding of the vital role a strong, independent Church had to play in the nineteenth-century world, and his unshakeable belief in the ability of all people to respond to its fundamental tenets provided both inspiration for the Mission and the basis for its methodology.

Until his 1841 appointment as Bishop of New Zealand, Selwyn exhibited no particular interest in the colonial Church or a missionary calling. But he had a deep commitment to the institutional foundations of the Church and its long-range potential that left him 'bound to answer the call of the Archbishop as an officer is at the command of his superior'.[2] Moreover, in the wake of the reform legislation of the early 1830s, Selwyn came to see the established status of the Church of England as a threat to its strength and independence, a view shared by many of the Church's sympathetic critics. For the energetic young bishop a primary source for the revitalization of the Church of England lay in the creation of a dynamic colonial and missionary Church. The new see in New Zealand and the mission to Melanesia included in his letters patent provided Selwyn with a chance to act on his vision of an independent, synodical Church. Far from being mere dependencies and institutional responsibilities of the home Church, these new fields of Christian endeavour might well become a 'new church', with the power to inspire and energize its parent.

On his arrival in New Zealand, Selwyn had to establish an Anglican Church for the growing European population, integrate his episcopal role with the existing CMS mission to the Maoris and begin laying the institutional groundwork for his vision of the new Church. His High Churchmanship and his conviction that mission should come under the purview of the institutional Church strained his relationship with the previously independent CMS while the increasing encroachments of settlers on Maori lands jeopardized relations with that population. But Selwyn persisted, supported in part by generous grants from SPG that enabled him to secure matching funds from the New Zealand Company to support his work. In addition to the New Zealand effort, Selwyn clung to his broader vision of the Church in the Pacific. Neither the grandeur of the project nor the additional commitment presented any difficulty for this most self-assured of Victorians, but even Selwyn could not ignore the practical problems involved.

In a period when the supply of recruits for the mission field did not keep pace with demand, Selwyn's resources hardly sufficed for New Zealand. Moreover, the sheer number of Melanesian islands with their diversity of languages and cultures, the distances involved and a climate considered unhealthy for Europeans combined to make the existing model of resident European missionaries virtually impossible. Rather than rely on resident Europeans or Polynesian teachers – missionary practice used elsewhere in the Pacific – Selwyn determined to create a Melanesian ministry that could Christianize island communities from within. This approach, however, depended on a belief in the equal capacity for understanding in all human beings. Selwyn quarrelled with contemporary use of such terms as 'poor heathen' and 'perishing savages'.

> To go among the heathen as an equal and a brother is far more profitable than to risk that subtle kind of self-righteousness which creeps into mission work, akin to the thanking God that we are not as other men are.[3]

By extension, if islanders could not be defined as irredeemably savage, neither could their culture. Thus, from the time of his earliest voyages, Selwyn advocated non-interference with Melanesian customs unless they presented a clear conflict with Christian principle.

Further development of the Mission's methodology depended on the work of John Coleridge Patteson (1827–71). Recruited by Selwyn specifically for the Melanesian work in 1854, Patteson was a thoughtful, scholarly man with a gift for languages. After Selwyn secured the creation of a missionary bishopric for Melanesia in 1861, Patteson became the Mission's principal architect. Under his guidance, the Mission's Norfolk Island college, St Barnabas, combined the principles of formal education conducted in Mota, the Melanesian language of choice of the Mission, with the discipline of regular work in the college's gardens and shops. By 1871, Patteson could report an enrolment of 145 scholars, collected from the island groups by the mission ship, *Southern Cross*. Yet despite Selwyn's best efforts to incorporate financial responsibility for mission into the structure of the colonial Church in New Zealand and Australia, the Mission's work until 1880 relied on Patteson's private funds, contributions from interested friends in England and a £300 per annum grant from the Society.

By the time of Patteson's death in 1871 at the hands of islanders in the Santa Cruz group, however, the Mission had developed a distinctive and enduring approach to its task. Among members of the Mission itself, the policies developed by Selwyn, Patteson and Patteson's closest associate in the field, Robert Codrington (1830–1922), became virtual holy writ. Use of a Melanesian language as the teaching and liturgical language of the Mission, rotation of students between the mission school and their home islands, development of a Melanesian clergy and respect for local tradition and custom remained fundamental long after the isolation of the early years had disappeared.

Missionaries and Victorian intellectual life

This distinctive approach evolved in response to the pragmatic considerations already indicated and to the intellectual and spiritual resources of the Mission's members. Scholarly discussion of the latter has emphasized the relatively high level of education among members of the Victorian High Church missions as a primary factor in their more sensitive approach to indigenous culture. Certainly, the percentage of missionaries holding university degrees was relatively greater in these missions than among their evangelical counterparts, and their leadership clearly saw university education as part of the profile of the ideal missionary. Any correlation between levels of formal education in the mid-nineteenth century and cultural sensitivity must, however, be treated cautiously. The classical curriculum of the English public schools and universities that the founders of the High Church missions encountered remained overwhelmingly classical until the last third of the nineteenth century. While it doubtless contained much of linguistic and philosophical value for mission, there is little to connect this curriculum *per se* with the sympathetic predisposition of the missions' leaders.

The greater awareness certain university-educated men had of the broad spectrum of Victorian intellectual life must, however, be taken into account. Well-educated clergymen like Selwyn, Patteson and Codrington had to engage at least to some degree with developments in the natural sciences, language studies, history and the infant social sciences that transformed Victorian intellectual life or else retreat into biblical literalism and obscurantism. Patteson capped his undergraduate career at

Oxford with a year's residence abroad – largely in Germany – pursuing his scholarly interests in languages and theology. He became a Fellow of Merton College, Oxford, upon his return in 1852, and he might well have pursued an academic career had he not felt compelled to join Selwyn. Like many other Victorians, he would hardly have known what to make of our too-easy assumption that the pursuit of new knowledge in the nineteenth century inexorably led to a diminution of faith. 'A man needn't be unbelieving,' he wrote, 'because he doesn't like to be credulous.'[4]

Patteson indeed went to considerable pains not to be credulous. He kept abreast of intellectual issues to a degree that astonishes when one considers his location and the press of his duties. He never returned to England in the years between his departure for the mission field in 1855 and his death in 1871, but his reading in Melanesia included a wide range of current and often controversial works that challenged traditional views of biblical authority, history and the natural world. He knew Sir Henry Maine's *Ancient Law* (1861) which posited a connection between ancient and modern legal perceptions, also Sir John Seeley's controversial life of Christ, *Ecce Homo* (1865). *Essays and Reviews* (ed. J. Parker, 1860), which brought down heresy charges on its authors, found its way to Melanesia, as did the writings of such innovative biblical and missiological scholars as Lightfoot and Westcott.

In striving to come to terms with both current intellectual challenges and an exotic environment, these educated men of faith formed very distinctive habits of mind. These included careful examination of sources, a willingness to utilize different types of evidence, an enlarged sense of historical time and a strong preference for the comparative. That this intellectual perspective subjected traditional religious values to new critical scrutiny is widely recognized. We tend to forget that it also served to revitalize an Anglicanism that, in the view of many committed individuals, still had a critical role to play in the world. Defined by both their faith and these new critical perspectives, such individuals found in Anglicanism a vital intellectual and emotional resource for the mission enterprise itself *and* a mission methodology that sought to incorporate rather than destroy indigenous culture.

Anglican sources, mission application

Although Patteson, the chief intellectual force of the Melanesian Mission, relied on Victorian developments in comparative linguistics and historical studies to provide further support for the Mission's methodology, his greatest inspiration appears to have come from his critical reading of those most venerated and orthodox Anglican theologians, Richard Hooker and Joseph Butler.

Hooker's *Treatise on the Laws of Ecclesiastical Polity* (1593–97) and Butler's *Analogy of Religion* (1736) formed an important part of the Anglican canon and appeared in the ordination preparation of most Anglican clergy in the nineteenth century. For Patteson, however, they represented considerably more than an academic exercise. Until the end of his life, he praised the excellence of Hooker's and Butler's thought, and utilized their writings for training both his European ordinands and his senior Melanesian pupils. Although he consistently advocated openness in theological discussion, Patteson staunchly defended the contemporary relevance of Hooker's ideas. Of Butler, he wrote shortly before his death in 1871, 'I do really and seriously think that a great and reverently-minded man, conscious of the limits of human reason – a man like Butler – would find his true and proper task now in presenting Christian teaching in an unconventional form.'[5]

Although Patteson had little quarrel with the Anglican orthodoxy represented by Butler and Hooker, his comments suggest that he found in them, not a refuge from change and difficult questions, but justification and support for the central theme of his mission – presenting universally applicable Christian teaching in an unconventional form. What exactly did a Victorian missionary bishop find germane for this purpose in the theology of an Elizabethan defender of the Anglican compromise and an eighteenth-century apologist?

In formulating a systematic response to the Puritan critique of the Elizabethan Church, Hooker unwittingly gave the first complete expression to an Anglican theology that could still be appreciated and applied three centuries later. Clearly, Hooker maintained, the Scriptures have primacy, but the Church, with its cumulative wisdom, has the authority to develop and interpret the implications of Scripture for each succeeding generation. Scripture itself provides neither its own methodology of interpretation nor knowledge of matters available through science, philosophy and experience. Hence both the authority of the Church and the claims of other, non-scriptural, knowledge must be given due consideration. Moreover, as the ultimate authority for natural law is God, the legitimacy of natural law cannot be less than that of Scripture. Reason as well as revelation leads to the acquisition of moral knowledge. Thus the proper relationship between moral and natural philosophy and revealed religion is not conflict but completion.

As for human nature, Hooker focused on creative human potential. Whereas Puritanism saw man as a creature destroyed by sin and in dire need of God's mercy and forgiveness, Hooker saw him in terms of unrealized possibilities. That man does not always achieve his own realization can be attributed to the perversity engendered by original sin. But that does not obviate God's original vision of man as good. The realization of human potential is a gradual process; Hooker does not expect man to manage this transformation on his own. The Church is there to provide support, through its ministry and its sacraments, in restoring him to his rightful, natural place in God's plan. Once that process is under way, man becomes a creative agent in the building of society. Variety in forms of culture simply reflects this rich human potential. As to when man might be trusted to take on the role of responsible agent, Hooker sets no hard and fast rules but relies on the common sense of the Church's teachers.

Hooker was therefore the source of a broad, developmental view of morality that became an important strain in Anglican theology. A thoughtful reader of Hooker – a reader such as the first Bishop of Melanesia – could put Hooker's views on the value of tradition, the possibility of multiple sources of truth, the validity of reason, the realization of human potential and the value of human cultural variety to good use in mission. When, for example, Patteson spoke of the sort of missionary he envisioned for Melanesia, he dwelt on the need for 'strong religious common sense', for men who could successfully adapt Christianity to local practice without compromising doctrinal truth or principles of conduct. Mission teaching must take existing belief as a point of departure, and the best missionaries would be those who could discern elements of truth or at least the yearning for truth in the midst of error and superstition.[6]

The relationship between Melanesians and missionaries, as Patteson saw it, was less that of the elect pointing out the error of their evil ways to wretched sinners than that of reasonable, spiritual men helping God's creatures realize themselves more fully. This could be accomplished through the slow, undramatic exercise of sound learning, reason, patience and the ministrations of the Church. The imposition of forms which might signify 'progress' to outsiders, for example, Sabbath observance, the wearing of clothes, the abolition of dancing and other local practices, had, in fact, little relevance for indigenous peoples themselves.

All of this seemed so basic to Patteson even at the outset of his work in Melanesia that ordinary mission methods completely appalled him. 'It seems,' he wrote, 'as if common sense and ordinary observation were to be regarded as "unspiritual leaning on the arm of flesh": as if the knowledge of the human heart and the application could never be practically taught and learned.'[7] The failure to recognize variety and potential, to underplay reason and practical knowledge in man, and to confuse form and substance were, for Patteson, the principal sources of mission failure everywhere. The Anglican tradition as embodied in Hooker's writings, by contrast, provided a world-view in which natural law and reason as well as Scripture and revelation revealed God's truth. The possibility could at least be entertained that an indigenous culture could create something worthwhile even without the benefits of Christianity. The role of Christianity was to complete and enhance; it did not always need to replace or destroy.

Joseph Butler's place in Anglican thought rested on the definitive response to the deist attack on Christianity he presented in *The Analogy of Religion Natural and Revealed to the Constitution and Course of Nature* (1736), a treatise in which he sought to establish the analogy of natural and revealed religion with what is observable in nature. By Patteson's time, his theology was seen by many as an inadequate response to the challenges of modern life. In Butler's approach to changing conditions and new challenges and in his ethical theory, however, there remained much to appeal to the Victorian missionary. Butler espoused the view that for religion to be meaningful it had to be understood through general experience. While the unique truth of Christianity depends on divine revelation, this 'miracle' has to be appropriate to the human condition and address human concerns. The role of the theologian is therefore not so much to 'prove' the Gospel as to point out its meaningfulness and to mediate between the direct experience all people recognize and the specifics of Christian thought. Christian understanding must be built on familiar, existing belief. The Gospel must be presented in such a way that its relevance is apparent to general human conditions. Again, the possibilities for the application of this hallowed Anglican intellectual position to mission methodology are apparent.

An even stronger case for Butler's influence can be found in a consideration of his view of man's moral sense or moral feeling. In contrast to the rationalist, utilitarian approach in which self-interest determined human ethical behaviour, Butler felt that the empirical evidence supported the concept of a separate faculty with the capacity to discern moral goodness. Without this faculty or conscience, disinterested actions or motivations cannot be explained; yet the empirical evidence for both is undeniable. Moral sense is not, for Butler, a matter of rational distinction but an innate human faculty.

For the leaders of the Melanesian Mission, the assumption of the innate ability of all people to make moral distinctions was critical. Interestingly, it seems to have been part of their intellectual perspective when they arrived in the field rather than a result of greater familiarity with the indigenous peoples they served. In 1856, shortly after his arrival in New Zealand, Patteson was already firmly of the opinion that 'the capacity for the Christian life is there; though overlaid it may be with monstrous forms of superstition or cruelty or ignorance, the conscience can still respond to the voice of the Gospel of Truth.'[8]

That being the case, the concept of 'savage' had little meaning. Neither the moral failings nor the moral successes of Pacific islanders differed in any essential way from those of Europeans. 'It is strange to be living so peacefully among nations accounted savage and fighting each other,' Patteson wrote after three years in the mission field, 'while you highly educated and civilized individuals act your barbarism on a more exalted scale and with a far greater refinement. It is very savage indeed to spear 3 or 4 men, but exceedingly valiant to leave about 3000 dead on a field slain by the Enfield rifle.'[9]

This fundamental perception of moral consciousness may also have influenced the Mission's approach to teaching and, ultimately, the decision to rely on an indigenous clergy. For if islanders failed to recognize Christian truth, the fault did not rest with them. They had the capacity to make moral judgements, and if they did not do so, the Mission personnel could attribute this to either harsh living conditions or inappropriate presentation of truth. Melanesians, Patteson believed, demonstrated that they could think perfectly well if principles were put in terms they understood. And despite the Mission's use of Melanesian languages, its sensitivity to existing belief and the patient, long-range nature of its goals, he was never certain a European missionary could fully accomplish this. An indigenous clergy was another matter. A Melanesian priest like George Sarawia had, in Patteson's view, a decided advantage, based not just on language ability, but on his mastery of such cultural subtleties as the language of gesture and expression.

Those pillars of orthodox Anglican tradition, Hooker and Butler, seen through the eyes of critically minded Victorians could provide an important intellectual foundation for the Mission's methodology. The exercise of mission, however, also requires an element of imagination and emotional commitment that one would be hard-pressed to find in the cool, common-sense reasoning of Hooker and Butler. Important support for this requirement would be supplied by the Oxford Movement. The Movement combined two critical elements: Anglicanism's High Church tradition, with its emphasis on episcopacy and the authority of the Church fathers, and the emotionalism of nineteenth-century Romanticism. In Chadwick's opinion, the Movement's high regard for history and the mystery and poetry of religion were its most distinctive features.[10] This intensified religious feeling and an almost mystical devotion to the Church had obvious implications for mission, a venture that by its very nature attracted the most determined of Christians.

Patteson resisted identification with any specific Church party and deplored the extremes of ritualism and formalism that he observed in some of his colleagues, but he had numerous personal links to the Tractarians and a considerable affinity for some of their views. His own student days at Oxford came after John Henry Newman's defection to Rome when most of the furore had abated. Still, he recorded his favourable impressions of a sermon on penance and absolution he heard Edward Pusey preach in 1846. His family maintained a particularly close friendship with John Keble and his wife. Patteson himself corresponded with Keble from Melanesia, and both Keble and Pusey contributed to the building of the Mission's ship, the *Southern Cross*.

More to the point, Patteson was thoroughly familiar with Tractarian literature. Pusey's books, he wrote from Melanesia, provided one of his chief delights. On reading the whole of the *Apologia* for the first time in 1866, he professed his astonishment at the profundity of Newman's thought. But it was Keble, 'one of the Saints of God' as he called him, who attracted him most.[11] *The Christian Year* along with the *Meditations* of Thomas à Kempis formed the core of his own devotional reading, and he fantasized over the intellectual delight of having Keble to himself for a couple of days in order to question him to his heart's content.

Patteson particularly shared the Tractarian sense of the role of devotion and worship and the ultimate limits of reason in religious understanding. The Bible must be read, he maintained, for devotional as well as intellectual and theological content. Reason alone could never accomplish the surrender of the will he associated with spiritual growth. Given these predilections, he also proved extremely sensitive to the aesthetics of Anglican worship stressed by the Tractarians. As far as Melanesia was concerned, opposed as he was to the imposition of inappropriate forms on islanders, he still hoped to have some day, 'a small but exceedingly beautiful Gothic chapel'. As 'a really noble Church is a wonderful instrument of education', Patteson saw no incongruity in this desire.[12] The Mission eventually acquired such a chapel though not without an element of tragic irony. SPG appealed for a memorial fund following Patteson's murder and allocated £2000 of the £7000 raised for this purpose. The remainder went to a new *Southern Cross* and a permanent endowment for the Mission.

The severity and discipline that formed an important part of the Tractarian conception of religious life also had significance for this High Church mission. Religion, according to the Movement's leaders, was not meant to be a comfortable thing. Self-denial became an important test of religious earnestness and discipline. Patteson, perhaps because of his horror of the self-righteous missionary, tended to play down the hardships of mission life. 'It is,' he exclaimed in 1857, 'the happiest life a man can lead, full of enjoyment, physical and mental, exquisite scenery, famous warm climate, lots of bathing, yams and taro and coco-nut . . . and such loving gentle people.'[13] His trials were nothing compared to those sustained by the clergy working in the slums of London. But mission life *was* in fact difficult, uncomfortable, and often dangerous. Patteson's own health had begun to fail well before his fortieth birthday. Yet his correspondence and diaries convey the sense that had the missionary's lot been an easy one, it would have had limited value in furthering the spiritual growth he sought. 'If you think impartially of me,' he wrote his favourite sister, 'you will see how soft and indolent I was, how little I cared to exert myself and try and exercise the influence a clergyman may be supposed to possess.'[14]

The Mission's founder, Selwyn, provided perhaps the best insight into the role of self-denial in mission. If by self-denial one meant asceticism and withdrawal from the world, he maintained, one came dangerously close to self-indulgence. Why did not those who complained of the lack of self-denial in the Church of England not 'throw themselves into the dark wastes of our manufacturing towns, or upon the millions of the unconverted heathen . . .?'[15] Anything less smacked of hypocrisy, for surely self-denial was as well practised in missionary life as in a monastery. Selwyn articulated the precise relationship of self-denial, one of the key contributions of the Oxford Movement to Victorian Anglicanism, to the world of Christian activism. For churchmen like Selwyn and Patteson, suspicious of the ascetic and ritual extremes of the Movement but mindful of its insights, the merger of action and self-denial in mission proved a fortuitous outlet for their own 'determined Christianity'.

The Oxford Movement also provided the Mission's leadership with a sense of historical connection. In its 'rediscovery' of the early Church, it brought to light historical models of mission organization and methodology that proved extremely useful in Melanesia. The Tractarians, in their zeal to establish the historical legitimacy of the Church of England, sought to establish direct links between Anglicanism and the Church of the first five centuries. Their scholarship emphasized and glorified this early epoch of Church history, an epoch that also encompassed the first phases of Christian mission. Thus Victorian High Church missions had at their disposal, through the scholarship and concerns of the Oxford Movement, historical models and images of mission including some very different from the prevalent focus on Christian home and family.

The High Church missions saw themselves in terms of the religious community. In describing St Barnabas' College to his aunt in 1867, Codrington likened it to the ancient monasteries of England and Germany in its view of work and education.[16] The daily routine indeed had a monastic orderliness, with daily services and classes interspersed with work on the Mission farm and meals of plentiful but decidedly plain food. Melanesian students and European staff shared the work, and the entire Mission sat down together for meals. When discipline was required, Patteson quite consciously borrowed from the example of the early Church and found it entirely effective. A council of Melanesian communicants sat in judgement on the transgressor and determined appropriate punishments. Usually this involved banishment from services for a stated period. If the culprit was a Melanesian teacher, he might also be barred from teaching and sitting at the 'high table' of the dining hall.

Patteson also found in the example of early Church mission arguments for employing an indigenous clergy with limited formal training. The entire matter of the training and education of the indigenous clergy was problematic. Thorough training in theology, Church history and the languages necessary for biblical studies assumed critical importance. In his own preparation for ordination and in that which he and Codrington provided for the European ordinands of the Mission, he insisted on rigorous standards. But should this standard be applied to the Melanesian clergy? Despite his confidence in their ability and intelligence, Patteson thought not. Their job did not entail teaching theology to educated Christians. They had, rather, to convey the elements of Christian truth to people completely ignorant of it. Again, he found his point of reference in the Church's earliest missionaries. Many of these men, Patteson noted, had scarcely been literate and had yet accomplished much of value. A Melanesian clergy ensured the proper communication of Christian truth and, consequently, the proper establishment of a Melanesian Church. As long as the Christian message came only from Europeans, it ran the risk of being perceived as the foreigner's religion and not as God's universal gift.

Thus, when George Sarawia, an SPG missionary but a Melanesian, took his ordination vows in Mota alongside Charles Bice who took his in English in 1868, Patteson expressed his overwhelming feelings of hope and thankfulness at the realization of a Melanesian clergy. He might also have credited his own particular understanding of Anglican tradition; a tradition that, thanks to both the orthodox Anglican divines of past centuries and the Tractarian interpreters of the nineteenth century, provided him with a critical framework for the development of his own religious life, the methodology of the Melanesian Mission and the vision of a truly Melanesian Christianity.

⋗≡⊙⊂≖⋗

Dr Sara Sohmer has written on various aspects of the British Empire in the Pacific region. She is presently an instructor in history at Texas Christian University, Forth Worth, in the USA.

Notes

Portions of this essay originally appeared in *The Journal of Religious History*, Dec. 1994.

1. Hilliard (1978), p. 56; Whiteman (1983), p. 425.
2. Selwyn to Gladstone, Jan. 1841, Gladstone Papers, British Library.
3. C. E. Fox, 'History of the Melanesian Mission', Typescript, p. 18, Bishop Patteson Theological Centre, Solomon Islands.
4. Patteson to his sisters, 1 Aug. 1871, quoted C. M. Yonge (1874) *Life of John Coleridge Patteson, Missionary Bishop of the Melanesian Islands*, London, II, p. 510.
5. Patteson to his sisters, 6 Aug. 1871, *ibid.*, II, p. 537.
6. Patteson to his uncle, 18 Mar. 1859, *ibid.*, I, p. 405.
7. Patteson to his sisters, 23 Sept. 1869 [Patteson Papers].
8. Yonge, *Coleridge*, I, p. 298.
9. Patteson to his sisters, 27 Aug. 1859 [Patteson Papers].
10. Chadwick (1960), p. 30.
11. Patteson to his sisters, 28 June 1867 [Patteson Papers].
12. Patteson to his sisters, 25 Oct. 1863; Yonge, *Coleridge*, II, pp. 78–9.
13. Patteson to his uncle, 8 Dec. 1856, *ibid.*, I, p. 301.
14. Patteson to his sisters, 30 May 1856, *ibid.*, I, p. 254.
15. Evans (1964), p. 20.
16. [Codrington Papers 4].

7

✦⇒◁✦

Wives of missionaries working with the Society

DEBORAH KIRKWOOD

Introduction

Were Priscilla and Aquila the earliest examples of a married couple engaged in missionary work together? St Paul sent greetings and messages to missionary women as well as men but there is little to indicate whether or not they were married. Circumstances have changed very slowly. In reading the earlier records of the Society it is difficult to discern the presence or absence of wives, with or without children, alongside their husbands.

They become briefly visible when their husbands die and they become widows. Thus, in 1706 'Mr. Thomas' widow was voted two months' salary from the Society and a gratuity of £25 in consideration of the great worth of her husband and his ministerial office and for the encouragement of missionaries to undertake the service of the Society.'[1] In 1799, 'on the death of Mr. Housel his widow appealed for financial help'.[2]

> One quarter's salary was due to him and she has taken the liberty of drawing on this and hopes that the Society, in their wisdom, will grant her some small allowance, she being infirm . . . and destitute . . . however, the Rules of the Society will not admit of their settling on her an annuity but she will have leave to draw on half a year's salary.

On 8 December 1843, a grant of £100 was agreed to the widow of A. L. Irwin on the understanding that 'no further claims can be entertained'. On occasion widows chose to remain in the place where they

314

had been with their husbands. In 1842 Mrs Irion, recently widowed, requested help. The Minute suggests that she wished to continue to be associated with her late husband's work. It was proposed that she could maintain herself in India by keeping a school. In 1848 the Madras Committee recommended that as she had become very frail she should be granted an annual pension of £50. At Arawak in Guiana, the widow of the late catechist was placed in charge of the mission, assisted by her sister, Miss Reed. Subsequently, this arrangement was found to be working well.[3]

The deaths of the wives were seldom included in the obituary notes in the *Mission Field* unless they had been particularly known for their contribution, like the wife of Dr Hose, the Bishop of Singapore, 'Though her name was not on the Society's list she had herself been an effective missionary for the last thirty years.'[4]

Hardships and dangers

These were many and varied, some trivial, others life-threatening. Poverty was a major and recurring experience for missionaries and their families. Standing Committee for 6 February 1835 confirmed that the Society could not consent to increase the salaries of missionaries in proportion to the number of their children except in cases where salaries did not amount to £100. Over the years there were many similar pronouncements.

Among the more trivial hardships, J. Gamage wrote from British Columbia regarding the high cost of living and the shortage of funds, so that 'Gentlemen clean their own boots, cut their own firewood and do other similar work; ladies are their own cooks and housemaids, dressmakers and almost everything else; there are no servants and even the Governor has no female servant in his establishment.'[5] In December 1859, R. Dowson wrote from Vancouver, 'I have had my wife laid up with an attack of fever for three weeks and I have had to be nurse and cook and everything myself . . . Little comforts which in England we look upon as actual necessaries in a sick room are lacking.' Mrs Dowson's illness was the result of an upset to their canoe after a sudden thaw while on a journey, forcing them to wade through freezing mud. In 1860 the Dowsons returned to England because of his wife's health.

Conditions had been harder in eighteenth-century North America, but by the nineteenth century missionary households in Asia and Africa probably faced greater challenges. In 1892 Mrs Gregory in Madagascar was severely wounded by robbers and never fully recovered the use of her right hand. Also in Madagascar, three years later, Mr and Mrs Johnson and their child were killed during a Malagasy revolt. In 1900 Frances Emily Scott, wife of the Bishop of North China, died from an illness due largely to the strain of the bombardment of Tientsin by the Boxers.

If children accompanied their parents to tropical climates they were exposed to health as well as other risks. If left in Britain they became virtual orphans even if cared for by relatives. Parents too suffered the deprivation of family life and separation from children for long periods. Bishop McDougall and his wife Harriette, sailing for Borneo in 1847, left their eldest son, Charles, aged two, with friends and took the infant Harry with them. By 1851, he and three more sons had all died in infancy and Harriette wrote to her sister-in-law,

> When I think of pour little Edward, Tom and Robert lying side by side at Sarawak, and Harry at Singapore, I wonder that I do not hate the place and everything belonging to it. However, it is equally true that I do not, that the place seems consecrated to me by sufferings, and I feel that it is really worth while living here without the children that Frank may follow his vocation.

Later, Charles, left in England, died as a result of an accident. How many other wives may have suffered, displaying the same commitment to their husband's calling?

Wives, was there a policy?

Probably in the early years SPG had no policy. In most cases, unless they enjoyed personal wealth, wives were dependent on their husbands, with little option but to join them in their work wherever it took them. However, by the mid-1850s the wisdom or desirability of wives' presence alongside their husbands began to be debated.

A correspondent to the *Mission Field* in 1859 regarding the need for more missionaries in China and Japan, wrote, 'The harvest is truly great but the labourers are few. We want, in short, a larger number of well qualified labourers *at first unmarried.*' Bishop Callaway, however, in South Africa, thought differently,

> It is desirable especially to exhibit practically to the heathen world what a Christian wife and family really are . . . [and] the holiness and blessedness of Christian married life.[6]

In 1875 the question was discussed again in the *Mission Field*, while in 1878, Priscilla, wife of Robert Winter of Delhi, refuted an episcopal statement deploring the presence of missionary wives in the field. She composed a lengthy address which was read by her husband on her behalf at the anniversary meeting of the Associated Missions in India, urging that some missionaries' wives of Indian experience should be chosen as leaders 'to help facilitate easier relationships with both unmarried and married women'.[7] Lobengula in southern Africa was in favour,

> The Roman Catholics tried to force their way in, but were sent south. Lobengula asked them where their wives were. They told him that they did not believe in wives. He then asked them where were their mothers and they are said to have given some answer to the same effect. His reply was, 'I do not wish anyone to teach my people who does not believe in wives and mothers.'

Bishop Knight-Bruce commented, 'I dare say he knew as much on the subject as many who have settled the question whether married or unmarried missionaries are best.'[8] The Bishop's own wife provided a different model. Laura Knight-Bruce was unable to tolerate the climate in southern Africa and remained in England. However, she was untiring in publicizing the work in Mashonaland. The Bishop returned to England and died a year later of blackwater fever. He dedicated his *Memories of Mashonaland* 'To Her, without whose Sympathy and Help there would have been no Material for these Notes.' After his death, she continued to edit the *Mashonaland Quarterly Journal* and to raise funds for the Society.

The debate continued into the twentieth century. Here, an indirect reference to the missionary wife as a potential financial asset occurred. Regarding women's work in Korea, the *Mission Field* commented in 1909, 'This is not supported by the SPG grants except in so far as Mrs. Hillary (wife of the Revd. F. R. Hillary) who is now in charge of the women's work in Kanghwa may be said to be provided from that source.'

In China in 1911 the need for single women missionaries was emphasized. 'The wives of missionaries have done what they could in holding classes and training women, but the duties of married women are so multitudinous that they cannot give daily teaching or study.' Further views were offered in 1913 in the *Mission Field*, where it was observed that some work could be done better by married missionaries, 'but many climates put a disproportionately heavy strain upon a young

married woman . . . and make married life impossible. Young missionaries must take no step towards engagement until after the first furlough.'

While the desirability or otherwise of wives accompanying their
husbands was periodically debated, there was concern at the problems of
families, at home as well as abroad. In 1874 a committee was formed to
superintend 'The Education and Guardianship of the Children of
Missionaries in Tropical Countries', with a Children's Home to be
established to facilitate the education of such children.

In 1879, a further step was taken with a Missionaries' Children's
Education Fund established. It was noted that the income of missionaries
was always small and sometimes variable and uncertain. In many cases it
appeared necessary to remove children from 'heathen' influences and
deadly climatic conditions. On occasion families had been left homeless
and dependent on charity, especially in cases when the missionary himself
had died. Initial contributions to the Fund were raised through an appeal
in the *Mission Field*.

What did the wives of missionaries do?

Certainly they shared the invisibility of most wives in the recorded
history of the work and achievements of men. They might be compared
with the wives of home-based clergy. Janet Finch suggests that many of
these 'see their own role very much in helpmeet terms and being very
active in . . . "the women's work" of the church . . . and the quasi-
domestic tasks associated with Church activities'.[9] Missionary wives had
opportunities for a broader and more active role; indeed this was usually
required of them, though perhaps not always specified or even imagined
in the very early days. In the second half of the twentieth century, wives
were expected to participate in the preparatory training provided for
most missionaries.

Teaching was always the most regular demand on their time and
energies. Of prime importance were scriptural and catechetical instruction, especially of girls. Pascoe, writing of South Carolina in 1711, noted
that 'Mrs. Haigue and Mrs. Edwards were formally thanked for their
good example in instructing the negroes; no less than 27 prepared by
them were baptised.'[10] A view reiterated by missionaries, also by colonial
administrators, was the need to educate the women in the 'receiving'
societies so that they could partner husbands in an emerging class of
'white-collar' professional men. This required classroom teaching as well
as more informal instruction in social behaviour and domestic virtues; it
was believed that missionary wives could usefully do this. Zenana work

among élite women in India exemplified this, though later carried out also by single women missionaries.

Pascoe writes of Eliza, wife of Robert Caldwell, 'An impetus to the cause of female education was given by her at Edeyengoody in 1844 when she introduced lacemaking amongst the women and established a boarding school for girls. Both ventures were highly successful.' Robert Caldwell had said, 'From the beginning of the world it had never been known (in Tirunelveli) that a woman could read or write.' At the start there were only six girls but progress was rapid. When the girls were received, 'they were of the wildest . . . but now they have learnt to be quiet and behave'.

> They are taught a little English and in the event of their marrying husbands that have learnt a little English, they may be able to carry on with the study of it together. Upwards of forty young women who were educated at boarding school are now married and settled in various parts of the mission.

Eliza Caldwell added that 'They give us great comfort by their uniform good Conduct.' Subsequently, in 1887, a Girls' Normal School of the diocese, supported by the Society, was the first in South India to send up Indian girls for a university matriculation examination.[11] Shortly after their deaths, a memorial tablet for Bishop and Mrs Caldwell was unveiled at Idyangudi, commemorating their 43 years work there, she being described as a 'mother in Israel'.[12]

In the *Mission Field* in 1875, William Drew wrote regarding the school run by Mrs. Drew that there was little acknowledgement of such schools. 'For some reason it has not been thought fit to receive such reports formally. It devolves on me therefore to submit a few remarks on the condition and working of this, the only school for girls in the Society's Southern Bengal Missions.' He gives details of the number of pupils and their successes: another example of the 'invisibility' of missionary wives and their work alongside their husbands. Pascoe refers to the work of an unnamed teacher, 'The girls' school has always had the advantage of the influence and care of a European lady, the wife of one of the missionaries. The girls get a good education as well as acquiring habits of cleanliness and neatness.'

Mrs Winter's zenana work in Delhi during the 1860s and 1870s is described elsewhere in this book. After her death in 1881, when St Stephen's Hospital was erected in her memory, the Bishop of Lahore remarked, 'There are few perhaps to whom the healing and saving bodies as well as the souls of our fellowmen could be such a passion and such a longing and burning desire.' From Madras in 1878 Isabella Wyatt wrote an account of her zenana work in the *Mission Field*,

> I think we should regard with great thankfulness this movement among our women who endeavour to do good to their own sex now lying in darkness and the shadow of death . . . People at home say 'how shocking women should stay at home and not go about the country.' I think only lukewarm Christians can raise this objection . . . all the good is undone by women who have not heard what their husbands have heard and there is no way for them to hear it unless women go and tell them.[13]

In 1876 the Prince of Wales visited India and in Tirunelveli was greeted by a line of women and girls. He was escorted by Bishop Sargent who explained,

> Here you see the work voluntarily and gladly undertaken by the Missionaries' wives and daughters. When the Missionaries found any promising girls they brought them home with them and the wives and daughters took those girls under their care and into their hearts and while they taught them the Bible as the basis of all good teaching, they also included useful knowledge of every kind.

During a famine in India, James Kearns referred to '3,000 orphans – a very large number, but I feel quite equal to it. My wife will find it a field that will give her pleasure'. The solution was an orphanage, training the children 'to do useful work as early as possible . . . so they may earn their own bread. Their education shall not reach higher than the three R's but they shall have careful instruction in the Bible and Christian Catechism.'[14] Similar low-key accounts of wives teaching effectively are widespread, Mrs Gregory in Madagascar in 1878, Mrs Williams in Punjab, in the 1890s, and many more. In 1900 a Girls' Training Institution at the Rorke's Drift Mission in Natal, South Africa, was established,

> The House is under the care of Mrs. Johnson, (wife of Archdeacon Johnson) whose assistance in the Mission work generally can never be fully estimated in this world. In addition to her services to education it was noted that, during the Boer War . . . the fact that Mrs. Johnson and her children remained quietly at Rorke's Drift when all their neighbours had fled had a quietening influence on the surrounding natives and the missionaries helped to keep them from attacking the Boers.[15]

Ashram art. *The Visit of the Magi,* by Alfred Thomas, at the Christa Seva Sangha in western India

'... bringing the universe together at one point'. Members of the College of the Ascension,
Selly Oak, UK, 1988

'The power of educated womanhood in the world is ... the power of skilled service'.
Zenana and medical workers, Delhi, 1877

'Patients in purdah.' How women patients in Delhi travelled

'...the fundamentals of the Christian religion grafted upon the sound stock of Confucian morality'. Roland Allen and theological students, Peking, 1899

'...the descendants of slaves ... origins shrouded in anonymity'. Theological students at mas Codrington Commendation Day, 1961

Missionaries on tour, some in a wheelbarrow, North China, 1924

Archdeacon Leary and assistants, South Africa, c. 1930

Medical assistant with bike, Zambia, 1920s

Priest with motor-bike, Kuching, 1978

'Lobengula replied, "I do not wish anyone to teach my people who does not believe in wives and mothers."' Missionary wife and daughter, Central India, 1950; and missionary household, Canada, 1925

SUNDAY COLLECTION FOR THE S. P. G.
(Little Pedlington.)

After Morning Service.
OH—ER—I 'M COMING AGAIN THIS AFTERNOON, YOU KNOW."

After Afternoon Service.
"OH—ER—I WAS HERE THIS MORNING, YOU KNOW."

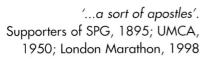

'...a sort of apostles'.
Supporters of SPG, 1895; UMCA, 1950; London Marathon, 1998

St Peter and St Paul's Anglican Church, Kanghwa. Local Cultural Property No 111

대한성공회
성베드로.
지방문화

'...without undue or conspicuous self-assertion'.
The local idiom in churches at Kanghwa, Korea, 1900; Mehrauli, India, 1927

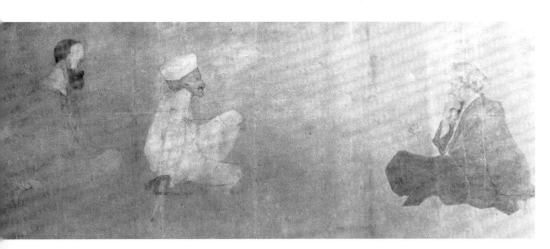

..atheists of empire'. C. F. Andrews with Gandhi and Tagore; A. S. Cripps beside his rondavel at Maronda Mashanu, Mashonaland

'...church of the future'.
Bishop Dinis Sengulane with children, Mozambique, 1983

Many people were kept from starvation by the Johnsons. These comments perhaps illustrate the point made by Groves that the presence of wives may have been interpreted as indicators of peaceful intention, giving missionaries hope that they might be received as friends, as in the case reported by Groves, 'Sebitoane gave Livingstone a warm welcome and deeply appreciated the presence of Mrs. Livingstone and the children.'[16]

In Mashonaland, George Broderick reported from Bonda in 1912 that 'Mrs. Broderick received the highest praise from government inspectors for the organisation of special classes for girls in sewing, laundry and general housework.' A small boarding school for girls was under her supervision. All the girls had been in trouble because their relations had tried to force them into marriage. They were 'saved from relapse into heathenism, or being taken by the Roman Catholics who have a large staff at the mission nearby'. He noted that the women's work was not big enough yet to require two white workers but was a big strain on his wife by herself. Bonda's later St David's girls' school, with, after independence, a Zimbabwean headmistress and over 800 ambitious pupils anticipating careers in medicine, business studies, administration and education, and the Bonda Hospital training nurses and paramedicals, stood in direct succession to this wife's endeavours.

Teaching was of course blended with care and friendship in mission work. Reporting from Swaziland in 1912, Canon Mercer describes the school at an outstation opened by Susie Mercer, 'We have commenced the boarding and industrial school, my wife having volunteered to go and look after the boarders.'[17] In 1915 after eighteen years of service the Mercers retired from the Mission of the Holy Rood; it was said that,

> Mrs. Mercer will be sadly missed, 'Who will get up in the middle of the night to give us medicine?' said one old lady before she left. Mrs. Mercer had one particular mixture which instantly stopped coughs in school.

Friendship, hospitality, evangelizing

These provided an important link between missionaries and the host community and women were perhaps more effective than men in this sphere. Care of sick children appears to have led to the conversion of parents, especially mothers. Nursing was increasingly professionalized with the introduction of improved hospital training by Florence Nightingale in the 1860s. The Society's Ladies' Association was established in

1866, coinciding with this, and within a very short time unmarried women were being recruited for overseas missionary work as nurses, and in due time doctors, as well as teachers. At the Annual Meeting of the Women's Committee in 1907 the Bishop of Ely commented on the fact that the advance of women's education in England coincided with the great advance in single women's participation in missionary work. Meanwhile wives continued to serve the Society as they had done for so many years.

Some wives, moved by the plight of children, are remembered for specific acts of kindness and compassion. Sometimes these initiatives created unanticipated problems. In Southern India in 1859 Mrs Coyle responded to an appeal that she should take into her home a young child whose mother seemed to be on the point of death.

> She received the helpless little thing and brought her home . . . With proper care and nursing the infant, named Mary, gradually revived and is now a Christian child. The mother too recovered, but being a caste woman is prevented from receiving back into her bosom her child which had already been fed by Pariahs.

'Is there anything more wicked and unnatural than caste?' asked the writer in the *Mission Field*. Also in India, in 1869 Charles and Mrs Wheeler were reported as running an orphanage in Kanpur for boys and girls. The orphans included five little girls under ten who had been sold by their parents 'into a life of infamy'. The boys were trained in tailoring and carpentry and the girls instructed in 'all manner of useful housework', a further example of the close link of education with compassion.

Over the years the positive role of wives was reiterated; 'Christian ladies too can do much good by visiting the married quarters of workers on plantations and in towns to show sympathy with women and children.' Pascoe, writing with reference to Bengal in 1895, described

> A cherished plan of Mrs O'Connor (the wife of the missionary) whose medical skill has proved of great service in the district . . . to teach nursing from house to house to some of the more capable native women.[18]

In 1877 at the time of the Indian famine, a *Mission Field* correspondent paid tribute to the wives of missionaries, who had 'taken a personal interest in saving the lives of children all but dead from want'. Mean-while, in the Canadian industrial town of Frankford, Niagara, where there was a very mixed community of workers, the bishop told the Synod,

> The men were brought to a sense of their sins through Mrs Welsh and devoted ladies whom she has interested in Christ and his Church. Many whom she had sought out were hard, ungodly, if not drunken men and women. Kindness and Christian spirit led them into the way of righteousness. Bible classes and Sunday School attracted high attendance and 1,500 have been counted on occasion.[19]

Recalling work in British Columbia, Pascoe paid tribute to the late Jane Ridley (wife of the bishop), who had died in 1896, a hospital erected as a memorial to her at Claxton:

> She left a record of missionary spirit and devotion rarely equalled. After the departure of a fellow missionary and his wife, who recoiled from the horrors of savage life and suddenly left for England . . . to save the work from collapsing, Mrs Ridley, taking a year's provisions, went herself – a dismal journey of fifteen days, camping and sleeping on the snow being but the least of the discomforts – and for a year dwelt among the Indians and miners, the only white woman within 170 miles, her entire household consisting of two Indian schoolboys. Such was her isolation that the Bishop visited England and returned without her ever knowing it. When she left the miners said she was the best parson they ever had and the Indians called her 'mother' to the day of her death.[20]

Wives were sometimes quite as effective evangelists as their missionary husbands. An unnamed Hindu wrote 'The Story of an Indian Convert', in the *Mission Field* in 1909. He describes his friendship with the Bexells. 'Mrs Bexell helped me in clearing my doubts . . . she introduced me to the Revd. Pakenham-Walsh . . . and with the help of that lady we became correspondents . . . which led to my baptism.'

Writers of letters, books, reports, etc.

Those wives who wrote and whose writings were published acquire 'visibility' and offer a personal dimension and insight to their experiences. Frances Colenso and Harriette McDougall were sisters who married missionary bishops. Frances Colenso's letters were happily preserved and eventually published.[21] Harriette McDougall, too, was an indefatigable letter-writer. *Letters from Sarawak, addressed to a Child* was addressed to their eldest son Charles, who died before receiving it. Frances and Harriette, born respectively in 1816 and 1817, grew up in an evangelical family; their father Robert Bunyan, a businessman, was closely involved with the CMS. They were inseparable companions and as well as their shared Christian commitment both enjoyed music and art. Harriette was eager for missionary life and is said to have persuaded Frank McDougall to turn down a secure appointment at the British Museum in favour of accepting an offer to go as a missionary to Borneo; they embarked on the five-month voyage to Sarawak in 1847. Frances, however, had no wish to leave England and life in a new colony held no attractions for her; the Colensos left for South Africa in 1855. As well as carrying out the usual obligations and responsibilities of missionary wives, both sisters were married to men who experienced serious difficulties in the course of their ministries. Bishop McDougall had to maintain a delicate relationship with Rajah Brooke, the founder of the settlement of Sarawak and in a sense patron of the Borneo Mission. The McDougalls, despite the high cost of living and many shortages, entertained generously and Harriette recorded that one Christmas they had 'seventy Christians to dinner at the school house and eighteen more at our own table'. She loved the country, especially the flowers and exotic fruit. Her drawings and paintings provide the only pictorial record of life in Sarawak during those years.

As the years passed strains developed with Brooke and members of his family. Frank McDougall came to depend greatly on his wife's support and vigorous loyalty. There were also the problems of an unhealthy climate, and they were subjected to a violent attack from Chinese goldminers, the women and children having to flee temporarily. They had to leave Borneo permanently in 1867 when Harriette contracted 'Labuan fever'. She survived, and in due course had four more children. She died in 1886, six months before her husband; he wrote to a friend, 'My life is broken now . . . and all the brightness centred in her is gone.' A memorial to her in Winchester Cathedral records, 'She first taught Christ to the Women of Borneo.'

The problems faced by Frances were of a different order. Soon after John Colenso and she met in the early 1840s, he remarked that she was far the better theologian. Certainly she was strongly supportive in the theological and ecclesiastical conflicts he faced in Natal, and of his liberal attitude in race relations, which alienated them from some of the colonial settlers. There was a further cost in estrangement from her evangelical family at home because of her husband's views. In marked contrast to Harriette, she was shy and reserved; some criticized her on this score but others praised her for her commitment to her missionary vocation. Mrs

Forcett, wife of a fellow missionary, remarked that she 'had only seen her three times in ten months and she was scarcely to be seen outside her own house . . . always pale and anxious', but Alice Mackenzie, sister of the archdeacon, wrote,

> Mrs Colenso I love very much. She is a thorough lady . . . in every thought and feeling, and such a worker, at the same time fancying she does nothing . . . governess to her own children, and others . . . overseeing a troop of black girls . . . indeed the whole community up here comes to her as their Mother in any kind of sickness and trouble, for she is their doctor as well . . . then besides all this she is fond of music, drawing, poetry and flowers. Above all, she is in love with the African people.[22]

She always preferred the little wooden chapel on the mission station at Ekukanyeni to worship at the cathedral. She was fortunate that their five children grew up to be a major support in the work of the Mission. Their daughter Harriet (named after her aunt) wrote extensively, especially in support of the Zulu people and in defence of King Cetewayo. John and Frances Colenso remained in Natal, with periodic visits to England, and both died at Bishopstowe, their official residence, he in 1883, she ten years later.

Many wives wrote reports of their work and progress and some of these have been quoted here. Elaine Lloyd, a nurse at St Faith's mission at Rusape, Southern Rhodesia, wrote regular descriptions of life and work there with her husband, Edgar, for the *Mashonaland Quarterly Journal*. She helped with a few in-patients as well as a daily clinic at St Faith's. Itinerating and outstation work were an important part of mission life and she frequently accompanied her husband; she writes evocatively of a visit to a nearby kraal, 'White women are rare and this was perhaps the first time one had visited the kraal.' She describes another trip to an outstation where she helped to save a baby sick with malaria, and where, also, with the help of the teacher, Stephen, 'we were able to do a little translating work'. In 1919 she gives a long account of a seven-week trek from Rusape to Wreningham to visit their friend, the poet-priest, Arthur Shearly Cripps, who had officiated at their marriage in 1910. 'We always enjoy setting out on trek, and indeed enjoy it all the time, but I am not sorry to get home again as the packing and unpacking all one's things every one or two days gets boring.' They visited many old students from St Faith's on the way, now with their own missions. They stayed with Cripps at Maronda Mashanu for a week. 'To sum up, we shall have done 350 miles and packed and unpacked thirty six times.' They travelled partly on foot, partly on donkeys. When not trekking, she was very busy at St Faith's. In 1922 she was appointed to a committee for translation and publication work and was appointed editor of a quarterly paper; a hymn book in the vernacular was a pressing need and she arranged the translation. Another major interest was indigenous craftwork. Reporting on an exhibition which she had arranged she wrote, 'We Europeans have lessened the joys of the natives. We came to . . . [stop] tribal fighting and limit hunting, while our cheap wares have destroyed the native crafts they were skilled in. We have left the sole joy of drunkeness which will continue to grow unless we put some higher joy in its place.' Woodcarving, for which Rusape became famous, was one such.

Missionaries marrying missionaries

With the growing numbers of women missionaries that followed the formation of the Ladies' Association in 1866, it would have been surprising if there had not been marriages between missionaries. There is little specific documentation regarding these, though some stand out in the annals of the Society, like that of Priscilla Sandys, a zenana worker, to Robert Winter in Delhi in 1863. In the *Mission Field* for July 1909 there is reference to 'Two clergy wives – Mrs Cowie and Mrs Davie – both qualified doctors'. Charlotte Ferguson-Davie had married the Bishop of Singapore and wrote extensively on the work of the Church in Malaya. There were countless other missionary couples and inevitably the policies regarding marriage were reviewed periodically, for women workers as much as for men from the later nineteenth century. The Committee for Women's Work (CWW) ruled in 1902 that women candidates should not enter into any agreement of marriage for at least three years. This implied 'no disparagement of married life'. Such a pledge enabled them 'to give themselves wholly and without distraction to the work to which they were sent out to fulfil'. Nevertheless, 'it is not true to say that women are lost to mission work if they marry other missionaries'. The possibility of regarding missionary wives as salaried workers was also discussed, but no conclusion seems to have been reached at this stage. Though not explicitly stated, the discussions seemed to relate to marriage between missionaries rather than to the possibility of women considering marriage to men outside the circle of the Society. In 1928 Notes on Marriage Regulations were issued and the following points were made: (1) The Church must have a *flying squad* of unmarried people. (2) The Society cannot make any proclamation about marriage and only Bishops can give permission to marry. (3) If the Society supports someone on unmarried rates, it is not to be assumed it will support that person after marriage.

In 1915, the jubilee year of women's work was celebrated. CWW members were reminded that before women's work was organized, 'wives played a very significant role'. It seems, however, that wives were still destined to receive only marginal attention; each monthly issue of the *Mission Field* contained a section reporting women's work, always placed on the last few pages, but with rarely any reference to work by wives. In 1937 it was noted that training was available for fiancées; applicants for this were required to agree to take a full share in their husband's work and that any work that they undertook should be definitely in connection with the Society. Fifty years on, revised policies reflected some of the changes which had taken place in the wider world, decolonization and equal opportunity expectations in particular. All policy and regulations including training now applied to both men and women. There was no restriction on the appointment of women to key posts. In the selection process, all women, if married, were treated as being separate from their husbands with regard to application references, medical examinations, review and appointments. Financially there was usually only one salary unless the wife actually had a separate appointment to a separate job, when she would be paid accordingly.

Conclusion

The whole archive of the work and the writings of missionary wives deserves closer scrutiny. A consistent theme in missionary literature has been the importance of establishing contact with the women in the 'receiving' societies. On the assumption that such contact could be made more effectively by women, the celibate orders and sisterhoods were enrolled for this work; where missionaries were permitted to marry it seemed logical that wives also could play an active role in this. If there was a conscious policy regarding wives accompanying their husbands it was perhaps based partly on the following considerations: first, the presence of wives might serve to indicate peaceful intentions in a potentially hostile environment; second, it was hoped that wives and children might serve as models of Christian family life; third the presence of wives could reduce the risk of sexual temptation to which a single man might be subject, though this was not explicitly stated. In this brief essay I have tried to illuminate the roles and achievements of the missionary wife by selecting individuals from throughout the Society's history and from a broad geographical perspective. I have suggested their status as being that of a 'muted group', a term adopted by some social anthropologists to describe categories who appear to have little voice in the affairs of the community in which they live and work.[23] However, it could be argued that by the very nature of their lives and work they had motivation and scope and fulfilment. Their letter-writing is almost legendary and provides a rich resource of descriptive information. The need to educate Christian women to be 'suitable' wives is frequently mentioned, but there were contradictions: it was reported from Zululand in 1909 that it was difficult to find enough Zulu churchmen for the girls to marry 'as . . . women were attracted to Christianity in greater numbers than men, there at least'.

How far those early missionary wives perceived a role for themselves remains uncertain. They probably anticipated poverty and danger and endured these with fortitude. In many cases they had the opportunity, if not the obligation, to fill an active and responsible position in the work of the Society. No doubt there were loneliness, boredom, health hazards and homesickness as well as challenges and adventures. Beyond any doubt their contribution to the work and achievements of the Society has been incalculable if not always recognized.

⋅→≡◉⋐←⋅

Deborah Kirkwood is an anthropologist and sociologist with a special interest in education in Zimbabwe. She contributed to and co-edited *Women and Mission: Past and Present* (1993) in association with the Centre for Cross-Cultural Research on Women, Oxford.

Notes

1. Pascoe, p. 15.
2. Standing Committee, 9 June.
3. *Mission Field*, Jan. 1860.
4. *Ibid.*, Oct. 1904.
5. *Ibid.*, Aug. 1839.
6. *Ibid.*, 1874.
7. *Ibid.*, 1878, pp. 369–70.
8. Pascoe, p. 362a; G. W. H. Knight-Bruce (1895) *Memories of Mashonaland*, London, pp. 74–6.
9. Janet Finch (1983) *Married to the Job: Wives' Incorporation in Men's Work*, London, p. 102.
10. Pascoe, p. 15.
11. Pascoe, pp. 544, 553d.
12. *Mission Field*, Feb. 1903.

13. *Mission Field*, 1878, p. 123.
14. *Mission Field*, 1877, pp. 585–7.
15. Pascoe, p. 341c.
16. C. P. Groves (1948) *Planting of Christianity in Africa*, London.
17. *Mission Field*, 1912.
18. *Ibid.*, 1874; Pascoe, pp. 500f,g.
19. *Mission Field*, 1878–9, p. 77.
20. Pascoe, p. 191c. .
21. Rees (1958).
22. Rees (1958), p. 40.
23. Ardener (1980), *passim*.

8

❖⇒◦⇐❖

Building a home-grown Church

JEROME T. MORIYAMA

A humble beginning

In the history of Christian mission the development of an indigenous Church with an indigenous ministry in the second half of the nineteenth century was the especial achievement of the Universities' Mission to Central Africa (UMCA). However, the intention of developing an African Church with an African ministry was not an original part of the official policy set by the Committee in 1859. This was mainly due to the fact that the formation of the Mission was largely a response to the lecture given by Dr David Livingstone at Cambridge in 1857 in which he appealed for English initiatives to carry out a civilizing mission comprising 'commerce and Christianity' to put a stop to the slave trade.

The training of Africans to be missionaries to their own people in the interior of Africa was pushed to the front as the most urgent and practically the only work of the Mission, as a result of the disaster of the first mission on the Zambezi during 1861–63 in which out of fourteen missionaries five were dead within two years, including the first bishop, Charles Mackenzie (1861–62), and four had become invalids. The second bishop, W. G. Tozer (1863–73) saw the interior of Africa was too inhospitable for English missionaries, too remote, with no reliable or regular means of communication with the coast, and too unsettled politically. Thus he removed the Mission from the Zambezi altogether at the end of 1863 and transferred it to Zanzibar in August 1864, hoping it would make the best place for ultimately reaching Central Africa through established caravan routes by trained African missionaries.

If Zanzibar can be made into a School of the Prophets, we shall have cause to rejoice in that day when all work shall be tried, and every jewel counted up.[1]

With this idea Tozer set out to establish a training school in September 1864 with five freed slave boys given by Sultan Seyed Majid. With the arrival of two female missionaries in June 1865, the training of girls also began: they were to be made good Christian wives to go along with their evangelist husbands for the conversion of their people in the interior. The number of pupils increased to twenty in 1866 and the boys' school was promoted to the status of a 'college', St Andrews, Kiungani.

As a practical step to advance the African ministry programme before proceeding to full deacon's orders, Tozer revived the old Catholic practice of a subdeacon's order. The progress of the boys, however, was advanced more rapidly than expected by the shortage of available English missionaries. Thus, in early 1870 George Farajallah and John Swedi were made subdeacons, while the sudden death of Farajallah brought forward Francis Mabruki to the same office early the following year. By 1872 the Mission had received 105 freed children, of whom 65 were boys and 40 were girls. The development of these boys and girls was affected, however, by the Mission's close contact with the Anglo-Arab power and civilization in Zanzibar. Its effect began to show in the character development of the boys, particularly through their identifying with the English and through the comparatively high living standard provided by the Mission. Tozer's ideal of an African ministry, with his emphasis on the adaptation of African indigenous culture, in practice clashed with the general orientation of the Mission: his English-medium principle in training also proved to be incompatible with his theory of adaptation to the local context, for which Swahili, the lingua franca of East Africa, would have been essential.

Ironically, the more Tozer proclaimed the importance of an African ministry the fewer missionaries applied for the work. He broke down shortly after the cyclone in 1872 and in the spring of the following year officially resigned. Whatever his ideals of African ministry might have been, he did establish on a permanent basis the work of training African boys for the future ministry and girls as their faithful wives.

Reform of the training scheme

The UMCA had from the outset entrusted its missionary bishop to a great extent with power and authority for decision-making and the application of missionary methods. Consequently there were often major changes when the headship changed. Thus, Edward Steere, the third bishop (1874–82), who had first joined the Mission in 1863 as adviser and chaplain to Bishop Tozer, brought much change to the course of development of an African ministry through his sympathetic attitude, emphasis on moral development and the vernacular principle.

Steere held the view, like Mackenzie, that 'a something of English' was not a blessing but a curse to an African boy. He decided therefore to amend the system of education 'to give all alike first a plain education in Swahili . . . and then to give the best scholars a thorough grounding in English'. For that purpose he had at once put into print the results of his study of Swahili, and by the end of 1872 the Mission was able to supply a range of school books in the language. He also reformed the method of recruitment of the pupils: his theory was that the candidates should be recruited primarily from the mission stations on the mainland. In October 1872, he despatched a party of young English subdeacons with several African workers to reoccupy the mission station at Magila in Usambara area on the mainland, which had been unattended since 1870. Steere soon began to use the mission stations on the mainland for the completion of the training of the ex-slave Africans for the office of subdeacon, later that of reader.

Steere did not consider that English missionaries could ever be qualified to be in charge of stations as the permanent ministers to the African people. He thought this could be done only by African ministers, who could 'speak to the people not only in their own language, but according to their own modes of thought – a matter of great importance and scarcely even within the ability of any foreigner'.[2] He envisaged that the African Church must be developed into 'a really native, home-grown Christianity' through a process of 'self-improvement' which would work 'slowly and from within', and that the African missionaries would be the best and only instruments for the development of this home-grown Christianity. Consequently he laid considerable stress on character and moral development in the training of African missionaries to sustain this weighty and lengthy task.

Meanwhile, the improvement of Kiungani school had been furthered by the increased number and better quality of missionaries sent from Britain. Translation of the Bible and Prayer Book into Swahili were carried out so rapidly that by 1 May 1879 the whole liturgy was able to be conducted in the language for the first time. By 1880 the training programme for the development of African ministry was firmly established:

The most promising are taught English and by degree are made pupil-teachers, teachers. catechists, readers and sub-deacons.[3]

Yet Steere firmly maintained his strict standard for ordination:

> For Ordination a man must show steadiness and capacity. We must know him for some years and let him work as Reader and Catechist for at least two more. No length of probation could justify want of power or steadiness.[4]

At length, however, John Swedi's nearly nine years of steady work and successful ministration broke through the strict standard set by Steere and he was ordained deacon on 18 June 1879, supported by SPG for the first two years of his ministry, and the first African of the Mission to enter Holy Orders.

Progress on the mainland

The existence of the freed-slave African workers certainly made it possible for the mission to form a party for the mainland mission. The party sent on to Magila in June 1875 consisted of two English missionaries and six of the ex-slave workers among whom were a subdeacon, Francis Mabruki, and a reader, Acland Sahera. The actual situation of the area around Magila, however, was nothing like 'a nation'. The area was occupied largely by the Bondei, who lived in numerous small villages scattered all over the area without any centralized authority. A method for evangelizing in such a situation was soon found by making good use of the ex-slave African workers:

> The European members of the staff will live at Magila or Umba, and work . . . [the villages] from one or other of these places, putting a native teacher in as resident, in accordance with the Bishop's scheme.[5]

Thus, by the end of 1881, the Mission in the area was able to establish three English-resident stations with several sub-stations around each of them served by resident ex-slave African readers.

The ex-slave workers in the Ruvuma Mission around Masasi in the south also played an important role: there were four Kiungani students in the first party led by W. P. Johnson. As in the north around Magila there was no centralized indigenous authority in Masasi, and the Mission hoped that the settlement of the Nyasa freed-slaves would become the centre of 'light and life' in the area. By September 1880 there were more than five stations outside the colony opened and worked by the ex-slave workers, including John Swedi, now deacon, who joined the Masasi Mission towards the end of 1879.

The ex-slave workers were successful especially in teaching and school work under the management of the missionaries-in-charge, such as Farler in Usambara and Johnson in Ruvuma, but there remained the question of their direct contribution to evangelism and pastoral work among the local people. According to Steere, there were four major advantages that the African workers were supposed to possess on the mainland in comparison to the English missionaries, physical fitness for the climate, adaptability to the local living standard, familiarity with the local language and better comprehension of the 'mode of thought' of the local people. There were, however, problems.

First of all, the local climate around Magila was found to be not ideal for the ex-slave African workers, as had been hoped. Although their death rate was much lower than that of the English missionaries, they were not entirely free from attacks of fever and ailments such as foot diseases. This caused the Mission constant problems in finding ways of keeping the regular work going, especially at sub-stations. Their long stay and boarding-school life in Zanzibar, moreover, seem to have affected not only their physical constitutions but also their lifestyle and living standards as a whole.

As for the question of the vernacular languages of the mainland, by the time they were sent there they had almost lost their original tongues. Swahili was at that time understood sufficiently only by headmen and chiefs of villages, the majority of the villagers possessing very little knowledge of it. Understanding the "mode of thought"' of the local people, therefore, was beyond the ex-slave workers. In addition, their lack of kinship ties with local people made it doubly difficult for them to enter into a knowledge and understanding of the people and their customs. Consequently their work was restricted to teaching and cate-chizing within the stations.

Even within the stations, the ex-slave workers, who were mostly in their twenties, found it extremely difficult to minister in spiritual and moral matters to the elders, some of whom were chiefs and headmen, to discuss with them the building of schools, chapels and mission houses, and to establish church customs, such as Christian burials, against the strong opposition of the Muslims.

Furthermore, there was a strong tendency among the local people, for example, the Bondei in Usambara, to identify the Mission with 'English' or 'white' men: many of their requests were specifically for 'an

English teacher'. The ex-slave workers were expected by the Mission to identify themselves with the local people, but the latter were keen on identifying themselves directly with the English missionaries, so bypassing the ex-slave workers.

The Mission consequently began to incline to looking for the future of the African ministry from among the free-born inhabitants of the land. Preparation for the recruitment of free-born children made good progress around Magila among the Bondei. The number of children in the school at Magila increased from twelve in 1876 to nearly 40 in 1881. The school at Umba, the second station, had eight children in 1881, among whom were Samuel Sehoza, Peter Limo and Hugh Kayama, all of whom were to play important roles later in the Mission's story of African ministry. The freeborn converts also took full advantage of the Mission's vernacular language policy. The first reader among the freeborn Bondei, Lawrence Kombo, was said to know no English when he was made reader in September 1880 and he was practically in charge at Magila for a short time, over the heads of ex-slave workers. The major disadvantage of the ex-slave workers, despite their longer training, was their rootlessness: it would take many generations for them to re-establish themselves and be accepted.

These aspects of the success and failure of the mainland work were clearly reflected in Steere's new presentation of his ideal for an African ministry:

> Our desire is to cultivate an independence of spirit. We don't want them under our orders, but we think that the sound principle is that they should be able to rely upon individual efforts, so that if the whole European superintendence were withdrawn, the Church we have founded and the society we have founded might be able to stand by itself.[6]

When Steere died in August 1882, he left behind some 34 English missionaries and 26 African workers. Although the majority of the African workers were still Kiungani-trained ex-slaves, two out of six readers were already freeborn mainland Africans.

Creation of an ideal African Church

The breakthrough of the ex-slave workers from dependence on the missionaries to being independent workers came through Cecil Majaliwa. In June 1886, he was placed at Chitangali in the Ruvuma Mission which had hitherto been regarded as far behind the Usambara Mission in terms of the development of an African ministry. Cecil Majaliwa was a freed-slave Yao who was received by Steere in the early 1870s and was educated at Kiungani. He was made a teacher by 1878. In 1879 he married an ex-slave teacher, Lucy Magombeani, and was made a reader and worked at Mbweni. He was said to be the brightest of all the ex-slave students at Kiungani and towards the end of 1883 he was sent to St Augustine's College, Canterbury, for further education.

After his return from England, he worked at Mbweni for a year and was ordained deacon in April 1886. The new bishop, C. A. Smythies (1884–94), immediately took Majaliwa with him to start his 'new scheme' at Chitangali. The place was a Yao community and the chief, Barnaba Matuka, was an early convert of W. P. Johnson at Masasi in 1880. He had also had some education at Kiungani. By the time the Mission was opened in his town, two of his sons had already been educated by the Mission, the elder, Yohana Abdallah at Kiungani, the younger at Newala. Thus, Smythies hoped that great things would come of Chitangali, knowing also that chief Barnaba Matuka would have a good chance of being chosen as Nakaam, the supreme chief in the area.

It was Majaliwa's first working experience on the mainland and he had to carry out everything entirely by himself. He soon realized that his experience at Mbweni was not applicable here. However, with the aid of the sons of Barnaba Matuka as teachers, he began to have constantly between 25 and 30 children in school. He picked up the Yao language quickly and within two months he was able to say in Yao at least such set formulae as the Ten Commandments and the Liturgy. Meanwhile, he visited the people on the Makonde Plateau and secured a chief's promise to give him his sons and other children for education at Chitangali. At the end of the year he returned to Zanzibar with Smythies, as had been originally planned. While he stayed in Zanzibar, Chitangali was reoccupied in June 1887 by an English missionary with an ex-slave teacher, Harry Mnubi, who had also been educated in England at about the same time as Majaliwa. Barnaba Matuka had been invested Nakaam in November 1887 and on the same day was confirmed by Smythies, while his son, Yohana Abdallah, was taken a second time to Kiungani and on Advent Sunday 1887 'definitely offered for a missionary life'.

Abdallah obviously told Majaliwa about the state of the Mission's work at Chitangali. The missionary had evidently made little progress in getting adults and children for instruction and school. Majaliwa accepted for a second time a call to the work at Chitangali, and returned there in May 1888 with his wife and children on the departure of the missionary for furlough in England. The presence of a Christian Nakaam provided for Majaliwa a comparatively peaceful and stable situation which enabled him to concentrate on the work of evangelism. The Nakaam also helped him by making Christians of most of his relatives and taking an active part in the work as interpreter and a sort of churchwarden. Most significantly, though, he was the defender of the Church from the incursion of Islam into the area. The Nakaam's sons made their contribution through work as teachers and then readers. Yohanna Abdallah even stood in for Majaliwa for a time in 1893 when Majaliwa, who had been ordained the first African priest of the Mission in January 1890, was called to the Synod in Zanzibar. Assisting with Abdallah was Cypriani Chitenge, and these two were to be ordained in a few years' time.

Although the existence of these favourable elements must be recognized, the personal qualities and ability of Cecil Majaliwa were the decisive factors in the success of the Mission at Chitangali between 1888 and 1894. His maturity and courage, in the first place, were clearly demonstrated when the whole village evacuated to the hills for fear of Ngoni attack. Majaliwa sent his wife and four children to the safety of the hills and remained at his post till the danger was over, in doing so winning the respect of the people. His linguistic ability also helped him to win the hearts of the people. He soon became fluent in Yao, so important for pastoral work since the majority of the people were not conversant with Swahili. He exploited to the full personal contacts with friends in England to obtain funds for school prizes, presents at baptism, teaching materials and so on, in order to keep his station abreast of the European priests' stations in the standard of material provision. At the same time, he clearly had a programme for self-reliance. Churches were built entirely by the offertory and free labour of the people, alms in kind were sold to raise money for the upkeep of the church and portage for church goods was provided free by the people.

Majaliwa did not confine his work to the Yao or to Chitangali. He frequently visited the Makonde people, and it was he who produced the first converts of that race. He sent them teachers and built schools and churches at places such as Miwa and Mwiti. By 1893, Chitangali had become the ecclesiastical centre of a wide area and Majaliwa became almost 'archdeacon' of the Ruvuma district. He went over to Masasi to administer the sacraments when there was no priest there; he went over to Newala to hear the confessions of the Christians, for there was no other priest who was able to hear them in Yao.

Thus, by his assimilation to the local life, his physical fitness for the work, his language ability and his understanding of the mode of thought of the people, it appears that Majaliwa became the embodiment of the ideal of the African ministry which Steere had advocated. Smythies recognized the significance of Majaliwa's work and in his address to the Synod in 1893 he encouraged other missionaries to follow his example.

The Usambara area, despite earlier promising signs of African ministry under Farler, was slower to achieve a breakthrough such as Majaliwa had effected. Future Bondei clergy were, however, being prepared from the early 1880s, among them Peter Limo, Samuel Sehoga, John Mdoe and John Saidi. Finally, in March 1894, Peter Limo, educated in England at Dorchester Theological College, was ordained the first freeborn priest in the Mission. The Bondei Christians were delighted with this promise for the continuity of ministry among them, while one of their missionaries hailed it as 'a landmark in the history of the Mission . . . distinctly a new beginning'.

A. C. Madan, one of the teaching staff at Kiungani, was cheered by these developments and reconfirmed Steere's view on the role of the missionaries:

> An African Church must be founded, spread and worked by Africans themselves. The business of its European members is to do their best to start them on this career, help as they may, and then pass out of sight.[7]

Smythies, sharing this view, began to look ahead to the realization of the ideal of the Mission, first in the Ruvuma district and centring upon Cecil Majaliwa:

> I hope in four or five years time we may see four or five native priests from the district. Then it will be time to talk about making Cecil a Bishop for which I think in many ways he would be admirable.[8]

End of the early ideal of an African Church

The African ministry on the face of it enjoyed continuous and fast progress under Bishop W. M. Richardson (1895–1901). He declared at the beginning of his episcopate that he would continue the line of Smythies. Thus the number of African clergy increased from two priests and two deacons in May 1894 to four priests and six deacons in November 1901 in the East African sphere of the UMCA. The number may not seem to be impressive compared with the CMS in Uganda, with 24 African clergy by 1900, but the quality of the UMCA African clergy was 'undoubtedly superior to the general African ministers' in East Africa.[9]

The most damaging impact on the development of the African ministry occurred in 1897 with the withdrawal of Cecil Majaliwa to Zanzibar. Majaliwa had lost the support and co-operation of the Nakaam, who had become an agent for the German colonial government from September 1894. When the chief moved to Chiwata he asked to come under the superintendence of the 'white' missionaries at Masasi or Newala. To Majaliwa's disappointment, Richardson agreed to this. Thus Majaliwa lost both Nakaam and Chiwata at once. He tried fresh work at Mwiti, about ten miles south-west of Chitangali, but even after more than a year the church building was not completed. After eight years' continuous work on the mainland, early in 1896 he asked for 'a year's holiday in Zanzibar', but this was refused. Then, his home at Mwiti was burgled during his absence for the Synod at Zanzibar in October 1896. He must have felt that he was no longer respected by the people as he had been at Chitangali. Majaliwa decided to act. He left Mwiti in August 1897 'to settle down at Zanzibar' for the sake of his children. His self-allotted semi-retirement from active missionary work on the mainland thus aggravated the missionaries' assessment of the African ministry.

Furthermore, the 'lenient' personality of Richardson began to weaken the unity and cohesion of the Mission and its policy. The resignation of experienced missionaries accelerated change, and the method of developing an African ministry by a non-directive approach encouraging growth 'slowly and from within' was replaced by specific models introduced from the Catholic wing of the Church of England. At the same time, the relationship between the English and African clergy shifted from one of trust between equals to a strict supervisory one, the English over the Africans, the latter regarded as too 'immature' to maintain by themselves the organization and standards of the Church of England. Thus, Woodward at Magila, who was baffled by the manner of Sehoza, wrote to the Secretary in January 1901:

> Even Padre Sehoza came back from Zanzibar with a new spirit and wanted to know the difference between a European priest-in-charge and an African![10]

The state of internal anarchy in the diocese and his own physical weakness forced Richardson's resignation, and J. E. Hine (1901–9), the Bishop of Likoma in Nyasaland, was translated to Zanzibar in December 1901. Recognizing the importance of the African ministry, Bishop Hine ordained one priest and four deacons between December 1901 and

February 1903, but by then had come to believe that, compared to Likoma, Zanzibar Diocese was morally 'corrupt' and too 'luxurious materially', especially at Kiungani, the backbone of African ministry. After a case of failure of an African deacon, Hine decided in 1903 to ordain 'no more native priests for ten years'. He also established a new pattern whereby an English missionary priest would be in charge, but with African clergy 'doing the work'.

The rising self-assertion of the missionaries and the slowing down of the Africanization of the ministry was seriously challenged in Ruvuma district by events following the Maji–maji rising, which began its indiscriminate attack upon 'the white man' in August 1905. At the rising, all the missionaries were evacuated promptly to the coast. For the next six months the entire district was left in the hands of an African priest, Daudi Machina, and his five African deacons. The Mission took this as a test case for the African ministry as to whether it was able to 'stand alone' with 'no European to lean on'. At the Anniversary Meeting in England in 1906, Hine declared proudly,

> So they can stand alone. They can rise to their vocation. They can carry on work just as if we were not in Africa, faithfully and devotedly and sincerely.[11]

He now saw the African ministry as indispensable and independent, not merely supplementary to the ministry of missionaries. Thus he resumed the ordination of Africans after a break of four years, first a deacon for the Usambara district in February 1907, and then in August three more for the first time locally at Masasi in Ruvuma district. In April 1908 he ordained Daniel Usufu priest. Now the district was staffed by two old English missionary priests, two African priests and seven African deacons for seven stations. The district was hailed as 'the most native part of the Mission' and 'the ideal of the Mission'.

Hine's change of heart, however, was put in jeopardy as a result of the consolidation of German colonial power after the rising. He wrote to the Secretary,

> Daudi Machina is excellent, but the district with the German government complications needs absolutely a European in authority and can't be left to native clergy only.[12]

Along with the intensification of colonialism, denominational rivalry reinforced the perception of the need for missionary direction. Additionally, missionaries' health conditions were continuously improving with the use of advancing medical aids and means of transport, including railways. These various factors all served to promote the seeming permanence of missionaries in their work in the earlier twentieth century, and in turn rendered more distant the realization of a self-governing African Church with an African ministry.

-->≡◎⊜≡<--

Often the development and direction of African ministry had been drastically altered by the views of different bishops in each period. The idea of making Majaliwa a bishop for Ruvuma district died with Smythies, and was not revived by Richardson or Hine. The idea of advancing African clergy to higher positions, revived by Hine, though only to the rank of archdeacon, such as Sehoza for Usambara and Machina for Ruvuma district, had no guarantee of implementation after his departure. In fact, no member of the African clergy was promoted beyond the status of honorary canon in the UMCA dioceses until after Tanzanian independence in 1961.

The ideal of a home-grown African Church thus came to an end completely at the resignation of Bishop Hine in 1908. It is some satisfaction that the grandson of Cecil Majaliwa, John Ramadhani, ordained priest in 1976 at the cathedral built by Bishop Steere in Zanzibar, was consecrated bishop in 1980 and became the third African Archbishop of Tanzania in 1984.

-->≡◎⊜≡<--

Dr Jerome T. Moriyama is a Japanese Africanist specializing in East African economic development and in the history of Christian mission in East Africa. He taught in the 1970s at St Mark's Theological College, Dar es Salaam, Tanzania, and from the 1980s until recently worked in the City of London as a senior executive.

Notes

This essay is based on my PhD Thesis (see Bibliography).

1. G. Ward (ed.) (1902) *Letters of Bishop Tozer and his Sister*, London, p. 86.
2. E. Steere (1875) *The Universities' Mission to Central Africa: A Speech delivered at Oxford 1874*, London, p. 7.
3. *Kiungani* (1880–1), p. 59.
4. [Steere to Heanley, 2 Jan. 1878, A1(III) B:456].
5. *Annual Report 1879–80*, London, p. 30.

6. *Report of the Proceedings at a Meeting in Liverpool for UMCA, June 1882*, Liverpool, p. 14.
7. *Central Africa*, May 1892, p. 66.
8. [Smythies to Travers, 10 Jan. 1893, IX(18):3].
9. Neave (1974), pp. 223–4.
10. [Woodward to Travers, 10 Jan. 1901, B2:318–19].
11. *Central Africa*, July 1906, p. 177.
12. [Hine to Travers, 30 Nov. 1906, A1(X–XI):334].

9

From medicine chest to mission hospitals:
the early history of the Delhi Medical
Mission for women and children

ROSEMARY FITZGERALD

Introduction

In the early 1860s, a sharp-eyed observer walking at daybreak along the
misty western banks of Delhi's holy River Jumna, might have chanced
upon an unusual sight. At dawn, several times each week, a young
English woman slipped quietly through the Water Gate in the city wall
to take a path, past the temples and Brahmin houses, down to the
bathing steps at the riverside. According to Hindu belief, here Krishna
once played his flute while Radha danced. Each morning, Hindu
women of all classes, including those normally veiled by purdah, gathered at the female bathing place to make their religious vows and dip
themselves in the sacred waters. The solitary European figure in the
jostling crowds of Indian women would make her way to a ruined hut
where, opening a medicine box carried with her, she dispensed simple
remedies and rudimentary cures among those troubled by disease and
sickness.

This English woman was Priscilla Winter, wife of the head of the
SPG Mission in Delhi. Her riverside dispensary for women led to the
founding in 1867 of the Delhi Female Medical Mission (DFMM) – the
first women's medical mission established in India. By the century's
ending, the scope and scale of the work that Priscilla Winter had
initiated, with 'no further medical qualification than a medicine-chest',
was so developed that the SPG regarded the agency of women medical
missionaries as 'the distinctive feature of the whole mission at Delhi'.[1]
The history of the Delhi Female Medical Mission, from its difficult birth
in the 1860s through to its rise to prominence as a missionary institution
in the first decade of the twentieth century, saw the forging of the

Mission's reputation for caring for the sick in the city destined to become the capital of modern India.

'The germ of the endeavour'

Priscilla Winter was born in Calcutta in 1842, the daughter of a CMS missionary, Timothy Sandys. In 1858, after a childhood in England, the sixteen-year-old Priscilla rejoined her family in Calcutta where she threw herself 'with all the fresh enthusiasm of her youth' into zenana work – a newly emerging missionary method designed to reach purdah women who were deeply secluded within the zenana, the female quarters of the Indian home.[2] Although the poorest communities could not afford to confine their womenfolk to a life of such intense privacy, most Hindu and Muslim households of the 'better classes' observed purdah customs that prohibited women's public visibility and contact with men outside the immediate family. The curtain of purdah proved an impenetrable barrier for male missionaries and the mission world eventually began to concede, in the 1860s, that female agents were needed to gain access to the women and the homes of India's élite and middle classes. Before that time, the male authorities of Church and mission generally viewed the appointment of female missionaries with grave misgivings.[3] The originators of zenana work at mid-century were, therefore, usually missionary wives, daughters and sisters – women who laboured 'silently and unassumingly', without pay or title, alongside their menfolk, the 'real' missionaries.[4] These pioneer zenana visitors offered secluded women home tuition in needlework, reading, writing and arithmetic, in the hope of finding opportunities for also teaching Christianity. Priscilla Sandys worked as a Calcutta zenana teacher for four years, until her marriage in 1863 to the SPG missionary, Robert Winter. As a new bride she moved to Delhi, a city still shrouded in bitter memories of the Mutiny and Rebellion of 1857.

The SPG Delhi Mission had only been in existence since 1854, but it already had an eventful history. The first Society agents sent to this historic city, the one-time capital of Mughal India, were two Cambridge men, J. S. Jackson and A. R. Hubbard.[5] They started work on a tide of optimism for, even before their arrival, the East India Company chaplain, M. J. Jennings, had baptized two eminent Delhi citizens – the mathematician Ram Chandra and sub-assistant surgeon, Dr Chimman Lal. By December 1856, a visiting bishop declared Delhi one of the 'most promising and hopeful of our Indian Mission fields'.[6] But only months later, in May 1857, the Indian Mutiny and Rebellion engulfed the

Mission. News of the siege of Delhi filtered back to England, and eventually, a bleak message was received by the Society, 'The Delhi Mission has been completely swept away.' Hubbard, two young catechists, Louis Koch and Daniel Sandys (Priscilla Winter's elder brother), Jennings and his daughter, Chimman Lal and other members of the Church had all perished in the uprising.[7]

SPG resolved immediately to 're-establish with increased strength, and on a broader foundation, the Mission which has been for the moment quenched in blood'.[8] While the Society arranged to send out Thomas Skelton at the end of 1858 and Robert Winter in 1860, the surviving Indian Christian community, led by Ram Chandra, initiated the work of reconstruction. Nevertheless, when Robert Winter took over the headship in 1863, the year of his marriage to Priscilla, the Mission had barely begun to recover from the trauma of its near obliteration. In the years that followed, missionary work was successfully rekindled with the development of a range of agencies and institutions — evangelistic, educational and medical — far wider and more diversified than was usual in the missions of that period. The swift and ambitious expansion of activities reflected the character and talent of both the Winters who, in equal measure, left their stamp on Christian work in the Delhi district. As one fellow missionary wrote, at the time of Robert Winter's death many years later, their 'names must always be coupled in speaking of the Delhi Mission'.[9]

Although the 'hidden service' of missionary wives usually received little official recognition in this era, Priscilla Winter's 'ever-ready' energy and determination, combined with her reputation as 'fiery' tempered, made it difficult for her male contemporaries to overlook her achievements.[10] She was acknowledged to be the chief architect of the rapid growth in 'women's work', the most outstanding development in the Mission during the 1860s and 1870s. On her arrival in Delhi, she had found 'not a single zenana open for instruction in the Punjab and North-West Provinces'.[11] Apart from a short-lived attempt to provide lessons for the Mughal princesses (now destitute after British reprisals for the 1857 uprising), missionary work for the women of Delhi consisted of just two schools, one for orphans and Christians and another for low-caste girls. Such public institutions, catering for the poor and marginalized, held no appeal for families of wealth and substance whose social standing was gauged largely by their adherence to purdah customs. The Winters were convinced that missionaries should make every effort to bring the high-born and the low, both men and women, within the orbit of Christian teaching. Priscilla Winter first attempted to reach the households of secluded women by establishing a system of zenana visitation and instruction according to the Calcutta pattern. In 1865 two zenana teachers were obtained through the London Auxiliary of the Calcutta Female Education Society and, after 1866, others were supplied by the newly founded SPG Ladies' Association. But in the conservative climate of north India, these first women missionaries found that their notions of female education were often rejected by the city's more prosperous families.[12] Searching for other routes into the homes of the higher classes, Priscilla Winter's 'quick eye at once detected the importance of *medical* work amongst the women of Delhi'.[13]

Priscilla Winter first glimpsed these medical possibilities during the fever and cholera epidemics of 1863 and 1864 when she nursed sick women in their homes and began distributing medicines at the female bathing steps on the River Jumna. This was a period when it was not uncommon to find missionary personnel, with no hint of medical qualifications, attempting to 'doctor' local people in times of sickness. The term 'medical missionary' had barely been coined and it was only later in the century that officially designated medical agents began to enter the missionary ranks in any number. In the days before medical missions were established on a professional basis, missionaries generally believed that their inexpert aid was at least preferable to leaving the sick and injured in the hands of indigenous healers. To the European mind, the deficiencies of indigenous medicine were most starkly revealed in the case of India's women who were said to suffer untold pain and loss of life through the 'murderous doings' of the *dhai* (traditional midwife). Female patients were unlikely to turn to government medical services as an alternative to attendance by the 'dangerous dhai'. There was sparse provision of public hospitals and dispensaries for the mass of Indian people and, more importantly, these male-staffed institutions were abhorrent, not just to purdah women, but to the bulk of the female population. Indian sentiments on female modesty were so intense that few women were prepared to subject themselves to examination by a male practitioner of Western medicine, especially in cases of childbirth or 'diseases peculiar to women'. In these circumstances, missionary wives, like Priscilla Winter, felt justified in giving whatever medical relief they could if women and children appealed to them for aid. But, as she readily admitted, it was far from ideal to consign this work to amateurs; her medical limitations had soon been revealed by the severity of the diseases that she was called upon to treat. As she explained, the work demanded 'more knowledge and time than I possessed, and as I did not give medicines for *every* disease, the women got angry, and believed I *would* not give them advice, not that I *could* not.'[14]

The founding of the Delhi Female Medical Mission

Returning to England on furlough in 1865, the Winters resolved to find a way of placing the Mission's medical work on a firmer footing. However, the idea of a female medical mission was then so novel that neither SPG nor any other missionary organization was willing to finance such an unproven (and to many minds, unlikely) missionary method. In October 1866, the Winters resorted to forming their own association of English friends and relatives to raise funds and publicity for their scheme. In November of that year, the Association published an inaugural pamphlet announcing its intention to establish 'a Medical Mission among the native women of Delhi, with the double object of alleviating much physical suffering, and of taking a knowledge of Christianity to them in their secluded homes'. It was suggested that a female medical agent would be widely welcomed, even into homes resolutely closed to zenana teachers. A lady with 'a knowledge of medicine' would be appointed to develop three departments of work – domiciliary care for purdah women, dispensary services for less secluded females and training classes for Indian nurses. Readers were assured that only a woman could carry out this work, as many Indian women would rather die than consult a medical man.[15]

However, finding a suitable lady medical worker proved a formidable problem. The British medical profession was still effectively closed to women and women's access to medical education remained a deeply controversial issue. Among those of a conservative mind, the very idea of the woman doctor was an outrage against all notions of propriety.[16] In the absence of women doctors, the Winters turned to the world of nursing. But even here, it was far from easy to find a candidate with the qualities of commitment, character and refinement thought essential for a 'lady missionary'. In the 1860s, nursing was not yet considered a noble calling and nurses were, in the main, placed on a par with domestic servants, like Charles Dickens's character, Mrs Gamp. The campaign to reform nursing was under way, but changes were of such recent origin that the new breed of Nightingale nurse was only just emerging. The Winters entered into negotiations with one of Florence Nightingale's protégées, Lucy Osburn, but this candidate's missionary aspirations soon evaporated. Miss Osburn had seen a letter in which the Delhi Civil Surgeon described the medical work awaiting her in India, concluding, 'She must be a Heroine who would undertake so Herculean a task!' Miss Osburn promptly withdrew, declaring she was neither heroine nor Hercules.[17] The Winters eventually appointed Mrs Browne, a 30-year-old midwife, admittedly not one of the highly prized 'new nurses' but a woman with prior experience of work in India. In September 1867, Mrs Browne sailed for India and that autumn the Delhi Female Medical Mission was launched officially.

Unfortunately Mrs Browne did not last a year, being dismissed in June 1868, on suspicion of improbity. Medical work was temporarily halted until Mrs Littler was recruited in November 1870, a midwife with hospital training. Mrs Littler and her Indian assistant, Mariam, activated work in two directions – attending secluded women in their homes and opening a female dispensary in a rented room in the Chandni Chowk, a bustling thoroughfare in the heart of Delhi. These services were said to be 'in great request', the register of cases for December 1870 to October 1871 showing that '1,446 visits had been paid to 191 patients in the Zenanas, and that 1,917 visits had been made to the Dispensary, by 305 patients'.[18] Towards the end of 1871, a 'native house' in the Chandni Chowk was turned into a dispensary and a ten-bedded 'temporary' hospital. It was hoped that in the future there would be a more permanent hospital site and structure; meanwhile, this makeshift arrangement at least provided a place for training Indian nurses and for tending the few women willing to accept in-patient treatment. Robert Winter was now able to report that the original threefold plan was 'fairly in operation'. On the thorny question of 'spiritual fruitage', he was confident that medical work offered 'one of the most appropriate and hopeful means of influencing the women of India' although he was equally clear that patients should not be coerced into Christianity.[19]

However, these buoyant reports were soon followed by the sombre news of Mrs Littler's sudden death in May 1873. The future of the DFMM was once again in jeopardy. Although temporary help was drafted, these interim arrangements failed to satisfy the Winters who were convinced that missionary operations should be run 'on principle and not haphazard'.[20] But, despite their undoubted organizational powers, their medical plans had to weather 'the storms of many disappointments' and, as in other emerging female medical missions, the early work progressed in a discontinuous and uneven fashion.[21] Yet the Winters' enthusiasm for missionary medicine remained undimmed. In their opinion, there were few better demonstrations of the Christian message of love and mercy than caring for the sick and suffering. As Robert Winter explained: 'our object [is] to show the people of Delhi that we have their real welfare at heart, and that we seek the benefit of their minds and bodies as well as their souls'.[22] Showing an unusually expansive and far-sighted understanding of mission, he wrote:

We should try to come before the people, not merely as preachers of a new religion, a capacity in which they care for us little enough, but as friends and sympathisers . . . we should aim at benefiting *the whole man*.[23]

1875–91: 'years of mingled trials and progress'

The DFMM entered a more settled period when Miss Engelmann took charge of the work in 1875. Like most of the first wave of single women missionaries of the 1860s and 1870s, Miss Engelmann began mission service as a zenana teacher. On joining the Mission in 1871, she was assigned to the chief branch station in Karnal, a country town 70 miles north of Delhi. In this particularly disease-ridden district, Miss Engelmann's educational work soon took on a medical flavour. By 1875 she was back in Delhi as the newly appointed head of the DFMM, a post she held for the next sixteen years. Her scanty preparation for this work was typical of the first generation of female medical missionaries, many of whom gleaned their elementary medical skills from 'the hedgerow of experience' rather than from any formal course of study. In Miss Engelmann's case, she simply took 'a training (such as it was in those days) in midwifery and, "by sitting beside a doctor in his consulting room, learned to use the stethoscope and something about eyes"!'[24]

In 1875 the DFMM was still 'in an embryo state of existence' – the dispensary was open only on alternate days and the average attendance at a session amounted to no more than 30 patients.[25] However, the work developed substantially under Miss Engelmann's 'vigorous administration'.[26] Between October 1876 and September 1877 the Mission treated over six thousand women and children in the dispensary and over a thousand more in their own homes. During that year Dr Bose, a Bengali Civil Surgeon on furlough from government service, gave valuable assistance, providing advice on difficult cases among the women and children and running a separate male dispensary that treated almost two thousand men in its first year of operation. Furthermore, eighteen local women, supported by scholarships from the Delhi Municipality, were enrolled in the nursing class, by now a two-year course of instruction examined half-yearly by the government Civil Surgeon.[27] With Dr Bose's unexpected death in December 1877, however, the already overburdened Miss Engelmann was once again left in sole charge of the medical work. Despite repeated appeals for reinforcements, two years passed before the Mission secured another permanent medical worker – Deaconess Jacobina Zeyen, an experienced nurse from the famed Kaiserwerth community in Germany.[28] Six months later, in May 1881, Deaconess Zeyen extended the Mission's medical work to the Karnal outstation. Although the next year was a comparatively healthy season, the Karnal branch reported an annual return of over 7000 individual patients with a total of 11,583 consultations. Meanwhile in Delhi the figures for 1882 surpassed all previous years, with over 13,000 cases and 43,690 consultations, bringing the daily average to 140 patients.

Although these statistics indicated growing public confidence in the DFMM, Indian women were often highly reluctant patients. They did not easily accept the strange procedures of Western medicine, particularly in the mission setting where an unfamiliar form of medical care was allied to an equally alien religious system. The ostensible 'blessings' of Western medicine, so confidently asserted by Europeans, were not so apparent to the people of India where many segments of society, not least the women, remained strongly attached to their own medical traditions. In India, as elsewhere, indigenous healing systems proved more resilient than their detractors expected and medical intrusions from the West were long-regarded with suspicion. At the founding of the first female medical missions, and for many years after, missionaries commonly complained that patients were brought to them in a moribund condition and only after all indigenous therapies had been exhausted. As Mrs Winter lamented: 'The natives try their own systems of medicine, and as a last resort fly to the Englishwoman: a succession of bad and hopeless cases is the result.'[29]

To encourage women to come for early treatment, '*before* having their disease aggravated by months or years of mal-treatment or neglect', female medical missions took great precautions not to violate purdah customs.[30] In Delhi the patients' entrance to the dispensary was situated in a quiet side lane, leading into a private courtyard where purdah women could alight from their bullock carts, *ekkas* (horse-drawn carriages), *dolies* (curtained palanquins) or even covered bedsteads, without fear of attracting male attention.[31] Once safely inside this exclusively female environment, all the women, poor and wealthy, were assembled for hymn singing and Bible teaching while awaiting their turn for treatment. However, even with the help of Indian Christian Bible-women, it proved difficult to capture the attention of a crowd of women and children seeking cure not conversion. Domiciliary care continued to be supplied to secluded women who refused to leave their zenanas, but missionaries were agreed that, in both educational and medical work, house-to-house visitation was too expensive and impracticable to be undertaken on any extensive scale. Increasingly, the advantages were emphasized of treating women either as dispensary out-patients or, better still, as hospital in-patients. But, while growing numbers were prepared to pay a fleeting visit to the dispensary, most still refused to be admitted into the hospital. A host of social and religious sentiments militated against a sick woman leaving her home and for many years only the desperately ill and the very poor would consent to in-patient treatment. Nevertheless, in the later decades of the century, medical missionaries became convinced that the best results, both medical and spiritual, came with the kind of intensive treatment only possible within a hospital.

From the late 1870s 'the melancholy refrain that a Hospital is wanting' appeared increasingly often in the reports of the Delhi Mission.[32] The existing Chandni Chowk dispensary could accommodate a few in-patients but the building was hot and cramped, plagued by monkeys and mosquitoes, in every way miserably unsuitable quarters. These conditions, Robert Winter wrote, 'would make the hair of English people . . . stand on end' and had stretched even missionary ingenuity to its limits.[33] In 1881, following the death of Priscilla Winter at the age of 39 from complications following the birth of her tenth child, the Mission decided to build a women's hospital to commemorate her life's work among Indian women.[34] By 1883 a suitable site had been found in the Chandni Chowk, overlooking a park, the Queen's Gardens, and work commenced, with financial aid from the Punjab government and Delhi Municipality as well as from private donors, both Indian and European. The new hospital provided wards for some twenty in-patients as well as more airy accommodation for staff and dispensary patients. Opening in October 1885, the building was named St Stephen's Hospital for Women and Children, the first institution of its kind in Delhi.

Similar developments occurred on a smaller scale at Karnal, where, in 1884, Deaconess Zeyen's dispensary moved from a Hindu house 'in the midst of the noisy bazaar' to the more spacious, peaceful setting of a Muslim mansion, the Shish Mahal or Glass Palace. This rented property was arranged around a central quadrangle, with two wards for fifteen patients and two huts for those with infectious illness or caste preferences for segregation; there was also a large dispensary and ample accommodation for the missionary and Indian nurses. The small bed-capacity of both hospitals indicated that the missionaries did not expect to attract many more in-patients. Furthermore, in their founding years neither Delhi nor Karnal hospital possessed an operating theatre. Although this might seem a strange omission, in the 1880s the Delhi station, like many other female medical missions of that era, still had no woman doctor, so that only very minor surgical operations were possible.

The advent of qualified medical missionaries

The DFMM finally acquired a qualified medical woman in May 1891, when Dr Jenny Muller took charge of St Stephen's Hospital and Miss Englemann retired, broken in health after twenty years of service. Jenny Muller, a young woman of Indian–German origins, had joined the Mission as a teacher–evangelist in 1884, but soon became Deaconess Zeyen's medical assistant at Karnal. In similar circumstances a decade earlier, Miss Engelmann had transferred from teaching to medical work with only a hastily improvised training. However, by the 1880s women were beginning to inch their way into the medical profession and, aided by grants from SPG and SPCK, Jenny Muller was able to train as a doctor, first at the Calcutta Medical School and later at the London School of Medicine for Women. Returning to Delhi in 1891 as the Mission's first woman doctor, she was believed to be the only fully qualified lady practitioner in a city of 200,000 inhabitants.[35] At first her work was greatly hindered by lack of staff and poor resources: 'Not only were there no proper assistants but there were no appliances, no clothes, no instruments worth speaking of, though there was, it must be admitted, a fairly good stock of drugs.' Her duties, 'many and mixed', initially even included hospital cleaning. As she later recalled ruefully:

> It was well I possessed both the hopefulness of youth and the energy of the proverbial new broom, for it was no light task that lay before me, looked at from the point of view of either a char or a medical woman.[36]

Jenny Muller's appointment marked the beginning of a period of substantial development. At the end of 1893 a second doctor, Mildred Staley, joined St Stephen's, allowing Dr Muller to go to Karnal where the medical work had lapsed since the marriage of Deaconess Zeyen in 1888. The arrival of qualified medical agents was a powerful incentive for improving conditions in both the Delhi and Karnal hospitals, with St Stephen's the first to undergo transformation. When Robert Winter died in 1891, after a ministry of more than 30 years in Delhi, plans were made to add a substantial frontage to the hospital so that the completed building would stand as a memorial to both the Winters. When the workmen ('the real bane of our existence' wrote Dr Staley) finally finished the new three-storey extension in 1895, the hospital had a handsome entrance and better facilities for staff and patients, including a proper operating theatre with white glazed tiles and a good supply of surgical instruments. The wards also underwent complete refurbishment – floors were retiled, tired quilts and blankets replaced and better furniture procured, with the traditional Indian charpoy (wood and rope bed) replaced by Lawson-Tait iron bedsteads; speaking tubes were installed to save staff countless trips up and down the many stairs.[37] By the close of the century, similar renovations, including an additional wing, were made possible at the Karnal hospital, now known as St Elizabeth's, by the generosity of their landlord, Nawab Rustum Ali Khan Sahib.

The Delhi Mission's medical work also expanded in other directions. Periodically in the cold weather season, a team of doctor, nurse and evangelist set off in the Mission bullock-cart to tour outlying villages. Pitching camp near the larger settlements, they held impromptu clinics offering immediate treatment for minor ailments or despatch to hospital for more serious cases. In addition, between 1898 and 1903, dispensaries were established at the Mission's sub-stations in Sonipat, Panipat, Rohtak and Rewari. These outreach programmes were important for advertising missionary medicine and extending its coverage to rural areas, although, by now, the development of city hospitals was clearly the core concern of female medical mission work in India. In Delhi, as elsewhere, the growth of in-patient services was seen as the surest sign of rising standards in mission medicine. This emphasis on hospital care would have seemed impossible in the days when the vast majority of patients and their relatives raised 'a perfect storm of opposition' at any suggestion of in-patient treatment; but by the opening of the twentieth century, Indian women were growing less wary of Western medicine.[38] Gradually, patients were presenting for treatment at an earlier stage of illness and showing greater willingness to consider hospital admission. As Jenny Muller observed:

> The dread of the 'Daktar miss' and her instruments seems to be disappearing. I remember the time, when a whole household had been in an uproar on the production of a clinical thermometer and in a very frenzy at the sight of a stethoscope. Now, if I do not happen to need these, the patient feels herself ill-used, and her case neglected![39]

The Delhi in-patient statistics underline this gain in popular trust. By the century's ending, the DFMM was registering more new in-patients monthly (some 50–60) than were admitted yearly in the 1870s. Some 1200 domiciliary calls were still made annually, but this was now deemed 'the most trying and unsatisfactory' aspect of the work.[40] Far better, in the missionary view, to remove patients from their 'unsanitary' homes and install them, freshly scrubbed and newly clothed, in the clean, bright wards of a mission hospital. The order, cleanliness and regularity of hospital life were seen as vital aids to recovery although, as Dr Staley noted, the patients often found the restraints 'most irksome'.[41] Indeed, Indian women were far from passive patients and the imposition of Western ideas of hospital discipline proved no easy matter, with many necessary concessions to Indian sentiment and tradition to induce female patients to stay inside the hospital. Purdah customs were, of course, observed as well as other caste and communal practices, most notably those concerning diet and cooking arrangements. It was also common for patients to enter hospital with an entourage of female relatives, to the dismay of staff who complained that these 'intruders' cluttered up the wards.[42] New staff, freshly arrived from England, were often amazed by the differences between a mission hospital and their training hospitals at home. Yet medical missionaries all agreed that hospital work was their 'chief delight' for they were certain that a Christian hospital provided the best setting for achieving the healing of both body and soul.[43]

The staffing of the DFMM was greatly strengthened in this period. In 1891, the young and inexperienced Jenny Muller had been the Mission's only doctor as well as chief nurse, evangelist and compounder. By 1895 she had reopened St Elizabeth's with a small group of Christian Indian nurses, while at St Stephen's there were two lady physicians, Dr Staley and Dr Thornett, plus two dispensers, a resident hospital evangelist and eight Indian nurses supervised by an English matron, Mary Roberts. In the following years a series of qualified medical women (almost all European) joined the Mission.[44] More fully trained English nurses were also recruited to superintend and raise the standards of nursing care and education.[45] In this era Indian staff served mainly as junior nurses and dispensers, not forgetting the vital workforce of maids and sweepers, cooks and cleaners. One Indian woman doctor, Martha Francis, was notable in the Mission at this period, working for decades as house surgeon and hospital assistant.[46] Despite considerable growth in medical and nursing personnel, staff shortages remained a perennial problem. The precariousness of health and frequency of sickness among the staff caused many disruptions in the work, and there were tragic losses. In 1903 Sister Roberts died of cholera and in 1908 there were three fatalities – Dr Hayes died from (probably) pneumonic plague, Sister Allen from typhoid and Dr Harding from dysentery.

New hospitals for the new century

By the beginning of the twentieth century, medical mission work had changed considerably. In Delhi, as in other missions, fully trained doctors and nurses were able to offer their patients an increasingly sophisticated range of medical and surgical therapies. Missionaries had once looked at empty hospital beds with sinking spirits, but now mission hospitals were often overcrowded, with cots and beds squeezed into every corner. In 1908 a new and enlarged St Stephen's Hospital for Women and Children was built outside the city walls, with 60 beds, an out-patient wing, isolation block, kitchens, chapel and staff quarters. Although all were glad to leave 'the smells and dust and heat of the Chandni Chowk', Dr Scott cannot have been alone in feeling that 'forsaking the old place' seemed 'like deserting a dear and trusty friend'.[47] In March of the same year St Elizabeth's also moved into a new building after an earthquake had irreparably damaged the original hospital. In 1910 Dr Muller wrote, 'With the rebuilding of the Hospitals at Delhi and Karnal a new era seems to have dawned for the medical work of the Mission.' Looking back to the quiet and humble beginnings of the work in the 1860s, she marvelled that Priscilla Winter's simple medicine chest had 'yet contained the germ of the endeavour which has brought healing and blessing to many thousands of Indian women'.[48] And the work continued and still continues. Although St Elizabeth's closed long ago, St Stephen's Hospital survived the many dramas of the twentieth century and stands today, a vibrant and now much expanded medical institution still caring for the sick and suffering at the beginning of a new millennium.

⋗⟫⊜⟨⋖

Dr Rosemary Fitzgerald is a medical sociologist and historian who has taught in universities in Britain and North America. Her current research is on medical missions, gender and health care in colonial India.

Notes

1. J. C. Muller (1910) *Some Personal Reminiscences of Work in The Delhi Medical Mission, 1884–1910*, CMD Papers, pp. 5–6.
2. 'In memoriam', *Guardian*, 18 Jan. 1882.
3. On changing Anglican attitudes to the commissioning of female missionaries, see Gill (1994), pp. 173–205.
4. J. Richter (1908) *A History of Missions in India*, Edinburgh, p. 332.
5. Apart from a small Roman Catholic community surviving from the time of the Jesuit mission to the Mughal court, sporadic work by the CMS and the efforts of a lone Baptist minister, there was little missionary interest in Delhi and its district until the arrival of the SPG: F. J. Western (1950) 'The early history of the Cambridge Mission to Delhi', (unpublished typescript), pp. 7–13.

6. Pascoe, p. 614.

7. V. H. Stanton (1908), *The Story of the Delhi Mission*, London, pp. 9–11.

8. Resolution of the SPG monthly meeting, 17 July 1857.

9. [G. A. Lefroy, Memorial to Revd R. R. Winter, 1891, DOS 8292, R. R. Winter].

10. *Report of the SPG and Cambridge Mission in Delhi*, 1880--81, p. 5; Western, 'Early History', pp. 84, 98–99.

11. *Report of the General Missionary Conference held at Allahabad 1872–73*, London, 1873, p. 154.

12. For many years, zenana teaching in Delhi was conducted in great secrecy because heads of households consenting to missionary visits feared the outraged reactions of friends and neighbours. On the beginnings of zenana visitation and teaching by the Delhi Mission, see Forbes (26 Apr. 1986), pp. WS 2–8.

13. *Delhi Female Medical Mission* (hereafter DFMM) *Annual Report for 1881*, p. 7 (emphasis added).

14. *General Missionary Conference, Allahabad 1872–73*, p. 157.

15. Pamphlet, *DFMM*, Nov. 1866 [CMD 88].

16. At the end of the 1860s, only one European woman, Elizabeth Garrett (the first woman to gain a medical qualification in England) was practising medicine with official approval: Bonner (1992), p. 29.

17. Lucy Osburn to Florence Nightingale, 23 Oct. 1866, Nightingale Correspondence, Greater London Record Office, HI/ST/NC2/V6/66.

18. *The Englishwoman's Review*, Oct. 1872, **11**, p. 268.

19. *DFMM Report for 1872*.

20. Pascoe, p. 616.

21. R. R. Winter (1885) *Delhi Medical Mission to Women and Children*, p. 4.

22. *Report of the Mission in Delhi and the South Punjab of the SPG* (hereafter *Report DSP*) (later Reports include 'and Cambridge Mission'), 1873–4, p. 11.

23. *Mission Field*, Sept. 1877, p. 383.

24. [Draft leaflet on St Stephen's Hospital, Delhi, 11 Dec. 1929, CMD 115].

25. *DFMM Report for 1882*, p. 2.

26. Winter, *Delhi Medical Mission*, p. 4.

27. Before the arrival of women missionary doctors, the DFMM depended heavily on the advice of sympathetic Civil Surgeons when treating serious cases.

28. The Kaiserwerth community, founded in 1836, cared for the sick and poor and was visited by prominent figures in the reform of British nursing, including Elizabeth Fry and Florence Nightingale.

29. *Medical Missions at Home and Abroad*, Jan. 1879, **1** (3), p. 47.

30. *Report DSP*, 1895, p. 20.

31. In Karnal, where conveyances were less easily available to secluded women, the Mission instituted evening clinics so that these patients could walk to the dispensary under cover of darkness. Women from the poorer classes, less restricted by purdah customs, came on foot to the dispensary even during daylight hours.

32. *DFMM Report for 1882*, p. 7.

33. *Report DSP*, 1875–6, p. 9.

34. At the time of Priscilla Winter's death, after eighteen years in Delhi, she had established eight Indian girls' schools, two Normal schools for training Indian women teachers, a female industrial school, a Christian girls' boarding school, a European day-school, a refuge for 'fallen women', training classes for zenana missionaries, Sunday schools and Bible classes for Indian Christians and the DFMM. The staff of women workers included some twenty European missionaries, a similar number of Indian Christian teachers and several non-Christian assistants. The work was carried out not only in Delhi, but also in a large number of outstations.

35. An Indian Christian woman doctor was practising in Delhi at that time but she had studied medicine at a lower grade than Jenny Muller and was not therefore deemed fully qualified.

36. Muller, *Personal Reminiscences*, pp. 5–6.

37. *Report DSP*, 1895, pp. 18–21.

38. *Ibid.*, 1898, p. 23.

39. *Ibid.*, 1902, p. 37.

40. *Ibid.*, 1900, p. 44.

41. *Report DSP*, 1895, p. 22.

42. When a separate hospital kitchen could not be provided for high-caste Hindu patients, relatives brought food daily from the home to ensure there was no defilement of caste status. *Report DSP*, 1894, pp. 22–3.

43. *Ibid.*, 1898, pp. 22–4.

44. Apart from those already mentioned, the following women doctors joined the Delhi Mission before the First World War: Charlotte Hull and Annie Harding (1897), Mabel Stevenson (1902), Agnes Scott (1903), Marie Hayes (1905), Minna Bazeley (1908), Marcia Fishe (1909), Millicent Webb (1910), Helen Franklin (1913), Dorothy Scott (1914).

45. Pre-First World War European nursing staff arrived as follows: Mary Roberts (1895); Edith Field (1897); Sister Ansell (1901); Eva Roseveare and Agatha Allen (1904); Alice Wilkinson and Beatrice Ponzoni (1908); Mary Watts (1909); Wynifrede Bury (1912); Ida Thomas (1913); Eva Peters and Annie Buck (1914).

46. An orphan, she had been brought up first in St Stephen's Hospital (in Miss Engelmann's time) and then in the Mission's Christian Girls' Boarding School (renamed Victoria Girls' School in 1887). She took a shortened course at the Agra Medical College in the 1890s, leading to the lower qualification in medicine – Roseveare (1986), p. 61.

47. *Report DSP*, 1908, p. 83.

48. Muller, *Personal Reminiscences*, pp. 1–3.

10

⟡═◑═◑⟡

An archbishop for Greater Britain: Bishop Montgomery, missionary imperialism and the SPG, 1897–1915

STEVEN MAUGHAN

'These are great times and one feels the stir of an Imperial Christianity.' Thus did Henry Hutchinson Montgomery, Bishop of Tasmania, express his feelings to his friend and brother Bishop of Winchester, Randall Davidson, six days after the relief of Mafeking in the South African War.[1] Montgomery was voicing here a sentiment that resonated with the cresting wave of popular imperialism in the 1890s, that there was an organic connection between the religion of Britain and the success of its empire.

When appointed to the Secretaryship of the SPG fourteen months later, Montgomery determined he would use this connection to reorder High Church, and indeed all Anglican missions and make explicit the connection between English religion and imperial duty. Ultimately, this bid to weld Christianity and empire into a single popular programme failed, and Montgomery's efforts might be considered no more than a quixotic episode in the history of Anglicanism and popular imperialism. Closer inspection of Montgomery's career at the Society, however, illuminates several difficult problems in the history and interrelationship of Christian missions and the British Empire, particularly the dynamics that theology, party identity, local feeling and the imperatives of missions in the field brought to the complex process of constructing a viable missionary imperial programme.

Over the course of the nineteenth century, missionary societies became prominent among British imperial institutions, involving by the turn of the century over 9000 female and male missionaries, 60 missionary societies and roughly £2 million annually. Missionary presses accounted for a substantial outflow of 'missionary intelligence' on the empire and its 'regions beyond'. Yet, while SPG stood as the second largest missionary agency in Britain in terms of domestic charitable income, during Tucker's Secretaryship in the late-Victorian era it could not remotely match the vigorous growth and rising enthusiastic confidence of the CMS. There were 'grumbling and complaints as to the lack of spiritual fervour and enthusiasm in all connected with SPG as contrasted with CMS', while the marked failure of the bicentenary appeal, raising only one-fifth of its target amount, confirmed the position.[2] It was this perceived problem that H. H. Montgomery was recruited to address.

Despite his enthusiasm to construct an 'imperial Christianity', and the support he received from a cadre of enthusiastic younger clergy and the highest authorities in the Church, Montgomery failed to attain his most ambitious goals. While his work as Secretary was vigorously reforming in many respects, he was unable to move beyond simply renewing the Edwardian-era Society to achieving a sea change in missionary emphasis that would construct 'support of empire' as a fundamental motivation for action and Anglican corporate unity. Thus the case of the Society is especially instructive; while it was home to the most ardent missionary imperialists at the turn of the century, the disappointments suffered by Montgomery demonstrate that the equation between support of empire and support of missions was not an automatic one, and that the conversion of diffuse imperial enthusiasm into concrete action proved to be unexpectedly difficult. Montgomery and his followers discovered that the obstacles were not only the persisting divisiveness of theological and religious party issues, but also the contested nature of discourses on empire, nationality and race in missionary circles. In this atmosphere, the dream of constructing a unified Anglican 'Greater Britain' that was at the heart of Montgomery's ambitions dissipated in the face of conflicts over theology, church authority and religious identity.

⁘⟐⟐⁘

In the 1890s the CMS enjoyed particular success, adding hundreds of new missionaries and tens of thousands of pounds per year in contributions to its resources. These achievements, drawing heavily on 'holiness'-based revivalism, were important to spurring efforts at revitalization in SPG. Not all, of course, who recoiled from the evangelical CMS found a home in the Society, the UMCA in particular tending to attract the more extreme Anglo-Catholics, but it was something of a haven for moderate and non-partisan varieties of High Churchmanship. Many moderates, mostly High Church and Anglo-Catholic but also some traditional Low Churchmen, found good reason to maintain the older Society tradition of claiming to be above party by articulating a set of non-sectarian church principles.

Prior to the 1890s, Anglicans from the High and Low traditions had been bitter combatants. By the end of the century, however, damaging party strife had led to the evolution of powerful moderate parties in both camps and a growing desire within these to broker a reconciliation in the interests of church unity. At the centre of these developments were several English bishops, many of the younger clergy and a growing student missionary movement which advocated ecumenism and 'scientific' methods of missionary planning. The central organizations supporting this movement among Anglican students and younger clergy were the Society's activist Junior Clergy Missionary Association (JCMA), founded in 1891 with the encouragement of Henry Scott Holland and Bishop Temple of London, and the largely evangelical but increasingly ecumenical Student Volunteer Missionary Union (SVMU). The JCMA particularly held strong ideals of church unity, imperial engagement and enthusiastic activism, uncharacteristic emphases within the conventional 'high and dry' party the Society had strongly represented in the past. Because of this unconventional enthusiasm, and also the association of many of its leaders with Anglo-Catholicism, the JCMA was perceived by staff of the Society as challenging its traditional appeal, its deference to church hierarchy and its commitment to co-operation with the state. Over the course of the 1890s, the JCMA, with a supportive intervention by Bishop Montgomery of Tasmania in 1897, clashed repeatedly with the Society's traditionalist Secretary, Henry Tucker, and his colleagues.

Despite resistance from Tucker, the JCMA gained considerable influence with the bishops and Standing Committee by recruiting talented university graduates, revitalizing the Society's local organization and developing an increasingly coherent imperial vision of 'a Missionary Empire whose contribution to the world's progress shall be the making permanent those ideas of liberty, truth, justice and love, which we ourselves have learned from Christ', as its chairman, John Ellison, put it.[3] It carried its programme in the Society when, after the failure of the bicentenary appeal, a commission of bishops determined to appoint a new Secretary. The moderate High Churchman and imperial enthusiast Bishop Henry Montgomery was selected in 1901 by a committee of six English bishops, and given a mandate to 'remake' the Society.[4] His larger dream, however, was to reinvigorate the Church itself by directly linking the fortunes of Anglicanism with the British Empire. Through a missionary programme relying heavily on episcopal authority, Montgomery and his JCMA supporters hoped to broker a reconciliation between the parties of the Church while marshalling party energy, hitherto employed in fruitless bickering, against the religious doubts bred by the modern world. In pressing this vision of an imperial missionary Church, the 'progressives' in the Society sought to force a sweeping reconsideration of the role of the Church of England in the empire.

Educated at Harrow as a 'Broad Church Evangelical' and trained for ordination as a conservative High Churchman, Montgomery's diverse religious background encouraged him to strive for Anglican unity. Additionally, born in India to an influential East India Company official of the 'Punjab School' and strongly influenced by the environment of his first episcopal appointment, the white-settler colony of Tasmania, Montgomery developed an elevated view of British imperialism. With encouragement from the English bishops he saw the Secretaryship as an opportunity to transform the worldwide Anglican Communion. His imperial fervour came to maturity in the 1890s, when public support for imperial ideologies was at a historic high point.

Both the party of the liberal imperialists led by Lord Rosebery and the conservative Tariff Reformers under Joseph Chamberlain suggested that empire could help relieve the social problems of an urban industrialized England. Montgomery transferred these assumptions to the Church by arguing that missions could excite denominational unity, defuse party tensions at home and encourage the acceptance of the status quo in matters of church authority. He made these plans public with his book *Foreign Missions*, written on his England-bound steamer from Tasmania in 1901, including his conviction that 'the clergy are officers in an imperial army' who, when 'full of the Imperial spirit, not merely of the empire of England, but of something still greater, the empire of Christ', could remove the primary obstacles to missionary success, 'party spirit' and a 'want of missionary zeal'.[5] Fulsome imperial sentiments were common at this time, but they held a special significance coming from Montgomery because of the specific religious programme to which he attached them. He imagined himself an 'Archbishop of Greater Britain', with the 'dearest dream to make SPG the "centre of reconciliation"' in the Church.[6]

Montgomery's enthusiasm had marked him as a natural candidate for the Secretaryship, but by the time he was appointed in 1901 the new century had come to present unanticipated challenges. After the South African War the flood of missionary and imperial enthusiasm began to recede as attention shifted to the need for social improvements at home. Within the Church, the parties were confronted with the new religious challenges posed by theological modernism and declining levels of worship. Montgomery sought to meet these challenges by co-ordinating Society efforts with those of Anglican evangelicals and advocating an outspoken imperialism that linked missions and the formal empire in explicit and concrete ways. In this way he attempted to emulate the success of the CMS, replacing the evangelical enthusiasm for revivals and campaigns, repugnant to High Churchmen, with enthusiasm for the empire.

By 1905 Montgomery had reorganized the Society, paying special attention to the integration of women into the home organization. The Women's Missionary Association (WMA), founded in 1866 as the Ladies' Association, and renamed in 1895, had been treated cautiously hitherto as a supporting auxiliary operating entirely independently, but under Montgomery, it became the Committee for Women's Work and was given a degree of autonomy and influence that women at the CMS regarded with envy. Montgomery's reorganization led to increased income at a time when many missionary societies saw contributions static, and a strong perception of increased 'warmth' in the Society.[7] Under Montgomery, and with strong support from Randall Davidson, Archbishop of Canterbury from 1903, SPG began to usurp the reputation of the CMS, while his plans facilitated levels of Anglican collaboration that would have been unthinkable in the midst of the earlier ritualist controversies. Financial troubles at the CMS caused by its rapid overseas expansion in the 1890s influenced its leaders to emphasize their moderate loyal churchmanship as a strategy to consolidate the loyalties of 'respectable' Anglicans. Their moderation created a more favourable atmosphere for Montgomery's bid for Anglican leadership.

During this period, many churchmen, accustomed to thinking of colonies as a defence of nation, came to imagine foreign missions as a potential defence of the Church and vital to the Church of England's life and health. To prosper, the Church had to address questions of imperial scope. In a letter to Davidson in 1899, Montgomery had argued that a 'marriage of High & Low' was needful to absorb the enthusiasm of evangelicalism and redirect it to 'great social questions', which would benefit church projects at home as well as abroad.[8] Soon after becoming Secretary, he told Standing Committee,

> The expansion of SPG which is to be the new factor in this century is in a sense to revolutionize Church ideals and make the ancient Church of England more completely an Imperial Church – the unit being the world and not the United Kingdom.[9]

Success would mean that the Society 'might help to check the falling off in men in Holy Orders in England as well as supplying the world'.[10] Similarly, Eugene Stock at the CMS came to embrace more fully the idea of using missionary societies to ameliorate party strife. Montgomery's goal was the creation of a 'Pax Evangelica' in which the Society could re-establish its historic claim to be the truly non-sectarian representative of Anglican missions. Furthermore, in an atmosphere in which the increasing radicalism of extreme Anglo-Catholics was beginning to fragment such unity as had been achieved among High Churchmen following the Oxford Movement, Montgomery's imperial programme can be seen as an attempt to claim a broad Anglican middle ground opening between Anglo-Catholicism and 'holiness'-inspired Evangelicalism.

Montgomery was exceedingly talented in articulating an ideal of imperial co-operation that appealed to the enthusiasm of young High Churchmen. However, while he developed the ideal of 'imperial Christianity' and in the process revitalized the Society, his larger project to unify the Church through an appeal to the empire was less successful. In fact, very little materialized beyond his successful agitation for an international and comprehensive Pan-Anglican Congress in 1908. Montgomery wanted to direct the attention of a troubled home Church overseas, and thereby create an area of consensus. However, he had no means of compelling acceptance of his imperial rhetoric, especially in a Church that was home to historically antagonistic parties, and that had largely ceded independence to foreign bishops in their dioceses several decades earlier. One of the chief difficulties of Montgomery's scheme, which Davidson recognized from the beginning, was that a vision of church unity achieved through an engagement with empire was alarming to many in the Church who prized the independence which the historically broad Anglican Communion provided.

Within ten years, Montgomery's imperial missionary bid to unify the Church and infiltrate the empire had collapsed. There appear to be three major reasons for its failure. First, the old divisions between Evangelicals, Anglo-Catholics and 'rigid' High Churchmen flared up, despite their common abhorrence of liberal theological modernism. Second, the Anglican clergy remained preoccupied with domestic problems. Third, churchmen disagreed over the basis for a meaningful Christian imperial engagement. Montgomery's programme was launched with several practical steps: the Society was reorganized to embrace 'enthusiasm', the JCMA worked to attract clergy to service overseas and plans for the Pan-Anglican Congress were undertaken. From 1903 Archbishop Davidson aided the effort, emphasizing Lambeth Palace as a clearing house for worldwide episcopal correspondence and encouraging promising public-school boys 'to offer themselves as Missionaries in the Imperial work of the Church of England'.[11] Soon, however, circumstances conspired to undermine Montgomery's vision. Ultimately the failure lay in the limited power of foreign activity, itself contested on many levels, to overcome the religious anxieties of Edwardian Britain and displace the local concerns on which the social reality of English religiosity was based.

⸱⸱⸩═◉═⸨⸱⸱

One of the greatest obstacles to any programme for Anglican unity resulted from the stubborn persistence of party divisions. For generations competition and sectarian identity had been a primary factor in generating missionary support. Doubtful as Montgomery's original premiss was that missionary preoccupations could heal party rifts within the Church of England, even more doubtful was the idea that unity within the Church would increase levels of support for foreign missions. The experience of generations suggested instead that it was precisely competition and sectarian identity that most strongly animated supporters. If many Evangelicals were becoming more comfortable within the Church, and embraced the novel idea that the use of episcopal influence could strengthen Evangelicalism, the ever-closer relations between the CMS and SPG also reirritated old wounds originally inflicted in the battles over ritual. Strikingly, the chief opposition that arose to Montgomery's 'Archbishop of Greater Britain' rhetoric came not from anti–imperialists, but from three different religious quarters: from Evangelicals who claimed he had been 'appointed by a set of Ritualists to advocate Ritualism all round the world', from Anglo-Catholics who opposed any move perceived to increase the power of church authority above the level of the diocese and from exclusivist supporters of the Society themselves who resisted co-operation and association with Evangelicals and Nonconformists.[12]

The system of independent voluntary missionary societies persisted so strongly in England because of the paramount importance of theological and party alignments in forging religious identity. Davidson found that the situation required him to dampen the plans of enthusiasts who envisioned abolishing the societies to create a unified church missionary structure to serve a unitary empire. He wrote to one JCMA enthusiast,

> It must always be remembered that the real supporters of Missions in the Church of England have for generations past been mainly those who belong to the Evangelical School. Even now, for one High Church layman who is really aglow with belief in Foreign Missions, you have ten or twenty Evangelical laymen.

Trust Bishop Montgomery quietly to advance unity in church missions, Davidson advised, but respect the societies for their function of raising both interest and funds, while waiting in the knowledge that unified church missionary boards were the ultimate, if distant, goal.[13] Despite Montgomery's pleading, the more unbending of High Churchmen continued to accuse Evangelicals of fostering 'Pan-Protestantism', while Anglo-Catholics criticized them for hindering reunification with the Eastern Churches and Rome. The strong opposition of many in the Society to collaboration with Nonconformists was underlined by the attempt, ultimately unsuccessful, to prevent Montgomery and others representing the Society at the World Missionary Conference in Edinburgh in 1910.

Party identities also took on new meaning in the age of theological modernism. The burgeoning Student Volunteer movement was ironically involved in the re-emergence of party strife. Although it emphasized ecumenical co-operation, through its advocacy of 'scientific' missions it questioned both biblical infallibility and the emotionalism of 'holiness' based evangelicalism. These positions added fuel to the fires of controversy ignited by the advance of theological modernism. One of Montgomery's primary goals was to integrate as many 'advanced' students as possible and reconstruct the Society as modern, open and progressive. This meant taking an open and even adventurous approach to missionary problems. *The East and the West*, the Society's new 'issues and problems' publication, was launched to engage supporters with the concerns that drove the student missionary movement. Instead it brought the wrath of traditionalists upon the Society. Two articles in the journal's first issue, in October 1903, explored biblical criticism, the most theologically sensitive of subjects. The response was an immediate denunciation of the Society for promulgating 'sceptical theories'. Montgomery was forced to back down, and a public expression of regret 'settled' a matter of controversy that pitted 'the old and the young' against each other.[14] Older issues of party had been transformed by modernism. The youthful imperial enthusiasms of university-based Christians were essential to any Anglican imperial programme, yet the concerns of those same Christians to engage 'modern' subjects, both theological and imperial, were increasingly at odds with the anxieties felt by the deeply orthodox supporters of the missionary societies.

A second factor undermining Montgomery's programme was the continuing preoccupation of the majority of the clergy and bishops with the domestic problems of the Church. From the beginning, many doubted the realism of Montgomery's plans, including his own Commissary of thirteen years, who asked Archbishop Temple, 'Have you weighed up the exact value of my friend's high-sounding phrases, "Archbishop of the World of Missions", "Worldwide oversight"? Are they not a trifle inflated?'[15] He also hinted at a deeper problem, that

English clergy were unlikely to focus strongly on missions when the Church was facing important domestic challenges. This became rapidly evident to Davidson after 1903 when, as Archbishop of Canterbury, home problems were pressing, including the need to reconcile orthodox conservatives, both High and Low, to theological modernism, and the need to attract able people to the Church. These problems revived older criticisms that foreign missions drained much needed clerical resources from the home shores.

By 1905 Davidson and the bishops regarded the plans of 'imperial' Anglicans with increasing scepticism. When the JCMA requested from Davidson and individual bishops another 'authoritative' call for missionaries, Davidson resisted. He asked the leader of the JCMA to imagine what might happen if this call were issued:

> I wonder if you can yourself picture what would occur if I as Archbishop were to send, say, to the Bishop of Worcester, or Hereford, or Norwich, a definite request for, say 10 or 12 of his best younger men to be sent up within a year for me to despatch them over the world . . . Are the Colonial members of this committee to take into account or to disregard English needs and English conditions?[16]

As a pragmatic leader of a Church that was governed largely through consent and good will, Davidson was forced to question the grandiose imperial rhetoric of both the JCMA and Montgomery and to recognize the fundamentally local nature of religious experience in England. In a broad English Church concerned first and foremost with local affairs, the prosecution of foreign missions had to operate by persuasion rather than compulsion. Regardless of the expansive rhetoric of the JCMA and Montgomery, the attention of the English bishops, who largely controlled the training and assignments of the clergy, was never deeply engaged with an imperial missionary programme. Montgomery's arrival at the Society and his prosecution of a self-important programme for the Society did not change this.

The problem of how precisely to define the nature of imperial missionary engagement, in the face of both conflict in British politics and the rise of colonial nationalisms, provided the third and final straw that broke Montgomery's programme. Increasingly the question of the nature of the British Empire was becoming a topic for debate and division in the missionary world. The student movement embodied in the SVMU was implicated in this through criticisms made by some of its prominent leaders of British imperial practice, while Montgomery and the Society encountered the new attitudes very directly in the person of a one-time JCMA member, their own Delhi missionary, C. F. Andrews.

The student world's criticisms of the cold, formal, distant imperial policy of colonial rulers, as well as their emphasis on the need for 'a Christianized world with a juster and nobler order of society', were seen as dangerously naïve to more strident imperialists at the JCMA and the older stalwarts of the Society.[17] Imperial sympathizers instead emphasized the 'responsibilities' of empire and the 'backward' nature of colonial subjects. Firmness and morality at home were paralleled by the assertion that firmness and Christianity were the backbone of imperial rule and missionary activity. These were the notes most commonly sounded in the volume published in preparation for the Pan-Anglican Congress of 1908, *Church and Empire: A Series of Essays on the Responsibilities of Empire.*[18]

The Congress, embodying Montgomery's scheme to draw the entire Church together to face its challenges corporately, only reinforced the problems of securing church unity under the banner of empire. The Pan-Anglican Congress was the 'special "child"' which Montgomery had advocated in a sermon preached before the Society in St Paul's on taking up the Secretaryship. As Eugene Stock openly acknowledged, however, a Congress which was originally conceived to advance foreign missions came to focus primarily on the internal order of the communion and the home problems of the Church.[19] After the Congress, Montgomery could no longer ignore the fact that imperial rhetoric, which roused gatherings at the JCMA, was more difficult to sell as relevant to solving the diverse problems of the entire Communion.

Furthermore, given emergent colonial nationalisms, the rhetoric of an imperial Church produced problems of definition in the colonies and positive hostility in India. In 1904 Davidson had refused to provide official church endorsement to the celebration of Empire Day because, while in parts of Australia and Canada it had rapidly become a popular public holiday, in India and other territories less heavily influenced by English settlement Anglican bishops perceived its celebration as positively detrimental to the interests of the Church. The former Delhi missionary, G. A. Lefroy, now Bishop of Lahore, warned in his *Church and Empire* essay that educated Indians found 'the very word and thought of Imperialism . . . in the highest degree obnoxious', and 'resented bitterly the claim of racial superiority' and 'coldness' in English manners.[20] In this respect, a clear weakness in Montgomery's position was its openly racist basis. While encouraging 'sympathy' toward other races, he insisted upon each race occupying 'the place reserved from the beginning for it', with a clearly subordinate position for all outside the 'Anglo-Saxon' race.[21]

Capitalizing thus on notions of race allowed Montgomery to shape his distinctive rationale for church unity. For, while he imagined the 'imperial Church' to be an expression of Christian unity through worldwide Anglicanism, he also imagined this union to be racially divided. Anglicanism could embrace many races, but could be led by only one. Once the 'Church of the race', the Church of England, was educated to the essential reality of its Anglo-Saxon racial unity, internal divisions could be vanquished and the Church could fully embrace its destiny to lead. Furthermore, division within the world Anglican Communion could be diffused by a patronizing tolerance of racial difference on the part of the Church's 'natural' leaders. Awareness of racial hierarchy, then, formed the basis of an understanding that could unify the Church, strengthen the empire and brace the loyalty of its subjects.

This open theorizing about the fixity of race and the hierarchy of functions that it set for the various Anglican 'racial' Churches of the world, not unusual theorizing at this time, was Montgomery's choice as an ideological underpinning for his imperial programme for Anglicanism. Rapid changes in the mission field, however, ensured that Montgomery's programme would suit neither indigenous Christians, whose legitimacy in places like India was contested by nationalists, and missionaries in the field who, like G. A. Lefroy, preferred, as wiser, missionary ideologies that would not unnecessarily antagonize the ethnic, racial or national identities encountered.

⋅⊶⩴◉⩴⊷⋅

Bishop Montgomery's imperial vision was attractive to many when he first shared it with the JCMA in 1897, but it had grown out of Australian conditions. His primary assumption was that the reflexive support of empire characteristic of Australian Anglicans could be easily extended throughout England and the empire. As the debate over what sort of empire the British should have unfolded in the Edwardian period, Montgomery advanced an ideal of imperial federation in which colonies would be tied with the bonds of Anglican spiritual loyalty to the mother country. But Montgomery miscalculated the appeal of this because of his misperception, in part as a colonial, that Britain could operate as a powerful metropolitan engine of empire if only its people could be educated to their duty. This misperception was reinforced in the Society, with its exceptionally high involvement in areas dominated by settler populations. These elements combined to support an imperial vision tending to concentrate on common cultural, national and racial identity.

Following the Pan-Anglican Congress, Montgomery stopped pressing for an 'imperial Church'. By 1910 the obvious course open to Anglican missionary societies was to attempt to reclaim older Victorian strategies that had gathered support in the past. Hopes that Anglican unity would be achieved through the student movements, ecumenical co-operation and imperial progress were thwarted by university heterodoxy, re-emerging party factionalism and discomfiture with contending imperial models. While the core ideologies of the Victorian Anglican missionary movement continued to have a force and resilience through the Edwardian period, delivering stability in income and even modest growth, the bid to unify foreign missions in the shape of heroic imperial Anglicanism had failed.

In June 1915 Montgomery gave a revealing address to the home workers of the Society at the Summer School in Eastbourne. The Anglo-Saxons, Montgomery explained, were an impatient race from a temperate climate advancing through the lethargic tropics. As they progressed they were constantly diverted by internecine squabbles, being a people ruthlessly critical of themselves as well as others. This critical British nature expressed itself nowhere more virulently than in the most important project the race was undertaking, the planting of Churches in every land. While Montgomery had not abandoned his imperial and racial paradigms for explaining missions, he had reversed his stand on imperial church unity, suggesting instead that restless, critical, individualistic chauvinism was at the heart of British strength.

The shift in course was undoubtedly influenced by the Anglican infighting that resulted from the 1913 Kikuyu Controversy. The partisan rhetoric unleashed by Kikuyu helped to re-establish the importance for the Society of maintaining an identifiable and distinctive religious identity. Openness to Protestant ecumenism was increasingly incompatible with holding the allegiance of the Society's Anglo-Catholic constituency. With this last pre-war controversy, Montgomery's hope of building church unity through imperial enthusiasm was finally and irrevocably dashed. Imperial ideas were useful when general and amorphous, but could not bear the weight of a concrete programme because, just as Victorian Christians could not agree on dogma, they could not agree on what 'imperial Christianity' should entail. The attempt to co-opt the diversities of the missionary movement for pan-Anglican purposes after 1900, instead, generated more sectarian feeling and activity within the Church, returning the movement to its Victorian footing on the eve of the great social and theological changes that would emerge after the First World War.

Dr Steven Maughan is Associate Professor of History at Albertson College of Idaho, USA. He has published a number of articles on foreign missions and British culture, and is currently preparing for publication *Greater Britain and the National Church: Culture, Faith and Imperialism in the Missionary Project of the Church of England, 1870–1914.*

Notes

A longer version of this essay, with a broader focus, is to appear in A. Porter (ed.) *Imperial Horizons of British Protestant Missions 1880–1914*, Curzon/Eerdmans, due 2000/2001.

1. Montgomery to Davidson, 24 May 1900, Lambeth Palace Library, Randall Thomas Davidson Papers [DP].
2. Circular letter of Bishop of Qu'Appelle to members of Standing Committee *c.* July 1894, Lambeth Palace Library, Edward White Benson Papers.
3. [Speech of 11 May 1898, X 540].
4. Montgomery to Davidson, 4 Oct. and 13 Dec. 1901 [DP].
5. H. H. Montgomery (1902) *Foreign Missions*, London, pp. 1–2, 110, 145.
6. Montgomery to Davidson, 27 May and 21 July 1901 [DP].
7. [H. H. Montgomery typescript, 'Survey of my stewardship, 1902–1918', H. 3].
8. Montgomery to Davidson, 12 July 1899 [DP].
9. Montgomery to Standing Committee, 17 Aug. 1901 [DP].
10. Montgomery to Davidson, 13 Dec. 1901 [DP].
11. M. M. Montgomery (1933) *Bishop Montgomery: A Memoir*, London, p. 53.
12. Montgomery to Davidson, 21 Aug., 8 Sept. and 4 Oct. 1901 [DP].
13. Davidson to A. W. Bedford, 15 Oct. 1901 [DP].
14. *Church Times*, 18 Nov. 1904; Montgomery to Davidson, 3 Nov. 1904 [DP]; [Circular letter, 15 Dec. 1904, H.37].
15. F. D. Cremer to F. Temple, 10 July 1901, Lambeth Palace Library, Frederick Temple Papers.
16. Davidson to J. Ellison, 17 Oct. 1905 [DP].
17. Dr Cairns, quoted in T. Tatlow (1933) *The Story of the Student Christian Movement*, London, p. 250.
18. J. Ellison and G. H. S. Walpole, (eds) (1908), London.
19. E. Stock (1916) *History of the CMS*, London, Vol. 4, p. 549.
20. J. Ellison and G. H. S. Walpole (eds) (1908), pp. 66–8.
21. Introduction to H. H. Montgomery (ed.) (1907) *Mankind and the Church*, London, p. xii.

I I

Arthur Shearly Cripps

MURRAY STEELE

At first sight he was a typical colonial missionary of the first half of the twentieth century. He came from a traditionally conservative upper middle-class Home Counties family and like the founder of the colony where he spent most of his life, Cecil Rhodes, he was a product of that greenhouse of late Victorian imperialism, Oxford University. Extant photographs and descriptions seemingly confirm first impressions: a tall, khaki-clad, athletic figure, an embodiment of the muscular Christianity that formed the spiritual counterpart to the brawn of empire. But outward appearances deceive. Arthur Shearly Cripps (1869–1952) was a most unusual missionary: a rebel against authority, ecclesiastical and temporal; an exposer and relentless critic of imperial cant and humbug; a prophetic voice; a poet who could write bitingly satirical, as well as lyrically pastoral, verse; a champion of the weak and oppressed; a missionary who, as Adrian Hastings has succinctly put it, went out to teach but remained to learn; a priest who lived a life of strict self-denial, gave his substance to the poor and, above all, identified with the black people he lived amongst.[1] Cripps' calling to Africa and its people was the result of two formative experiences.

First, the influence of Charles Gore, Scott Holland and 'Jimmy' Adderley, which brought him into the Christian Social Union. Undergraduate visits to the Trinity Mission in London's East End provided a practical element, further deepening his social as well as spiritual awareness, resulting in an early decision to enter the Church. It was during this time his lifelong conviction developed that upper-class priests who chose to live in comfort had no business to be preaching to ordinary people that they should have no thought for the morrow. As a corollary to this, he resolved to remain celibate: as he told his brother much later, he felt that marriage got in the way of a priest's pastoral responsibilities. His identification with the poor is expressed vividly in the collection of poems published on his departure from Britain in 1900, *Titania and Other Poems*, which reflect his experiences of life in the East End and in rural Essex, where he had served as a vicar from 1894.

Second, there was the revelation of Olive Schreiner's political fable *Trooper Peter Halket of Mashonaland* (1897) with its frontispiece (suppressed in subsequent editions), a photograph of Africans hanged as suspected spies by the administration of the British South Africa Company ('the Chartered Company') during the 1896 Matabele Rebellion. Schreiner's literary method was to have a strong influence on his output, although she wrote from the standpoint of an agnostic.

Thus, Cripps arrived in Africa with an inherent sympathy for the underprivileged, a deep suspicion of Rhodes' 'civilizing' enterprise in Southern Rhodesia and a readiness to condemn hypocrisy. As early as 1904, he was to write to his sister:

> Don't for Heaven's sake believe all the claptrap about the misery and horror of Mashona paganism you may hear from one or other of our missionaries: there are many things in Mashona paganism that are a glory and an honour to the Light That lighteth every man that cometh into the world. The economic cry of pseudo-necessity for breaking up the old Arcadian life in the interests of white men's industries has surely much to do with the slanders.[2]

The most striking expression of these anti–imperialist views may be found in another early document, Cripps' remarkable verse play *The Black Christ* (1902), where British imperialism is presented as an Antichrist figure in a nightmarish vision of the Last Judgement and the Crucifixion:

> I see a hooded Fiend in judgment set
> Red, white and blue the flappings of His hood,
> Beckoning the rich with one obsequious Hand
> With the other warning off the sad dark faces
> . . . On Thy Cross's Arms
> I see a leering laughing Thing astride,
> Its cruel thin thirsty Lips they sponge with blood,
> About its Loins a flag of Empire gay.[3]

To the end of his life, Cripps sustained his relentless battle against the exploitation and maladministration of Africans by the Chartered Company; and, after 1923, by successor Southern Rhodesian settler governments. He conducted an extensive correspondence with a wide circle of friends from Oxford days, many in positions of influence, supplemented by contacts of later provenance with pressure groups such as the Anti-Slavery and Aborigines' Protection Society and, after 1940, the Fabian Colonial Bureau.[4] The essentially lyric character of his poetry gave place to the harsher tones of satirical political verse, of no great quality though not quite descending to the depth of 'creaking political philippic' as that conservative historian of colonial Rhodesia, L. H. Gann, has termed it.[5]

His campaigns had one common ingredient, a dislike of any form of compulsion. This included compulsion by direct methods – forcing people to work for private employers, or for the government on rural roads and other public works, obliging herdsmen to sell 'surplus' cattle, allegedly to preserve grazing areas, and to 'improve' their agricultural methods along 'scientific' lines. He also opposed indirect compulsion by such means as raising the level of taxation, or taking or threatening to take land away from so-called Native Reserves, thus forcing men out to seek employment. Cripps employed a variety of means to denounce administrative oppression and malpractice: apart from pleas to overseas sympathizers and pressure groups, he wrote letters to the press in colonial Zimbabwe and Great Britain, poems of the type already illustrated and pamphlets. His 1936 tract, *How Roads Were Made in the Native Reserves of Charter District* . . ., outlined the methods, some in breach of international law, utilized to get local people to make roads that were in reality for the benefit of Native Department and other white officials rather than local people. With not a little justice, he had earlier remarked to his brother William that Southern Africa was greatly in need of 'legal' missionaries to defend the rights of black people.

Meanwhile he had enthusiastically greeted the first tentative efforts of black Zimbabweans to organize themselves politically. He made contact with Clements Kadalie, leader of the Industrial and Commercial Workers' Union in South Africa, and with the local branch of the Union set up on an independent basis from the parent body in 1930. During the Second World War, he corresponded with and encouraged many of the new black leaders who emerged. He also gave strong support to the first multiracial political organization, the Southern Rhodesia Labour Party, though blindness from late 1940 onwards severely restricted his activities. By this stage, his identification with the black majority had become complete: 'I have come to realise what it feels like to be an African in Southern Rhodesia.'[6]

In his lifetime, however, his various political campaigns achieved little for those he championed. His one major 'success', the Administration's decision not to take land from the Sabi Reserve for the projected

Mvuma-Odzi rail-link, in fact seems to have been determined by the post-First World War depression, and not by pressure from Cripps and his allies. His significance as a political activist lies rather in his prescience, his skill at reading signs and anticipating how later generations would respond. Thus in 1935 he saw Mussolini's Abyssinian aggression as playing a role in Africa's future history analogous to that of the Russo-Japanese War of 1905 in Asia's. And as early as 1912, he foresaw a future in which the Shona 'rebels' killed by Rhodes' troopers in the 1896 Rising would be seen as heroes and patriots:

> Here on this hill did many patriots die –
>   Looking a wide last look on land and sky.
> Hark! Was it only that a wind went by?
>   Or was it some strained bough or night-beast shy?
>
> Or was it haply – ? Nay, I know not, I.
> Here where we stand, an altar-stone is nigh
> And souls or saints will under altars sigh, –
> Blood, too, at whiles will cry.[7]

Similarly, he took issue with the common belief that the pre-colonial Great Zimbabwe complex could not possibly have been built by 'backward' Africans and must be the work of Arab or Indian master builders:

> About the quiet graves we fill
>   Blind moles of strangers delve and pry,
> And they that work our children ill
>   To us their sires our walls deny, –
> 'Would artless men so nobly will?'
>   'Would low men leap to task so high?'
>
> What name of Ind or Araby
>   They take in vain, it matters not . . .
> Through all the world His Wind is free
>   To blow at will man's embers hot:
> In colour-blind perversity
>   He gave to us His Vision's glee, –
> Vision our children have forgot,
>   Visions our children yet may see.[8]

Since his death in 1952, events have borne out his prescience: archaeological research has confirmed his belief that Great Zimbabwe was an African achievement, and the leaders of the Shona Revolts in 1896–7 have been hailed as forerunners of the 1970s' liberation war leading to the creation of independent Zimbabwe. However, in the last months of his life, he was to welcome the first major stride of black Africa towards freedom, the grant of internal self-government to the Gold Coast, later Ghana.

His struggle with church bureaucracy was at times almost as fierce as his battle with the temporal power. A perusal of the SPG archives uncovers his unwillingness to respond to authority's request for routine reports and statistics, a shortcoming the diocese and Society seem to have accepted with weary resignation: it is thus impossible to make any quantitative assessment of his pastoral work, although those in charge of women's work at his mission seem to have reported on it at times. Symbolically, he never accepted the diocese's essentially political decision in 1915 to adopt the name 'Southern Rhodesia', and to the end Cripps observed the former usage in correspondence, describing himself as a 'Missionary in Mashonaland' to disassociate himself from the colony's 'Founder'. He was similarly unhappy about the way the Church had become dependent upon the colonial state for the provision of mission school education. Shortly after an administration had been set up, the Chartered Company had introduced the South African system of providing grants-in-aid to mission schools, but these were conditional upon the provision of regular European supervision, satisfactory reports from government inspectors and a satisfactory level of pupil attendance. Cripps objected to the compulsion implicit in this latter requirement, and in more general terms to the way in which he felt that, by accepting finance from the state, the Church was implicitly accepting its authority, and so would be less inclined to query those policies towards Africans which it would otherwise condemn. Accordingly, he refused to accept grants-in-aid for his mission school, although financial hardship, and presumably the pleas of local black Christians, forced him to compromise in the years just prior to his death, and to introduce a scheme managed by local European friends.[9] His views on such issues were shared by several Anglican and Roman Catholic priests between the Wars, but no one expressed them more vehemently than Cripps.

Also, within the government of the Church itself, he was highly critical of Synod's differential treatment of white and black Christians, and condemned the decision, implemented after the First World War, to impose an annual assessment, the *rutsigiro*, on black, but not white church members, and to deny the sacraments to those who failed to pay. Leonard Mamvura, who helped him during his years of blindness, has quoted Cripps' characterization of the *rutsigiro* and the state's Native Tax as 'two white calves sucking on a black cow'.[10] His disillusionment with diocesan practices culminated in his surrendering the bishop's licence in

1926, and, because SPG supported diocesan practice on grants-in-aid, severing his connection with the Society after 26 years. After a four-year stay in Britain, during which he became increasingly homesick for Africa, he returned to operate as an independent missionary, a 'Clerk in Holy Orders in Mashonaland'. Ironically, the bishop concerned, Edward Paget – with whom it should be said Cripps retained warm personal relations – took the local Church a good distance down the road towards racial equality during his long episcopate.[11] However, just prior to his departure for England, Cripps had condemned the bishop's 'modern' methods of mission administration in a poem that deserves extended quotation, 'Missionaries of a New Age':

> How many sheepfolds here are shut and lost
> In hope to save a few poor pence at most!
> How many pounds these new flock-masters cost!
>
> These tend an office rather than a fold,
> So rotting sheep-pens strew the brooding wold.
>
> Gloating o'er schedule-drafts and typescript reams
> These scorn the poverty of pastoral dreams
>
> These, stinting pasture for a sheep to browse,
> Build or rebuild to please a shepherd's spouse.
>
> Busied with engines, oil and cars' upkeep –
> What time have these to track one straying sheep?
>
> How little heed they – these so overwrought
> With shearing flocks – to feed one sheep Christ bought!
>
> Haply old names anew He confers: –
> 'These be no shepherds, but sheep-traffickers,
> Hirelings, thieves, robbers, fleece-wrapt raveners!'[12]

His reference to the use of motor transport for missionary work underlines a characteristic feature of Cripps' African ministry, his practice of walking often vast distances to visit as well as to take services.

The name of Arthur Shearly Cripps in modern Zimbabwe has become indissolubly linked with the place to which he returned in 1930, his mission at Maronda Mashanu 'the Five Wounds [of Christ]', located a short distance from the modern town of Chivhu, formerly Enkeldoorn. At the focal point, beneath a hill that may be said to represent the 'Acropolis' at Great Zimbabwe, he built his church, modelled not on the usual Gothic pattern of so many early mission churches, but incorporating some of the features of the Great Enclosure (the 'Temple') at Zimbabwe, and supported by five pillars representing the Five Wounds of Christ. The Mission itself was located on three farms totalling about 7500 acres, purchased with funds left by his mother shortly before the First World War. To these farms came local Africans, some driven off adjacent European-owned land, some escaping the exactions of land companies and their managers and some, like Cyprian Tambo, later to be ordained priest, who were originally labour migrants from elsewhere in the colony. Cripps allowed them to stay at Maronda Mashanu without obligation, requiring neither payment in cash nor in kind, nor compulsory church and school attendance, conditions imposed by mission superintendents elsewhere. John Doyle Jr, the author of the most substantial critical appreciation of his literary work, has described his mission as 'one of the most remarkable experiments of the twentieth century'.[13] Perhaps inevitably this open-handedness was regarded by many of his white contemporaries as evidence of an innate naïve credulity and an inability to distinguish between the deserving and undeserving. But in fact Cripps was made of sterner stuff than this: between the wars he was regularly punishing moral lapses in his Christian flock for sexual impropriety, expecting the guilty to make a public penance, following the practice of the English Church a century earlier. In one case that came to the notice of the colony's Native Department, he gave a man notice to quit when he said he proposed to divorce his wife, whom he had married in church, because she had taken up prostitution in the colony's capital. We are reminded again of the fact that saints are not always very tolerant people.

For much of his ministry in Zimbabwe, and especially during the last two decades of his life, between 1930 and 1952, when he worked as an independent missionary, Arthur Cripps was seen by his contemporaries as a 'loner', an isolated and increasingly eccentric figure who had deliberately turned his back on the modern, 'civilized' world and retreated into some kind of unreal and incongruous medieval Arcadianism. Evidence may certainly be found to substantiate this view. Much of his early verse and prose work reflects his admiration both for the pre-Reformation (and pre-capitalist) age of late fifteenth-century England, and for a rather idealized vision of Mashonaland, where 'Daphnis and Menalcas stray; And reap and fold and sing and love', and where young men work with cheerful effort to earn the marriage cattle they need to satisfy prospective fathers-in-law.[14] His rather idiosyncratic — and, for some authors, quite inexcusable — espousal of the racial segregation of land ownership in 1927 in his book *An Africa for Africans*, at a time when other so-called 'liberal segregationists' were abandoning their earlier advocacy, was in truth an attempt to protect Africans and African families against white land rapacity, and the socially corrosive vices of urban areas.[15] A careful reading of *An Africa for Africans*, with its condemnation of white capitalist greed, especially in the fourth chapter, 'Land-Lust', will anyway disabuse anyone who believes that Cripps was just another segregationist. And in time, having seen the manifestation of black immiseration that lay at the heart of the official segregationist policy, he recanted of this view.

His self-imposed exile from 'civilization' enabled him to enter fully into the universe of the underprivileged and dispossessed, and to see in it the immanence of God and the Black Christ, a presence that is expressed in the poem that most succinctly summarizes his faith, and furnished with a title that contains a typical Crippsian litotes, 'Seen Darkly in Africa':

> To me – as one born out of his due time –
> Christ hath revealed Himself – not as to Paul
> Enthroned and crowned, and marred, despised, rejected –
>
> The Divine Outcast of a terrible land,
> A Black Christ with parched Lips and empty Hand.[16]

The Black Christ is a constant companion in his literary output, a descendant of the unidentified 'Stranger' in Olive Schreiner's *Trooper Peter Halket* and an antecedent to the Christ of modern Black Theology. He is the Christ who suffers, who shares in and with the experiences of the hungry, the homeless, the oppressed, who walked abroad in Mashonaland and stretched out to the poet his 'Nail-grooved, hoe-hardened Palms'.[17] In the same way, the continent of Africa, taken by strangers who have imprisoned its rightful owners, is 'God's own Country', destined to be crowned by the King of Heaven as his Queen.[18] The master–servant relationship these strangers have enforced on its people is likened to that between Dives and Lazarus, while Cripps does not shirk from pointing to the moral of that particular parable:

> O dark, meek Mephistopheles,
> Safe in your hand a soul you hold:
> Th'inevitable end he sees
> No more than Dives saw of old.[19]

His service as chaplain in the 1914–18 East Africa campaign seems to have played a major role in deepening his empathy with African suffering. Over a period of eighteen months he witnessed the privations

of the black Carrier Corps, caught up in a white man's civil war that
ravaged large parts of their continent. It was an experience that moved
him to write his saddest and bitterest poem, 'The Dirge of Dead Porters',

> Who reaps the guerdon of their footsore pain,
> Of flies', and suns', fevers' and fluxes' drain?
> England – that must be snatching ere her time
> Fruit like to drop? Heroes – a few that climb
> On these poor bodies' waste, and crow their day
> As cocks on dung-hills thron'd?
>   No, rather say
> The gain's their own. For are they not away
> From Africa – the home that's no more home
> To her own children? God, Thy Kingdom come:
> Grant these to find Thy Mercy in that Day![20]

In his somewhat underrated volume of war poetry, *Lake and War . . .*,
he rightly predicted that despite contemporary propaganda about German
colonial 'frightfulness', once peace was restored, the 'colour bond'
between white nations would lead to the creation of a more rigid colour
bar.

Cripps' identification with Africa and Africans led him to employ the
local black idiom to express his Christian faith. While he was not unique
– recent research has shown that many white missionaries in the early
twentieth century had realized that God had not depended on the
proselytizing efforts of their predecessors to manifest himself to pre-
Christian societies – he must be counted amongst its most prominent
advocates.[21] His Zimbabwe-type church at Maronda Mashanu has already
been mentioned. In his retelling of the Chaminuka story for African
schools, he uses the significant subtitle 'The Man Whom God Taught'
to describe Chaminuka, the Shona folk hero killed by Ndebele soldiers a
few years before the colonial occupation. His ability to work miracles is
one conferred by a God who is indubitably the God of the Bible. He
could make rain, an important attribute of Shona mediums like Chaminuka, but he had been taught by God how to do this. His final act
before going out to confront the Ndebele was to peg out an oxhide on
to a solid granite rock with wooden pegs, using the skills conferred by
'the Power that was with him'. His powers were so great and so
commanding that he could not be killed by the Ndebele, but only – and
at his suggestion – by an innocent child.[22] In Cripps' less well-known
retelling of the martyrdom of Perpetua and Felicity in third century
Carthage, he emphasized their Africanness, and presented Felicity as a

black woman willing to share in the martyrdom of her mistress. Reference is made to the Uganda martyrs, together with comments about Roman imperialism, with a contemporary allusion:

> One might have argued that, in nation after nation, Rome had crushed a native art and culture, and put in its place a very dull and mechanical civilization, with little life, or beauty, or power of growth; that it took the heart out of local religions, and put in their place a dead official ceremonial. But such arguments would have been met with an incredulous smile, as similar arguments are met nowadays.[23]

However, it is unlikely that Cripps' future reputation will lie in his literary work, which is now difficult to get hold of in Britain and has been reprinted only to a limited extent in Zimbabwe. The abiding memory is that of *Baba Chapepa*, 'He who cares for people', who lived a life of self-denial in an ordinary African thatched hut and gave away the very clothes on his back to those in need. It is a memory renewed in an annual festival of commemoration held over the first weekend of August at his church, recently restored by the local community, and attended by Christians with Maronda Mashanu connections from all over Zimbabwe. Local people still tell stories about him, including many testifying to his success in praying for rain in times of drought: there is a written record confirming his success on one occasion at least, though typically Cripps did not allude to this when telling his brother that the drought had been broken at last. However, the abiding spiritual legacy of Arthur Shearly Cripps rests in and with the community of black Christian farmers he created at Maronda Mashanu, and which continues to flourish at the time of writing under the pastoral leadership of his devoted helper, Leonard Mamvura.

⊷⊷◉⊷⊷

Dr Murray Steele was based at the University of Zimbabwe in the early 1970s, when he got to know Maronda Mashanu. He has written several articles on Cripps and his community. Until retirement, he was Head of Afro-Asian Studies at Edge Hill College of Higher Education, Ormskirk, in England.

Notes

My thanks go to the staff of Rhodes House, Oxford, the British Library, the National Library of Scotland and the National Archives of Zimbabwe; also to the USPG, University of Zimbabwe and Edge Hill College of Higher Education for supporting this research; and amongst many individuals who have helped, Leonard Mamvura, Terry Ranger and George Shepperson, who first introduced me to Cripps over 30 years ago.

1. The chief biography is Steere (1973).
2. [A. S. Cripps to Edith Cripps, 23 Feb. 1904, X.630, Box 1].
3. From excerpt in A. S. Cripps (1939) *Africa: Verses*, London, p. 54. This collection contains the best of his poetry over 50 years.
4. In addition to Steere (1973), see Steele (1975), pp. 152–74.
5. Gann (1965), p. 310.
6. 'Is our Colour Bar to cross the Zambezi', 4 Feb. 1942, published as a pamphlet by the author, Enkeldoorn, 1942.
7. A. S. Cripps (1912) *Pilgrimage of Grace: Verses on a Mission*, Oxford, p. 11.
8. A. S. Cripps (1916) *Pilgrim's Joy: Verses*, Oxford, p. 21.
9. Thus Mary Prior, Cripps' WMA worker, 'Mr. Cripps objects for conscience reasons' [Report, Dec. 1911, E.66b (1911)].
10. L. Mamvura to author, 22 Jan. 1973.
11. See the rather understated biography, Gibbon (1973).
12. *Africa: Verses*, pp. 90–1. For Paget's methods, see [letter to the Society's Overseas Secretary 5 Mar. 1926, CLR 142 Mashonaland].
13. Doyle (1975), p. 75.
14. *Ibid.*, p. 31.
15. London, 1927.
16. *Africa: Verses*, p. 52.
17. A. S. Cripps (1917) *Lake and War: African Land and Water Verses*, Oxford, p. 119.
18. *Africa: Verses*, p. 47.
19. *Ibid.*, p. 58.
20. *Lake and War*, p. 73.
21. e.g., Gray (1990), especially p. 84.
22. A. S. Cripps (1928) *Chaminuka: The Man whom God Taught*, London. For the significance of Chaminuka to black Christians more recently, see Ranger (1982).
23. A. S. Cripps (1928) *Saint Perpetua: Martyr of Africa*, London, p. 7.

12

⵹⵺⵻

'Ethiopia shall soon stretch out her hands to God': the Order of Ethiopia and the Church of the Province of Southern Africa, 1899–1999

MANDY M. GOEDHALS

In 1899, James Mata Dwane, in a quest for valid orders and autonomy for the Ethiopian Church, approached the Anglican bishops, a process which led to the formation of the Order of Ethiopia within the Church of the Province of South Africa. In 1999, the Provincial Synod of the Church of the Province, now Southern Africa, passed a resolution put forward by his grandson, Sigqibo Dwane, Bishop of the Order of Ethiopia, which recognized that 'the Order has now developed to the position of having its own Episcopal leadership and seeks the realisation of its original desire to be a church which is in full communion with the CPSA'.[1] The synod agreed that a new relationship between the CPSA and the Order of Ethiopia should be explored: it had taken a century for the CPSA to recognize the relationship with the Ethiopians which James Mata Dwane had envisaged in 1899.

Ethiopianism

Ethiopianism is an expression of Christianity rooted in Africa, part of the rich indigenous contribution to the Catholic faith. The nature of the nineteenth-century Christian mission from Europe to Africa was the painful spur which produced the desire for Christianity in an African idiom. European missionaries regarded their work as one of many positive by-products of imperial rule, and had little insight into the alienation caused by colonialism, loss of political independence and lands, poverty and demands for waged labour, together with the imposition of

382

Western cultural norms. Missionaries regarded Western culture as infinitely superior to African, and as integral to the Gospel, and showed little appreciation of African heritage or of the effect of their rejection of African culture.[2]

In its religious and cultural dimension, Ethiopianism involves the search for an authentic African Christianity, and an assertion of the legitimacy of African culture. Ethiopianism has been described as embracing the totality of African experience.[3] Just as in traditional African society, religion and politics are integrated, so Ethiopianism also contains a nationalist element, not necessarily expressed as direct political involvement, but as a concern for African rights, and encouragement of African self-reliance and dignity. Growth of Ethiopian Churches is often associated with a charismatic leader, whose own painful encounter with missionary failure to practise the Gospel they preached, usually through experience of racial prejudice and denial of leadership opportunities, precipitated the establishment of an indigenous Church. Ethiopianism also grew at a time when economic and political opportunities for Africans in the secular world were shrinking.

In 1884, a Wesleyan minister, Nehemiah Tile, established the Thembu Church in which loyalty was given to the Thembu paramount Ngangelizwe, rather than to Queen Victoria. Although this was a regional development, it was a formative influence on Ethiopianism and the Order of Ethiopia. From the 1880s, mineral discoveries drew Africans to the Witwatersrand from all over southern Africa, and common experience contributed to the creation of a national identity. In this context, Ethiopianism emerged, when another Wesleyan minister, Mangena Mokone, resigned in disgust at discrimination he encountered at a church conference in Pretoria, and shortly afterwards established the Ethiopian Church in Johannesburg in 1892.[4] The Church expressed what its African members regarded as important: Wesleyan class meetings, lay preaching and extempore prayer were retained, but priority was given to African responsibility and leadership. James Mata Dwane joined this body in 1896.

Born of a chiefly family in the eastern Cape in 1848, Dwane had begun to attend Wesleyan services in about 1858. He was brought up in the household of a Wesleyan missionary, Robert Lamplough, baptized in 1867 and made a lay preacher. Dwane's enrolment and success in the Fort Beaufort state-supported school sparked objections from white parents and he was removed to the mission college at Healdtown for teacher training. He was ordained in 1881, and served in various eastern Cape circuits. The Wesleyans made great use of African agents, but were slow to ordain and entrust significant responsibility to African clergy. In

1894, supported by prominent white Methodists, Dwane visited England and successfully raised money for an African college at his station. On his return, he was required to deposit the sum into general Wesleyan funds. Resentful of the slur on his trustworthiness, Dwane handed in the money but resigned from the Methodist Church.

Dwane was briefly associated with the Lovedale newspaper *Imvo Zabantsundu*. He attended the 1896 conference of the Ethiopian Church which decided to seek union with the African Methodist Episcopal Church (AMEC) in America, and Dwane was delegated to visit the United States and explore this. The AMEC, formed in 1816 in response to racial discrimination in the Methodist Episcopal Church in the United States, had three orders of ministry, bishops, elders and deacons. Their first bishop was consecrated by ministers of several denominations, including an Anglican priest, and through this, the AMEC claimed connexion with the apostolic succession. Dwane was impressed by what he found in America, and accepted appointment as AMEC superintendent in South Africa. In 1898, AMEC Bishop Turner came to South Africa, ordained Ethiopian lay preachers as deacons and elders and consecrated Dwane as vicar-bishop. Enthusiasm for Ethiopianism raised church membership to 10,000. However, Dwane's subsequent visit to America in March 1899 was less than successful: the Ethiopian Church was not regarded as an equal partner, and AMEC leaders in the USA had reservations about his consecration as vicar-bishop. In any case, Dwane was beginning to doubt the validity of the AMEC claim to apostolic succession.[5]

Back in South Africa, in Queenstown in the eastern Cape, Dwane faced a dilemma. He favoured separate churches for blacks and whites, not only because of his personal experience of racism, and explained to the local Anglican rector, Julius Gordon:

> His people had customs and traditions which we white people could not understand. Rightly or wrongly, they believed that the missionaries classed all these things as sin, and when they became Christians they gave up these things, even to the wearing of bangles. 'We do not like to lose our customs,' he said. 'Let our people become Christian; but they need not become English.'[6]

At the same time, Dwane wanted Ethiopianism to be demonstrably part of the Catholic Church. Gordon lent him literature which expounded the Catholic, ecclesiastical and sacramental aspects of Anglicanism, and recommended that if he wanted to connect the Ethiopian Church with the apostolic succession, he should seek communion with the CPSA.

In August 1899, Dwane wrote to the Archbishop and Metropolitan, William West Jones, proposing that the Anglican bishops consecrate a bishop for the Ethiopian Church, so that it could have a valid priesthood and sacraments. He offered a compromise, 'if absolutely necessary',

> we might be satisfied to take the position of a missionary order within the Church for the purpose of evangelizing and building up the native people, provided that this order receive a constitution with ample powers and the right to hold property and provided that the head of the order should receive episcopal consecration and be empowered to ordain Priests and Deacons for work within the limits of the order. In order to retain the loyalty and devotion of our people, it would be necessary . . . to keep the title 'Ethiopian Church' as expressive of our order. This is the popular name whereby we are universally known, and we attach the very greatest importance to its retention.[7]

West Jones agreed that, 'for cultural reasons there ought to be a black Province of the Church, with black priests and bishops and freedom to adapt such things as ceremonial to the black ethos', and that 'the Ethiopian bishop should hold . . . the position of a Diocesan Bishop, subject to Provincial Synod, in which he should have a seat'.[8]

Full of hope, Dwane proposed that the Ethiopian Church conference to be held in October 1899 select a man from the Church to present to the Anglican bishops for consecration. The incipient South African War prevented Transvaal and Free State delegates from attending, but a majority of those present agreed to sever the AMEC connection. Mangena Mokone was among those who opposed the measure on the grounds of black solidarity. Under Dwane's leadership, the conference also resolved to request the CPSA bishops 'to give our body a valid Episcopate and priesthood, and . . . to include our body within the fold of the Catholic Church on the lines indicated in our Superintendents' letters to the Archbishop of Cape Town'.[9] When West Jones began to explore ways of giving effect to this proposal, objections were raised which prevented the realization of his own and Dwane's hopes.

Compact, conflict and constitution

Representatives of the Ethiopian Church accepted a Compact with the CPSA in Grahamstown in August 1900. It was far from a negotiated settlement, and more like a capitulation on the Ethiopians' part: Charles

Cornish, Bishop of Grahamstown, reported that Dwane and his delegation 'did not wish to make terms . . . but desired absolutely and without reserve to place themselves in the hands of the Bishops'.[10] In terms of the Compact, the Order of Ethiopia was set up under a Provincial, appointed by the bishops. With a chapter, half of whom would be appointed by the Metropolitan, he would superintend the affairs of the Order. While the Provincial could recommend clergy for missions of the Order, appointment would rest with the diocesan bishop, and any expansion of work would take place in consultation with him. Diocesan bishops in areas where the Order was working would also be responsible for individual examination of candidates for baptism and confirmation. Ethiopian clergy were to be examined before being licensed as readers, catechists or subdeacons, and arrangements would be made for training Ethiopian clergy for ordination in accordance with CPSA regulations. Dwane alone was received into the CPSA and confirmed in August 1900 in Grahamstown Cathedral.

Why did Ethiopian Christians accept this one-sided compact, such a far cry from their original vision? First, they were profoundly committed to the apostolic succession, and to obtaining valid orders and sacraments. Second, they had severed the AMEC connection in 1899, and had no access to the sacraments: numbers were dwindling, and decisive action was needed. Third, the siXhosa name, *Ibandla lase Tiyopiya* (Congregation of Ethiopia) was not specifically rejected, and Section 12 of the Compact referred to the possibility of a bishop for the Order. Fourth, the Compact was not the final document, and Dwane may have hoped for more gains in the constitution, which was still to be drawn up.

Growth of Anglican work in South Africa had been initiated by episcopal leadership, with the support of the SPG. Given this pattern, and given indications of the Society in England's evident 'sympathy with the movement' and recognition of 'the principle of revolt against the tendency to denationalize native converts', it would not have been illogical to appoint a bishop for the Order of Ethiopia.[11] The bishops had a vision of the future, 'when all the nations shall walk in the light of the City of God and shall bring their glory in to it'.[12] They also saw the Order as exercising a missionary vocation among African people which the CPSA was unable to fulfil, and hoped it might draw in other Ethiopian bodies. The fact that the Ethiopian Church had a large number of members on the Witwatersrand, where Anglican converts among Africans totalled less than a thousand, perhaps also influenced them. The racial prejudice in South African society, and among the bishops circumscribed the kind of liberating generosity which might have been extended to the Ethiopian Church.

Objections to the Compact came from those who thought it went too far, and from those who thought it had not gone far enough. Colonial officials and many white Anglicans regarded Ethiopianism as a dangerous manifestation of African nationalism, and the church hierarchy found it necessary to placate the secular authorities on this score. The Metropolitan persuaded the Prime Minister of the Cape that 'the Ethiopians who belong to the order under the guidance of the Church are less likely to be dangerous than those who continue in independent sects of their own.'[13] Dwane himself was 'grieved and pained' at allegations of disloyalty to European authority, declaring that no more loyal people could be found 'anywhere on the face of this Earth'.[14]

Because the AMEC ordination of the Ethiopian clergy was no longer recognized in the Order of Ethiopia itself, and because the Compact required individual preparation of Order members for confirmation as well as substantial additional training for their clergy, chaplains from the CPSA were appointed for the Order of Ethiopia. SPG made a substantial grant for this, also providing missionaries, Alfred Kettle, the first chaplain, who died soon after starting work, and F. W. Puller SSJE, chaplain from April 1901 to April 1902.[15] The Secretary, Montgomery, provided generous moral support for the Order, and then recommended William Cameron, who was chaplain from August 1902 to November 1903.[16] Both Puller and Cameron felt that the Order should be allowed initiative and freedom. Puller pointed out the dangers of delay in ordaining their clergy: 'The dissenters twit the Ethiopians as being a religious body without ministers. Of course that is very foolish, but the Ethiopians are not philosophers, and the combination of circumstances tends to damp their ardour.' He added that the experience of Ethiopian clergy as preachers and evangelists should outweigh their 'lack of technical knowledge' in examinations.[17] When Cameron left South Africa, the Order of Ethiopia had 1389 'definitely attached adults': 410 were confirmed, 698 passed for confirmation and 281 prepared for examination.[18]

Puller and Cameron felt the potential of the Order of Ethiopia was hampered by the attitude of the Bishop of Grahamstown. Whereas West Jones had envisaged adaptation of the provincial system to accommodate the Ethiopians, Cornish saw the relationship as a one-way process with all the adjustment on the Ethiopian side. Cornish ordained Dwane deacon in 1901, but found it difficult to recognize Dwane's authority as Provincial of the Order of Ethiopia. The Metropolitan and Dwane expected Cornish to seek and follow Dwane's advice on Order affairs, whereas Cornish understood consultation as giving Dwane 'an attentive hearing' and then endeavouring 'to make my course of action plain'. Anglican missionary work among Africans in Southern Africa began in the Diocese of Grahamstown, and several of the first generation of Society-supported European missionaries were still at work, and hostile to the Ethiopians. Some of their attitude must have rubbed off on Cornish, although he understood that they were partly motivated by jealousy.[19] In November 1903, Edward Courtney West came out from England as chaplain to the Order, and at the Order conference in April 1904 he was openly critical of Dwane's financial administration, and spoke dismissively of the diaconate: in addition, he had visited Ethiopian congregations without consulting the Provincial. In 1905, Arthur Cardross Grant joined West as assistant chaplain. Both were appointed by Cornish, and supported by SPG. Puller described West and Grant as 'zealous' and 'masterful'.[20] Dwane felt that they had contravened the Compact, now ratified by Provincial Synod, but saw no point in complaining to Cornish 'because he had so clearly sided with Mr. West. He no longer believed in me and always treated me with suspicion.'[21] In October 1905, Cornish appointed William Stead, a long-serving Society missionary to St. Philip's church in Grahamstown. St. Philip's was a CPSA congregation, but the priest there ministered to the Order, and in view of Stead's rabid opposition to the Ethiopians, whom he described as 'disobedient, disloyal and ungrateful . . . a menace to the church and to the country', it was an extraordinarily insensitive exercise of episcopal authority.[22] For Dwane, history was repeating itself, and he wrote that he was 'so disappointed and downcast that I did not know what to do'.[23] Dwane complained to the Archbishop, but also initiated something of a rebellion. Order members were instructed to stay away from Holy Communion administered by West and Grant, and in spite of a ban from Cornish, he convened a conference which appointed catechists without consulting the bishop. Enraged by what he regarded as contumacy, Cornish withdrew Dwane's licence. Determined to preserve the Order, and sympathetic to allegations that Cornish had contravened the Compact, the Metropolitan summoned a conference in August 1906 to draw up a constitution for the Order of Ethiopia. Cornish was in England at the time, and resented the action, but West Jones saw the matter as of provincial importance. This constitution recognized the Order as extra-parochial, and in spite of strident protests from Grahamstown, Episcopal Synod agreed that it should be in force from February 1907 until Provincial Synod could meet and approve the final constitution. The constitution which was eventually drafted and approved by the 1910 Provincial Synod was the work of white clergy of all shades of opinion, but Dwane's was the only Order voice. Although the constitution confirmed its extra-parochial status, and was accepted by the Order of Ethiopia, the constitution was, once again, imposed rather than negotiated, and did not reflect their full aspirations.

The breach between Dwane and the Bishop of Grahamstown had still to be healed. Episcopal Synod appointed William Cameron, now a bishop, as Provincial and it was agreed that Dwane would go and work in the Transvaal. A subsequent Commission of Enquiry into the objects, method and work of the Order of Ethiopia was critical of Dwane's response in 1905–6, but recognized that he had encountered provocation. Cameron pointed out that policy in the Diocese of Grahamstown, including delays in the ordination of Ethiopian clergy, had hampered the work of the Order, and prevented it from 'winning over any of the other bodies of Ethiopians'.[24] Thanks to Cameron's tact, the 1908 Conference of the Order, at Dwane's initiative, passed a resolution regretting disrespect shown to the Bishop of Grahamstown in 1906. Cameron was stern in dealing with the chaplains, and reprimanded Grant:

> There is nothing which tends so much to produce antagonism . . . and to hinder my efforts to bring about a feeling of brotherliness and mutual help, as this miserable system of constantly renewed petty persecution, and grudging the Order its covenanted rights. I have written strongly because I feel strongly, and I think you ought to know it.[25]

Cornish and others continued to express strong opposition to the 1907 interim constitution, but once the constitution was adopted by Provincial Synod, the situation seems to have settled down. In 1911, Dwane was ordained priest at St Mark's in the Diocese of St John's, and was again appointed as Provincial. By 1913, Cornish was able to report that the Order was working 'in a most satisfactory way'.[26]

Episcopacy

Political developments in South Africa and a changing ecumenical view of the Church shaped the second half-century of the relationship between the Order of Ethiopia and the CPSA. Another powerful influence, preserved as oral tradition within the Order of Ethiopia, was the conviction that the CPSA bishops had promised to create a bishop for, and to recognize the separate identity of, the Order of Ethiopia.[27]

Verryn described the history of the Order from 1912 to 1955 as 'the first long peace'.[28] Developments were less dramatic than in the early years, but racial tensions, both within the CPSA, and between the Province and the Order, were accumulating. The 1914 Order of Ethiopia conference requested Episcopal Synod to consecrate Dwane as bishop, but the request was turned down, 'for the good of the whole church', according to Archbishop Carter.[29] Dwane died in 1916, and William Gcule was elected as Provincial. The Order was sufficiently established for the leadership transition to take place peacefully.

The CPSA held firmly to its dictum that the Church should be a symbol of unity, but racial inequalities, especially the denial of leadership opportunities to African clergy, were increasingly apparent. In the 1940s, African clergy from the CPSA proposed the creation of an African branch of the Catholic Church, envisaged as a parallel diocesan structure within the province. At the same time, in 1944, the Order of Ethiopia petitioned Episcopal Synod for a bishop. Clearly, the bishops could not agree with this without also yielding to the other request.[30] Archbishop Darbyshire attended the Order conference in 1945, and explained their objections, which related to the creation of a separate Church with a specifically African identity. The Archbishop attempted to end on an encouraging note: because 'the Bishops have never failed to realise that the time must come when Africans shall rise in the Church to the highest office', he suggested that the Order should look forward to producing a bishop for the CPSA as a whole, rather than one for the Order of Ethiopia.[31]

Most members of the Order of Ethiopia lived in the Diocese of Grahamstown, where the authoritarian Archibald Cullen was the bishop from 1931 to 1959. His chief complaint was that the Ethiopians regarded themselves as a Church, and he reported that although he tried to be friendly, he actually felt that the Order ought to be absorbed into the CPSA.[32] A 1951 commission set up by Episcopal Synod to investigate the Order of Ethiopia reveals the prevailing paternalistic attitude in the CPSA: the commission consisted of a bishop and two white clergy.[33] Cullen advised that the Order should not be informed of its existence.[34]

The Order complained of bishops who blocked their progress, and of being relegated to the servants' quarters in the CPSA household. Its own members were never comfortable with the English name of the Order of Ethiopia: the siXhosa name, *Umzi wase Tiyopia*, which translated as 'household of Ethiopia', reflected their self-understanding more accurately, but the desire to be a separate Church was never far from the surface.[35] At a 1959 conference, the Order set out their vision of the relationship with the CPSA in no uncertain terms: freedom from control by diocesan bishops, election of their own head, control of their property and intercommunion with the CPSA. Fearing schism, the CPSA delegates undertook to present the Order position to the bishops. In February 1961, Archbishop Joost de Blank addressed the Order conference, but the text of his response was only available in November 1962, and contained an unequivocal rejection: 'We must repudiate any suggestion that either now or in the future the Bishops will be prepared to consecrate a Bishop for the Order.'[36] He did, however, encourage discussion. Throughout, the Order of Ethiopia showed absolute determination to retain the apostolic succession. In resolutions of 1964, they expressed 'joy' at being part of the Anglican Communion, 'deep appreciation' of the link with the CPSA, while complaining of 'arbitrary domination' and 'unco-operative and inconsiderate bishops'.[37] Further negotiations were held in the 1960s and at this stage the CPSA was in dialogue with other denominations, so that an ecumenical spirit, greater reciprocity and flexibility characterized discussions with the Order, which nevertheless proved inconclusive.

In 1975, the Order of Ethiopia applied to join the South African Council of Churches as an independent body. This again forced the CPSA to examine the relationship with the Order. By this stage, Black Consciousness had emerged as a strong force, and the CPSA was beginning to recognize, with some discomfort, the extent to which it had conformed to the racial norms of the wider society. The CPSA was seeking unity with Methodists and Presbyterians, and the relationship to the Order of Ethiopia was increasingly untenable. In June 1976, yet another commission was appointed. This focused on the collegial aspect of the apostolic succession, recommending that the Order of Ethiopia be formed into a diocese and that a diocesan bishop with personal rather than territorial jurisdiction be consecrated for them.[38] The bishops felt unable to accept this, but acknowledged that they had 'delayed far too long' in responding to the Order's request for a bishop, expressing sorrow for their part in this. They were prepared to consecrate a bishop for the Order, but he would only be able to function as an assistant to diocesan bishops. They recognized that the Order might, as a result, feel bound to cut ties with the CPSA.[39] On the contrary, though, the Order accepted the offer as 'good tidings from on High'.[40] The 1979 Provincial Synod passed a Canon which repealed the 1900 Compact and made provision for a bishop for the Order of Ethiopia, but once again, the Canon was imposed rather than negotiated with the Order.[41]

The Elective Assembly of the Order of Ethiopia met in Port Elizabeth on 17 August 1982, and delegated the appointment of a bishop to Episcopal Synod. The Provincial, Ephraim Hopa, was already past 70, and the bishops chose Sigqibo Dwane as Bishop of the Order.[42] A section of lay members objected, but not on canonical grounds: they accused Dwane of having earlier abandoned the Order to join the CPSA, and of being a 'puppet' of the bishops.[43] The grandson of the founder was nevertheless consecrated, and in spite of a disruption occasioned by protesters armed with sticks and stones, installed as Bishop of the Order of Ethiopia on 8 May 1983.[44] Pockets of resistance resulting in schism continued into the 1990s.[45] Under Dwane, however, the Order has pursued its vision and vocation of autonomy and African Christianity. In 1989, Canon 48 of the Provincial Canons was amended to give the Bishop of the Order of Ethiopia episcopal jurisdiction over members of the Order in the various CPSA dioceses where the Order exists, without a licence from the diocesan bishop.[46] The next major step was the 1999 Provincial Synod decision. The way ahead has yet to be explored, and will probably involve a change of name for the Order, symbolic of more profound changes. Bishop Dwane concluded his address to the 1999 Provincial Synod with the words:

> When a young person comes of age, his/her relationship with the parents does not terminate but matures. So the Ethiopians believe that the parent relationship should not terminate but mature.[47]

Over the last century, it has not only been the Order of Ethiopia which has matured. The Church of the Province of Southern Africa itself has become deeply rooted in Africa and committed to an African expression of Christianity, and therefore more willing to trust African vision, leadership and initiative than the bishops who were first approached by the Ethiopian Church a century ago.

--◦==◦--

Dr Mandy M. Goedhals is Professor of History in the University of Durban-Westville, Republic of South Africa. She has edited and contributed to a number of studies of the Church of the Province of Southern Africa.

Notes

1. *Provincial Synod of the CPSA*, Durban, 1999.
2. For a critique of missionary activity, see Goedhals (1989), pp. 104–29.
3. S. Dwane, (1988) 'The Order of Ethiopia', lecture at St Paul's College, CPSA Archives, University of Witwatersrand (CPSA Arch.), AB2546.

4. On the early history of Ethiopianism, and the role of James Mata Dwane, see Balia (1991); Dwane, 'The Order'; F. W. Puller, (1903) 'The Ethiopian Order', *The East and the West*, pp. 75–91; Verryn (1972).

5. J. M. Dwane to Archbishop Jones, 21 Aug. 1899 (CPSA Arch. – unless otherwise stated, all correspondence is from the CPSA Archives).

6. Quoted in E. Farmer (1900) *The Transvaal as a Mission Field*, London, pp. 98–9.

7. J. M. Dwane to Archbishop Jones, 21 Aug. 1899.

8. Quoted in Verryn (1972), pp. 79, 81.

9. Dwane, 'The Order', p. 7.

10. Quoted in Verryn (1972), p. 88.

11. Pascoe, pp. 305, 304e.

12. *Pastoral Letter issued by the Archbishop and Bishops*, Cape Town, Aug. 1900, p. 8.

13. *Mission Field*, Oct. 1903.

14. J. M. Dwane to Archbishop Jones, 21 Mar. 1906.

15. C. Cornish to Secretary, 28 June 1903, SPG microfilm, Diocese of Grahamstown. The Society's grants for the Order continued to 1923; thereafter, significantly, they were simply added to the block grant for the Diocese of Grahamstown.

16. Secretary to Archbishop Jones, 19 Feb. 1906; Cameron had been a Society missionary in St John's Diocese from 1884.

17. F. W. Puller to Archbishop Jones, 20 Dec. 1902.

18. W. Cameron to Archbishop Jones, 8 Jan. 1904.

19. C. Cornish to Archbishop Jones, 14 Nov. 1906; 21 July 1902.

20. Letters, 12, 31 May 1906.

21. J. M. Dwane to Archbishop Jones, Whitsun 1906.

22. W. Y. Stead (1908) *The Order of Ethiopia and its Relation to the Church*, Grahamstown.

23. J. M. Dwane to Archbishop Jones, Whitsun 1906.

24. W. Cameron to W. M. Carter, Archbishop-elect, 28 Oct. 1908.

25. W. Cameron to A. C. Grant, 29 Jan. 1909.

26. C. Cornish to Secretary, 9 Feb. 1913, SPG microfilm, Diocese of Grahamstown.

27. Verryn (1972), p. 187.

28. Verryn (1972), pp. 162–70.

29. Archbishop Carter to Provincial, Order of Ethiopia, 6 Feb. 1915.

30. A. Cullen to Archbishop Darbyshire, 18 Mar. 1942.

31. *Petition*, 8 Oct. 1944; the Reply, 29 Jan. 1945, CPSA Archives AB941/C.

32. A. Cullen to Archbishops Darbyshire and Clayton, 24 Nov. 1944 and 14 June 1952.

33. Archbishop Clayton to A. Cullen, 14 Nov. 1951. For the report, CPSA Arch. AB941/B.

34. A. Cullen to Archbishop Clayton, 14 Nov. 1951.

35. Verryn (1972), pp. 174–80, 189.

36. Archbishop de Blank to Provincial, Order of Ethiopia, 27 Dec. 1962.

37. Resolutions of Select Committee of Order of Ethiopia, 23–4 May 1964, CPSA Arch. AB1363/04.

38. Report, CPSA Arch. AB1363/04. S. Dwane chaired the Commission, other members being G. W. Ashby, E. Mosothoane, J. N. Suggit, M. Nuttall.

39. Archbishop Burnett to Provincial, Order of Ethiopia, 23 Apr. 1977.

40. Provincial, Order of Ethiopia to Archbishop Burnett, 29 Apr. 1977.

41. S. Dwane to Archbishop Tutu, 27 Feb. 1987.

42. Archbishop Russell to Canon Hopa, Provincial, Order of Ethiopia, 11 Nov. 1982.

43. Petition of lay members, 22 Nov. 1982, CPSA Arch. AB1363/04.

44. *Eastern Province Herald*, 9 May 1983.

45. For details, CPSA Arch. AB2546; also *Eastern Province Herald*, 23 Mar. 1992.

46. S. Dwane to Bishops of the Province, 13 Apr. 1989.

47. S. Dwane (1999) *Address to Provincial Synod*, Durban.

13

·✦·⇒◯⇐·✦·

The evolving role of the Church:
the case of democratization in Zambia

MUSONDA T. S. MWAMBA

The Church in Zambia is undergoing a revolution. This is perceptible in the role it has played in the democratization process. The Church's advocacy for a healthy and democratic society is a new stance in relation to politics. I trace the development of this emerging trend, and explore what it signals for the future of Church–state relations in Zambia.

Let me clarify my use of the term Church. There are three main Church bodies in Zambia: the Roman Catholics or Episcopal Conference of Zambia (ECZ), the Christian Council of Zambia (CCZ) and the Evangelical Fellowship of Zambia (EFZ). I employ the term in a generic sense to refer to all denominations in their concerted role in the democratization process.

The ecumenical role is significant in that the Churches have had different theological orientations and colonial records. In spite of the differences, a common thread clearly evident was the apolitical nature of the Church. But I suggest that there is crystallizing a change in theological thinking amongst the Churches in perceiving their pastoral role in society as also encompassing politics.

This change has arisen in a pastoral context, caused by a politico-economic collapse which has ruined the quality of life of most Zambians. The pastoral concern for the welfare of the poor has motivated the Church to address the political source of this suffering. The reasoning is simple: structures that impinge upon the vulnerable in society are a religious concern for the Church. 'The Gospel not only affects the human being's inner self but it is also relevant for *all* areas of life and culture.'[1] This holistic approach is the essence of the silent revolution in the Church. In following this trend I draw examples mostly from the Anglican Church as representative of the changing view of the Church *vis-à-vis* politics.

The Anglican Church

The Anglican Church in Zambia was established by the Universities' Mission to Central Africa (UMCA) at the time of its Jubilee in 1907 as the Diocese of Northern Rhodesia. The Church is now divided into four dioceses, the Dioceses of Lusaka, Central Zambia, Northern Zambia and Eastern Zambia. The Church forms part of the Church of the Province of Central Africa (CPCA), comprising the Anglican Church in Botswana, Malawi, Zambia and Zimbabwe.

Active around the country, the Anglican Church is, for example, involved at Chipili in the north of Zambia with a rural health centre, primary and secondary school; Katete in the east has St Francis, a major referral hospital, which from the 1980s has been jointly administered with the Roman Catholic Church; Mapanza in the south has a major secondary school for boys. There are other activities such as homecraft, trades training and agriculture that the Church is involved in. Most of the work has been and is assisted by USPG. This invaluable partnership between the Society and the Anglican Church in Zambia cannot be measured in terms of pounds and pence, for five pounds from a caring, willing and generous community of faith is worth more than a million pounds without love. The bond of affection has been described by Archbishop Makhulu at a recent consultation between the Society and the CPCA at Harare in February 1998, when he spoke of 'bonds of mutual understanding and love'.

Reflections of the West

The Church and state in Zambia are constructs of a Western view of Christianity and the nation-state. Every society is shaped by its political, economic, religious and cultural values, evolved over a period of time, and usually not without struggle. Ultimately, these societal values find their vitality and legitimacy through popular and consensual acceptance by the people, thus forming the foundations of society. A person's attitude, for instance, concerning religion is shaped within a certain cultural context. Thus Christianity in the West evolved from its Palestinian character into one illustrative of the European context. Logically, the Christianity brought to Africa by the missionaries was dressed in a Western garb.

However, instead of allowing Christianity to find expression in the African cultural context, the conversion of Africans to Christianity was presented as involving the adoption of Western values. Williamson demonstrates this when writing on the Akan of Ghana, 'an invitation to accept the Christian religion was also a call to participate in a Western interpretation of reality'.[2] Similarly, John Taylor has candidly pointed out how:

> The missionaries of the Christian Church have commonly assumed that Western civilisation and Christianity were two aspects of the same gift which they were commissioned to offer to the rest of humankind. This assumption was sometimes quite ·conscious and was explicitly stated. More often it was quite unconscious and would have been indignantly denied.[3]

It is not my intention here to discuss the complex issues related to colonialism, or the downside of the missionary endeavour. I simply seek to show a legacy of these enterprises that still defines the Church and African states, that is, the matter of *identity*. Most Africans, unfortunately, still think that progress, excellence, modernity and culture must be measured by European standards. Similarly, inherited Western structures still influence the life of church and government institutions, without regard to their historical origins and purpose, and above all their suitability to the African environment.

The Anglican Church, for example, in hierarchy and structure reflects the Church of England. Worship is also modelled on English liturgical forms, and even takes over cultural specificities, so that it is not uncommon to sing 'In the bleak mid-winter', in the bright African sunshine at Christmas!

In theory, the Africans were expected to perceive themselves as in a new culture and suppress their past. However, in practice it symbolized an identity crisis, which Frantz Fanon succinctly described by the title of his book, *Black Skin, White Masks* (Eng. trans. 1967) The problem of identity was not only personalized, for example, in times of adversity like illness where African and European beliefs clashed. It went deeper to the African's whole perception of cultural, political and social issues, which were marginalized to irrelevancy.

Divorce of Church and state

The missionaries had naturally a Western view of the separation of Church and state. Various stages were passed in European history culminating in the separation of Church and state. Prior to this, society from its medieval heritage was a *Respublica Christiana*, a Church and state fused wherein morality and legality were indivisible. Early Protestantism maintained the link of a 'church civilization', one in which a unitary spiritual creed governed both Church and state, but substituting for the Catholic priestly hierarchy and sacramental ritual the certainty of Scripture and decisive acts of faith. In the burning furnace of the Enlightenment, Protestantism shifted to what we may call 'modern' Protestantism. This basically shunted religion from the public into the private realm, and recognized a dichotomy between Church and state. It replaced the absolute authority of the Bible with a humanistic, subjective spirituality based upon inner conviction. Hence Christianity turned inward to personal piety and to its rituals. The state learnt to get on without religion, and this left the public realm with no accountability towards religion.

In contrast, the African traditional understanding assumed a fusion of religion and politics, spiritual and physical, and insisted upon an ethic that is social and utilitarian rather than individualistic and pietistic. Thus what we have is religion animating the political and social fibre in African society. The significance of this should not be overlooked, a point made by Busia, who placed first in his treatment of factors to be considered in Africa's search for democracy what he called the 'religious heritage'.[4] However, the religious factor permeating society, as perceived by Africans, was degraded in the Church's teaching.

The Church in a colonial context

The Church in Zambia since its inception helped fashion the country. The Church's major contribution has been in health care and education. This is manifest in the work of the Anglican Church. It is in the field of education that the Church significantly influenced African lives. The Church facilitated the universalizing of African horizons, a process which was crucial in the transition into the expanded world that came with Western contact.

In spite of its noble contribution, the Church strongly discouraged practical political activity. Many Africans were disillusioned with their orthodox 'Mission' churches on account of their failure to speak out on the major political issues of the times, such as the federation. There was a 'passive acceptance of the superior wisdom of Government' on the part of the Church.[5] Europeans expected the Church to co-operate with the government loyally by putting across a religious viewpoint which was in harmony with the government's approach. A caveat should be allowed, in that the political voice of the Church was articulated by some individual missionaries, such as UMCA's Anglican Rector of Luanshya, Fred Sillet, and the Methodist, Colin Morris, who spoke up for the rights of Africans.

For example, Morris in *The Hour After Midnight*, detailed his experience and the coming to terms with Zambian nationalism by the mission Churches. He rightly observed that the Church's non-involvement in politics could only result in the Church becoming a 'pathetic assemblage of personal pietists running away from that creative encounter with the world which enables religion to come alive'.[6] The outspoken clergy were attacked by the government and by the Church, keen to preserve its apolitical role.

African Christians felt that more clergy should take a stand on political issues on which their destinies depended. Ironically, the African clergy, with few exceptions, were devoted pastors but political quietists. The reason was twofold. First, their training at the hands of missionaries was not about being equipped to judge and act politically from Christian premises. Pheko has argued that the Africans' academic and theological training was inadequate and aimed basically at upholding the colonial system.[7] The African clergy could therefore not be critical of the forces at play in society. Second, the African clergy served under their European colleagues and thus lacked the power to initiate political change to any degree. Those who opted out to join the African Independent Churches, like the African Methodist Episcopal Church, although religiously nationalist were basically neutral in politics.

The effect of the Church's failure to speak out politically was that the ordinary Zambians at independence surrendered their political conscience to the political leaders.

The Church after independence

After independence the Church still eschewed its prophetic witness, partly because of its old habit, and also for fear of offending the new black government. But President Kaunda, son of a Church of Scotland minister, was a dedicated Christian, with immense respect for the Church. A charismatic leader, he exuded integrity and charm.

One night in 1967 Kaunda briefly resigned as President for a couple of hours because of divisions within the United National Independence Party, UNIP. Church leaders, led by the Anglican Bishop, Filemon Mataka, went to State House to urge him not to go, and out of respect he rescinded his decision. Thus the Church had a respected position in the state, but was never critical of government.

The first critical opposition from the Church occurred in October 1979, when government attempted to introduce the teaching of 'Scientific Socialism in the school curriculum. The Churches opposed this strongly and wrote a pastoral letter to all their members entitled 'Marxism, Humanism and Christianity'. The government abandoned its plans to introduce 'Scientific Socialism'. This encounter demonstrated the potential the Church had to influence policy in Zambia.

Root of problems

Zambia's current political and economic crises are rooted in the pattern of economic development inherited from the colonial period. Tordoff and Molteno rightly observed, 'the colonial system not only shaped the nationalist movement which emerged to oppose and eventually overthrow it, but has also had continuing consequences for Zambia since independence'.[8]

There are two major features from the colonial era which affect the present profoundly. The first is the economy. Zambia was developed according to British interests on a mono-economy based on copper. The infrastructure was developed with the needs of the mining industry in mind. This exclusive concentration on copper meant that the manufacturing and agricultural sectors were neglected. The Zambian government, whilst giving top priority to copper production and industrial expansion, did very little to improve agricultural production throughout the 1960s and 1970s.

The second is political and concerns the authoritarian nature of the colonial system. The colonial government had wide-ranging and arbitrary powers which restricted civil liberties. These powers were inherited by the post-colonial state and used liberally.

It remains indisputable that the colonial era did little to develop a political culture in Zambia to validate limited government and respect for individual rights. Similarly, Bishop Taylor has stated that the problem with the new African states is that they were not prepared for independence. Very inadequate preparations were made for the countries to govern themselves. The irony of the British colonial system was that Britain prided herself as the mother of democracy, with Her Majesty's Opposition leader drawing a salary, and comfortably ensconced at Westminster. In the colonies, however, there was no opposition to Her Majesty. The opposition was usually in jail.[9]

At independence

Zambia had immense promise. It was one of the richest and most industrialized countries in Africa. There were great expectations in all sectors. The workers who had been underpaid in colonial times saw substantial improvements in their wages. The government embarked on social development projects, building schools, hospitals and health centres, roads, housing estates and other necessary infrastructure. Government also introduced social reforms by providing free education and health for all. Economic reforms brought about the nationalization of crucial areas of economic activity as part of the government policy of achieving economic independence.

The government also created parastatal institutions such as the Zambia Industrial and Mining Corporation (ZIMCO). These economic reforms made the state the largest employer in the country. By 1982, the state controlled 70–80 per cent of economic activity in Zambia.

Interestingly, none of the measures taken by the government were designed to change the colonially determined structures and patterns of production and exchange in order to mobilize the people and bring them into the main stream of politics and power. The structures of potential discontent were merely eclipsed for a time by an economic boom and popular support.

Consolidating power: the one-party state

For nine years after independence, Zambia had a multi-party democracy, which according to Kaunda presented considerable difficulties both at election times and in tackling the problems of national integration and development.[10] The one-party state was therefore introduced in 1972, ostensibly because it reflected the style of 'traditional' African democracy. That is, it could avoid dissensions and commotion that were merely obstacles to national unity and social harmony and promote economic development on account of its alleged capacity to reduce social tension and mobilize people's energies.

The one-party state was, however, in fact a strategy employed by the ruling party to control dissent within the one party as well as the opposition outside the party. It came at a time when the party was losing support and faced the formidable threat posed by the former vice-president, Simon Kapwepwe's formation of the United Progressive Party (UPP). The one-party system heightened the authoritarian streak of the government.

The slide to decay in economy and state

Zambia's economic good fortune was short-lived. When the world market price for copper dropped sharply in 1975 in the context of a world economic recession which carried over into the 1980s, the Zambian economy was affected. Higher oil prices in the early 1970s exacerbated the crisis as Zambia's economy is oil-dependent, and it was downhill all the way, as copper prices dropped sharply on the world market. The obsessional dependence on copper has been the main cause of Zambia's vulnerable position in the world economy.

The overall effect was that the capacity utilization in all major industries declined. Industries that were heavily dependent on imported inputs were the hardest hit. Some firms had to be closed because of lack of spare parts and basic inputs, resulting in thousands of workers being made redundant. In the construction industry employment dropped from 80,000 to 30,000 in ten years. With the extended family system in Zambia, a lot of people were affected. The effect was registered by increased malnutrition, infant mortality and a rise in crime.

As revenue diminished it became difficult for government to support and subsidize the parastatal sector and institutions such as hospitals, schools and other public services institutions. These sectors deteriorated rapidly as drugs, equipment, educational and other basic facilities became difficult to obtain, and 'free health and education was nothing but a hollow slogan'.[11]

The deepening economic crisis inevitably had political and social ramifications, with the shoots of democratization breaking through the ground.

Democratization in Zambia and its immediate causes

We can isolate two causes of the democratization process in Zambia, the external and the internal. The former can be traced to the end of the Cold War and events in Eastern Europe and the pressure from international donors, such as the International Monetary Fund and World Bank. The latter lie in the structural and political areas we have just traced. It is the convergence of these causes, commencing in 1989, that defined the democratization process. In this context, democratization in Zambia was not simply a reaction to events in Eastern Europe. The events in Eastern Europe merely bolstered the internal causes embedded in the general development of the country.

In spite of being a one-party state there was a coup attempt in October 1980, allegedly staged by prominent business people. The attempt indicated that all was not well in Zambia.

The trade unions also posed a threat to the UNIP government. The unions played an important role in the independence struggle. When Zambia became a one-party state, UNIP made the Zambia Congress of Trade Unions (ZCTU) a branch of UNIP. The rapid decline of living standards after 1975 and cuts in subsidies broke down the symbiosis between union and government. This led to hostilities and workers' resistance in the 1980s.

By December 1986, the stringent IMF conditions imposed in 1985 led government to adopt a policy of desubsidization, which in turn led to a massive, nationwide riot, widespread destruction, especially on the Copperbelt, and the death of fifteen people. The government was forced to reintroduce the subsidies.

IMF pressure, however, compelled the government in 1990 to more than double the price of maize meal, a staple food. Public protest erupted into violence and in three days of rioting 26 people were killed. During this period, the second coup attempt occurred. This received widespread support all over the country, and was the catalyst for political and constitutional reform in Zambia. The coup plotters were quickly pardoned, an indication perhaps that President Kaunda felt politically vulnerable.

In July 1991 Kaunda's leadership of UNIP was challenged by Enoch Kavindele, a member of the Central Committee. Kavindele later withdrew his candidature in the interest of the party and Kaunda was re-elected President of UNIP in August 1991.

Clearly, the government had lost the ability and capacity to undertake socio-economic programmes necessary to improve the people's welfare. In tandem was leadership 'fatigue' resulting in loss of legitimacy and alienation from the people. The people were ready for change.

The role of the Church up to 1991

The government in the name of nation-building had consolidated its power in all sectors of society so that there were no alternative power bases. The Church became 'the only tolerated countervailing power to that of the state' and was able to act as an instrument of political substitution.[12] Events pushed the Church to shed its apolitical cocoon and become instrumental in pressing for democratic change.

The strength of the Zambian Church lies in its wide constituency.

It permeates all classes of society. Working among the poor and daily witnessing their worsening conditions compelled the Church to voice its concern as UNIP rule became more oppressive. So the church leaders became more critical, attacking unfair distribution of wealth between rich and poor, corruption and intimidation of non-party members. For example, the Anglican Bishop of Lusaka, Stephen Mumba, preached a sermon in which he criticized the government for failing to address the plight of the poor. This was out of character for him and the Church.

In this vein, however, the Church pressed its opposition through preaching, pastoral letters and Christian media, such as *The National Mirror, Icengelo* and *Workers' Challenge.* The reporting raised the political consciousness of the readers and provoked angry outbursts from President Kaunda. I recall the President complaining to the Anglican Archbishop of Central Africa, Dr Makhulu, about the way the Church was carrying on. The Archbishop retorted that it was necessary to have a 'critical solidarity' between Church and state. With the government suffering from 'church phobia,' another front opened up.

The MMD

The Movement for Multi-Party Democracy (MMD) was formed in July 1990. MMD became an alliance of all opposition currents, led by Mr. Frederick Chiluba, Chairman-General of ZCTU. Chiluba is a Christian, with Pentecostal verve.

> Christian motifs were introduced into the political struggle – the diminutive Chiluba being frequently referred to as David challenging Goliath, and even more frequently being portrayed as Moses, about to bring his people to freedom after almost 40 years of fruitless wandering in the wilderness.[13]

There were now two Christian leaders seeking to lead their people to the 'promised land'. In December 1990, a parliamentary amendment to the constitution was passed enabling other political parties to be formed in Zambia. By July 1991, a hitch had developed. A new multi-party constitution drafted by a UNIP team in response to popular pressure was rejected by the MMD. There were other matters such as failure to publish official registration lists and to lift the state of emergency to allow for free campaigning, and the public media was manifestly partisan. Fearing meltdown, the Churches facilitated a meeting between President

Kaunda and the MMD leadership. This took place at Lusaka's Anglican Cathedral, on 24 July 1991, chaired by the Anglican Bishop, Stephen Mumba. The meeting successfully resolved much of the tension. An ecumenical service called by the Churches was later held at the Anglican Cathedral, to pray for a peaceful transition to the Third Republic.

The input of the Churches was also vital in the preparation for the elections. They joined to form the Christian Churches Monitoring Group, which was then a major force in the formation of the Zambia Election Monitoring Co-ordinating Committee (ZEMEC), which set out to train people to observe procedures at all polling stations on election day, and to provide voter education. They also called for a day of prayer on the Sunday preceding the elections.

On 31 October 1991, the MMD Party won a landslide victory, and with immense dignity President Kaunda graciously conceded defeat and handed over power to Chiluba. To commemorate the successful transference of power an ecumenical service was held at Lusaka's Anglican Cathedral, at which President Chiluba was anointed by Bishop Mumba to discharge his state duties with God's blessing.

After Kaunda

The Church played a critical role in the democratization process. To borrow a phrase, it acted 'as a midwife' by encouraging and facilitating the change.[14] At the same time, without Kaunda's respect for the Church, the MMD victory would have been that much harder to attain.

The Church's role in the democratization process contrasts sharply with its inactivity in the colonial struggle. The context and the leadership within the Church has effected this change. The Church is no longer a 'missionary' Church, but a vital integral part of the evolving Zambian society. Therefore, as a component of the society or culture, it is drawing upon a common stock of symbols, commenting upon relations of inequality both local and more global and communicating its message beyond its own expected confines of religion. Awakened by the plight of the poor, the Church in Zambia is embarking on redefining the political and religious structures. Thus it has to be *relevant* in correctly communicating and signalling the reality of the Zambian context.

This implies a change in the church leaders' theological thinking from one based on foreign contexts, a decoupling from a Western Protestant belief system that projects its values of individualism and a dichotomy of spiritual and material, replacing this with a more communal and holistic approach implicit in the African world-view. All this process is giving form to an authentic Church-and-state identity, brewed – so to speak – in an Africa pot. Emerging is an identity that seeks to facilitate a wholesome development of society, built on traditional African values, but adapted to modern times. This demands the restructuring of institutions to allow for a relevant expression of the political and spiritual will. In Zambia, the democratization process, to be a success, will require a radical transformation of the present structures of economic and political governance to reflect the religious, cultural and social values of the Zambian people.

Hitherto, this radical restructuring of the context and content of politics had not happened. Having more political parties to choose from is not democracy. But having an open environment conducive to the full participation of the people, free exchange and competition of ideas, on an equal basis, is the essence of democracy.

The reading of African democracy calls for a communal bias or 'traditional' democracy rooted in African societies, involving the popular participation of everyone in the affairs of the society, as well as 'people's organisational genius at solving community problems'.[15] This participatory attribute should drive the democratization process in Africa in creating a stable society. Thus, an inclusive rather than adversarial political system would best fit the African context, built on the 'religious heritage' and philosophy of *Ubuntu*.[16]

The MMD were voted into office in the belief that they would initiate a new culture of full democratic participation by the people, accountability and transparency, but instead revealed a spirit of intolerance towards the opposition parties and those with dissenting views. The democratization process was in jeopardy by the continuity of old styles of political behaviour reminiscent of UNIP under a one-party state. There was in practice a *continuity* between the UNIP and MMD governments. Kaunda, for example, found himself the victim of a relentless campaign to discredit him. The MMD government went so far as to bar him from running for the Presidency by amending the constitution, with the provision that only those whose parents were born in Zambia could be eligible to contest the Presidency. Kaunda's parents were born in Malawi. The Church protested and called for a special assembly to discuss and approve any new constitution, rather than the totally MMD-dominated parliament. To no avail, the MMD got its way and passed the amended constitution.

Further, without consulting the Church, President Chiluba declared Zambia a Christian nation, thus giving Christianity a formal constitutional status. The Church became more critical of Chiluba because of this action. After the general elections in 1996 he created a portfolio of

Minister of State for Religious Affairs. This move was not, however, a mechanism for controlling the Church, but rather an indicator of the importance President Chiluba attached to religion.

In spite of its overt Christian policy, the new political dispensation lacks a visionary programme that effectively builds on traditional and modern political principles of governance to develop. The MMD, having achieved power, uses the same repressive, inefficient and unstable structures as before to promote its form of democracy. In short, the identity of the state does not yet resonate with the Zambian culture.

The Zambian Church is just beginning to define its political ministry. Consistently, Christianity has to be mediated in the Zambian context as a Gospel that addresses the whole person and the material environment. Paradoxically, spirituality thrives only in relation to life in its totality. Apart from the 'stuff of life', the Church's existence and mission is an illusion.

It has taken the crucible of political and economic suffering for the Church to find its heart, to come alive and offer hope. In this context, then, it has to continue to provide definitions, principles of judgement and criteria of perception. It has to offer a reading of the world, of history, of society, of time, of space, of power, of authority, of justice, of ultimate truth. It has to inculcate a particular way of perceiving, experiencing and responding to reality. Consequently, in the democratization process in Zambia the Church is seen as legitimating new aspirations, new forms of organization, new relations, a new social order. Every religion, in a sense, involves struggles to conquer, monopolize or transform the symbolic structures which order reality. All these are issues for political analysis, and issues that are missed if questions of the political role of religion are asked purely in terms of Church versus state.

It is clear from present developments in Zambia that the future of the Church and state will be complementary. The ministry of the Church is to affirm and make whole the lives of people so they can realize their potential to the full. Consequently, as politics affects the lives of ordinary people, the mission of the Church will always be actualized in striving to enhance their well-being, whilst vigorously opposing those policies and actions, such as the debt crisis, that diminish and rob individuals of their divine image.

Everything in life is interconnected. Zambia's creation and political and economic development have given shape to its present status and to the role of the Church within it. From its initial apolitical stance the Church is evolving to face the challenge of the interconnectedness of life and to play an active role in transforming society into a healthy and democratic entity. We all live in what Turner described as a 'sacramental universe'.[17] The re-emerging voice of African spirituality speaks to the evolving Church and state in Zambia.

·→═◎═◁·

Musonda Mwamba was born in Zambia. From 1987 to 1997 he was Provincial Secretary of the Church of the Province of Central Africa. He is now a worker priest, continuing to serve the Church in the Province while Company Secretary and Secretary to the Board of the Standard Chartered Bank of Botswana.

Notes

1. Thielicke (1995), p. 236.
2. Williamson (1965), p. 170.
3. Taylor (1963), pp. 5–6.
4. Busia (1967), *passim*.
5. Morris (1961), p. 143.
6. *Ibid.*, p. 100.
7. Pheko (1982), p. 8.
8. W. Tordoff (ed.) (1974) *Politics in Zambia*, Manchester, pp. 3–6.
9. Observation of John Taylor, interview Oxford, 17 Mar. 1998.
10. K. Kaunda (1997) 'Does democracy have a future in Africa?' Address to the Oxford Union, 10 Nov. 1997, p. 4.
11. H. C. Mpuku and I. Zyyuulu (eds) (1997) *Contemporary Issues in Socio-Economic Reform in Zambia*, Hant, p. 2.
12. Joseph (1993), p. 246.
13. Gifford (1998), p. 193.
14. The phrase was used by Nelson Mandela in a speech to the Free Ethiopian Church of Southern Africa, 14 Dec. 1992.
15. D. Olowu, (Apr. 1989) *Newsletter of the African Association of Political Science*, Lagos, p. 13.
16. Fundamental to African culture, this sees a person's life as having meaning and value through interdependence with others, and all working for the common good. In short, a person is a person through other persons.
17. Turner (1977).

14

The Anglican Church in Ghana and the SPG

JOHN S. POBEE

Gratitude for the work of SPG

This chapter is written by one who is most conscious of the influence the Society has exercised in his life. For one thing, I am an Anglican. For another, I am, through my mother, a descendant of Philip Quaque, the first African to be trained as a priest by the Society. Thirdly, I was educated at Adisadel College, formerly SPG Grammar School in Cape Coast, Ghana. So this chapter is critical but grateful. The Akans of Ghana, whose wisdom is couched in proverbs, say 'the monitor lizard says mine is to help to build up and not let down my state'. I believe that the lessons of yesterday and today can help us cope more efficiently with life today and tomorrow.

A new context for a new account of the Society

This is not the first centennial consideration of the work of the Society. However, one undertaken at this point in time is rather different from earlier efforts. First, it is looking into a new millennium at a time of rapid change. So the task is not just to chronicle history, but to attempt also to evaluate the work done over the past 300 years, learn its lessons and plot new directions. Second, this volume is being undertaken following a shift in the demography of world Christianity, with the centre moving from Europe and North America to the south especially Africa. The 1998 Lambeth Conference vividly displayed this shift; the Nigerian bishops alone were about 50, not to mention other African provinces. Of course, this change has sometimes been facilely trumpeted.

Recalling the history of the fate of the Church in Roman North Africa, which in its time produced the vibrant theologies of Augustine, Cyprian and Tertullian, such trumpeting should set before its eyes the critical question: is the African Church doing everything required to sustain its viability? If not, then the seeming growth in numbers will ultimately be to no effect.

It is my concern, then, to ask about the viability and sustainability of the work which was initiated by the Society. Is our Church in Ghana a viable member of the Anglican Communion?

The Church in the Castle – a chaplaincy or a mission?

SPG came to the Gold Coast at the invitation of the Royal Africa Company. In 1720, the Company asked the Society 'to recommend proper persons to be chaplains to their factories abroad, offering to allow them 80 or 100 pounds sterling per annum with diet at the Governor's Table'.[1] This invitation means that the Society's initial forays into the Gold Coast were primarily chaplaincies. Hastings gives an instructive description of the life of a chaplain:

> The function of a chaplain was to take services on a Sunday, to baptize babies (mostly mulattos), to take the frequent funeral services, and to run a small school for the children of the garrison. Occasionally the sons of a black king might join the mulatto children.[2]

Thus for all practical purposes, what purported to be a missionary operation was primarily pastoral, caring for the English overseas and their dependants. In fairness to Thompson, the first chaplain, his ministry went beyond the Castle as he went evangelizing to Anomabo, Tantum and Winneba. His chaplaincy was a base for a growing mission bringing Christ from the Castle to the people and turning his schools into a nursery of the Church. The Company's invitation also gives us a peep into the nature of the operation. The chaplains were subject to political personalities even if recommended by the Society, and were on the staff of the Castle, their services paid for by the governor. The story of the work after Thomas Thompson, the first missionary to the Gold Coast, was not significantly different. Even Philip Quaque, an African, who succeeded him, from 1766 to 1816, although styled 'missionary, school master and catechist to the Negroes on the Gold Coast', and although he endeavoured to be this, was treated primarily as a chaplain to the Castle. Nor were his missionary efforts greatly successful, for he had very limited preparation for this. He did not appreciate that Christianity had to be Africanized rather than Africans Christianized and Europeanized.

This linking of Anglican mission with the Castle has dogged the Anglican Church almost to today. For nearly 250 years, the Prayer Book services prayed for the English sovereign but not for local kings and chiefs. In Fante it was and continues to be called *abanmu asor*, the Church of the Castle, the government's Church, a privileged Church.

From mission to Church

Initially, evangelization in Ghana was a missionary project of the Society. It was only with the appointment of Nathaniel Hamlyn in 1904 as assistant to the Bishop of Western Equatorial Guinea, with responsibility for the Gold Coast, that we can properly talk of a diocese in the making. Broadly, the period 1751 to 2001 represents the Society's association with Ghana in the growth from mission to Church, from a colonial to an autonomous Church. It further represents the development from an Anglican tradition in the Gold Coast, content to be in the image and likeness of the Church of England, to a Church at least beginning to speak of Africanization.

Political tapestry for the story

The Bond of 1844 established British 'power and jurisdiction' in the Gold Coast, 'moulding the customs of the country to the general principles of British Law'.[3] This and subsequent imperial impositions ensured that mission done in this context would be a dance of missionaries with traders, colonial officials and adventurers.

When the missionaries first arrived, what later became the Gold Coast, and later still Ghana, consisted of a congeries of some 40 loosely knit tribes. For the Society, however, this was not the focus. That was provided by the location of the colonial administration and mercantile activity, so that the missionaries were located in Cape Coast, Accra, Winneba, Sekondi and Kumasi. The work of Bishop Hamlyn was on the railway routes constructed to bring gold, bauxite, manganese and diamonds to the coast for trans-shipment. Anglican establishment did not require going to the four corners of the Gold Coast. The later division of the one diocese of Accra into seven dioceses was driven by a vision of breaking out of this earlier colonial vision to reach out to every tribe and tongue in Ghana, and that had to wait for African leadership.

In the 1950s the Society's work was called the English Church Mission. Other denominations alleged that Bishop Aglionby won over members of other Churches with the slogan 'Join your King's Church'. Whether this was true or not, the allegation reflects the perception that the mission of the Anglicans amounted to proselytism with colonial trappings rather than propagation of the Gospel. In any case, the African Anglicans seemed to pride themselves on the Church of their colonial rulers. This suggests they had an identity crisis. The Church was seen by many as élitist, belonging to the white clergy and others, who out of their kindness and generosity had extended it to the Africans.

Thus, right into the 1950s the Anglican Church was perceived as the colonial Church, a foreign body on the Gold Coast. On the other hand, 1950 was more or less the time when the independence movement in the Gold Coast was gathering momentum, with the coming into being of organizations like the United Gold Coast Convention and the Convention People's Party. 1951 saw the creation of the Church of the Province of West Africa, comprising the Dioceses of the Gambia–Rio Pongas, Gold Coast, Sierra Leone and Niger (Lagos). One interesting point about this creation is that the CMS and SPG co-operated in support of the province, with CMS interest in Sierra Leone and Nigeria and SPG in Gambia–Rio Pongas and the Gold Coast. But this also points to the strange situation of Church of England mission, with two major societies of one Church within the one Communion collaborating but seemingly incapable of integrating. The mission is not about calling people into a denomination or a missionary society, it is about inviting people into the One Holy Catholic and Apostolic Church and taking the structural consequences. The further consequences, for developing an ecumenical vision of mission, hardly need pointing out.

The links with colonialism carried with them the perception of Anglicans, at least the official Church, as lackeys of the colonial government. Thus, in 1950 an African Anglican priest, V. K. A. Saifah was sent to prison for publicly supporting Kwame Nkrumah and the CPP's demand for freedom for the Gold Coast. The official Church was silent. Again, while in prison, his only son and his wife died. The authorities refused to let him go to bury his family, as African custom demanded. On neither occasion did the official Anglican Church speak on his behalf. Saifah's only comments was, 'If that is the price I have to pay for liberation of Mother Ghana, I am prepared even to lay down my life so that my country shall be free.'[4] In the perception of the African, the Anglican Church was evidently an outpost of the colonial administration. The Saifah story was not an isolated case.

The principle of self-governance

It is illuminating to test out the three-self principles with the Ghana story. First, regarding self-governance and the achievement of local leadership.

In earlier times, from Bishop Hamlyn on, the incumbent bishop in consultation with the Society chose and recommended his successor to the Archbishop of Canterbury. Bishop John Daly had wanted his successor to be an African in 1956, but the African clergy were bickering about it, many candidates pushing their cause. When no consensus proved possible, another Englishman was appointed, Richard Roseveare SSM. In the case of a Church judged to have been closest to the colonial government, white leadership in a nationalist age was a liability and embarrassment. Thus, when Bishop Roseveare complained of incipient atheism in the ideology of the CPP in 1962, something other church leaders also did, he alone was subjected to attacks in the CPP press, being called, among other things, 'saboteur' and 'rabble rouser' and being temporarily deported. The bishop was a soft target for the nationalists because he was not only European but also head of the Church most closely identified with the erstwhile colonial masters.

The first African diocesan, Ishmael LeMaire, was appointed in 1968 when Ghana had been independent eleven years. Compared to other historic Churches, native leadership in the Anglican Church came late. As early as 1949 when African nationalism was gathering momentum, the Methodists elected Gaddiel Acquaah as their first African President of Conference. Similarly, in 1958 the Roman Catholics appointed their first African auxiliary bishop, John Amissah.

Again, the Church in the Gold Coast was late in getting a constitution of its own. Even the beloved Bishop Aglionby used to say 'the bishop is the constitution', which was a colonial way of defining a bishop. It was his successor, Bishop John Daly, who in 1952 summoned the first synod of clergy and elected members and through it put in place a constitution for the Diocese of Accra. That coincided significantly with two things: the diocese was about to become part of the new province, and the independence movement in the Gold Coast was in full swing.

However, the self-governing principle needs some qualification. It focuses too much on the structures of the mission. Important as structures and who controls the structures may be, it is perhaps more important to see mission as the overriding concern. A casual observer of the Anglican Church in Ghana cannot fail to recognize that the African bishops are busy maintaining the structures bequeathed by their forbears. Some are still referred to as 'the Lord Bishop'. Synods meet and pass resolutions but they are often not implemented, which is a sign that the process involved has not been appropriated by the diocese. Dialogue seeking consensus, African style, which is time-consuming but innately democratic, is rarely seen. These reveal the limits or shortcomings of the principle of self-governance.

A self-propagating Church

The second of the three-self principles would see Africans as missionaries to ourselves. One of the bright spots of the Anglican story in Ghana is that from the beginning the vision of native people taking ownership of the project of mission was articulated. Partly in response to the high mortality rate on the west coast of Africa, Thomas Thompson stated and implemented the vision of training Africans to lead the mission, and so sent Philip Quaque to England to be trained. Nathaniel Hamlyn, the first assistant bishop with responsibility for the Gold Coast, set up in 1910 the SPG Grammar School, now Adisadel College, to be the ground for generating priestly vocations and other enlightened African leadership for the country. The college has, since 1968, produced almost the entire leadership of the Anglican Church. So the vision of Thompson and Hamlyn took time to come to fruition in church leadership. But it did come to pass.

Similarly Bishop O'Rorke mooted the idea of a theological college in Kumasi to train local personnel to lead the mission in the Gold Coast, but it was only in 1925, after Aglionby had taken over and found a diocesan staff of three English priests, three African and one African deacon, that it was begun. In 1928, he wrote 'beyond all things, West Africa needs leaders of its own race in every department of life but above all, men of spiritual power'.

Local clergy could never do all the work that needed to be done. So there was developed, especially under Aglionby, the peculiar African creation of the catechist as critical and frontline agent of Anglican mission. Bishop Aglionby bore this testimony in 1945: 'the work which our catechists do is indispensable and their withdrawal from the field or any diminution in their numbers will be disastrous ... It is only after years of patient teaching and the example of a certain life lived among them, that one by one lives are changed, souls are saved, a church built, a school opened and seeds of our holy religion are sown and fostered.'

The Catechist School had its ups and downs, often for financial reasons. But there were deeper issues. One was that clarity about Ghana's development was needed. Increasingly African church life was being defined by differing modes of economic activity, including traditional culture and the rural peasant economy, and popular culture and the urban industrial economy. This distinction is helpful in addressing the identity issue and the consequent human resources needed for ministry and mission. The story of the catechist shows that the Church has not exactly understood the distinction and difference between mission in the rural and the urban area. In the latter, more sophisticated personnel were needed, while in the rural areas the less sophisticated catechist was right in his element. A real strategy of mission would have been clearer about this, targeting two distinct vital resources. When in 1968 the first African diocesan was in place, the urban-centred, élite-led Church was ill-equipped to compete with the more progressive mainline Churches and the new charismatic, Pentecostal and African-led Churches.

There was a further issue: in Ghana Anglicanism's High Church tradition, the Church was clergy-centred and the catechist consequently relegated to a limbo, his centrality in rural mission overlooked. For this reason, there were never enough of them. For example, the whole of the Western Region of Ghana, now the Diocese of Sekondi, had only three paid catechists, slowing evangelization almost to a halt. A further aspect of this was that the catechists were never canonically recognized and were treated as errand boys for the clergy. Thus the self-propagating and self-governing principles intersect. When the story of the Church is told, it is often the missionary and the clergy who are mentioned when in point of fact it was the catechist who was doing the work. Their story is yet to be told. A Church that chooses to be oblivious to such a vital and vibrant asset is the loser.

However, the principle of a self-propagating Church needs further nuancing. Worship and spirituality in Ghana continued, and continue, to be a regurgitating of the received English tradition. With the principle of self-propagation must go a commitment to being self-contextualizing, focusing on the quality of the message and the identity of the Church. The Anglican Church in Ghana today has to be an African minting of the One Holy Catholic and Apostolic Church reaching us by way of its English minting, and this is a more serious question than one of introducing drums, Kente or adinkra symbols.

The testimony of Bishop Aglionby with regard to the catechists may be illustrated with the story of Joseph Quashie (1900–83). Schooled initially at Methodist schools in the Western Region, he completed his education at St Peter's Anglican School, Tarkwa, in 1927. By today's standards such education was very elementary, but with it he got a job as clerk at the Aboso Gold Mines, indicating that for his time he was intelligent and able.

In 1936, Quashie went for a one-year catechist training at St Augustine's Theological College, Kumasi. He was then stationed as catechist in Bogoso, a mining town. His leadership and drive established a mission station there with a church, a residence for church personnel and an Anglican school. Bishop Daly laid the foundation of the school building.

In 1952, Daly transferred him to Mampong, Ashanti, to help with the training of catechists and, thereafter, he established mission stations with schools and churches at various places in Western, Central and Eastern Regions. On retiring in 1972, he settled at Madina near the University of Ghana, Legon, where despite failing health and sight, St Peter's Anglican Church was established by his leadership and drive.

As a bonus for mission, his son Kobina Quashie, a soldier who became Paymaster-General of the Ghana Armed Forces and then Commissioner for Trade in the military government, offered for worker-priesthood, becoming subsequently Funding Officer of USPG and Bishop of Cape Coast.

The story of Joseph Quashie substantiates the tribute of Bishop Aglionby to catechists. By today's standards, his education was minimal, but his achievements bear testimony that he was a mover for God. He has been an unsung hero in the Anglican Church history of Ghana. With the catechists he trained and the stations he founded, the foundations were laid of the Dioceses of Sekondi (Western Region), Cape Coast (Central Region) and Koforidua (Eastern Region).

The principle of self-support

The financial backing of the missionary bishops was characteristic of SPG. The case of Bishop Aglionby is instructive. He was looked upon as a great bishop partly because he disbursed funds to his clergy. Talking with the older clergy there is a distinct impression that they thought the funds came personally from Aglionby, who was claimed to be aristocratic and rich, whatever the facts. They hardly mention the Society in referring to him. It is clear that he was seen as the support of the Church out of his bounty. Likewise, they hardly if ever mentioned the Accra Diocesan Association, the other main provider, which his brother Peter Aglionby, a clergyman in England, ran. Of course, reports of the Association were always summarized at the back of the Association journal, *The Golden Shore*, but few in Ghana will have actually read these.

The sum total of this construct is that the Church developed a dependency syndrome. The beloved Aglionby, only partially understanding the situation, commented: 'As long as people believed as they did, that they were the government church, supported by government funds, it is no wonder that they were content to fold their hands and open their mouths to see what would drop into them.'[5]

This dependency syndrome has been deeply imprinted on the psyche of the local churches with the result that their real potential has sometimes been smothered. It is not only a question of too quickly looking abroad for finance. There was a failure to recognize other resources at hand. Why, for example, would a church, which had for decades had most efficient catechists, accept a European director of evangelism? Why would the dioceses in Ghana send people to England to study church administration and mission, when back home the structures were not present to uphold whatever they might learn abroad? In the meantime, we rarely developed local resources on the spot for these continuing tasks.

At the same time, when LeMaire, a black, became diocesan bishop, funding from the Society dwindled and the relationship grew frosty. What Bishop Roseveare had received from both the Society and his order to run the Diocese of Accra was many times what Bishop LeMaire subsequently received. LeMaire's clergy noticed the difference and indeed blamed him for the reduced support. The laity were so used to receiving that it was a most serious challenge to every local bishop to get the local church to support the Church's mission.

A further instructive point relates to the division of the Diocese of Accra in 1980. There was no actuarial or professional assessment and equitable division of historical assets. Indeed, each of the four new dioceses – Cape Coast, Koforidua, Sekondi and Sunyani-Tamale – received £300 from the balance on account at SPG as at 18 October 1981. For the Church in Ghana, the division was for the sake of mission; the Society opposed it for financial reasons. Subsequent history largely vindicates LeMaire's position. More progress was made than would otherwise have been made. Nor were there adequate infrastructures for the new dioceses. It is clear that the preceding English leadership did not foresee an increasingly vibrant future for the Church in Ghana and so did not plan for it, especially in financial terms.

We are still close to those days, and it is perhaps wise not to be overly critical in our evaluation. There is documented evidence that when whites depart from the Third World scene, funds dry up. In the Society, nevertheless, successive Secretaries in the 1980s, James Robertson and Humphrey Taylor, utilized an International Budget Group as a way of minimizing the raw faces of power and control. It is also the case that at about the time of LeMaire's accession to office, there were the beginnings of rumblings with regard to moratorium. Whether this actually influenced the attitudes of those concerned needs careful assessment.

The financial straits in which the Anglican Church in Ghana by and large finds itself suggests that there has not been much careful thinking about how the necessary resources can be generated for mission. Further, the language of self-support needs to be nuanced. We should be talking rather in terms of a Church that is self-motivating, a more dynamic concept.

The three-self formula was a significant insight, but lessons learned in the African Independent Churches have exposed its limits and invite its reformulation as self-motivation, self-contextualization and self-criticism.[6] An evaluation of the work of the Society in Ghana, such as the Provincial Consultations are intended to deliver, but which, at the time of writing have not yet reached Ghana, might hope to discern whether this renewed formula has been realized. In the light of that, we might hope to achieve a relationship that would be liberating for all concerned, breaking with foreign categories of thought, forms of institution and acts of faith, and opting for models that foster the clear identity of each party to the relationship.

Spiky High Church

Under Bishop Hamlyn early in the century, the mission in the Gold Coast took a High Church turn, even though before his arrival he had been a CMS missionary in Lagos. Bishop O'Rorke pushed this tradition further, with 'Catholic practice and . . . vestments', while the coming of the Benedictine monks to train our priests at St Augustine's further entrenched it. On the threshold of the twenty-first century, the Anglican tradition in Ghana is still firmly High Church – strictly 1662 Prayer Book, incense, bells and candles, chants and music originating in England, very much as an admirer, an English military officer, wrote of Gold Coast Anglicanism in 1924, 'the real presence in the Eucharist . . . beautiful and stately rites . . . the altar . . . it is the Mass that matters'. He concluded, 'to an impartial observer living in the Diocese of Accra it must be apparent that the form in which the Anglican Church presents the Catholic Church is immeasurably more suited to the spiritual needs of the people here than that of other church bodies, worthy though they be'.[7]

I have no doubt that aspects of High Church spirituality and worship suit Africans. On the other hand, the idiom of 1662 is not the African's idiom. What the Roman Catholic Bishop of Kumasi says of his Church is applicable to Anglicanism in Ghana too.

> It is evident that traditional Catholic worship is anything but religious worship to the genuine African! It is dull, uninspiring, almost without emotional appeal. The prayers are defective in one hundred and one ways. Composed with a Latin mentality, their structure, syntax and concepts are unintelligible to the African. What their words, even when translated into vernacular, are meant to convey is anybody's guess. They are composed without reference to the occasion. They are therefore, at best meaningless, at worst a waste of time.[8]

The virtues of our High Church spirituality and worship, which *prima facie* must be attractive to Africans, are obscured in effect because its precise idiom does not speak to Africans and their condition. The telling thing is that Anglicans who by day are in the Anglican Church, by night are in the African Independent Churches.

There are lessons to be learnt here. Since the cornerstones of religion are belief, ritual and religious experience, the assessment and renewal of the life and work of the Anglican Church must be done through those three, particularly ritual and religious experience. Worship and spirituality are a crucial test. The Society's missionaries brought what they knew and valued at home, but did they not offer them in ways that invited an African appropriation. Their African successors have been excessively faithful to the received tradition. Not only do they continue with the 1662 Prayer Book, but also their attempts at a West African provincial liturgy have amounted to no more than a selection of assorted texts from the Anglican Communion, or translations of English texts. The essential question is, in what does fidelity to tradition consist? It cannot be regurgitating or reparcelling English originals. The key is to discern in the received tradition what is biblical, apostolic and Catholic. These should be guideposts for developing an African worship and spirituality.

This is critical if the Church is to find its soul and place in the landscape of Ghana in the third millennium. Thanks to the work of SPG, the Anglican Church in Ghana stands by those pillars of Anglicanism, Scripture, Tradition, Reason and Historic Episcopate. But tradition can be deadly unless tested from time to time in the light of new challenges. We have to ask what is essential to Anglicanism, non-negotiable even in our non-English context, and what is accident, dispensable? And when that discernment is done, there is the other necessary exercise to shape an African expression of those non-negotiable

419

essentials. Here is a fundamental issue in which the founding mission, SPG, might renew its relationship as a challenging partner. Relations should not concentrate on finances but should dwell on issues that will make the relationship one of mutual support. Whatever the past, the question as we enter the third millennium is what measures should we take to further mutuality between the Society and the Anglican Church of Ghana? That is where we start in a Church whose self-understanding includes the word communion. Such could be the first step in mutual collaboration, to yield efficiency in mission, focusing less on projects and resources than on the essentials of spirituality that should bind us together as a communion.

Anglicans in Ghana and the ecumenical imperative

Under the impact of the Missionary Conference at La Zoute, Belgium, in September 1926, the historical Churches in Ghana, excluding the Roman Catholic Church, established a Christian Council the following year. It was a platform and medium for speaking to government as one group on social, religious and educational matters. In 1960 the Christian Council also established a church union committee to discuss and negotiate with a view to the restoration of true and visible unity. From the start Anglicans were prominent in these developments. Bishop Aglionby was indeed the first Chair of the Christian Council. When the committee was established, Bishop Roseveare was an influential voice for some very radical agreements on ministry, but he was too advanced for his clergy. As soon as he left Ghana, the Anglican Church withdrew from the committee. That suggests a failure in ecumenical formation and education.

However, there was an additional explanation. The native clergy felt that to go into union in Ghana was to fall out of communion with the mother Church in England. Crudely put, the African Anglicans were afraid to lose access to the resources of SPG. So the link with the Society and with the Anglican Communion was a disincentive to following boldly the ecumenical and biblical imperative. The Society is not to blame for this. It is the natural instinct of a daughter Church suffering from the Peter Pan syndrome and not facing maturely the exigencies of the local mission. I had the privilege of chairing the liturgical and indigenization subcommittee of the church union committee. When our draft went to our Church for comments, one Anglican Archdeacon asked me, 'Are you Lambeth, that you are proposing a liturgy for us?' That question is the tip of an iceberg.

The future

The Society helped to give birth to the Anglican Church of Ghana, as well as to some of our problems. I see the situation as a kind of relay. SPG held the baton for a time. The baton is now in our hands. How are we running the race to make up for lost ground and to have a successful finish? At this stage we need partners to encourage us on. That is the significance of the word 'communion' in our self-description as an Anglican Communion. In identifying and applying the instruments of a viable, healthy communion, our historic links with the Society could still have a part to play. The lessons from the past can teach us together to avoid the dangers ahead and to develop a self-critical, self-contextualizing and self-motivating African Church.

--⊶═◉═⊷--

Dr John Pobee, now living in Ghana, is an Honorary Canon of Accra, Cape Coast and Tamale Cathedrals. He was Professor of Religions and Dean of the Faculty of Arts in the University of Ghana, and for fifteen years with the WCC, during which time he was President of the International Association of Mission Studies. He has published widely, most recently, with E. Oshitola (1998) *African Initiatives in Christianity*, Geneva.

Notes

1. Pascoe, p. 254.
2. Hastings (1994), p. 177.
3. 'Parliamentary Papers, Commons 1842', Vol. XI.
4. *Evening News*, 21 May 1952.
5. *Golden Shore*, Jan. 1926.
6. Nussbaum (1994), p. 2.
7. *Golden Shore*, Apr. 1928; Jan. 1924.
8. *Standard: National Catholic Weekly*, 11–17 Apr. 1977.

Select bibliography

For information on sources for study of the work of SPG, and a bibliography to 1950, see Thompson, pp. 723–35. UMCA and CMD records are now with those of SPG at Rhodes House, Oxford. Those of the United Society are at Partnership House, London. This select bibliography refers only to publications from 1950 to 1999, chiefly those used in preparation of this volume.

Theses

Chilton, R. H. (1993) *Euthanasia of a Mission: The work of the CMS in Western Canada Leading to the Society's Withdrawal in 1920 and the Consequences for the Canadian Church*, DPhil thesis, Oxford.

Clark, J. (1999) *Boards of Mission in the Church of England: A Study of their Precedents, their Formation, and First Seven Years' Activities (1887–1894)*, MA dissertation, London.

Devapackiam, M. (1963) *History of the Early Christian Settlements in the Tirunelveli District*, MA thesis, Madras.

Edwards, D. A. (1998) *A Study in Paradox: Some Contradictions in Anglican Attitudes to Mission in the Mid-nineteenth Century as Embodied in the Life of Francis T. McDougall and his Work in the Borneo Mission*, PhD thesis, Edinburgh.

Harper, S. B. (1991) *Azariah and Indian Christianity in the Late Years of the Raj*, DPhil thesis, Oxford.

Jayakumar, S. (1998) *The Impact of SPG Missions on the Dalits of Tirunelveli 1830–1930*, PhD thesis, Open University.

Lee, J. A. (1998) *Architectural Anglicanism: A Missiological Interpretation of Kanghwa Church and Seoul Anglican Cathedral*, PhD thesis, Birmingham.

Maughan, S. S. (1995) *Regions Beyond and the National Church: Domestic Support for the Foreign Missions of the Church of England in the High Imperial Age, 1870–1914*, PhD thesis, Harvard.

Moriyama, J. T. (1984) *The Evolution of an African Ministry and the Work of the UMCA in Tanzania, 1864–1909*, PhD thesis, London.

Neave, D. (1974) *Aspects of the History of the Universities' Mission to Central Africa 1858–1900*, MPhil thesis, York.

Nelson, J. K. (1962) *Anglican Missions in America, 1701–1725: A Study of the SPG*, PhD thesis, Northwestern.

Sands, K. C. (1998) *The Anglican Church and Bahamian Cultural Identity . . . 1784–1900*, PhD thesis, Edinburgh.

Stanley, B. (1979) *Home Support for Overseas Missions in Early Victorian England c.1838–1873*, PhD thesis, Cambridge.

Talltorp, A. (1988) *Sacrament and Growth: The Sacramental Dimension of Expansion in the Life of the Local Church in the Theology of Roland Allen*, Licentiate of Theology thesis, Lund.

White, G. (1968) *The Idea of the Missionary Bishop in Mid-Nineteenth Century Anglicanism*, STM thesis, New York.

Books published since 1950

Allen, H. J. B. (1995) *Roland Allen, Pioneer, Priest and Prophet*, Cincinnati.

Amaladass SJ, A. and Young, R. F. (1995) *The Indian Christiad: A Concise Anthology of Didactic and Devotional Literature in Early Church Sanskrit*, Anand.

Anderson, O. (1988) *Jamestown Commitment: The Episcopal Church and the American Indian*, Cincinnati.

Anderson, O. (1997) *400 Years: Anglican/Episcopal Mission Among American Indians*, Cincinnati.

Anderson-Morshead, A. E. M. (1909) *History of the Universities' Mission to Central Africa, Vol. 1: 1859–1909*, London.

Appleton, G. (1990) *Unfinished: George Appleton Remembers and Reflects*, London.

Ardener, S. (ed.) (1980) *Perceiving Women*, London.

Axtell, J. (1981) *The Indian Peoples of Eastern America*, New York.

Axtell, J. (1985) *The Invasion Within: The Contest of Cultures in Colonial North America*, New York.

Axtell, J. (1988) *After Columbus: Essays in the Ethnohistory of Colonial North America*, New York and Oxford.

Baago, K. (1969) *Pioneers of Indigenous Christianity*, Bangalore.

Balia, D. (1991) *Black Methodists and White Supremacy in South Africa*, Durban.

Barbara Noreen, Sr CSMV (1994) *Crossroads of the Spirit*, Delhi.

Batumalai, S. (1990) *A Malaysian Theology of Muhibbah: A Christian Witnessing in Malaysia*, Kuala Lumpur.

Beeson, T. and Pearce, J. (1984) *A Vision of Hope: The Churches and Change in Latin America*, London/Philadelphia.

Bennett, J. H. (1950) 'The SPG's plantations and the emancipation crisis' in S. C. McCulloch (ed.).

Bennett, J. H. (1958) *Bondsmen and Bishops: Slavery and Apprenticeship in the Codrington Plantations of Barbados 1710–1838*, Berkeley.

Bickers, R. A., and Seton, R. (eds) (1996) *Missionary Encounters: Sources and Issues*, London.

Blackburn, R. (1997) *The Making of New World Slavery*, London.

Blood, A. G. (1957) *History of the Universities' Mission to Central Africa, Vol. 2: 1907–32*, London.

Blood, A. G. (1962) *History of the Universities' Mission to Central Africa, Vol. 3: 1933–57*, London.

Bolton, S. C. (1982) *Southern Anglicanism: The Church of England in Colonial South Carolina*, Westport.

Bonner, T. N. (1992) *To The Ends of the Earth: Women's Search for Education in Medicine*, London.

Bosch, D. J. (1991) *Transforming Mission: Paradigm Shifts in Theology of Mission*, New York.

Bowie, F., Kirkwood, D. and Ardener, S. (eds) (1993) *Women and Missions: Past and Present*, Providence/Oxford.

Bridenbaugh, C. (1962) *Mitre and Sceptre: Transatlantic Faiths, Ideas, Personalities and Politics 1689–1775*, New York.

Broomfield, G. W. (1957) *Towards Freedom*, London.

Broomfield, G. W. (1965) *Supplement to the History of the UMCA 1957–1965*, London.

Buhlmann, W. (1976) *The Coming of the Third Church: An Analysis of the Present and Future of the Church*, Slough.

Bultmann, W. A. (1950) 'The SPG and the foreign settler in the American colonies', in S. C. McCulloch (ed.).

Busia, K. A. (1967) *Africa in Search of Democracy*, London.

Butler, J. F. (1986) *Christian Art in India*, Madras.

Calam, J. (1971) *Parsons and Pedagogues: The SPG Adventure in American Education*, New York.

Cannan, E. A. (1992) *Churches of the South Atlantic Islands 1502–1991*, Oswestry.

Carrington, P. (1963) *The Anglican Church in Canada: A History*, Toronto.

Chadwick, O. (1959) *Mackenzie's Grave*, London.

Chadwick, O. (1960) *The Mind of the Oxford Movement*, Stanford.

Christadoss, D. A. (1950) *History of the Nazareth Mission*, Tirunelveli.

Christadoss, D. A. (1976) *Rhenius, Apostle of Tirunelveli*, Danishpet.

Christensen, T. and Hutchison, W. R. (1982) *Missionary Ideologies in the Imperialist Era: 1880–1920*, Aarhus.

Clark, J. C. D. (1985) *English Society 1688–1832: Ideology, Social Structure and Political Practice during the Ancien Regime*, Cambridge.

Clement, M. (1973) *Correspondence and Records of the SPG Relating to Wales 1701–1750*, Cardiff.

Cnattingius, H. (1952) *Bishops and Societies: A Study of Anglican Colonial and Missionary Expansion 1698–1850*, London.

Cochrane, J. (1987) *Servants of Power: The Role of English-Speaking Churches in South Africa 1903–30*, Johannesburg.

Cocker, M. (1998) *Rivers of Blood, Rivers of Gold: Europe's Conflict with Tribal Peoples*, London.

Cole, L. (1996) *China Passages: An Amity Teachers' Anthology*, Hong Kong.

Copley, A. (1997) *Religions in Conflict: Ideology, Cultural Contact and Conversion in Late Colonial India*, Delhi.

Cox, J. (1992) 'Independent English women in Delhi and Lahore, 1860–1947', in R. W. Davis and R. J. Helmstadter (eds) (1992) *Religion and Irreligion in Victorian Society*, London/New York.

Cox, J. (1994) 'George Alfred Lefroy 1854–1919: a bishop in search of a church', in S. Pedersen and P. Mandler (eds) (1994) *After the Victorians: Private Conscience and Public Duty in Modern Britain*, London and New York.

Daly, J. (n.d.) *Four Mitres: Reminiscences of an Irrepressible Bishop* (4 parts, privately printed).

Davies, J. D. (1983) *The Faith Abroad*, Oxford.

Davis, K. (1983) *Cross and Crown in Barbados. Caribbean Political Religion in the Late 19th Century*, Frankfurt.

De Gruchy J. W. (1997) 'Grappling with a colonial heritage', in R. Elphick and R. Davenport (eds) (1997) *Christianity in South Africa: A Political, Social and Cultural History*, Oxford and Cape Town.

Dent, M. and Peters, W. (1999) *The Crisis of Poverty and Debt in the Third World*, London.

De Silva, K. M. (1965) *Social Policy and Missionary Organizations in Ceylon 1840–55*, London.

Dettman, P. R. (1967) *The Forgotten Man: The CSI Laity in Historical Perspective*, Madras.

Dewey, M. (1975) *The Messengers: A Concise History of the USPG*, London.

Dharmaraj, J. S. (1993) *Colonialism and Christian Mission: Postcolonial Reflections*, Delhi.

Donovan, V. J. (1978) *Christianity Rediscovered: An Epistle from the Masai*, Indiana.

Doyle, J. R. (1975) *Arthur Shearly Cripps*, Boston.

Emmanuel, G. (1975) *Diocese of Mauritius (1810–1973)*, Port-Louis.

England, F. and Paterson, T. (eds) (1989) *Bounty in Bondage: The Anglican Church in Southern Africa*, Johannesburg.

Erickson, C. (ed.) (1976) *Emigration from Europe 1815–1914*, London.

Evans, J. H. (1964) *Churchman Militant: George Augustus Selwyn, Bishop of New Zealand and Lichfield*, London.

Fabella MM, V. and Torres, S. (eds) (1983) *Irruption of the Third World*, New York.

Fahey, C. (1991) *In His Name: The Anglican Experience in Upper Canada 1791–1854*, Ottawa.

Farrant, J. (1966) *Mashonaland Martyr: Bernard Mizeki and the Pioneer Church*, Cape Town.

Fingard, J. (1972) *The Anglican Design in Loyalist Nova Scotia 1783–1816*, London.

Foucault, M. (1991) 'Madness and Civilization', in P. Rabinow (ed.) (1991) *The Foucault Reader*, London.

Frey, S. R. and Wood, B. (1998) *Come Shouting to Zion: African–American Protestantism in the American South and the British Caribbean to 1830*, Chapel Hill.

Frykenberg, R. E. (1978) 'The impact of conversion and social reform upon the Society in South India during the late Company Period', in C. H. Philips and M. D. Wainwright (eds) *Indian Society and the Beginnings of Modernization*, London.

Gann, H. L. (1965) *History of Southern Rhodesia: Early Days to 1934*, London.

Gibbon, G. (1973) *Paget of Rhodesia*, Bulawayo.

Gibbs, M. E. (1972) *The Anglican Church in India 1600–1970*, Delhi.

Gifford, P. (1998) *African Christianity: Its Public Role*, London.

Gill, S. (1994) *Women and the Church of England: From the Eighteenth Century to the Present*, London.

Gilley, S. and Sheils, W. J. (1994) *A History of Religion in Britain: Practice and Belief from Pre-Roman Times to the Present*, Oxford.

Goedhals M. M. (1989) 'From paternalism to partnership? The CPSA and mission, 1848–1988', in F. England and T. Paterson (eds).

Goodridge, S. S. (1981) *Facing the Challenge of Emancipation: A Study of the Ministry of William Hart Coleridge, First Bishop of Barbados 1824–42*, Bridgetown.

Gow, B. A. (1979) *Madagascar and the Protestant Impact: The work of the British Missions 1818–1895*, London.

Grafe, H. (1990) *History of Christianity in India: Tamilnadu in the Nineteenth and Twentieth Centuries*, Vol. IV, Part 2, Bangalore.

Gray, G. F. S. (1958) *The Anglican Communion: A Brief Sketch*, London.

Gray, R. (1990) *Black Christians and White Missionaries*, New Haven.

Guha, R. (1999) *Savaging the Civilized: Verrier Elwin, His Tribals and India*, Chicago.

Guy, J. (1983) *The Heretic: A Study of the Life of John William Colenso 1814–1883*, Pietermaritzburg.

Handy, R. T. (1976) *A History of the Churches in the United States and Canada*, Oxford.

Harriss, H. M. (1964) *Outward and Onward: Ireland and SPG 1714–1964*, Omagh.

Hastings, A. (1979) *A History of African Christianity 1950–1975*, Cambridge.

Hastings, A. (1986) *A History of English Christianity 1920–1985*, London.

Hastings, A. (1994) *The Church in Africa 1450–1950*, Oxford.

Hayes, V. (ed.) (1977) *Australian Essays in World Religions*, Bedford Park.

Hilliard, D. (1978) *God's Gentlemen: A History of the Melanesian Mission 1849–1942*, St Lucia.

Hobsbawm, E. J. (1968) *Industry and Empire*, Harmondsworth.

Hobsbawm, E. J. (1994) *Age of Extremes: The Short Twentieth Century*, London.

Hodgson, J. and Kothare, J. (1990) *Vision Quest: Native Spirituality and the Church in Canada*, Toronto.

Hollenweger, W. (1976) *Evangelism Today: Good News or Bone of Contention*, Belfast.

Howes, P. H. H. (1995) *In a Fair Ground: or Cibus Cassowarii*, London.

Iliffe, J. (ed.) (1973) *Modern Tanzanians: A Volume of Biographies*, Historical Association of Tanzania.

Iliffe, J. (1973) 'The spokesman: Martin Kayamba', in J. Iliffe (ed.).

Ion, A. H. (1993) *The Cross and the Rising Sun: The British Protestant Missionary Movement in Japan, Korea, and Taiwan*, Waterloo.

Jacob, W. M. (1997) *The Making of the Anglican Church Worldwide*, London.

Jarrett-Kerr, M. (1972) *Patterns of Christian Acceptance: Individual Response to the Missionary Impact 1550–1950*, London.

Jarvis, W. A. W. (1991) *William Teape*, Cambridge.

Jayakumar, S. (1999) *Dalit Consciousness and Christian Conversion: Historical Resources for a Contemporary Debate*, Delhi/ Oxford.

Jeffery, R. M. C. (1980) 'When all are Christians none are: Church and mission in the teaching of Father Benson', in M. Smith (ed.) *Benson of Cowley*, Oxford.

Joseph, R. (1993) 'The Christian Churches and democracy in contemporary Africa', in J. Witte (ed.) *Christianity and Democracy in Global Context*, Boulder.

Kairos (1985) *The Kairos Document. A Theological Comment on the Political Crisis in South Africa*, Braamfontein.

Katjavivi, P., Frostin, P. and Mbuende, K. (eds) (1989) *Church and Liberation in Namibia*, London.

Kiernan, V. G. (1972) *The Lords of Humankind: European Attitudes to the Outside World in the Imperial Age*, London.

Labode, M. (1993) 'From heathen kraal to Christian home: Anglican mission education and African Christian girls, 1850–1900', in F. Bowie, D. Kirkwood and S. Ardener (1993), pp. 126–44.

Lambert, F. (1999) *Inventing the Great Awakening*, Princeton.

Lapsley SSM, M. (1986) *Neutrality or Co-option?*, Gweru.

Lewis, H. T. (1996) *Yet With a Steady Beat: The African American Struggle for Recognition in the Episcopal Church*, Valley Forge.

Limbrick, W. E. (ed.) (1983) *Bishop Selwyn in New Zealand 1841– 68*, Palmerston North.

Lloyd, R. (1966) *The Church of England 1900–1965*, London.

Lowther Clarke, W. K. (1959) *A History of the SPCK*, London.

Luscombe, E. (n.d.) *A Tale of Two Centuries: Scots and the Developing Anglican Communion 1688–1888*, (privately printed).

McCulloch, S. C. (ed.) (1950) *British Humanitarianism: Essays Honoring Frank J. Klingberg*, Philadelphia.

McDougall, H. (1992) *Sketches of our Life at Sarawak*, Singapore/Oxford.

Maw, M. (1990) *Visions of India: Fulfilment Theology, the Aryan Race Theory and the Work of British Protestant Missionaries in Victorian India*, Frankfurt/New York.

Millington, C. M. (1993) *An Ecumenical Venture: The History of Nandyal Diocese in Andhra Pradesh 1947–1990*, Bangalore.

Millington, C. M. (1996) *Led by the Spirit: A Biography of Bishop Arthur Michael Hollis*, Bangalore.

Mills, F. V. (1978) *Bishops by Ballot: An Eighteenth-Century Ecclesiastical Revolution*, New York.

Morris, C. (1961) *The Hour After Midnight*, London.

Neill, S. (1964) *A History of Christian Missions*, Harmondsworth.

Neill, S. (1985) *A History of Christianity in India 1707–1858*, Cambridge.

Nelson-Pallmeyer, J. (1989) *The War Against the Poor*, New York.

Newbigin, L. (1985) *Unfinished Agenda: An Autobiography*, London.

Newsome, D. (1966) *The Parting of Friends: A Study of the Wilberforces and Henry Manning*, London.

Ngewu, L. (1998) 'The CPSA Calendar: a case study of the martyrs of Mbokothwana', in J. Suggit and M. M. Goedhals (eds).

Nockles, P. B. (1994) *The Oxford Movement in Context: Anglican High-Churchmanship 1760–1857*, Cambridge.

Nussbaum, S. (1994) 'African Independent Churches and a new threefold formula for mission', in S. Nussbaum (ed.) *Freedom and Interdependence*, Nairobi.

O'Connor, D. (1990) *Gospel, Raj and Swaraj: The Missionary Years of C. F. Andrews 1904–14*, Frankfurt.

O'Connor, D. (1993) *Din-Sevak: Verrier Elwin's Life of Service in Tribal India*, Bangalore.

Oddie, G. A. (ed.) (1997) *Religious Conversion Movements in South Asia: Continuities and Change, 1800–1900*, London.

Oliver, R. (1952) *The Missionary Factor in East Africa*, London.

Paradkar, B. M. (1969) *The Theology of Goreh*, Bangalore.

Parsons, G. (1997) 'Rethinking the missionary position: Bishop Colenso of Natal', in J. Wolffe (ed.).

Pato, L. (1989) 'Becoming an African Church' in F. England and T. Paterson (eds).

Paton, A. (1974) *Apartheid and the Archbishop: The Life and Times of Geoffrey Clayton, Archbishop of Cape Town*, London.

Paton, D. M. (ed.) (1996) *Christian Missions and the Judgement of God*, Cedar Rapids.

Paul, J. P. (1975) *Mozambique: Memoirs of a Revolution*, Harmondsworth.

Paul, R. D. (1961) *Chosen Vessels*, Bangalore.

Perham, M. (1964) *Colonial Reckoning*, London.

Pheko, S. E. M. (1982) *The Early Church in Africa: First to Seventh Century and Today*, Lusaka.

Philip, T. V. (1982) *Krishna Mohan Banerjea: Christian Apologist*, Bangalore.

Piggin, S. (1984) *Making Evangelical Missionaries 1789–1858: The Social Background, Motives and Training of British Protestant Missionaries to India*, Abingdon.

Raboteau, A. J. (1978) *Slave Religion: The 'Invisible Institution' in the Antebellum South*, New York.

Ranger T. (1972) 'Missionary adaptation of African religious institutions. The Masasi case' in T. Ranger and I. N. Kimambo (eds) *The Historical Study of African Religion with Special Reference to East and Central Africa*, London.

Ranger, T. (1973) 'The Apostle: Kolumba Msigala', in J. Iliffe (ed.).

Ranger, T. (1983) 'The invention of tradition in colonial Africa', in E. Hobsbawm and T. Ranger (eds) *The Invention of Tradition*, Cambridge.

Ranger, T. (1999) *Voices from the Rocks. Nature, Culture and History in the Matopos Hills of Zimbabwe*, Harare.

Rees, W. (1958) *Frances Colenso: Letters from South Africa*, Pietermaritzburg.

Robertson, I. (1990) 'The Jando and initiation in Southern Tanzania', in D. R. Holeton (ed.) *Liturgical Inculturation in the Anglican Communion*, Nottingham.

Robin, A. de Q. (1976) *Mathew Blagden Hale: The Life of an Australian Pioneer Bishop*, Melbourne.

Roden, J. (1999) *Northward from Cape Town: The Anglican Church Railway Mission in Southern Africa 1885–1980*, Appleton Roebuck.

Roseveare, R. (1986) *Delhi, Community of St Stephen, 1886–1986*, (privately printed).

Rotberg, R. I. (1965) *Christian Missions and the Creation of Northern Rhodesia 1880–1924*, Princeton.

Rowell, G. (1983) *The Vision Glorious: Themes and Personalities of the Catholic Revival in Anglicanism*, Oxford.

Sachs, W. L. (1993) *The Transformation of Anglicanism: From State Church to Global Communion*, Cambridge.

Sadiq, J. (1984) *Surprised by Love: Autobiography of Bishop John Sadiq*, Delhi.

Said, E. W. (1978) *Orientalism*, London.

Sardar, Z., Nandy, A. and Davies, M. W. (1993) *Barbaric Others: A Manifesto on Western Racism*, London.

Sargent. N. C. (1962) *The Dispersion of the Tamil Church*, Delhi.

Saunders, G. (1992) *Bishops and Brookes:The Anglican Mission and the Brooke Raj in Sarawak 1848–1941*, Singapore/Oxford.

Shaw, G. P. (1978) *Patriarch and Patriot: William Grant Broughton 1788–1853, Colonial Statesman and Ecclesiastic*, Melbourne.

Shevill, I. (1998) *Between Two Sees*, Worthing.

Shirai, T. (1999) *Yukichi Fukuzawa and the Missionaries: The Untold History of Anglo-Japanese Relations 1874–1901*, (Japanese) Tokyo.

Singh, B. (1999) *The First Protestant Missionary in India: Bartholomaeus Ziegenbalg 1683–1719*, New Delhi.

Skelton, K. (1985) *Bishop in Smith's Rhodesia*, Gweru.

Smith, M. (ed.) (1980) *Benson of Cowley*, Oxford.

Stanley, B. (1990) *The Bible and the Flag: Protestant Missions and British Imperialism in the Nineteenth and Twentieth Centuries*, Leicester.

Steele, M. (1975) '"With hope unconquered and unconquerable . . .:" Arthur Shearly Cripps, 1869–1952' in T. Ranger and J. Weller (eds) *Themes in the Christian History of Central Africa*, London.

Steere, D. V. (1973) *God's Irregular: Arthur Shearly Cripps*, London.

Stradling, L. E. (1960) *A Bishop on Safari*, London.

Suggit, J. and Goedhals, M. M. (1998) *Change and Challenge: Essays Commemorating the 150th Anniversary of the Arrival of Robert Gray as First Bishop of Cape Town*, Marshalltown.

Sugirtharajah, R. S. (1991; new edn. 1995) *Voices from the Margin: Interpreting the Bible in the Third World*, Maryknoll/London.

Sugirtharajah, R. S. (1998) *Asian Biblical Hermeneutics and Postcolonialism*, Maryknoll.

Sundkler, B. (1954) *Church of South India: The Movement Towards Union 1900–1947*, London.

Sykes, S. and Booty, J. (eds) (1988) *The Study of Anglicanism*, London.

Symonds, R. (1986) *Oxford and Empire: The Last Lost Cause?*, Oxford.

Tatz, C. (1999) *Genocide in Australia* (Australian Institute of Aboriginal and Torres Strait Islander Studies), Canberra.

Taylor, B. (1983) *The Anglican Church in Borneo 1848–1962*, Bognor Regis.

Taylor, J. V. (1963) *The Primal Vision*, London.

Taylor, R. W. (1975) *Jesus in Indian Paintings*, Bangalore.

Thielicke, H. (1995) *Notes from a Wayfarer*, tr. D. R. Law, Cambridge.

Thompson, H. P. (1954) *Thomas Bray*, London.

Tinker, H. (1979) *The Ordeal of Love: C. F. Andrews and India*, Delhi.

Titus, N. (1983) *Missionary Under Pressure: The Experiences of the Rev. John Duport in West Africa*, Barbados.

Turner, H. W. (1977) 'The primal religions of the world and their study', in V. Hayes (ed.) *Australian Essays in World Religions*, Bedford Park.

Tutu, D. (1999) *No Future Without Forgiveness*, London.

Van Den Berg, J. (1956) *Constrained by Jesus' Love: An Inquiry into the Motives of the Missionary Awakening in Great Britain 1698–1815*, Kampen.

Van Horne, J. C. (1985) *Religious Philanthropy and Colonial Slavery: The American Correspondence of the Associates of Dr Bray 1717–1777*, Urbana/Chicago.

Varghese, K. (1961) *Herbert Pakenham-Walsh: A Memoir*, Delhi.

Verryn, T. D. (1972) *A History of the Order of Ethiopia*, Cleveland.

Waddy, R. P. S. (1954) *Philip Loyd, Missionary and Bishop*, London.

Walker, D. A. C. (1985) *Paterson of Cyrene*, Gweru.

Walls, A. F. (1996) *The Missionary Movement in History: Studies in the Transmission of Faith*, New York.

Ward, B., and Dubos, R. (1972) *Only One Earth: The Care and Maintenance of a Small Planet*, Harmondsworth.

Ward, W. R. (1999) *Christianity under the Ancien Regime 1648–1789*, Cambridge.

Webster, A. B. (1954) *Joshua Watson: The Story of a Layman 1771–1885*, London.

Webster, J. C. B. (1976) *The Christian Community and Change in Nineteenth Century North India*, Delhi.

Weller, J. C. (1971) *The Priest from the Lakeside: The Story of Leonard Kamungu of Malawi and Zambia 1877–1913*, Blantyre.

Weller, J. and Linden, J. (1984) *Mainstream Christianity to 1980 in Malawi, Zambia and Zimbabwe*, Gweru.

Whitehead, R. L. (ed.) (1989) *No Longer Strangers: Selected Writings of K. H. Ting*, Maryknoll.

Whiteman, D. (1983) *Missionaries and Melanesians: An Ethnohistorical Study of Social and Religious Change in the Southwest Pacific*, Pasadena.

Whyte, Bob (1988) *Unfinished Encounter: China and Christianity*, London.

Wickeri, P. L. (1988) *Seeking the Common Ground: Protestant Christianity, the Three-Self Movement, and China's United Front*, New York.

Wilkinson, J. L. (1993) *Church in Black and White: The Black Christian Tradition in 'Mainstream' Churches in England: A White Response and Testimony*, Bonn and Edinburgh.

Williams, C. P. (1990) *The Ideal of the Self-Governing Church: A Study in Victorian Missionary Strategy*, Leiden.

Williamson, S. G. (1965) *Akan Religion and the Christian Faith*, Accra.

Wilson, A. (1968) *The Clergy Reserves of Upper Canada*, Toronto.

Wingate, A., Ward, K., Pemberton, C. and Sitshebo, W. (1998) *Anglicanism: A Global Communion*, London.

Winslow, J. C. (1954) *Eyelids of the Dawn: Memories, Reflections, Hopes*, London.

Wolffe, J. (ed.) (1997) *Religion in Victorian Britain. V. Culture and Empire*, Manchester.

Woolverton, J. F. (1984) *Colonial Anglicanism in North America*, Detroit.

Wynne, R. (1985) *The Pool That Never Dries Up*, London.

Yates, T. E. (1978) *Venn and Victorian Bishops Abroad*, Uppsala.

Young, R. F. (1981) *Resistant Hinduism: Sanskrit Sources of Anti-Christian Apologetic in Early Nineteenth-Century India*, Vienna.

Periodicals

Bentley, M. (Apr.–June 1966) 'Philip Quaque', *Church Quarterly Review*.

Ch'en, J. (1960) 'The nature and character of the Boxer Movement', *S.O.A.S. Bulletin*, **xxiii** (2).

Davidson, A. K. (Dec. 1990) 'Colonial Christianity: the contribution of the SPG to the Anglican Church in New Zealand 1840–80', *Journal of Religious History*.

Forbes, G. H. (26 Apr. 1986) 'In search of the "pure heathen": missionary women in nineteenth century India', *Economic and Political Weekly*, **21** (17).

Frykenberg, R. E. (Feb. 1986) 'Modern education in South India 1784–1854', *American Historical Review*, **91** (1).

Gibbs, M. E. (Sept. 1965) 'The catechist in the Tinnevelly Missions in the first half of the nineteenth century', *Bulletin of the Church History Association of India*.

Hinderaker, E. (July 1996) 'The "Four Indian Kings" and the imaginative construction of the first British Empire', *The William and Mary Quarterly*.

Hinkelammert, F. J. (July–Aug. 1990) 'Changes in the relationship between Third World countries and First World countries', *Pasos*.

Hodgson, J. (July 1987) 'Kid gloves and cricket on the Kei', *Religion in Southern Africa*.

Hodgson, J. (Advent 1993) 'Liberating Anglican theology in Africa', *Anglican World*.

Kumaradoss, V. K. (Jan. 1996) 'Negotiating colonial Christianity: the Hindu

Christian Church of late nineteenth century Tirunelveli', *South Indian Studies*.

Lin, M. M. (Jan. 1998) 'A modern Chinese journey', *International Review of Mission*.

McVeigh, M. J. (Apr. 1999) 'Peacemaker *extraordinaire*', *Missiology*.

Pennington, E. L. (Mar. 1951) 'The SPG anniversary sermons 1702–1783', *Historical Magazine of the Protestant Episcopal Church*, **XX**, pp. 10–43.

Porter, A. (1985) 'Commerce and Christianity: the rise and fall of a nineteenth-century religious slogan', *Historical Journal*, **28**.

Ranger, T. (1982) 'The death of Chaminuka: spirit mediums, nationalism and the Guerilla War in Zimbabwe', *African Affairs*, **81**.

Ravindiran, V. (Jan. 1996) 'The unanticipated legacy of Robert Caldwell and the Dravidian Movement', *South Indian Studies*.

Ray, N. R. (July–Dec. 1964) 'Bishop Middleton and Raja Rammohun Roy', *Bengal Past and Present*.

Singh, B. (Jan.–Feb. 1982) 'Three characters in search of an author: E. M. Forster, C. F. Andrews and Verrier Elwin as heroes of colonialism', *New Quest*.

Sohmer, S. (Dec. 1994) 'Christianity without civilization: Anglican sources for an alternative nineteenth-century mission methodology', *Journal of Religious History*.

Spear, T. G. P. (1970) 'The early days of Bishop's College, Calcutta', *Bengal: Past and Present*, **89**.

Tengatenga, James (1996) 'The good being the enemy of the best: the politics of Bishop Frank Thorne in Nyasaland and the Federation, 1936–61', *Religion in Malawi*, **6**.

Thapa, V. J. (6 July 1998) 'Top ten colleges of India', *India Today*.

Titus, N. (Spring 1980) 'The West Indian mission to Africa: its conception and birth,' *Journal of Negro History*.

Warrior, R. A. (Dec. 1989) 'Canaanites, cowboys and Indians', *Christianity in Crisis*, **49**.

White, G. (1992–3) 'Frank Weston and the Kikuyu crisis', *Bulletin of the Scottish Institute of Missionary Studies*, **8–9**.

Conference Papers, Lectures

Hodgson, J. (13–17 Jan. 1997) '"Stones the Builders Rejected": Ecclesial Communities of the Excluded within the Anglican Church in Southern Africa'. (Conference on African Initiatives in Christianity, UNISA).

Robertson, J. S. (Jun. 1977) 'The dynamics of mission from Britain 1925–75' (Scottish Episcopal Church Missionary Lectures, Edinburgh).

Robertson, J. S. (1981) 'Images of mission in the Anglican Communion' (Sprigg Lectures, Virginia Seminary).

Index